Natural Lives
Modern Times

Natural Lives
— Modern Times

PEOPLE AND PLACES OF
THE DELAWARE RIVER

Bruce Stutz

CROWN PUBLISHERS, INC.
NEW YORK

Copyright © 1992 by Bruce Stutz

Designed by Nancy Kenmore
Map © 1992 by Jacques Chazaud
Illustrations © 1992 by Brian Callanan
Photographs © 1992 by Mary Waddington Smith
Permission to reprint the Roebling illustration granted by H. B. Longacre John A.
Roebling's Sons Company, Trenton, NJ (1898).
New Jersey State Museum Collection, Trenton.
Gift of F. W. Roebling, III.

Published by Crown Publishers, Inc., 201 East 50th Street, New York, New York
10022. Member of the Crown Publishing Group.

CROWN is a trademark of Crown Publishers, Inc.
Manufactured in the United States of America

Library of Congress Cataloging-in-Publication Data

Stutz, Bruce.
    Natural lives, modern times / by Bruce Stutz. — 1st ed.
        p.   cm.
      1. Delaware River (N.Y.-Del. and N.J.)   2. Delaware River Valley
(N.Y.-Del. and N.J.)   3. Natural history—Delaware River (N.Y.-Del.
and N.J.)   I. Title.
F157.D4S78   1992
974.9—dc   91-32188
                                                        CIP

ISBN 0-517-58225-2

10   9   8   7   6   5   4   3   2   1

First Edition

TO MY PARENTS

who taught me that everyone and
everything has a voice;
that one learns by listening
and listening well;
and that, wander among people
where you will,
as my mother always put it,
"If you have a mouth,
you can't get lost."

ACKNOWLEDGMENTS

My thanks first to Nixon Griffis and the Griffis Foundation, who, through Dery Bennett and the American Littoral Society gave me the financial support to get this book started. To Alan Ternes at *Natural History* magazine for the year's leave to do the research and travel, and to everyone who shared their time, knowledge, concerns, and visions of the river with me, especially those who don't get mentioned otherwise in the book. Biologist John O'Herron made sure I got out to see the riverfront from the river. Rusty Harvey of Delaware Wildlands in Odessa, Delaware, spent a day introducing me to my best sources along the river's Delaware shore. Delaware Riverkeeper Cynthia Poten and Mary Ellen Noble of the Watershed Association of the Delaware shared with me their knowledge of the intricacies of environmental actions along the river. Realtors Davis Chant, Scott Frazier, and Ed Carroll gave me a look at the nuts and bolts of the development business. Rick Radis showed me much of the birds and the botany. Richard Albert of the Delaware River Basin Commission shared some of his own experiences, as well as his files for his book on the Tocks Island Dam. Thanks to Nature Conservancy researchers for their time and information. The rest all have their say in the book. Thanks to my agent, Dominick Abel, and my editor, James O. Wade, for appreciating the book before it was one, and to Mary Frank for the vision of her art. Thanks to my wife, Sallie, and to Benjamin, Nathaniel, and Julia, for listening to my unedited river stories and traveling this long way along with me.

CONTENTS

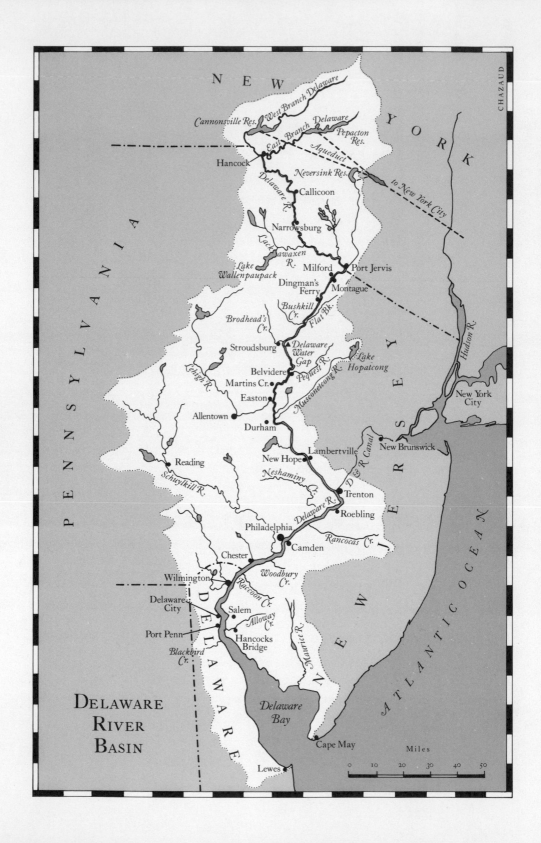

CHAZAUD

N E W   Y O R K

West Branch Delaware

Cannonsville Res.

East Branch Delaware

Pepacton
Res.

Hancock

Aqueduct

Neversink Res.

to New York City

Delaware R.

Callicoon

Narrowsburg

Lackawaxen R.

*Lake
Wallenpaupack*

Milford   Port Jervis

Dingman's
Ferry   Montague

*Bushkill
Cr.*   *Flat Bk.*

*Brodhead's
Cr.*

Stroudsburg   ▲ *Delaware
Water
Gap*   *Lake
Hopatcong*

Pequest R.

Belvidere

Martins Cr.

Lehigh R.   *Musconetcong R.*

Easton

Allentown   Durham

Reading   Lambertville   New Brunswick

New Hope

D & R Canal

Schuylkill R.

Neshaminy Cr.

Trenton

Delaware R.   Roebling

Philadelphia

Rancocas Cr.

Chester   Camden

*Woodbury
Cr.*

Wilmington   *Raccoon Cr.*

Delaware
City   Salem   *Alloway
Cr.*

Port Penn   Hancocks
Bridge   *Maurice R.*

*Blackbird
Cr.*

Hudson R.

New York
City

N E W   J E R S E Y

A T L A N T I C   O C E A N

P E N N S Y L V A N I A

D E L A W A R E

*Delaware
Bay*

Cape May

Lewes

DELAWARE
RIVER
BASIN

Miles

0   10   20   30   40   50

Old Walt Whitman
Went finding and seeking,
Finding less than sought
Seeking more than found,
Every detail minding
Of the seeking or the finding.

Pleasured equally
In seeking as in finding,
Each detail minding,
Old Walt went seeking
And finding.

LANGSTON HUGHES

As I was crossing the Delaware to-day, saw a large flock of wild geese, right overhead, not very high up, ranged in U-shape, in relief against the noon clouds of light smoke-color. Had a capital though momentary view of them, and then of their course on and on southeast, till gradually fading . . . the waters below—the rapid flight of the birds, appearing just for a minute—flashing to me such a hint of the whole spread of Nature with her eternal unsophisticated freshness, her never-visited recesses of sea, sky, shore—and then disappearing into the distance.

WALT WHITMAN

Part One

ANCIENT LIVES

BY THE DELAWARE'S BAYSHORE UNDER A MAY FULL
moon, I roll up my pants legs and wade out
into waters aswarm with hard-shelled, spike-
tailed, tarantula-legged horseshoe crabs,
which come ashore here each spring in a copulatory *arribada* like no other in the world.
Their ancestors plied the waters of the Devonian, some 400 million
years ago. The spring high tide drives them up from the soft sands
of the deep channels at the mouth of the bay. They drift in with the
lapping waters. The males, sometimes two or three at a time, grasp
the back of a female and ride her in as she sculls slowly toward
shore. Once there, the female claws her way up the beach, still
bearing the males, to the high-tide line, where she'll dig in and lay,
burying anywhere from a few to a couple of dozen clusters of shot-
sized, lime-green eggs, three thousand at a time—putting her
young, in her ancient mind's eye, out of harm's way of the predators of more lively ancient seas. But I can make out only minnows
flashing in the moonlit waters, drawn by the wash of milt and eggs,
swirling about the dark forms that loll silently in the shallows.

Humans have lived along the Delaware Bay and River shores for
at least twelve thousand years. Many of the natives knew the river
waters as Lenapewhihituck—"the swift waters of the Lenape." Europeans settling here in the middle of the seventeenth century
named the waters for the English Lord De La Warr, who himself
had never seen any part of them. The colonists next named the
natives for the river, calling them all "Delaware," no matter how
distant their bands or unique their lives. The natives and their
places as they knew them would be all but gone within a hundred
years of their renaming. The settlers fished the waters, diked,

3

drained, and farmed the lowlands, stripped bare the vast timber-lands, hunted and trapped the birds and furbearers, or drove them out of the diminishing wilderness toward extinction. In the same time the Delaware became the new country's maritime, agricultural, mercantile, political, philosophical, revolutionary, and industrial heartland. Its course served as border and transportation corridor for New York, Pennsylvania, and New Jersey, the growing nation's most populous states. Timber rafts and coal barges brought fuel for the homes, hearths, looms, and lathes for the steelmakers and the shipbuilders of Camden, Trenton, Wilmington, and Philadelphia. Here the river shores and tidal marshes suffered slagheaps, bulkheads, landfills and railyards, and the greatest collection of oil refineries on any shore but that of the Gulf Coast. The number of people who now live in the Delaware River Basin is greater than that of forty of the fifty states, and the river provides water to 20 million, 700 million gallons of it a day going to New York City alone.

All this presents a great opportunity. Here is a river so long settled and so much changed one can look at it anew, a modern river in an ancient course, an ancient river in a modern world. So I undertook to explore both its nature and its people, its past lives and present lives, its farm lives, industrial lives, city and rural lives—all, these days, river lives. And everywhere I found stories well worth the finding, and nothing that is unchanging.

Even the vision of the Devonian.

THE MIGRATION

AT DAWN THE BEACH IS LITTERED WITH CARNAGE, AS IF A RETREATING infantry had left behind shards of its armor in the sand. The tide has left many of the crabs helpless on the upper edge of the tide line. If their telsons—their hard, spiked tails—aren't damaged, they'll right themselves and dig into the sand. The crabs can hold on to enough moisture to live for a day or more out of water, provided some idle passerby doesn't come and turn them to view the curious ten-legged underbelly and pre-arachnoid gills, but most passersby can't keep from poking at the half-buried animal or imagine a thing so still can still be alive. If undisturbed, the crabs can await the next tide and then scrape their way along the sand back down to the water. Some will wash up and lay again. Many will die, desiccating among the windrows of algal wrack and unburied eggs. And in the heat the flies begin to swarm.

Now it happens that at this same time flocks of migrating shorebirds, which have come some three thousand miles from South America on their flights to Arctic nesting grounds, land in flocks of a hundred thousand and more on this same strip of Delaware Bay shore. Red knots, ruddy turnstones, and palmated sandpipers join dowitchers and the local stock of laughing gulls to glut themselves on fresh horseshoe crab eggs. As many as a million migrating birds, most with another couple of thousand miles to go, make this few miles of Delaware shore their last feeding ground.

By midmorning birds pack the beaches among the carcasses of the horseshoe crabs. Between the skittish migrants, squawking laughing gulls, and large young herring gulls that stand among the rest like dull sentries, there's often not an empty foot of shore. The flocks wing in and out like shoals of swirling reef fish. Feisty territorial challenges break out and little birds go beak-to-beak over a few square inches of sand. Sometimes, on this short stretch of narrow beach, nearly the entire western hemisphere's population of turnstones can be feeding. This is an awesome prospect for even the most worldly birder to contemplate: that one can be seeing half the world's population of a species at one time. Scenes of such abundance are so rare these days they can inspire giddiness among the most serious naturalists. I think of a birding friend's jubilant whoop at the sight of just a single great flock of gannets on the ocean horizon. As we watched, the birds caught sight of a school of leaping baitfish in the waters below them, and began to toss themselves, one by one, like a squadron of diving fighters, into the surface of a silvery ocean. In his rush to get his binoculars from the glove box, my friend nearly landed us and his old red pickup in a sand dune. Never mind, the sight of this abundance, feeding wildly upon even greater abundance, was nearly enough to bring tears to his eyes. But this inspirational gathering along the Delaware also makes biologists nervous, for it leaves nearly entire species vulnerable to any catastrophe from disease to oil spills. Here on the Delaware, the latter is more likely. This last refuge is within sight of the shipping channel, and no law limits the times of passage of the tankers that carry some 30 million gallons of crude oil a day up past these beaches to the refineries of Wilmington and Philadelphia.

By midday the dilettante watchers arrive. They drive down the narrow crushed-shell lane that serves the ramshackle beachfront shanties, park county-fair-style along the sides of the road, and then stroll around the wood-frame cottages to see the bird-congested beaches. Many flip intensely through pocket guides, looking down, looking up, distinguishing for friends the sanderlings from the semipalmateds. Photographers take aim across the roofs of their cars. Along a nearby stone jetty the better-equipped line up their tripods and focus and refocus their spotting scopes and five-hundred-millimeter lenses like an artillery battalion taking aim across a beachhead. Some self-appointed wardens try to keep the too-casual observers from wandering into the picture.

I have been working all morning with a group banding birds, but now all the activity on the beach is making the migrants skittish. They stay off from the net. Even state biologist Larry Niles, as laconic and mild-mannered a bird man as ever I've met, is beginning to set his jaw against the barrage of bystander inquiries as he weighs, inspects, notes, bands, and releases the birds. He has been at this for days now, and at dusk he has been taking flights over the marshes in a small plane to make counts of roosting migrants.

For Niles and other observers the problem is that the populations of many of these shorebirds have been declining—declining precipitously—over the past several years. The red knots are down some twenty percent, the sanderlings by perhaps twice that. Since the birds travel from South America to the Arctic tundra, just where and why the declines occur has been difficult to discover. It's certain that places where they once fed along their routes have been lost to development. Even this Delaware feeding frenzy may be a relatively modern occurrence. Crab eggs may be making up for the lost insect life upon which the birds fattened in the once-extensive flyway marshes. After all, barely half of the egg material is digestible. By one accounting, a fifty-gram fat-depleted sanderling, now seemingly of no more substance in the hand than the weight of its feathers alone, might have to eat some nine thousand eggs a day over its three-week Delaware stopover in order to double its weight for its northward journey. All told, in a matter of two weeks the birds on this stretch of Delaware beach may devour tens of billions of horseshoe crab eggs, some hundred tons.

It may be significant that only very recent accounts mention the numbers of birds feeding along the beaches. When Professor George H. Cook, of the New Jersey Geological Survey, reported on the scene in 1856, the horseshoe crab, known then (and locally still) as the king crab, was the major attraction:

> On about half a mile of the strand about 750,000 were taken in 1855, and 1,200,000 were taken on about a mile in 1856. The king crab deposits its eggs, and then leaves the shore entirely till the same season next year. But little if anything is known of their habits or localities during the interval. The number of eggs is very great. They have been so thick along the shore that they could be shoveled up and collected by the wagon-load. Great numbers have thus been gathered up and carried away to feed chickens. When they hatch the sand is fairly alive with the little creatures. On one occasion a vessel took in a load of sand on the shore, and in two or three days so many of these young king crabs appeared in it that the whole cargo was thrown overboard. Hogs will eat king crabs with avidity, and it is a common practice to gather them for that purpose during the season. They seem to act as a tonic to most hogs, and are very desirable food for them. The usual practice is to gather king crabs into pens and allow them to putrefy, forming a kind of compound, to be used as manure.

When the crabs came ashore with the tide to lay, they were trapped in wire impoundments. When the tide receded they were loaded onto wagons and piled into wood stockades ten feet high that might hold a quarter million and more.

> *We saw several which were filled to overflowing and had bursted, leaving great masses of the animals about their sides. They are frequently emptied and then filled again. By the method in vogue in fishing the pound, and continually adding crabs, there are always a number of live individuals in the pens. They, of course, are those forming the surface layer. The crabs live about two or three days, and as the pens are high and dry here and there those which had attempted to escape were always found dead or dying in the hot dry sand. They always appear to be more restless in the pens at the flood tide, when they produce more commotion than at other times. The king crab appears to be able to determine the time of high-tide even when far removed from the water. . . .*

Longtime residents recall that if the wind blew onshore, the stench of the putrefying crabs might cause the school picnic to be canceled. At season's end the crabs were carted off in boats and shipped upriver to be ground up for a fertilizer sold by the name of "Cancerine."

The great crab harvests are no more. But this aggregation of some two million, maybe more, remains the largest in the world. The three other horseshoe crab species live in the Far East, and their numbers are in serious decline. So these *Limulus*, as the Delaware species is known, attract, besides onlookers, researchers who bring in the crabs, take blood samples from them, tag them, and release them. They study its ancient eyes, the purity of its chitin, the simplicity of its nervous system. A clotting factor in the crab blood can be used in a laboratory to show contamination in a serum. Yet some basic information is difficult to know. The age of a horseshoe crab, for instance, is still best told by the age of the parasites that live on its back. It appears that the crabs come ashore to mate at seven to nine years of age, and live to twenty. Perhaps some quarter of a million of the crabs die each year. These, along with the billions of unviable eggs washing back from the beaches and marshes with the tides, make a considerable contribution of nutrients to the Delaware waters that spawned them. The waters here may be the bay's richest.

It's worth seeing. But take my advice and find a small, rutted, unmapped road to a silent marshy shore where, when the tide recedes, the crabs lie so thick you'd think the mud guts among the marsh reeds had been paved with their carapaces. The gray sands around them are coated with eggs. Dig a pocketknife in, and the clusters of eggs are as deep as the blade will go. The coupling crabs crowd so close together the birds have nowhere to stand and feed. So there's quiet. The water runs and pools in the tidal rillets. Now and again there will be a scraping, like a nuzzling, of one chitinous ancient against another.

MORE SLAUGHTER OF THE ANCIENTS

IN 1747 THE SWEDISH ACADEMY OF SCIENCES SENT PETER KALM, A thirty-two-year-old naturalist, to America to survey New World plants in the hopes that some might thrive in the northern climes of Sweden. Kalm, a favorite student of the great animal systemizer Carl von Linné, better known as Linnaeus, proved as irrepressible a journalist as a naturalist, and documented not only the fauna and flora of America, but its colonial society as well. He spent much of his trip along the Delaware befriending Philadelphia scientists such as William Bartram and Benjamin Franklin, and recording the recollections of old Swedish settlers who told Kalm of the changed nature of the river valley in the hundred years since New Sweden had been founded. By the time Kalm arrived, New Sweden was already part of history. The Swedes had surrendered

their Delaware forts to the Dutch under Peter Stuyvesant in 1655.
The Dutch in turn surrendered to the English barely ten years
later. So the old Swedes Kalm met could blame the ruin of their
fishing, hunting, and trapping on those who came after them, those
who diked and drained the marshes along the river shores and built
cities where none should have been built, along the unwholesome
lowlands, for instance, in places like Salem, New Jersey. As Kalm
wrote:

> *Experience has shown, that those who came hither from other
> places to settle got a very pale and sickly look, though they ar-
> rived in perfect health, and with a very fresh color. The town is
> easily distinguished about this time [early May] by the dis-
> agreeable stench which arises from the swamps. The vapors of
> the putrid water are carried to those inhabitants which live next
> to the marshes, and enter the body along with the air, and
> through the pores, and are thus hurtful to health. At the end of
> every summer, the intermittent fevers are very frequent. I know
> two young men who came with me from England to America:
> soon after their arrival at Philadelphia they went to Salem, in
> perfect health; but a few weeks after they fell sick, and before
> winter was half over they had both died.*

But across the river, David Stewart, a Delaware physician who
owned a great deal of this marshland, hoped to carve out yet another settlement. In 1764 Stewart ran an advertisement in Philadelphia's *Pennsylvania Gazette* promoting "a Town on the River
Delaware" to be known as Port Penn.

> *As the Erection of Towns in every County capable of them, is
> justly esteemed a public Utility, as it increases the Number of
> Inhabitants, enlarges Trade, and thereby contributes to the
> Strength of Government, and the Riches of a People, it is hoped
> this Scheme will meet with proper encouragement for this Town
> is extremely pleasant and convenient for Trade . . . the Navi-
> gation there is scarce ever interrupted by Ice; the County*

*around it is very fertile, and abounds with such Commodities
as especially suit the West-India Market. . . .*

Although it now seems evident that the best way to ruin a river
is to build a city along its banks, this was not always thought the
case. In fact, the first Europeans to the Delaware shores wondered
why the natives themselves had not built up a great civilization.
Why, with all the wealth of resources available, were they content
to live in temporary encampments, foraging, fishing, and hunting.
The size of their bands, twenty-five to thirty or so, was limited by
the number who could survive the most difficult times. When the
Europeans arrived, no more than fifty such bands may have lived
along the entire lower Delaware shore. But even were there twice as
many, here was a vast wilderness with very few inhabitants and a
wealth of resources such as no modern European had ever seen. The
colonists could only imagine that these were simply lazy savages
who had little appreciation of all the favors God had granted them.

As one incredulous Delaware diarist wrote in 1649, the men spent
their time making "traps, nets, and other such trifles," and "do
nothing but fish, hunt, and go to war." And while these natives
seemed to believe "in an Immortality of the soul; and have, like-
wise, some knowledge of the Sun, Moon and Stars, many of which
they even know how to name" and were "passable judges of weather," most seemed to have "scarcely any knowledge of God," and
were "unchaste and lascivious, without the least particle of
shame." Somehow this correspondent also knew "they make little
of death" and "despise all tortures that can be inflicted on them at
the stake, exhibiting no faintheartedness, but generally singing until they are dead."

"When we speak to them about God," wrote the Swedish Rev-
erend Johan Campanius in 1646, "they pay no attention, but they
will let it be understood that they are a free people, subject to no
one, but do what they please. I presume it would be possible to
convert them, but only with great labor."

The Indians took more readily to the use of firearms and became
crack shots, providing the colonists with a thriving fur trade. Yet

their continued lack of what the Europeans considered civilized ambitions peeved many of the colonists no end. Kalm relates the following story:

> *The old Swede once walked with an Indian, and they encoun-*
> *tered a red-spotted snake on the road: the old man therefore went*
> *to seek a stick in order to kill it, but the Indian begged him not*
> *to touch it, because it was sacred to him. Perhaps the Swede*
> *would not have killed it, but on hearing that it was the Indian's*
> *deity, he took a stick and killed it, in the presence of the Indian,*
> *saying: 'Because thou believest in it, I think myself obliged to*
> *kill it.'*

The lesson could not have been lost on the Indians who saw the colonists proceed to destroy everything in which the Indians believed, from the forests to the deer, bear, and beaver.

At the time Dr. Stewart ran his advertisement, the farms along the Delaware south of Wilmington were devoted to growing wheat on their uplands and salt hay along the marshy river shores. Boats came up the creeks at high tide, took on grain, and then ran out and up along the Delaware to Philadelphia. Stewart figured that ships coming up the bay into the river might be glad to cut their trip some sixty miles short. Besides, his port at the river's mouth was "scarce ever interrupted by Ice" and could boast better overland access to the Chesapeake Bay, which lay on the colony's western drainage. Stewart drew up an ambitious prospectus for Port Penn, even using a Philadelphia-style grid of streets named Liberty, Congress, Market, Merchant, Beaumaris, and Delaware. He plotted out the latter two on what was then and is now marshland. The plan therefore entailed the draining and filling of the marsh—at the time a job that was close to impossible. Stewart's plan, one history concludes, was "either very ambitious or overtly fraudulent."

In either case, Philadelphia was not to be so easily supplanted. As has been said, Penn and his Quakers came to the Delaware to do good, and did well. But even trading on Penn's name, Stewart's fancied port faced one bit of bad luck after another. In 1829 the canal that finally connected the Delaware with the upper Chesapeake Bay (and shortened the water route from Philadelphia to Baltimore by some three hundred miles) did so fifteen miles or so north of Port Penn. In 1838 the first lines of the Philadelphia, Wilmington, and Baltimore Railroad came south but northwest of the town. Twelve years later the Delaware Railroad from Philadelphia ran inland instead of along the coast. By then even the farmers who had once brought their grain to Port Penn began to take their wagonloads to the train, rather than shipping them to the Delaware shore.

When, after the Civil War, the migration to western farms began to ruin the local economy (a brief bright market in peaches was quickly extinguished by blight), the residents of Port Penn and the towns nearby turned to the marshes and water for their livelihoods—market gunning for wildfowl, working the nearby oyster beds, trapping muskrat, snapping turtles, and terrapins, and fishing for shad, white perch, catfish, and sturgeon.

Bob Beck, square-chinned, gaunt, and these days short of breath, who once did all of these things, recalls the killing of the sturgeon most of all.

"My God, I can remember the slaughter. The humongous slaughter, my God."

He stares out through the tiny-paned windows of his picturesque little house along the river just north of Port Penn, on the edge of what's known as Thousand Acre Marsh—his father's house and his grandfather's house and portrayed in miniature detail down to the purple martin houses and little grove of evergreens out front, in a primitive painting on the wall.

"I can remember as a kid, barges twice as big as this house, filled every day with guts and heads of sturgeon. You're talking about fish eighty to one hundred years old."

Fish a hundred million years old. While huge guns mounted on boats might shoot a hundred shorebirds at a time, and nets and weirs enmesh without regard to size every species of fish on its spring spawning run, the killing of the sturgeon had something of the magnitude of the killing of the buffalo on the Great Plains. When it came, and it came in the very same years as the great western slaughter, it came with an unusual ferocity. Like the buffalo, the sturgeon had something of the great ancient beast about them—these fish could be ten feet long and weigh some four hundred pounds—and seemed to move in undiminishing schools. The ardor with which they were hunted went beyond the value of their flesh and, in this case, their roe. And the killing only ended with both species of Delaware sturgeon nearly extinct. Beck, who worked for thirty-seven years with the Delaware Department of Natural Resources, says that even in the 1880s there were warnings about the demise of the sturgeon. No one wanted to believe them.

As late as the Civil War, sturgeon were appreciated more as curiosities than as food. They often came in schools of thousands up the river, leaping from the water as they moved upstream between Philadelphia and Trenton. As a reporter in 1890 recalled:

> *Many years ago there was a little steamboat which plied the Delaware above Philadelphia called the* Sally. *On each side, near her bows, were two large round windows, which, in the summertime, were often open. One day when the* Sally *was on one of its trips up the river, a large sturgeon in jumping made such a leap that it passed clear through one of these windows and landed in the vessel, where it was killed.*

Shad fishermen considered sturgeon a nuisance since they made their spawning runs at the same time as the shad, and could tear through the shad nets. Sturgeon meat sold for a few cents a pound. It was most often used for bait to catch eels. A whole uncut fish might bring only twenty-five to thirty cents because it was simply too much trouble to deal with.

But with the beginning of the commercial caviar industry in the 1850s, the value of the fish took its own leaps. By the 1880s the Delaware was the country's premier sturgeon river. Boats and nets crowded shore to shore. In 1890 the recorded catch reached some five million pounds (and commercial fishermen, unlike sportfisher-men, have always been notorious at underestimating the size of their catch). Each May, with the spawning run at its peak, the docks along the river from the aptly named town of Caviar (now Bayside), New Jersey, to Port Penn and Delaware City, were jammed with the fish being cut, gutted, and stripped of their roe. Crews bunked in houseboats along the shore. With the high tide they went out in two-man crews in sailing skiffs, setting deep nets to drift on the slack tide—deep nets because the sturgeon has an ancient toothless mouth on the underside of its snoutlike head and so feeds on the crustaceans of the river bottom.

Netted fish were gaffed with iron hooks and hauled up onto decks, where they lay still, their unfishlike heads with round, bead eyes giving them an almost doglike appearance. According to one account: "Although from 6 to 10 feet in length, they struggle very little when gilled. When being hauled into the boat they seem to lose all heart, and are generally rolled in like a log."

Loaded vessels quickly sailed up to the butchering wharves where the catch was sorted. The females with ripe, hard roe used in the preparation of caviar were called "cows." "Runners" were fe-male fish with roe too soft to process. "Slunkers" had already spawned. Males were "bucks," and young fish were "mammoses." An 1892 report to the Pennsylvania Fish Commission described the processing of the roe:

> *After the eggs have been removed from the fish, they are placed in large chunks upon a stand, the top of which is formed of a small-meshed screen. On the under side is arranged a zinc-lined trough, about 18 inches deep, 2 feet wide, and 4 feet long. The operator gently rubs the mass of eggs back and forth over the screen. The mesh is just large enough to let the eggs drop through, and as they are separated from the membrane by the rubbing, they fall through into the trough and are thence drawn off into tubs by means of a sliding door at the end of the trough. After all the roe has been separated, the tub is removed and a certain proportion of the best Luneburg (Germany) salt added*

to the roe, after which the operator carefully stirs and mixes the
mass with his hands. The most delicate part of the whole oper-
ation is in the manner of mixing.

Once drained, the salted eggs were transferred to oak or pine
casks that each held about 135 pounds of caviar. In 1885 a keg sold
for from nine to twelve dollars. In 1891 a keg sold for twenty. But
then the catch began to decline: from five million to four million,
and, by 1897, to two and a half million. The price of a keg of roe
jumped in turn to forty-six dollars. Even at that price, the fish were
becoming so scarce that many fishermen quit the business altogether. By 1898 the catch was down to a million and a half pounds.
The price of the roe shot up to seventy-three dollars a keg. By 1899
it was $105 a keg.

As the catch of the large Atlantic sturgeon declined and the value
of the roe and smoked fish increased, fishermen decreased the size of
their net mesh so they could catch even the smaller shortnose sturgeon. While both are long-lived fish, they reach reproductive age
late. Female sturgeons only begin to mature enough to breed at
twelve years. They were being caught long before then. So the crash
came suddenly.

Port Penn, Delaware, still has only four streets. But it's a wonderful small town on the edge of the Delaware marsh where one
could make all the introductions necessary in less than an hour.
There's Kelly's Liquors, John's Food Mart, the House of Furniture, the First Port Penn Church, the Augustine Inn, the white
clapboard post office, and even Dr. Stewart's old house. And there's
the cabin of a museum that Bob Beck helped the town develop in
order to preserve a little bit of its wild and woolly history. The state
of Delaware gave some money and in the enthusiasm of the Bicentennial celebrations a lot of bake sales helped pay for the upkeep of
the relics—from sturgeon gaffs to market guns—that people pulled
from their attics. But with attics cleaned, enthusiasm waned and
Beck began to have a hard time maintaining the place. When I
visited, it was closed more often than it was open. But Beck has his

own key, and as though it were his very own repository, he takes me through the collection with a thoughtful narrative of the decline of the sturgeon, the lives of the Delaware watermen, and the remote possibilities for a renaissance.

"In 1957 was a lot of fish. You'd see two hundred fish jumping on a tide, if you can visualize that. So somewhere around the turn of the century they had successful spawning. So now the young of those fish are forty to forty-five years old. And with the conditions of the river improved, I bet they're spawning as well."

Though sturgeon are occasionally seen rolling or, more rarely, leaping in the river, and shad fishermen sometimes catch one in their nets, the real numbers that now exist in the bay and river have become a mystery once again. As Beck puts it, it's difficult to get anyone to do a study of a fish that will outlive you. Those who have tagged and tracked the shortnose sturgeon believe there are thousands in the upper river, between Philadelphia and Trenton. But they warn that the continued dredging and deepening of the shipping channels may ruin even this last place of refuge.

Beck is doleful. "Oh, the younger generation doesn't know how bad this river was. I've seen it when it was pure shit floating up and down and it was hard to look at without gettin' sick. So I can appreciate the change. Now open space is a concern to me— waterfowl, woods, streams, croplands—I just hate to see houses coming at the rate they are. They wanted to put in a landfill here behind this marsh and I stood up—I was an activist, I guess—I stood up and fought and finally it was turned down. Then, goddamn it, there's going to be houses, and I don't know which is worse. And see, you're coming into a people now who don't know about sturgeon and will never fish for sturgeon."

He sees the little museum as a last window on those days.

"I sometimes think it was a mistake. I stood up and said make a museum. We had to sell a lot of pies and cakes to get it. But I'm proud because if we hadn't started, then all this stuff would've been sold in flea markets. First several years we could get volunteers. Now it's just almost only me and I worry about it. But it's served a lot of people—senior citizens, school groups—so I announced at the last meeting, I said we'd have to close unless we had help. But I'd hate to see the effort go down the tubes."

The latest news was that the state of Delaware would bear the minimal expenses of the place.

As for the fate of the sturgeon fisherman? Beck introduces me to Clyde Roberts of Port Penn, a trim, slightly stoop-shouldered retiree with a sun-pinkened face that colors his clear-framed eyeglasses.

When it comes to sturgeon fishing, Roberts seems to pretty much have the drift of the whole bay and river.

Sturgeon fishing has become a kind of retirement preoccupation for him. He takes nearly anyone who's curious out fishing, from reporters for the local papers to government scientists. In a well-rehearsed routine he pulls on his white rubber boots, hitches the trailer, with his white fiberglass fishing boat, to the pickup, drives down the half-mile to Port Penn's concrete boat ramp on the river, and puts in, his nets already stowed and ready to run.

The day we drift is humid and the fishing slow. This is not the sturgeon fishing of a hundred years ago; the pace is more Roberts's own. The slow drift of the boat recalls for him his days on the mail-train run from Philadelphia to Norfolk, long runs with breaks in Pocomoke and Philadelphia and the only excitement being when the train, without stopping, made its pickup, "hits the stick and dumps the sack," as Roberts puts it. It is, he acknowledges, a kind of pace, a kind of life, hard even for him to remember except out here, rocking on the water. We catch only a few fish, two to five feet long, leathery skin studded with five rows of rigid pinkish-tinged scutes running from barbeled nose to hard, vertical tail. They are as solid as logs, and with their pointed snouts and flat undersides they look something like alligators that have begun to sprout wings. Only the largest might be a keeper, but Roberts releases them all. They float a moment on the surface, then dive and disappear.

"I'm not the greatest conservationist in the world," says Roberts on our return, "but I can't see selling something that lives so long so cheap."

"Man gets accustomed to everything," Alexis de Tocqueville wrote in 1831:

> *He gets used to every sight. . . . [He] fells the forests and drains the marshes. . . . The wilds become villages, and the villages towns. The American, the daily witness of such wonders, does not see anything astonishing in all this. This incredible destruction, this even more surprising growth, seem to him the usual progress of things in this world. He gets accustomed to it as to the unalterable order of nature.*

But not back at Roberts's house, where pretty soon an argument is in progress.

RICK'S PLACE

ACROSS THE LITTLE KITCHEN TABLE FROM THE BESPECTACLED AND mild-mannered Clyde Roberts sits a stone-faced and mousy-eyed Rick "Muskrat" Davis, retired too, but still as intense as a scout, and at the moment sorely vexed over some long-past slight. And though the two of them have had this conversation before, perhaps often before, Rick gets no less lowdown as he harangues Clyde over the crooked deals that rooked his father out of a piece of prime property.

Clyde, seeming to agree, lowers his eyes and calmly nods, but then doesn't agree at all. Rick, he asserts, just simply never saw the will in question.

"But I knowed what was in it," blurts Rick, " 'cause she showed it to my daddy!"

"Maybe what she showed your daddy was different than what it was."

"I knowed it wasn't!"

"How do you know?"

"My daddy knowed it. I knowed it. Everybody knowed what they pulled!"

The sun pours in through the golden marsh reeds that sway just out back of Clyde's house. (The house sits right on the edge of the Delaware river marsh that never became a street, so each summer a crop of reeds blocks his view of the river.) How this argument flew in the window I wasn't certain, for barely a minute before the talk had been all about trapping snapping turtles and muskrat, which, for retired men and young boys along this low tidal shore of the Delaware River, have always been two of the major occupations. As it turned out, the property in question was a marsh where Rick's father had trapped muskrat.

A cranky old widow, "the Muskrat Queen of Delaware," had owned the farm and Rick Davis's father had trapped it for her, and the father had even suffered the humiliation each night before leaving of being shaken down by the foreman to check whether he'd stashed any stolen pelts on him—a humiliation that was still a nightmare to his earnest son, for Rick himself trapped the marshes and knew that if you did it right, you took the large and left the young, and like the Bible said, let a field lie fallow now and again, there was no more moral way to make a living. But somehow the marsh had been left to the undevout foreman.

"He fiddled his way into the farm," Rick insists. "It was left for his use, not, goddamn it, to give him the deed. *That* he took."

"You don't know that," says Clyde. "You just don't know it."

But one could tell this wind blew in whenever Rick's mind was in a storm as it was today. His snapper-trapping season had just begun: Should he raise his price for cleaned turtles from $1.50 to $1.75 a pound? And Clyde, always considerate, suggested that maybe Rick ought to just let his present price ride, seeing as how he had a ready market for his turtles. How much was he bringing in? Three to four thousand pounds a year. But the price had been the same for ten years. And the price of his pelts was down—muskrat from six dollars to barely two, coons from thirty dollars to three—

because the Chinese and the Russians had glutted the small-fur market with ranch-raised mink.

"So quit trapping and raise mink instead of chickens."

One could see by the cloud that came over Rick's face that that suggestion did not even rate a response.

A tidal marsh owes its existence to the rise of sea level. The view out Clyde's window twelve thousand years ago would have been of open spruce woodlands, a northern woods vista that included pine and fir and overlooked a plain of mixed woods and grasslands. Through the plain ran the cold, swift river, its mouth fifty miles off what is now the Atlantic Coast. The ice sheet, still only several hundred miles to the north, just north of the river's headwaters, dominated the weather. The Pleistocene forest was damp, cold, and rainy, but different still from today's northern woods. The late glacial scenery has been characterized, by those who have studied the fossil pollen found below the surface of the present shoreline, as a "disharmonious" mosaic, a hodgepodge of habitats rich enough to harbor not only the expected (and now extinct) woodland musk ox, but, as the Delaware archaeologist Jay Custer writes, an anomalous assemblage that might also include "grazing mammoth, browsing mastodon, giant moose of swampy forests, woodland peccaries, as well as white-tailed deer, caribou, elk, and giant beaver." He also cites evidence for smaller mammals: "moles, shrews, squirrels, lemmings, voles, and mice; various species of bat," and "carnivores such as wolf, skunk, otter, weasel, and fox." And, most likely, the adaptable muskrat, which even today lives in habitats as diverse as Hudson Bay and the marshes of the Gulf of Mexico.

As Pleistocene warmed to Holocene, the ice sheet melted further, receding north of the Great Lakes. The flow of the river increased and carved a course down through the hard upstream ridges, carrying along a load of fine grains of eroded rock. It deposited this silty "flour" as it flooded its lower plain. Sea level was rising, up to six feet every hundred years, and washing the shorelines back at least thirty feet a year (now a foot a century and three feet a year, respectively). At some point about ten thousand years ago, the combined effects of receding glacial ice and atmospheric changes brought about a relatively sudden warming trend.

Just as some paleontologists assert that evolution takes place in sudden bursts of speciation between long periods without change, so some climatologists see in the fossil record evidence that the climate may change abruptly, then settle down for a period of relative equilibrium. With this sudden Holocene warming—from 10,000 to 8,000 B.C.—the woodland mosaic vanished, and the still-enigmatic complexities of this never-seen-again patchwork of spruce, fir, pine, and meadowlands gave way to great stands of pine, which spread over much of the open land and left the great ancient grazing animals with precious little grassland. They became displaced, driven by the changing landscape to ever smaller refugia and, eventually, extinction. Mastodon and giant moose retreated northward where they might still browse in cool northern spruce forest, while deer, elk, and bear remained behind. A new array of transitional zones, called ecotones, replaced the patchwork of habitats. These places—the edge of the forest, the edge of the land—bridged one natural community with another and held their own riches.

For a long while the swift downstream flow of the river kept the rising tidewaters from moving inland, but the broad plain, flooding often, slowly filled in, and soon the course of the river itself disappeared beneath the broadening waters. For the next few thousand years the warming trend continued, and so did the changes in the land. Oak began growing among the pines, and new pine seedlings failed to grow under the denser oak foliage. Acorns provided food for turkey and squirrels; beech, hickory, elm, and chestnut provided mast for migrating birds like passenger pigeons, which came north "in numbers beyond conception" to nest, the beating of their wings in the woods sounding like a heavy downpour coming after their spring flights had darkened the skies with their passage.

A dry period then set in. Streams settled in their courses, the river slowed, the rush of silt diminished. The rise of sea level slowed. But with less rain and less fresh water coming downstream, the tide moved far up the bay and its tributaries. Some three thousand years ago the climate of modern times was established. Seasons came to these now-temperate climes. Along the shores of the growing bay, natural lives began to intertwine at the new confluences of land and water.

Sedges, cattails, wild rice, water lilies, arrow arum, sweetflag, and bulrushes took root and consolidated the drifting silt. The pulse of the tides circulated nutrients and oxygen. Algae thrived. The plants stored nutrients in their roots, rhizomes, and tubers. Snapping turtles, terrapins, ducks, raccoons, and muskrats fed on the plants. Fox and mink fed on the muskrat, raccoons, ducks, and turtle eggs (not much of anything will feed on a full-grown snapper). When the plants died, the growth of bacteria produced an enriched crop of detritus. Worms and insects fed on the detritus. Wading birds came to pick crustaceans out of the thick mud. Tirelessly cheering redwings tied their nests to the old stalks of cattail. Yellowthroats, marsh wrens, and scuttling rails came to feed or nest among the new plenitude of insect life. Fish and shellfish that, thousands of years before, had retreated to southern waters from the descending ice sheet—clams, oysters, crabs, sturgeon, striped bass, shad, and eels—followed the warming tidal waters north to these new feeding grounds. Ospreys, harriers, and eagles followed the feeders.

So did humans. Unlike the ancient and remotely imagined repavings of the geological landscape, humans were within view of the whole of tidal-marsh history—they felt the temperatures change, watched spruce give way to pine and pine to oak, and tracked the mammoth into extinction. Humans saw the sea rise, the shore retreat, the river flood and turn brackish and vanish beneath the tidewaters. And archaeologists know humans noticed. They have dated settlements along what were the spruce terraces above the Delaware as early as twelve thousand years ago, and have found evidence that as the climate and landscape changed, so did the prehistoric technology for dealing with it. Fluted jasper points of the Paleo-Indians of the mid-Atlantic coast were shaped to fit onto spear shafts, the weapon of choice for the nomadic big-game hunter.

The tool kit, as archaeologists call the collections of artifacts, also included knives and points for butchering and shaping hide and bone. In looking for places to encamp, such hunters kept base camps both close to hunting grounds and sources of stone—especially jasper and chert.

From the evidence—or, more correctly, from the lack of evidence—few finds along the river come from the very early Holocene. It appears that with the first warming trend and the change from spruce to pine forest, the Paleo-Indians retreated northward from the coast, following the larger game. But within a thousand years, artifacts begin to appear again along the river and its tributaries: stone sinkers designed to tie onto fishing nets, and tools that may have been used in agriculture. As the oak and mast-producing forests spread, the small game became more plentiful. The people carried a more diversified and sophisticated tool kit, with axes, adzes, celts, spear-thrower weights, and grinding tools. They made smaller spearpoints to take fish and smaller game. These natives recognized the advantages of the seasonal changes and, following the advance of the salt water, made camps farther inland as the head of the tide moved upstream. (These would be the spawning reaches of the herring, striped bass, and white perch.) On a wooded terrace above "the swift waters of the Lenape," one could hunt deer and turkey and small game, and collect acorns and chestnuts in the fall. On the floodplain below, one could harvest cattails or plant crops in the rich peaty soil; and in the spring, summer, and fall on the marsh and river, the freshwater mussels permeated the muddy banks, and the migrating fish and birds came to your traps and nets. And each year, life in river and marsh renewed itself.

In Lenape myth, the world was flooded and new land was brought to the surviving humans, in one legend by the muskrat, "which dived, scooped up some mud, but failed to come back to the surface alive. From a speck of earth, however, clutched in its dead paws, the world miraculously took its birth." By another account the new world took root on the moss-covered back of a turtle.

"We lived off the water during the Depression," says Rick. "We fished, snappered, trapped, hunted squirrel, rabbit, deer—I'd say my daddy just about fed Smyrna Landing. Took turtles into Philadelphia and ducks and rabbits into the King Street market in Wilmington. Then, after retiring from Sun Oil at sixty, he went back down to the water again."

Things on the river weren't so very good then.

"When I came out of the navy I cooked on a tug hauling out of Marcus Hook. The oil refineries used to wash their tanks out in the river—acid tanks—raw acid right into the river. You couldn't fish for the oil and the sewage. Them Jews at the market in Wilmington could lift a gill and smell oil on it. My grandmother would say to me, 'Go catch a mess of catfish for dinner, but don't go up to the head of Smyrna Creek.' That's where the sewage come out."

But things have improved, and the waters are cleaner, clean enough so that he could retire and begin living off the river. Now, Rick says happily, "I can live again like it's Depression times."

A small rowboat sits among black willows at the edge of a cove in Thousand Acre Marsh, which is a patchwork of high green reeds, cattail stalks as tall as August corn, and open water curtained by the reeds to the west and stretching to the Delaware River's early bright horizon to the east. Since the boat is small, Rick decides to stay on shore and let me go out with Joey Boyles, who, off and on, lives and works with Rick. Every bit as intense as Rick, Joey is in his twenties, lean, muscular, with tattoos on his forearms I can't quite make out for his flannel shirt. He has straight black hair and a little tuft of a chin beard. Joey refers to Rick sometimes as "Pop," sometimes as "Mr. Davis." He pushes us off and out into the marsh. The little electric motor moves us along into the open water of the cove. The going is slow but silent, the idea being to keep poachers from knowing where the turtle traps, known as fykes, have been set. ("You get a big outboard," Rick had told me soberly, "and soon you'll have everybody tending to your fykes.")

This is the broadening mouth of the river, where it opens into the bay, and is fed by the filamentary creeks that flow through the low wetlands. Where it can, where it isn't stopped by dikes or mill dams, the tide makes all these streams—Blackbird Creek, Hangman's Run, Augustine Creek, the Appoquinimink—into little estuaries. Fresh water flows from the wild-rice-and-cattail marshes of their upper reaches and meets and mixes with brackish water as it meanders slowly toward the salt marsh cordgrasses at the Delaware shore. Herring, white perch, and striped bass will run up these streams to spawn, their young finding safe havens in the shadowy grassy shallows. Young eels, spawned in the Sargasso Sea in the Atlantic Ocean, take to the creeks as their long migrations bring them up into the Delaware. Everywhere along the way the carp and dusky bullhead catfish go muddling the bottom. And in every pond or reedy stillwater there seem to be snapping turtles.

Dusky, scabrous, algae-covered, with sawtoothed shell, spiked tail, fleshy armored neck, and flattened hooked beak, the snapping turtle looks like the cantankerous survivor it is. Though the oldest fossils known are some 65 million years old, the snapper shows the long tail, armor, bone structures, and perhaps Triassic temperament of the big turtles of 200 million years ago. Its small undershell seems barely adequate to keep its massive body cinched within its carapace. Under the carapace the ribs arch away from the vertebrae, leaving a long tunnel through which the muscles run in one stretch from the neck all the way down to the pelvis. When a snapping turtle strikes, the muscles that control the strike contract all the way to the base of its tail. The bite comes together with a pressure of some four hundred pounds per square inch. (As big as the common snapper is, it can be dwarfed by its less common relative, the alligator snapper. One Indiana lake denizen known as "the Beast of Busco," was reportedly as big around as a dining room table and estimated to weigh five hundred pounds.)

The common snapping turtle most likely came early to the new unglaciated terrain, moving northward from drainage to melting drainage. They still have an exceptionally large northern range for reptiles—snapping turtles are a big, if not bigger, business in Canada—and adapt quickly to new surroundings. They seem to thrive so long as there are pondweed, water lilies, crayfish, or bullheads to feed on (though, like many turtles, they show a fondness for wild grapes), and so make themselves at home in farm ponds, fresh- and brackish-water marshes, lakes, creeks, and bogs. (Snapping turtles are common sights in the lake in New York's Central Park, and have been picked up crossing the surrounding avenues.) They prefer soft ground where they can nestle during the day, and dig in (sometimes in muskrat burrows) for hibernating through the winter. Nesting females need higher, preferably sunny ground to be able to bury their large clutches of two to three dozen Ping-Pong-ball-size eggs, but a nearby roadbed will do.

For the trappers, this is the second snapper season of the year. In early spring, just after the muskrat trapping ends, people on both sides of the Delaware go "proggin'" for turtles, walking out onto the just-thawing marshes with staffs, pounding the hard mud (this is also known as mudwhallopin'), listening for the hollow-log sound that means a turtle lies hibernating beneath the surface. A little digging shows the turtle, which is then grabbed by the tail and sacked. The proggin' season ends in early May, and in June the fyking season begins. What has enabled the snapper to survive a couple of centuries of trapping is that it lays so many eggs during its long reproductive lifetime (many more than most reptiles) that even with the number of eggs dug up and poached by raccoons (by some studies, as many as 90 percent) and young killed by fish and birds, the animal persists. Not that it can't be trapped out. In some Canadian waters that appears to have already happened.

They are meaty animals, long savored, along with terrapin and muskrat, on both sides of the Delaware. Archaeological digs at colonial privy sites nearly always turn up an abundance of snapper bones, and the deep, rich broth of snapper soup, thinned only by a touch of sherry, remains a delicacy in Philadelphia and Wilmington restaurants. This morning, before coming out to the marsh, Joey and Rick drove fifty miles to deliver four hundred pounds of cleaned snappers to a customer in Wilmington. Rick also bought two thousand pounds of uncleaned snappers from other trappers. The cleaning, skinning, and cutting up of the turtle into neck, tail, and limbs is time-consuming work, but the profit margin's higher than trapping alone. Turtles are a serious business, and with ever fewer acres of available marsh and open water, Joey and Rick don't take the threat of poachers lightly. A recent oil spill in the river has temporarily closed the crabbing, and now, as Rick puts it, "every bastard is out here snapperin' and floodin' the market."

They had set the tubular wire fykes the day before. These traps have been used at least since the Dutch settled the river in the seventeenth century. Originally a woven bag or basket shaped like a Chinese lantern with supports of grapevine or wooden hoops and used for trapping fish, the snapper fyke works by allowing the animals to swim in through a funnel-shaped entrance that they can't back out of. (The Dutch word *fuyk* referred to a V-shaped run used for trapping herds of deer.) Rick's wire fykes look more like wire wastebaskets. In the side is a wire pocket for bait ("Shad heads, bunker, anything that puts up a blood smell, anything Clyde has on hand," Rick says). Each trap is roped to a wooden pole, a thick tree limb staked into the marsh so that the top of the fyke stays just above the water, allowing the trapped turtles to come up for air.

As we approached the first trap we could see a turtle head poking just above the waterline. Joey cut the engine and let us drift up to the stake. He grabbed it as it came up to him in the stern and pulled us alongside. He untied the fyke from the pole, hauled it up over the boat, and shook out a snapping turtle whose head, tail, and claws would hang out over the sides of a good-size serving platter, and which began a serpentlike gaping and hissing. Joey lifted it by its spiny tail and, keeping it at arm's length—its claws flailing, its long neck arched, and its fist-size head looming just at knee level— lowered it into a canvas sack that he raised around the animal and knotted shut. He then pulled up the stake and set it in the boat with the trap. Joey estimated that the snapper weighed twenty pounds, above the average ten-to-fifteen-pounder and well above the weight allowed by the eight-inches-across-the-back size minimum. That minimum, as far as Joey's concerned, is far too generous. That's too small a turtle, he says, too young a turtle, although he knows a few trappers, like the infamous "Wire Man," who will keep everything they get. The biggest one Joey and Rick ever caught in this marsh weighed thirty-one pounds, but Joey's heard of snappers that weighed twice that.

When the next two fykes were empty, Joey became sullen, with unspoken suspicions running in his mind, silent but just as persistent as the hum of the electric motor. Not until he spotted turtle heads in the next fyke did his mood change. And each one thereafter had one or more turtles, and the additional poundage soon had the little motor laboring. Going so slowly and so low in the water with the boatload of hissing turtles I imagined us hauling sackfuls of adders on some Stygian mission, an image enhanced by Joey when he rolled up his sleeves to reveal neat tattoos of a skull and of a red devil with a pitchfork on his forearms.

But the marsh around us was in full bloom, the water gold-green with summer growth; the arrow arum had sent up its flower spikes, fish jumped, redwings and herons flew just over the tall spikes of cattail—a paradisal place, really, with a breeze that kept the curtain of reed blowing and the greenhead flies at bay, the flies being the one thing that can turn a marsh like this into a hellish place; long pants and long-sleeve shirts are a necessity even in the hot summer sun.

By eleven o'clock we'd picked up all the traps, and we went around to the other side of the cove to make another set. Drifting along the margins of the marsh, Joey chose a spot a few yards off from the stands of cattail, jammed in a stake, baited a trap, and tied it on the stake using two half-hitches—one wrapped one way and one the other—and making another wrapping around the rope itself "so when we come back we'll know if anybody's been here," and dropped it into the water. Joey and Rick will set this cove for five days and then move on.

As we completed the set, the little motor finally died. Joey took up the oars and began "a right good row," as he called it, back to the shore. The expression is distinctly southern, Eastern Shore, Chesapeake Bay, for though we're barely fifty miles south of Wilmington, this part of Delaware has more in common with the rural waterman's culture of the Chesapeake than with the city life of the Northeast urban corridor that begins not far upriver. (The

Chesapeake-Delaware Canal serves as a kind of cultural boundary. South of it, a man without a John Deere cap on his head is sure to be taken for a Yankee. North of the canal, stores carry the *Philadelphia Inquirer*; south of the canal, people read the *Baltimore Sun*. At the very southern end of Delaware they read the *Norfolk Pilot*. People will boast about how long it's been since they've been north to Wilmington or Philadelphia. Joey Boyles tells me he's only been out of Delaware four times in his whole life.) The Chesapeake connection is as strong across the river in New Jersey. South of Camden the landscape and lives are coastal plain, more of a piece with those of Delaware and the Eastern Shore of Maryland.

Joey rows without making the least splash, and now, his work done, he seems to feel free to talk.

"Oh, I like foolin' around on the water and whatnot, trappin', fishin'. But I'm the only one in my family to do it. So I learned everything I know from Mr. Davis. I knew him since I was eleven and I used to go through Townsend to Blackbird Creek on my bicycle and I started helpin' him with his house and we've been friends ever since. I'd help him do this and that and from there that went into trappin', then fishin', snapperin', a little huntin'.

"He's got a bad heart and his wife would like to see him get out of this, but he enjoys bein' out here and I don't let him do none of the hard work. Just let him run the motor. A lot of men gamble or chase women. He just enjoys bein' out in nature. Pretty soon you won't be able to move here for the people. And the same crowd everyone's movin' here to get away from is followin' them. When I was comin' up, there was only six houses on Blackbird Landing Road. Now there's fifty. The crime rate's up ten times what you had ten years ago."

The numbers, of course, are all relative. Most cities have more crimes in a night than Blackbird Creek has in a year or more. But while development has meant winter work—Joey does roofing—it has also cut down on the areas open for hunting, trapping, and fishing, making it harder for Joey and others like him to continue living the way they would, moving from livelihood to livelihood with the changes of the season.

"I don't like to be tied down to any one thing. I do a little bit of everything. There's always somebody out there needs something done, so there's always work if you're willing to do it."

He puts up the oars and we drift across the open water.

"What I'd like to do," Joey says, "is bring a fishing rod out here and make a whole day of it. There are eight-to-ten-pound channel cats in here. And bass. This cove is my favorite spot."

Ashore, we load the sacks of turtles into the back of the truck and drive back to Townsend.

Rick says his heart's holding up just fine. He isn't nearly ready to retire.

"Shit. I can't quit. My father used to always stay away trapping, stayed away for the season, and when he got home my mother made him take a bath and change his clothes. He done that all his life until he was eighty-three. Then she made him quit and stay at home in Lynwood, Pennsylvania, and he didn't last out a year."

Rick's place is part wooden shack, part cement block. A dog with a black and brown face trots barking alongside us as we pull up the drive. A goat grazes about its dusty, wire-fenced yard. We unload the turtles, haul them into the garage, and dump them into institutional-size metal sinks where fifty other snappers scrape about in several inches of water. If he puts too much water into the sinks, Rick explains, the larger turtles will crawl over the backs of the smaller ones and drown them. Rick spends a few days trapping and a few days slaughtering and cleaning. The killing is quick. He stuns each turtle with the back of an ax, then cuts off its head. It is, he says, a better way than scalding them. Some he knows, he says, scald the turtles while they're still alive, so that in crawling over each other they scrape off their own skins. The idea, he says, makes his own skin crawl.

Inside the long, narrow, low-ceilinged main room of the house, an air conditioner blasts from one end and a television is on. Through a door is Rick's study, a ten-by-ten paneled den with a hunting cabin's clutter, wildlife prints, a side table with a lamp made from a stuffed beaver kit (the kit is missing its big front teeth), a muskrat skin on the wall, a collection of turtle claws, and a sofa upholstered in a fabric printed with outdoor vistas. On the shelves is a collection of painted porcelain children and animals. Above Rick's desk, crowded with receipts and old issues of fur-trapping journals, is a collection of family photos in a single frame: kids, grandkids, son in navy uniform; Rick's photo of the USS *Biloxi*, on which he himself served in the Pacific from 1943 to 1946; and his certificate for crossing the Equator. Prominent on the wall opposite, an oil painting of FDR: "The only President," Rick avows, "that we ever had."

Rick says another of his sons joined the marines. He didn't want him to. He went to Vietnam and was wounded three times.

"He came back different," is all Rick will say. Within a year he killed himself. It was the second time Rick had told me this.

Out in the garage, Joey was cleaning things up. Rick's wife had come out and set up a lawn chair in the shade of the garage and sat silently, staring out at the yard and the narrow blacktop lane. Rick calls her "Mother." Rick begins to tell me how to prepare the snapper for soup.

"I don't like the soup at all, Pop," Joey says, "but I do like it fried."

Rick proudly displays a freezerful of cleaned and packaged turtle.

"Nothing's wasted. I'd rather quit than waste."

He shows me the old cedar shingles on which his father stretched muskrat hides, the woven snapper fyke his dad made and used, and his own old woven-oak backpack, which he used to carry into the marsh when he could still go trapping: "This here on my back filled with muskrat—like this—" he says, bending at the waist to show me how he'd carry the load, "and the water and blood dripping down my ass." Man and marsh become one.

A Turtle's Tale

SOME 110 YEARS AGO, CHARLES CONRAD ABBOTT, PHYSICIAN, NATU-ralist, and raconteur archaeologist (whom we will meet later and a little farther upriver), wrote and collected stories about the Delaware River marshes, including a few recollections by a neighbor whom he called Uz Gaunt, a rheumatoid eighty-year-old trapper and fisherman, still spry of mind and with "an eye as bright and piercing, at the last, as when, a score of years ago, he would point out the green head of a mallard in the tall grass and bid me shoot." Gaunt was Abbott's natural man, the quintessential river rat, a kind of gone-to-seed Deerslayer who had grown up, unlike Abbott, without civilizing influences in an increasingly civilized world. Abbott, a far greater realist than James Fenimore Cooper, made the cantankerous Uz his own surly spokesman. Here is Uz's turtle tale, a little river classic that takes place on an especially warm Christmas Day in 1877:

"The river was low, the meadows dry, and the crows as noisy as in April. I felt sort of restless-like, and I took a walk in the meadows. I left my gun home, and thought I'd just look 'round. Without thinking of them when I started out, I wandered over to your marshy meadow, and began pokin' about with my cane for snappers. You know I take kindly to a bowl of snapper-soup of my own fixin'.

"Well, I followed the main ditch down, jumpin' from hassock to hassock, and kept probin' in the mud with my cane, when, after a bit, I felt something hard at the end of my stick. It wasn't a stone or a stump, I knew at once. There was a tremble run up the stick so my hand told me that much. A sort of shake, as though you hit an empty barrel, as near as I can tell you. I'd a turtle down in the mud, and concluded to bring it out into the daylight.

"There's more than one way to do this, but none of 'em is an easy job to get through with. I kept probin' 'round him, to try and make out where his head was, and then I could feel for his tail, and pull him out. Now this does very well for one of your common snappers, but didn't work so easy in this case. I could sort of feel that turtle all over the meadow. Wherever I put my cane down, I seemed to come to his back shell; but after edgin' out a bit for some time I could make out the rim of it, and I tell you he was a whopper, accordin' to my probin'. That turtle seemed as big around as a wash-tub, and I got regularly worked up about him. I wasn't in trim for huntin', but didn't care. I'd found a turtle that was worth havin', and I meant to have him.

"Probin' showed that he was about three feet deep in the mud, but I made up my mind to locate his tail and then reach down for him. So I did, but it was no use. I felt about, and got one ugly scratch from a hind foot, but he kept his tail out of reach, or hadn't any; I didn't know which, then. After thinkin' a spell, I concluded I'd try to get a pry under him, and went for a fence rail. It took me some time to get what I wanted, and when I got back that turtle had got out. I probed all 'round, but he'd moved. This rather took me down, but I kept up my hunt, and after a bit found he'd moved straight for the main ditch, and was tearin' up the mud on the bottom as he went. This was all that saved him for me, and I no sooner learned his whereabouts than I went for him in earnest.

"I ran the rail I had right under him, and tried to lift him up. Thunder and lightnin', boy, you might as well try to lift a steer. I disturbed him, though, and checked his course a bit. Jammin' the rail down again, I guess I hit his head, for it riled him, evidently, and he raised right up. His head and neck came up out of the sand, and I was for standin' back just then. If ever you saw a wicked eye, that turtle had one, and his head was as big as my fist. Stickin' his head out, though, gave me the knowledge I wanted. I knew how he laid in the mud, and I ran my rail down under him as far as I could. It kept him from divin' down, and I went right into the ditch to try and get a hold on his tail if I could. This I did, after feelin' for it a bit, and no sooner had I got a good grip on it than the old fellow got free of the rail and commenced to goin' deep into the mud. I tugged and he dug, and it was a clear case of 'pull Dick, pull devil' between us.

"He was gettin' the better of me, though, for I was gettin' chilled in that water, and had nearly lost my hold, when the turtle gave an extra jerk, and if it hadn't been for the fence-rail I'd a lost him. I was pulled for'ard, but the rail was right in front, so I put one foot on it, to keep from sinkin' any deeper in the mire. This bracin' gave me the advantage now, and I put all my strength to it. The turtle came a little, and I seemed to gain strength. I tugged and tugged with all my might, and presently his hind feet showed. You see, he hadn't firm enough mud to hold on to. I backed slowly across the ditch when I got him in open water, and got a fair footin' on the ditch-bank at last. Still, I wasn't out of the woods by a long shot. That turtle weighed close onto seventy pounds, and I'd no means of handlin' him.

"Chilled through, with both hands needed to hold him, and in the middle of the mucky meadow, all that was left me was to try and drag him to the high smooth meadows. It was a tough job, I tell you. I had to walk backward, and he pulled against me like a frightened horse. I gained a little, slowly, and after a bit got on the high ground. Then I felt more at ease and took a rest. I couldn't take him home, of course, in the same fashion, but I had a chance to let him loose, and rest my hands. How I looked 'round for a bit of rope to bridle him! It was no use, though, and after all I was likely to lose him altogether.

"After a minute's thinkin', it occurred to me I'd make a hobble out of my shirt and then slip home lively for the right sort of tackle. I wasn't long in gettin' the shirt off, and I twisted it into a sort of rope and hobbled him with it. It was a desperate, odd-lookin' turtle when I got through, and I laughed at him a bit as I turned toward the house. You see, I left him on his back, and his legs bound so he couldn't use 'em to turn over.

"I skipped pretty lively, I tell you, for that mile or so 'twixt me and home, and was in a good glow when I got in. Hettie looked kind o' scared when she saw me, but I put her mind to rest in two words and soon was on my way back. A bit of rope and my sheath-knife was all I needed. I skipped over the fields pretty lively, and was soon again in sight. Now, I don't think it was an hour, by some minutes, before I was back on the high meadow, but, by gracious! it don't take long for scenes to change in natur' any more than it does in a theatre. Of all queer sights, that was the funniest I saw when I got back. The turtle had got half free of my old red shirt, and was pawin' the air like mad, tryin' to get on his feet again. I could see that much a long way off, and put on extra speed; but when I was about fifty yards off I stopped short. There was that turtle wrapped in my shirt, and a pesky skunk sort of standin' guard over him.

"Now, I hate skunks. They don't pay to trap, and they rob my hen-roost every winter. I was afraid to frighten him, too, for fear he'd spoil my snapper, and I wanted the value of a shirt out of the turtle, if nothin' more. I walked a bit nearer, to make sure how matters stood, and it was clear as day, the skunk thought he had a good thing of it, if he could only kill the snapper. I thought the same way, and didn't want to be bettered by a pesky skunk.

"I made up my mind to jockey about it, a little; and so, first, heaved a stone at the critter. It gave me a look and started a slow trot, but it was all up with me, sure enough. He shook that thunderin' old brush right at the turtle and—well! if he didn't sicken the snapper, he did me, that's certain. I stood the racket a bit, though, and tried to move the snapper, but it was no use; I couldn't keep at it long enough to do anything, and don't believe it would have amounted to much anyhow. I got a stick and put the snapper on his feet, as well as I could, without touchin' him, and he waddled off for the mucky meadow, with most of my shirt still stickin' to him, and plunged into the ditch as soon as he could."

"So you lost the turtle after all," Abbott said, not feeling sure he had heard the last of the story.

"No I didn't either," Uz replied quickly. "Don't set me down for such a fool as that. I knew well enough the turtle wouldn't wander far, so I kept him in mind, and the next April I went out in proper trim and hunted him up. I found him after two days huntin', when I got a dozen big ones besides, but he was the king of the lot. He couldn't turn 'round in a wash-tub, and weighed somethin' over seventy pounds. I looked all over him for some sign of my shirt, but there wasn't a thread left."

"How old do you suppose he was?" Abbott asked.

"I'm not sure I can say, but he was no chicken, that's certain."

"According to Professor Agassiz, a turtle a foot long is close to fifty years old," Abbott told Uz.

"Fifty years old! Then my big snapper came out of the Ark, I guess."

'Rats

*I*N WINTER IT CAN BE COLD WITH WINDS BLOWING OFF THE RIVER, BUT the trappers perspire in their rubber boots and coats, and when they lift their caps the vapor rises off their heads. The marsh is as silent a place as can be found along the river, even more silent than the deep woods. Silent, but full of signs. Flocks of snow geese pad the mudflats, tearing at tufts of grass. A bald eagle may circle. I saw one swoop down on a snow goose straggling behind its flock, knock it to the ground, and rise and circle again over the now-still, white, crumpled form of the bird, lording over its kill before returning to tear into it. Otter trails and fox tracks can be made out in the patchy snow. Black ducks may rise in a flutter and head off across the water. Turkey vultures may hold vigils over frozen remains.

As the tide recedes the trappers run their boats up the tidal creeks and guts. Flagged stakes mark their traps. They pull up the stakes to which the traps are chained (not leg-hold traps but body traps, looking like something made of a couple of croquet wickets), and remove the killed muskrats. Then, with the tide out and the boat anchored in the mud, the trappers traipse back out along the exposed cut, setting the traps at the exposed burrow entrances along the sloping and undercut banks, sinking the stakes into the muck.

Down in the gut the old reed stalks break the wind. The mud is thawed and damp, and where there are no reeds, there's no mat of root underfoot and boots can sink deep. And as the trappers kneel to their traps, gray silhouettes against the deep brown marsh, they inhale a warm, lickerish musk. Most of them will tell you this is the place they like best in the world.

The muskrat itself is a lickerish animal, gnawing with its sizable incisors at cattail, bulrush, wild rice, river willow, and ear corn, hankering occasionally for fish and crayfish, and baited by everything from apples to mussels to the musk of its own oil. It looks like a tiny beaver or an overgrown meadow mouse, but with a soft blackish brown to reddish brown fur and a long narrow vertically flattened and nearly hairless tail. It is a practical little waterproof rodent, native to North America and at home nearly everywhere on the continent except the Canadian Arctic and the American south, though it thrives in the marshes of the Louisiana Gulf Coast. It swims with its small forefeet held up under its chin, either sculling with its tail or kicking its hind feet in alternating strokes, the hind feet being fringed with a kind of webbing of stiff hairs. On land, its little legs leave it as floppy as a seal and easy prey for foxes or minks. So as long as it finds water surrounded by plants—a pond, a puddle, a drainage ditch, or a whole marsh—it can set up housekeeping: burrowing, lodge-building, and mating (which it does frequently, and preferably in the water), producing three or more litters, some two dozen or more kits a year.

They spend most of the winter huddled, sometimes a dozen together, in a many-chambered burrow or in a lodge of stacked cattail, which may also have several chambers. It is when they come out that they get caught, crawling or swimming through the steel wicket, catching the lever, releasing the bail, which stuns them if it doesn't kill them, and traps them firmly. In the spring the adults are up and about the marsh on their own, leaving their scent everywhere. The yellowish musk, produced in lima-bean-size glands beneath the skin near the genitalia, lingers even in the open air as much as several days to the human nose, and, in the dried muskrat glands, seemingly indefinitely. Colonists and Europeans in the

eighteenth century used the stuff straight to perfume themselves
and their clothing and bedding. In Revolutionary France, dandies
who shunned the restrained fashions of the time became known as
muscadins for dousing themselves with excessive amounts of musk.
Muskrat glands, which sell for about forty dollars a quart, are still
used in the manufacture of some perfumes and animal attractants.
(Nothing of the animal goes to waste. Trappers sell the glands, and
then can make nearly as much selling the meat as selling the pelt.)
The smell of the musk is best described as musky, and so they seem
to be muskrats in every language: *muskessu* in Algonkin, *mussacus*
in Powhatan, *desmansrattor* in Swedish, according to Kalm
(*desman*-rat or musk rat), *rats musques* in French, and *musquash* in
American colonial slang, which begat "talking muskwash" meaning "talking fur biz," as trappers, when they gather, still do.

Many of the Delaware River trappers meet on the New Jersey
side at T. Zander & Sons fur shed in Paulsboro, by the Mantua
Creek (around here known as "the crick") that runs by the Zanders'
small farm where horses graze and geese stroll the streambank. The
scene's a pretty timeless one for being only forty miles south of
metropolitan Camden and Philadelphia. But the people here struggle to remain outliers, even as the highways loop around them like
a tangle of unwelcome lifelines. Here one still wants to trap muskrat in winter; set nets up the creeks for carp and perch, and fish the
river for shad in the spring; run down the bay for crabs in summer;
and in autumn, hunt snappers and wildfowl. And here, when one
wants to do these things, one will be damned if one won't. These
days many feel just so intractable.

In one notable year, Harrod's of London announced it would no
longer sell animal furs; Aspen, Colorado, held a vote on whether
they wouldn't, either; and the Hudson's Bay Company, which began trading furs in 1670, announced it would close all its fur salons.
So there are some hard feelings down here by the Mantua, even
though the scene seems unchanged—a young black Labrador
romps around a tolerant fat old beagle who scrapes a paw against
the screen door in the hopes of being let in to the musty comfort of
the fur shed, where, after all, the cat lies asleep atop a sack full of

pelts among thousands of pelts, their deep, rich brown fur imparting an amberous glow to the dim interior. The screen door squeals open and bangs shut as each trapper comes in to deliver his pelts.

Though these days the shed is connected to Europe by Telex and cable "Zanderfur," Tom and Harry Zander have kept the atmosphere of a frontier trading post. Along the beams overhead, skins on wire stretchers hang like bats from a cave ceiling. Old traps and chains festoon the barn posts. The trappers lean along the grading benches, or up against the stacks of furs. And each man lingers to have a coffee or beer as his hides are graded, sorted, and priced. The prices, they are assured, are down, way down. So the muskwash is all about how things used to be.

"Used to be," the trappers say.

"Used to be able to catch a hundred and eighteen muskrats in Woodbury Creek in one day," Tom Zander recalls. "Now you don't catch a hundred and eighteen muskrats there a whole winter anymore."

"Used to be, the marsh I trapped," says a bearded Delaware trapper, "like the first day I would catch fifty-five muskrats. This year it took me three days to catch thirty."

"Used to be," says Harry, "the buyers would visit each trapper and put bids on the muskrat, and the high bidder would get them and take them to New York. Used to be you'd walk up to the fur district from Twenty-ninth to Thirtieth Street and it used to be store after store of fur dealers. Used to be small dealers who would buy. Now it's either computer stores or wholesale furs from China or Hong Kong. Now we bypass New York and sell directly overseas."

"Used to be," Tom assures me, "we had a lot more cold winters. Now it's fifty degrees in Vienna in February. No snow. Don't let them tell you the poppycock that the antis are affecting anything. If we have a cold December, sales skyrocket."

But he hasn't had a cold December for a while now, and the price of a muskrat pelt, which used to be (only a few years before) four or five dollars, is less than half that. With the glut of ranch-raised mink sinking mink prices and mink being the industry standard, the value of every other fur has dropped accordingly and the value of the muskrat—always, in these trappers' view, underappreciated anyway—went down sharply. Now even the best pelts, the dark "black 'rats" as they're called, with thick wool and good guard hairs, barely bring a dollar fifty a piece. The lower prices have driven many trappers out of the business, at least temporarily. What keeps the others in is that on both sides of the Delaware River, from this latitude down, the muskrat is prized as much for its meat as for its fur. Fewer trappers mean less meat, and so, even as the value of its pelt declines, the value of its flesh increases. Used to be the meat sold for fifty cents. Now the meat's worth as much as the fur. Yet even at twenty dollars a person, the Hancock's Bridge, New Jersey, annual muskrat dinner is sold out, they assure me, a year in advance.

Still, it's not the same. Many of the trappers have left the business.

"Used to be," Harry tells me, "two brothers who trapped opposite sides of a marsh near Gibbstown. One had good 'rats and one had bad, and I could always tell one brother's 'rats from the other's."

"Used to be a deaf mute lived down on the marsh. He used to take guys out ducking. Could just grunt. Couldn't understand a word."

"Oh, I could understand him," submits one old trapper, raising a small beer. "And he could cuss you up and down. 'Sombabitch this,' he'd say, and 'sombabitch that.' "

The first recorded fur trade with the Indians along the Delaware took place in 1616, though European whalers and fishermen landed on the mid-Atlantic coast even fifty years before and may well have carried on some informal barter. In those days, the animal of choice was the beaver.

Able to live up to the edge of the tundra, the beaver, by the time the Europeans arrived, had had thousands of years to settle the continent. Estimates of their precolonial numbers run anywhere from sixty to four hundred million (now some six to twelve million).

They had virtually landscaped the river and stream valleys. Beaver ponds formed basins for soils washing downstream and reservoirs for the nutrients the soils carried with them. When colonists extirpated the beavers and drained the ponds and flooded the meadows, they had (at least for a time) a highly fertile ground for raising hay.

The decline was quick. By the time the steel trap came to America in the late seventeenth century, the beaver was nearly gone from the lower Delaware Valley. Samuel Rhoads, in *The Mammals of Pennsylvania and New Jersey*, wrote that, by 1700, the only remaining evidence that the beaver had ever existed in these states were the names of creeks, rivers, lakes, meadows, and townships. Kalm, in 1748, wrote:

> *Beavers were formerly abundant in New Sweden, as all the old Swedes here told me. At that time they saw one dam after another raised in the rivers and brooks by beavers. But after the Europeans had come over in such great numbers and cultivated the country more, many beavers had been killed. Many, too, had just died out and some had moved further into the country, where people were not so numerous.*

Kalm could have substituted the word *Indians* for *beavers*. Their fates were intertwined. Beaver hats became the rage in Europe in the 1540s, and remained fashionable in one form or another for the next 350 years. The dense inner wool, combed out and processed, made a fine waterproof felt. But by 1600 the European beaver, mostly from Flanders, were almost gone. While cloth felt was available, it hardly seemed quite right for the seventeenth-century Cavalier's broad-brimmed ostrich-plumed hat popularized in Van Dyck portraits. More important, however, was that cloth felt would not help balance the trade deficit in the new colonies. In 1638, Charles I mandated that beaver and beaver alone could be used to manufacture hats. It was a decision that doomed the American beaver and speeded up the decline of the Native American cultures that hunted them.

Europeans had a fascination for the intricacies of both beaver and Indian societies, but little regard for the perpetuation of either. The Indians were always incredulous at the intensity of the Europeans' desire for furs. (At first, the most valuable beaver pelts were those the Indians had already worn, since the wearer's own body oils, combined with the animal greases with which the natives coated themselves for winter warmth, had already softened the hide, loosened the hairs, and made it easier to process into felt.) "The Beaver does everything perfectly well," a native reportedly told one Jesuit missionary in 1634. "It makes kettles, hatchets, swords, knives, bread; and, in short, it makes everything." Explained the priest:

> *He was making sport of us Europeans, who have such a fondness for the skin of this animal and who fight to see who will give the most to these Barbarians, to get it: they carry this to such an extent that my host said to me one day, showing me a very beautiful knife, "The English have no sense; they give us twenty knives like this for one Beaver skin."*

While settlers considered Indian men lazy for not plowing and planting, they did appreciate their patient and skillful hunting. While colonists set beaver traps nearby the dams and baited them with sticks, the Indians of the southern Atlantic coast rubbed snares with a secret bitter vegetable mixture called wysoccan. Soon the oil of choice for nearly all trappers was castoreum, which is the beaver's more fusty equivalent of muskrat musk. The colonists soon began supplying the Indians with steel axes and knives to cut through the brush of the beaver lodges and, contrary to the terms of many of their own treaties, guns to kill more efficiently than bows and arrows. Whatever the method—castoreum was diluted with peppermint, powdered sassafras root, nutmeg, and whisky— the success rate was high. Beavers were easy to locate and much slower and less wary than smaller rodents like the muskrat. Wrote Dutch journalist Adriaen van der Donck, "From December to the first of June, the skins are good, and then they (the beaver) are killed. The fall skins have the winter hairs in part, with very little fur. The summer skins and those taken from ungrown beavers are of little value. Still the Indians kill all they find when they are hunting." This killing for profit rather than for food, for exotic goods and liquor, began to destroy Indian society as much as that of the animals they hunted. Writes New Jersey archaeologist Herbert Kraft:

> *It required more time to hunt and trap a sufficient number of small pelts than it took to find and kill edible deer, elks, bears, or other large mammals, and it took the hunter much farther afield. Large animals provided both food and skins; small fur-bearing animals had little food value, and some, like weasel, were inedible. The preparation of many small pelts also added to the Indian women's workload. In exchange the Indians obtained some useful tools, weapons, and brass pots, as well as luxury items, that profoundly affected their way of life.*

Liquor had its well-known effects. Guns made the Indians further dependent upon the European trade. The Native Americans of the East Coast had not forged metal. Once they became dependent upon the guns, they needed the Europeans to make repairs and supply them with ammunition.

"If the Europeans should now refuse to supply the natives with muskets," wrote Kalm, "they would starve to death."

The egalitarian ways of the Indians annoyed the European traders. In order to have a single representative to deal with, the Europeans conceived the idea of creating chiefs among the river Indians. Although the Indians themselves didn't always buy the idea, Kraft says that "gradually the almost exclusive trading through male representatives for furs and land" began to alter the previously matriarchal nature of the native society.

As they traded away furs, the Indians became more and more enamored of cloth, especially red cloth. In the fight over the trade, the Indians could drive hard bargains and play the Swedes, Dutch, and English against one another. The Swedes had fewer goods to exchange than did the Dutch and English. The English may eventually have prevailed in part because they made a better scarlet cloth.

But once the beavers had been trapped out, the Lenape were left without goods to exchange. They had already traded away most of their lands. Now the colonists looked upon them as "poor rascals," in the words of New Sweden's four-hundred-pound governor Johann Printz (whom the Indians referred to as *Meschatz* or "Big Belly": "No governor of Delaware / Before or since / Has weighed as much / As Johan Printz"). Printz wrote to the Swedish West India Company in 1644, "Nothing would be better than that a couple of hundred soldiers should be sent here and kept here until we broke the necks of all of them in the river. . . ."

The Indians of the Delaware moved west. At first they went of their own accord, into the trapping and trading territories of their rivals, the Minquas, who had been defeated during the wars with the Susquehannocks. English traders equipped them with steel traps. Later, along with other survivors, they were moved by government decree. The U.S. Office of Indian Affairs supplied and repaired the traps. And they very nearly trapped the beavers to extinction. In 1846 a machine for manufacturing cloth felt was invented, and gradually the expensive beaver hat was replaced by felt bowlers, derbies, homburgs, fedoras, and silk top hats. The great trading companies got out of the trapping business. The muskrat came into its own.

Colonists along the Delaware had considered the muskrats pretty much a nuisance. As Kalm observed:

> *They make their nests in the dikes that are erected along the banks of rivers to keep the water from the adjoining meadows, but they often do a great deal of damage by spoiling the dikes with digging and opening passages for the water to come into the meadows.*

Many farmers sank wooden slats into the dikes to keep the muskrats from burrowing through. One Swede told Kalm he had only

finally rid his dikes of muskrat by smoking them out of their burrows with burning sulfur. But with the beaver gone, there was
money to be made on muskrat. The pelts could be used in hatmak-
ing, but were mostly made into coats. Sometimes the coats were
labeled "Hudson seal" (just as sometimes the meat was labeled
"marsh rabbit"). Before 1850 most steel traps were handmade, and
most imported from Europe. By the Civil War, new, cheap, mass-
produced steel traps allowed every man and boy to become a fur
trader. Farmers and ranchers could trap to supplement their in-
comes. And everyone trapped muskrat. In 1864 some three million
muskrat pelts were sold. By then the muskrat had become the most
trapped furbearer in America.

The largest dealer in steel traps became the Oneida Community,
of Oneida, New York. Oneida was a "biblical" commune, founded
in the 1850s by sexual reformer John Humphrey Noyes, who pro-
pounded, among other ideas, the theory that a perfect sexual union
could result in the conception of a superior child. Looking for a way
to support themselves in their quest for "scientific procreation"
(and "raising sexual intercourse to one of the social graces," as one
essayist put it), they had tried manufacturing and selling everything from brooms and mop handles to travel cases. They finally
struck it rich in the steel trap business.

It was a time when railroads, coal, steam, and immigrant labor
were building new industrial and urban worlds. Oneida, itself trying to reconcile the scientific and the sensual, found that nostalgia
for the rough sensuality of the quickly vanishing frontier could sell
their mass-produced animal traps. They created a legendary trapper by the name of Sewell Newhouse, a kind of New York Daniel
Boone or Kit Carson: woodsman, Indian trader, and inventor of
the steel trap, "the marvel of his neighbors and the envy of every
Indian for miles around." In 1857, Oneida made 26,000 steel traps.
In 1864 they made 275,000. They published a two-hundred-page
book on trapping, with testimonials to the Newhouse traps (not a
word on Noyes's notions of "coitus reservatus") and advice from
the old Oneida woodsman himself:

*The great question, after all, for the trapper as well as for the
soldier, is, how to live and keep himself comfortable while he
carries on the war. . . . The very first article of outfit that he
should equip himself with, I should say, would be a firm trust
in Providence. But as Cromwell told his soldiers to "trust God
and keep their powder dry," so the trapper will need to provide
some things for himself, while he trusts Providence.*

The book sold for a dollar in paperback and a dollar and fifty
cents hardcover; between 1865 and 1905 it went through twelve edi-
tions. The commune disintegrated, but the trap business boomed.
Between 1880 and 1905 they sold 25 million steel traps. They published trapping magazines and made special trapping kits for boys.
From 1911 to 1920 they sold an average of five million traps a year.

Fur demand rose quickly in the 1920s, when raccoon coats became the rage. Muskrat pelts went from fifty cents apiece to more
than three dollars apiece. The growing business brought some un-
wanted attention. A booklet, "From Thumbscrew to Steel Trap,"
with an introduction by actress Minnie Maddern Fiske, raised the
issue of the cruelty of the leg-hold trap. The National Anti-Steel
Trap League (later to become the Defenders of Wildlife) published
"The Steel Trap: Instrument of Torture." In 1925, to counter the
protests, two fur business associations, one neatly named the American Humane Association, offered ten thousand dollars to anyone
who could come up with a humane trap. The prize stood for the
next forty years. No money was ever paid out.

The problem was clear. An animal not killed immediately strug-
gled in the leg-hold. As one trapper told me, "They say a muskrat
chews their leg off, and that's a bunch of bull. Because what they
do is they're twistin' and they *break* their leg off." To most people,
hardly even a difference of degree. (Not that there were not more
expedient methods. Hunters once used to come up to a snow- or
ice-covered muskrat lodge, locate the huddled muskrat by where
their body warmth had melted the ice, and then spear the animals
through the side of the lodge. The Zanders' collection of old traps

includes a .32-caliber coyote "trap" in which a piece of meat was hung for bait. When the coyote grabbed the meat, it tripped the trigger, and the "trap" shot it in the head. Yet the suddenness of these deaths seems to leave in the mind a no less repugnant image.) Trappers claimed that the animals caught in the traps drowned quickly. But Paul Errington, a biologist and trapper who studied the animals for thirty years, found muskrats could live, and therefore struggle, for some five or more minutes underwater.

Not that this wasn't a concern for the trappers. "Wring-offs," as they called them, could mean a loss of as much as 25 percent of their catch. The invention of a second jaw to keep the animal from struggling helped some. But the problem remained until 1958, when Frank Conibear, a Canadian, invented a body trap for small game animals. This is the trap that many of the trappers along the Delaware use. In many New Jersey counties it's the only legal trap. When the bail closes, it usually kills the animal. Defenders of the leg-hold, and there are still many, insist it is the only trap that can be used on certain marshes where the muskrat burrows are too deep to set with body traps. They also claim the Conibear is far too efficient and can trap out a marsh.

The "antis," as they call them at Zander's, remain an annoyance, and everyone in the place is a bit too eager to dismiss them. Anyone who wears a leather belt or shoes or eats hamburger or chicken or fish, the trappers claim, has no right to criticize them. Tom Zander showed me a Christmas greeting card he received from the Animal Liberation Front of California. On the outside is a group dressed in terrorist black, with tight leotards and ski masks. On their laps they hold their pet dogs, cats, and raccoons. Inside it reads "Peace & Liberation."

By 1900 the beaver was nearly extinct across all of North America. But the muskrat trapping continued, at a rate of as many as ten million a year. How has the muskrat survived? Unlike the unusually social beaver, which bear and raise only a few young at a time and need running streams and dense woodlands, the muskrat can live closer to civilization while keeping its large broods together until they're able to go out on their own. They produce more off-spring than the beaver, and far more often. A good marsh can support some fifty muskrat per acre. What now may threaten the muskrat is the loss of good marsh.

"When. I first moved here twenty years ago," recalls Tom Zander, "this lake was solid cattails and hibiscus and lily pads. I used to catch thirty-five muskrats in a hundred yards. Now the cattails are history, the hibiscus is history, and the muskrats are history. Where there was sweetflag and cattail and hibiscus is now phragmites. And the muskrats won't eat it."

Muskrat populations appear to rise and fall in ten-year cycles, and no one seems to know why. The naturalist Aldo Leopold tried to correlate the abundance of muskrat in the Midwest with that of bobwhite quail, snowshoe hare, or grouse. But the relationships proved elusive. Many biologists as well as trappers relate declines along the Delaware River and other East Coast wetlands to the infiltration of phragmites (*frag-MITE-ees*), the common reed that, until this century, rarely if ever grew along the Delaware River.

The earliest scientific report on phragmites along the Delaware was made in 1862. The first collected specimen came to the botanical archives of the Philadelphia Academy of Sciences in 1865. Now its tall shoots, with their feathery top-plumes, appear wherever dredging, filling, plowing, silting, building, or garbage dumping—what biologists call "human activity"—disrupt the surface of a wetland or the salinity or depth of its waters. (The reed is not, as is often believed, an alien to American shores, brought in with ship ballast. It has shown up in New England coastal soil samples three thousand years old.) Thriving in nearly any moist soil, deep, shallow, flooded, or alkaline, and hardy enough to push up through asphalt, phragmites spreads on hard, woody, pencil-thick rhizomes that, as one botanist told me, "you can practically hear growing." Even muskrats can apparently have trouble burrowing through them. Phragmites clusters in dense colonies that can spread for acres or for miles, overwhelming every other bit of plant life, crowding out the spongy cattail rhizomes that muskrats prize and shading out other marsh grasses and plants. The accumulated mat of dead reed litter prevents other plant seeds from reaching the marsh soil to germinate. Birds such as the least bittern, king rail, moorhen, and marsh wren lose the cattails they need for nesting. The dense reed canopy can leave turtles fewer spots to bask.

But as much as phragmites has been cursed as a botanical pest, and sprayed, mowed, and cut where it invades, it's not certain that it's responsible for the decline of the muskrat. The accepted notion is that phragmites has little nutritional value—"You get flat 'rats," explained Tom Zander, "big, but without the fur of a regular 'rat. The leather's not heavy or greasy; whereas in the cattail areas you get a heavy, full 'rat." But European muskrats (which are all descended from transplanted North American muskrats) are evidently quite content to eat it. It may be that phragmites spread so quickly because there were already too few muskrats left to control it. Or that the muskrats continued to browse on their preferred food, leaving phragmites to take over unchecked. The reed is by no means worthless. Mollusks, crustaceans, and insects eat the reed litter, and these animals make up the base of the wetland food web. Europeans cultivate reed for paper pulp, mulch, and animal feed. (A reed harvest might be a better means of control than spraying and risking further ruin to the marsh.) In any case, the highly competitive phragmites, which overwhelms the diversity around it, has become, for many, the visible symbol of human disturbance to the wetlands.

Even as Tom Zander points with some pride to the golden, bronze, black, and silver pelts stacked in wooden bins in the fur shed's upper floor—from raccoon to red fox—he rues the decline in price and the number of trappers who might finally survive: only half as many trappers along the Delaware River as ten years ago, only half as many animals taken. (The Canadian trapping industry has suffered similar declines.) "We have to cover more area now just to get as many muskrats." But even the value of the best pelts, such as the cold climate Michigan muskrat with good, thick, blue underwool and heavy guard hairs, has gone down.

The old beagle has slipped in and lies asleep beneath the sorting bench. Zander nudges him with his toe. The dog looks up without lifting his head. Zander gives him a stern look and then just shakes his head. He recalls days out with his father.

"We used to catch snapping turtles. Used to catch catfish and sell 'em. And carp. We used to take the carp to Camden. Camden used to be a Jewish community, and I can remember going up there with my father when I was little and they had a big tank up there and they used to sell carp from it—live carp. And you used to get ten cents a pound for carp. But they had to be alive. It was the spring of the year. I don't remember exactly when. But the lady was a nice lady and she used to give me a cookie all the time. You don't forget that. We used to catch muskrat in Woodbury Creek, but I don't think I'd eat one from there now. I don't think I'd eat anything right from the river. Not even a muskrat. And I like muskrat."

Along the counties of the lower Delaware, everybody has a favorite muskrat recipe. Most soak the meat in salt, boil it until it falls from the bones, and then fry it in lard. Clyde Roberts had recommended a stew: "In a Dutch oven a layer of onion and bacon, a layer of muskrat, onion and bacon, muskrat, onion and bacon. Cook till it just falls off the bone, pour out juice and simmer it. Serve it with white potatoes and cornbread." Rick Davis recalled his mother cooked the muskrat head and all ("I once come to a piece of fur, and I never ate it after that").

Nana, a ninety-four-year-old nursing home resident whom my wife and I visit, tells us she's been a bit depressed lately because she had a gallbladder attack in the fall and since then hasn't been allowed to eat muskrat. The cure, we could see, was worse than the disease, and we assured her that we'd have a talk with the doctor before the season passed.

At Zander's, the take may decline but the muskwash remains plentiful.

"When things were good, a trapper could get three thousand to five thousand 'rats and make himself twenty-five thousand."

"No more."

"Is it the greenhouse effect?"

"The farmers clear more and more land and they spray on it from the air and the spray runs into the ditches. That's what got the eagles and ospreys. It's the same with the 'rats."

"Calvin's father was a fur dealer, and they were trappers all of their lives and he just got a job, he told me, working down at the nuclear plant driving a truck. Boy, now I couldn't believe that one. That's hard to believe."

"Now only the hard core'll go out in the mud and ice to do it."

"Now just the guys that like to do it do it. Hardly pay for your boots and your traps. 'Rats go down, traps go up. Boots go up. Used to buy boots for eight dollars. What are they now? Fifty? I heard my father say he sold 'rats for thirty-five cents. But that was thirty-five cents then. And we used to have a lot of muskrats years ago."

"We've fouled our nests."

"Part of the problem is people working where they're not living."

"Now I just do it to get out to where it's quiet."

Harry Zander had assured me Marvin Rankin was a gentleman. He didn't tell me how much of a gentleman he was. What they would have called in the old days a mountain of a man greeted me in an orange hooded sweatshirt, coveralls, white rubber boots, and a mud-spattered, tag-encrusted purple watch cap. Against the background of the flat southern New Jersey marsh and farmland, Rankin loomed large as he strode up the gravel driveway, stepping over the litter of a waterman's living—dried-up fish heads, muskrat feet and tails, crab shells, and a single Day-Glo orange rubber glove—like a kindly giant in a child's playroom. He had large hands and a large but unweathered profile (by no means what one would call rugged), and keenly attentive green eyes—a Bunyonesque figure who came to repose next to his old blue Custom Deluxe pickup, which goes by the name of Clyde. Behind him, crab traps were stacked high by the garage. Outside the garage a small, hand-painted signboard reads "FiSh"; off to the side stands a metal balance for weighing the catch, and a double-basin washstand in which to hose it down, the open drain connected to nothing, so the wash can run out and down the drive and keep it sparkling with the iridescence of fish scales.

The garage held a winter's worth of muskrat pelts hanging from the rafters on their metal stretchers. A bucket half-filled with musk glands lent the whole place a besotting, gamy sweetness, and the furs imparted a rustic warmth. To a young rural boy in winter, I thought, the spell of such a balm would be hard to break.

"I trapped," Rankin tells me, "since I was five and six years old. When I was a little kid, my Dad used to take me to the barbershop and I'd be sittin' there listenin' to all the men talk of catchin' fish and trappin' mus'rats, and I said to myself then, 'That's what I want to do.' " (The heady atmosphere of an old barbershop could heighten any young boy's suggestibility: the bright lights, the gleaming instruments arranged on white terry hand towels, and the jars of blue-green liquid in which the steel combs floated, everything reflected in the long mirror over the porcelain sinks. Above it all, the disconnected conversations—heard from behind and either side, while the speakers are seen reflected in front of you—and intoxicating musk made it seem like a cross between an operating theater and an opium den.)

Off in Clyde toward Rankin's marsh (box of Olin Super-x long-range shotgun shells spilling across the top of the dash as we come out the drive). Like most trappers, Rankin worries more over the fate of the marshes than over that of the muskrat. If the former is secure, the latter ought to thrive. But the marshes have changed. Higher tides have overflowed the dikes and drowned many places of once low but fast land.

"I now tend crab pots where there used to be a peach orchard. And the shoreline is still going back."

We walk down into one of his marshes (a meadow or "meddah," as he calls it), and there's the crack of old reed cane as we walk. Rankin points out the muskrat sign: "I like to see the scuttled-up mud [rhymes with 'wood'], and the places where they were chewin', where the water's kind of dirty-like, and where he's scratched around—there is a road he likes to travel. Now I put a Conibear ['cawnibear'] in there under water so he can't smell the iron ['oron'], you know.

"See, this used to be a really good meddah because we used to have water back there about that deep. And see, the mus'rat, he didn't have to walk on the mud. It tires ['tores'] him out, walkin' on the mud. Before [the mosquito commission drained the marsh] he could just lay along, swim along, and live happy. Now he's got to work for everything. He's got to walk across this mud, and it makes it easier for predators to come out and get him. Foxes, minks, and weasels will kill him. I've caught a few out here. And I've seen coyote tracks along the river shore."

Rankin has his suspicions about the commission.

"When I was a kid, right before a thunderstorm, I hear a fish hawk, and I see him with a fish. And then an eagle come, and I see that eagle hit that fish hawk and make him drop that fish and then catch that fish before it hit the ground. And here we have a mighty bird, isn't that right? Here he's king of the hill, and here he got done in by some DDT that's in some fish that he was eating that made his eggshells so thin they broke before they hatched. Now that was some roundabout way to do him in. And who would have ever dreamed it? So it might be the same way now with the mosquito spray. It could be doing harm. We just got back the ospreys, and I see eagles now every day." One might well wonder, if the trapping ends, who will there be who knows the marsh and has a stake in its fate?

We drive along a dike out through another meadow that he's trapped the last twenty years. When we get to the end of the hard road, Rankin points out signs of otter in the muddy bank. A quarter of a mile farther along what's now a dirt road, the truck squealing from its rear axle with each bump ("Clyde's got a sore foot."), we reach a small wooden dock on a creek ("crick") called Madhorse Creek, which winds out through the marshland a mile and a half to the Delaware shore. Here, Rankin will set maybe fifteen or twenty dozen traps in a day.

The quiet spreads as far as the eye can see.

"I come out here on this boardwalk and I could be having the worst day, but I feel better out here right away. I really like catchin' mus'rats."

Rankin's small, two-story clapboard house was about a third re-sided, with most of the rest wrapped in plastic against the winter. Inside it was warm, and humid from the steam of boiling water on the stove. In this house Rankin was born, grew up, and has raised his own children. The table in the small dining room was set for lunch with tablecloth and place settings, egg and tuna salads in glass bowls, a glass plateful of sweet pickles, and sandwich bread on a platter. Rankin's wife, June, as much of a presence as her husband (she drives a local schoolbus), though of a rosier complexion, and with a halo of soft, graying curls, served and then sat to eat.

"I'm worried about the mus'rat business," Marvin Rankin began. "I think it really looks bleak. I mean, maybe furs will come back in style—but I'm afraid, for the short term, a whole generation has a different attitude—I think it comes from people who don't any longer see their food caught or killed. Even my own kids. One of my kids' boyfriends, the family raised turkey, and, you know, she didn't like that fresh turkey. She wanted to have a turkey that was frozen like a rock. Guess he seems like he's deader when he's frozen hard. I mean, one time we had one of my nephews here for dinner and we had ham and I said, 'Would somebody please pass the hog?' and man, his eyes got so big, I thought—

"Well, now, I'm supposed to be a mus'rat killer, but yet, if I see one crossing the road in the summer, I'll get out of the car and help him across. In the summertime, he can do what he wants. And I wouldn't want to see the last mus'rat caught because I want to see the mus'rat here forever, and if I thought they was endangered, I'd be the first one to quit trappin'. As much as I love it. I wouldn't want to see them destroyed. But they're not endangered. As a trapper I can understand some of those people hunting endangered animals in Africa. There, they have no factories to work in, and no places to make a living, and they see this rhino walkin' by and they say, 'Well, there's enough to keep my family goin' for a whole year on that rhino's horn.' You know, I could see the guy's point. If I was in the same boat and a rhinoceros came walkin' up through this stoplight, I might try to take him myself, you know? I mean, they go after these poachers like it's a war. Maybe they wouldn't do so much poachin' if you gave them another way to make a dollar."

Phone rings. He takes the call and returns quickly.

"Damn, everybody wants fish [pronounced "feesh"] and I want to catch two hundred more mus'rats, yet." The spring spawning runs of shad and white perch come quickly on the heels of the trapping season. "Life," Rankin sighs as he sits, "is full of choices. We used to trap to the fifteenth of March and then we had a few days to get ready to go shad fishin'. Now the shad's here before we're done mus'rattin' and so we got to jump right in. And then we didn't used to start crabbin' until June. Now we could be makin' more money in April crabbin' than fishin'. The seasons just seem to come faster and faster."

A waterman's life runs on seasons and tides, and the uncertainties can be too difficult for many to bear, especially when alternatives like factory work with regular pay and good medical benefits are more readily available. Rankin himself worked at the county jail while he raised his family, but now, "When I get up in the morning I don't know whether I'll make a dollar or a hundred dollars that day. Where's the fun in life if you know what you're going to make this day and the next day and the next? Great day in the morning! How would you stand it?"

He decides to begin shad fishing next week and says he'll give me a call when he's geared up.

The Dukes of Delaware

THE HIGHEST POINT ON THE DUKES' RIVERFRONT FARM IN TAYLOR'S Bridge, Delaware, is twenty-two feet above sea level, but Jack Dukes swears that even during the worst storm tides the old 1850 farmhouse remains dry.

"Why, the marshes," he says, "take up all the water."

The Duke family owns four hundred acres of marshland and a hundred acres of upland, and has farmed this same fast land and trapped, hunted, and harvested these same marshes since 1730. Jack Dukes and I spoke first in the cavernous metal barn, among soybean and seed-corn sacks, the skeletal hulk of a John Deere tractor looming behind him, the only light from the just-opened door, and his deeply tanned narrow face coming in and out of shadow.

"My mother, who's eighty-nine, recalls her mother telling her about another house out in the field. And there used to be a house out closer to the river." But there's no longer fast land around the old foundations. "I can remember just in my time where my father used to till marsh grasses where we can't till anymore. These gradual changes, you know, hit hard all of a sudden."

Mrs. Edna Dukes herself had been recalling for me how her father had fished the Delaware for sturgeon from a small skiff.

"A sailing skiff?" I ask.

"Well," she scolded, "they didn't have motors then."

She sat in her rocker, steady gaze of blue-green eyes from beneath thick gray eyebrows, behind rimless eyeglasses. She wore a satin dress with large yellow polka dots, fastened across the bib top with matching yellow buttons. She didn't rock, but held her hands firmly to the arms of the chair and kept her head still as she spoke, and turned only to think, when she would press her still-rosy cheek to the chair, giving her a view out the window to where flocks of snow geese paraded across the damp winter fields.

Her father, she explained, worked alone, drifted his net on the strong tides here where the bay and river meet, and if the winds became too bad for him to return, he'd hie himself to a cove on the New Jersey shore, take shelter under his sail, and hold out till the storm blew over. And if they wondered at the house whether he was safe or heading home, someone could go up on the roof with their small telescope to see whether he'd decided to stay out for the night.

"Mother remembers they caught a lot of shad here in the river, and remembers that when she was four or five she'd help her mother bring vegetables and chickens out to the little shad cabins down by the shore where the men who tended the nets lived."

Mrs. Dukes insisted on her own version: "I can remember going down, my father taking me in the wagon down to the mouth of what we called Ray's Ditch, where there was a cabin boat where the shad fishermen lived, like a houseboat fastened to stakes by ropes to the shore. And boats from Port Penn and New Castle would come down the river and pick up the fish. Around 1910 that was going on, and the fish seemed to decline quickly afterwards."

Here is what she had to say about farm life in her time along the Delaware shore of the Delaware:

"It was, when I was growing up, typical of the farms around here. It was nothing to brag about and it wasn't one of the poorest farms. It was just a normal farm. Many larger, many smaller. For me, I grew up with it. It was just always here. We always had the hundred acres. At first it was just dairy cows, corn, and wheat, then later soybeans. Then we had the marshland, and there were spots we harvested salt hay that we used to cut and send on boats to Philadelphia. Sometimes boats would come up the creek into Taylor's Bridge and tie up at the bridge and you'd take grain there. All these creeks had little landings. Before we had automobiles you would take the steamship *Clyde* from the landing in Odessa to Philadelphia. They would load straw and ship calves from Clement's Landing. We'd take our wheat. I remember once with my father there was somebody down there trying to sell a bull and he was kind of wild, rarin' and pitchin' and so forth, and my father picked me up and put me on his shoulders to make sure I was out of that bull's way. Most of the corn was fed to the animals on the farm. We had turkey and chicken—I remember putting the eggs under the old hen. That was the only way you had babies, but my mother did have a little incubator that was heated with a kerosene lamp, and she would hatch some eggs in it and then give the chickens that hatched to mother hens to take care of.

"It was a time you prepared things yourself. You'd take some of your wheat to the mill at Smyrna, where they would give you so many pounds of flour for so many pounds of wheat. You did your own meat. Along in the fall you'd have hog-killing time and then that meat was salted down and you'd make sausage and scrapple and eat that during the winter. And then you had your ham and chickens and in the wintertime you ate wild ducks and muskrats if you caught them in the traps. Of course, we always trapped for muskrat. At some points the muskrat harvest was very profitable. It was one of our mainstays. My father trapped, my husband trapped, and it used to be years ago that a hired [pronounced 'hard'] man would live in the home with you, and you would give them so much per month and in the winter they would have the privilege of trapping so much marsh and they'd give back a share to the owner. As a very small child I remember my father giving me a nice, clean, dry muskrat to play with—a dead one, because they have very sharp teeth. The marshes had more cattails then, and some people would come out and cut them and bind them in bunches. I can't tell you why."

Jack Dukes and I had stood looking out over the marsh, watching a small boat maneuver in the rough waters along the river shore while, in the distance, a large tanker took the channel north toward Wilmington.

"We had a governor," he said, "who made a campaign promise to eliminate the mosquito along the Delaware shore. So after the War, in the forties or the fifties, about every two weeks the whole place would be doused with DDT. I forget how many millions of dollars they spent in ditching fragile marsh areas and spraying. We didn't know what would happen, but all of a sudden we didn't have any snapping turtles. No fiddler crabs. It was just a tragic mistake. We started noticing the decline in the muskrat about thirty years ago. And muskrats were the thing we were primarily interested in. We used to catch three and four thousand on this farm. Now they go in cycles, but now the peaks are lower and the low points are lower. I can remember not more than twenty-five years ago you could almost jump from muskrat house to muskrat house. Now these marshes are near a hundred percent phragmites. Even where we control the phragmites, the 'rats haven't come back like they should. Even in places that haven't been trapped in fifteen years there's less muskrat.

"Now, they say the Dutch drained these marshes and farmed them. Well, they had to have been a lot fresher then, because now even if you did that you still couldn't do anything with them for the salt. I'd like to have taken a peek back then when it was all fresh water, when white cedar grew here.

"I can remember three times in my life they had to move the monument here that marks where the river officially begins. The last time they put it back ten, fifteen feet up on the shore, put a lot of stone around it, but not long and the tide come up past it again. Now they moved it back and put it in concrete."

Mrs. Dukes:

"We didn't get electricity down here until after the Second World War. About fifteen years before that we did get a Delco plant where we had our own motor and our own storage batteries. That would light the house. The storage batteries were in the basement and you'd have to run the generator and I can remember you'd have to do the ironing in the parlor because that was closer to the batteries. And you had to run the motor when you were ironing."

"Was it a hard life?"

"It was just the way it was. Everybody was living the same way. We had no telephone. I can remember as well as can be—1913. One morning, came downstairs and had breakfast and my grandmother didn't come down and my mother went up to see what was wrong and she found her dead in bed. Well, what do you do? My father had to gear up the horse and go out and notify the authorities. You had to have a doctor come in here and pronounce her dead. And the undertaker came here and prepared the body, and the funeral was held here at the house. All done at home. And birth, too. Oh my Lord, yes. I was born right here in this house and three of my children were born here. You'd go for the doctor, but the midwife always got here first and the baby always got here before the doctor!"

Jack Dukes:

"This hasn't been the easiest way to make a living the last twenty years. My grandfather shot for the market, packed the birds in ice and sold them. Now they've all declined: green-winged teal, black ducks, mallards, pintails, mergansers, all. So if a farmer's lived here for twenty to thirty years and just made a living and someone comes along and offers him three or four hundred thousand dollars, he's going to take it. You couldn't start up a farm now. There's eighty thousand dollars in one combine. You can't buy the land and afford the interest payments. But we've always lived here and I enjoy hunting and this way of life, and this is where I'll stay."

Mrs. Dukes:

"It was rough going at times, but everybody else was in the same situation. Things got pretty tight during the Depression. I remember one time I had one good dress. And that was a gingham dress I'd made by myself. And that was it. But we lived through it. You lived according to what you had. We grew our food. We always had enough food. We never felt we would lose our home. We'd have social gatherings, birthday parties, things of that sort. And in the wintertime you'd have just parties where people would get together to enjoy themselves and they used to call them play parties. And games would be played like 'Bounce Around,' where we'd all be in a circle and they'd have some kind of music and you moved around and, well—kissing games! If you did something, you'd change partners and kiss one good-bye and kiss the other when you took up with them."

The pitch of her voice has been rising airily, and her small face has broken into an open smile. She straightens up to compose herself.

"Of course, they were very strong Methodists back early, and didn't believe in dancin' or drinkin'—not in public. So you'd have a freezer full of ice cream. You didn't have it in the summertime because you didn't have any ice. And if the ice was out from the marsh, you didn't have it in the winter either."

The Dukes farm has been a kind of matriarchy, passed on from daughter to daughter for at least four generations.

"Oh, I feel very happy to have been able to stay here."

She seems tired out.

"And now I'm getting ready to leave it."

I couldn't tell exactly what she meant by that—but it struck me that she said it with as much finality as her thinning voice could muster.

"I know what it means to have someone around who's getting along in age and can't take care of themselves. I had my father for years and I know what it means. So I want to go somewhere I'll be taken care of. I'm going into the Methodist Country House just above Wilmington—first day of April."

This is the first week of March.

I recall her father out alone on his sturgeon skiff, and now she herself sitting alone in this rocker, and this farmhouse sitting alone on this lone rise of land above the flat fields and marshland. I could see her taking the rocking chair, but what about the grandfather clock in the room, with the full moon rising over its dial? (The clock was right—this night a wonderfully full yellow moon would rise over the river.)

"Has it been a good life, the farm?" I ask.

"I have enjoyed it," she says.

It didn't seem to me that she'd be any kind of burden. She could point out to me the snow geese through the window a hundred yards away. She could still do the tatting on her pillowcases. But to leave after a lifetime here, for eighty-nine years seeing an unchanging vista of open land facing open water, and in her mind's eye, God knows, nine generations of this landscape—what will it mean? I wished Mrs. Dukes would just stay put.

What will she miss?

"Oh, everything has changed. We're not drawn together any longer. You can get in the car and go wherever you want to go—even if it's fifteen or twenty miles away. [In her mind this is still the measure of a considerable distance.] You couldn't do that years ago. You went to and associated with the people who lived close by. My father got an automobile in 1913. But in the wintertime he couldn't use the car, and it was back to the horses and mud road. When I grew up and started dating, the boy picked you up with the horse and carriage to go to the movies—that was your excuse, to go to the movies—and you'd just go out for a ride through the country aways. Go out one road and come back another one. Or picnic. Or Sunday night go to church. There was a family moved into the community not long ago and I went and called on them and I had a little cake—it wasn't iced or anything—I went and called on them and they never even invited me into the house. I stood outside and talked to them and gave them the cake and went on home. It wasn't like that. Now people live to theirselves."

These gradual things, as Jack Dukes had said, hit hard all of a sudden.

Perhaps too hard. I drive out between the row of cedars that line the Dukeses' drive and past the little "National Bicentennial Farm" sign. The radio whines a boozy country tune—this is south of the canal, after all—about how "country boys will survive" because they can still fish an' hunt an' ride with a shotgun in a four-wheel drive. But the "country" the song celebrates is going fast. Aside from the few who still live off the land and water, most country boys these days are part-time country boys, and their survival depends on the suburban economy. So the song turns out to be a mean-spirited anthem that equates the city with evil, the country with good, and all sung with not a little bit of xenophobic twang.

The next song was less surly, more authentic, and the lyric, it seemed to me, of far greater intelligence and genuine emotion: "There's a redhead from my hometown / That loves to let her hair down." Mrs. Dukes would dance to that if she could.

THE FAST LAND

"Folks hate to see the loss of farmland," Bernie Herman tells me, "but the greatest value of the land now is in selling it."

Herman is a student of change—of history, archaeology, architecture, and landscape. He goes wherever they lead him. Sometimes his red hair is long and he has a mustache. Sometimes he

wears a small black earring stud in his left ear. He raises rare peppers and collects waterfowl decoys. He's begun to dabble in
dendrochronology—taking a piece of wood from a house and examining its grain to find out where it came from, perhaps even the
climate in which it grew—and is hopeful that this might solve the
mysteries of a few questionable finds. And, since he makes his living
expounding on the distinctions of places and things in their times,
he rues the loss of diversity: in housing, in land use, in everything
"the growing uniformity of tastes, the loss of species beyond our
comprehension—off the awful meter on our scale of awful." He is
just getting started.

"I grew up at the mouth of the Chesapeake. When I was a kid,
people still used waterfowl decoys for firewood in the winter. People who collected them got them for thirty cents apiece. Now
they're an art carried on a market of historicism—the decoys have
become icons, standins for a disappearing way of life. Even the
Chesapeake itself has become an icon, in part because it and its
waterman's culture is being lost."

Herman holds a continuing palaver with the passing scene: he
looks, offers a proposal, then tries to run with it. Above all he wants
a good story.

"I mean I think this development is tremendously exciting historically. But it's happening in a way which is so destructive. We're
losing all the cultural and historical information encoded in the
buildings and the landscape—information you can't retrieve from
documents."

We drive one of the narrow blacktop roads that wind the high
ground amid the tidewater fields of the western Delaware River
shore. The peeling bark on the gnarled roadside sycamores makes
them look, even in bright day, as if they're spattered with moonlight. The rolling farmland looks to me as undisturbed a human-
made vista as I've seen along the river. But Herman looks at the
landscape as if it were the lifework of an artist painted on a single
canvas. Older shapes and colors show through the new; these entice
him to speculate on what the past works, the past worlds, might
have looked like.

"Now the land produces a crop of little houses sold as surely as the farmers once sold wheat or peaches. But now they've sold the last thing the land can produce. This brings about a whole series of tragic ironies. People ruin the land to possess it. People leave to get out of the city into the suburbs and find themselves out and in among the same people. People no longer derive income from the land or its natural resources, but they still try to tie themselves to it conceptually, naming their developments Wheatland, Cedar Ridge, or Mount Hope. They did something similar in the 1800s when they named the small towns around here Odessa, Smyrna, and Leipsic. It was a time when these lands along the Delaware were some of the richest agricultural lands in the United States."

Cargo schooners once crowded the prosperous little anchorages on the Leipsic River and the Appoquinimink Creek, waiting to take on the wagonloads of oysters, wheat, marsh hay, peaches, and furs for shipment up the Delaware River to Philadelphia. (Germany's Leipzig was the site of annual international fur auctions.) Shallops wound their way far up the Christina River from its mouth at Wilmington, passing the mills along the way till they came as close as they could to the narrow north-south ridge that separates the Delaware from the Chesapeake drainage. On the west side the Elk River runs down to the Chesapeake.

"There's this very narrow band of highland where the two watersheds fall away from each other, and it's a real important cultural divide. It separates the Chesapeake culture from that of the Delaware. Now, I don't know if it goes back to the prehistoric period or not, I suspect it does [the Minquas met the Swedes and Dutch here, just beyond the accepted borders of the Lenape lands and waters, to trade their furs], but if you look at just the historic housing, an early-eighteenth-century building, say, five miles west of the divide will have a greater similarity to a building near Williamsburg, Virginia, than to a building near Middletown, Delaware."

We have driven east across the divide, down across the farmland to the river, then come south, across the Reedy Point Bridge, past

Bob Beck's place with Thousand Acre Marsh and Rick's snapper-ing cove on our right, the river gleaming on our left.

"Okay," Herman finally says, an impatient curator having held his peace long enough to allow me my inexperienced look at the work. "Pull over and I'll expound to the sky."

The sky is about as large here as it gets along the East Coast, with an unobstructed view to the horizon across the river on one side and the marsh on the other, and the land beyond the marsh rising to rolling fields steeped in winter wheat.

"Now, if you think about how this landscape developed, there are several things that occur. You have Native American settle-ment. Then you have a period of contact by these more or less ephemeral European groups—ephemeral in what remains above-ground, but not ephemeral in terms of place names and perhaps more subtle aspects of cultural behavior. You have some Scandi-navian settlement, but most of it seems to have been marginal, and then a significant Dutch overlay which generally gets underrated. People build up the Swedes, who seem to have done not a whole lot, and downplay the Dutch, who seem to have done an awful lot in affecting the overall look of the landscape in terms of farming and even modes of house design. Why? Unreflective antiquarianism. U.S. history is still looked at from the view of the nineteenth cen-tury, when people began perpetuating the idea that older is better.

"The Dutch settled here fairly early. In the mid-seventeenth century you find names like Van Zant, Van DeGriff, Van Dyke. They sort of just get established when the door gets thrown open to British settlement in the 1670s, with Quakers coming in both here and to Salem County, across the river in New Jersey. They're from New England and they're refugees from Quaker emigrations from eastern Connecticut and Rhode island. And they bring with them a New England building style. But you have a period when these first English move in that we might describe as a period of non-durable building: a lot of houses built on posts in the ground, houses on wood blocks on the ground. Almost at the end of this first generation—say, beginning in the first years of the seventeenth century—on both sides of the river, you have the emergence of the first generation of durable buildings, of which this is one." He indicates a whitewashed, ramshackle, two-story brick Colonial amid a grove of trees on the first rise overlooking the marsh, the field, and the river.

"Built around 1704 by William Penn's first cousin—the white brick part—it is the wing to an earlier building which is completely gone, but which you can see the shadow of on the gable. This kind of building, and an identical one dated 1714 on the other side of the road, demonstrate the emergence of the architecture of a native-born elite, and the florescence of a Delaware Valley style of building. The landscape is changing and beginning to get organized. These are still one- and two-room houses, sometimes three, but they're bigger and they're fancier and more elaborately finished. It represents a new generation of folks able to acquire land, clear land—the woodland begins to disappear—and wheel and deal the local economic power.

"These folks were growing corn and wheat from day one—very little evidence here of tobacco. And they're able to undertake these building projects because of the stability of these grains and a stable European market—especially where constant wars needed provisioning. At this time these are really provincial European settlements—part of Europe, although they're across the Atlantic. And the Delaware River is a highway to Europe and back. So while they're involved with the local and regional markets, they're very much engaged in sending produce and staples to an international market. For instance, this was part of the butter belt of the United States, producing an incredibly high amount of butter by pound per farm. And a whole domestic sphere goes along with it. They raise lots of salt hay for the cattle—both dairy cows and steers. And this butter is not only for the English muffins of Philadelphia, this is for the English muffins of England. By the early nineteenth century this has changed. These people have become much more insular, and the markets they respond to are regional markets. Some goes to Wilmington, or to the mills along the Brandywine, which then goes out along the Atlantic Coast or upriver to Philadelphia.

"This is not subsistence agriculture—from day one. Folks are interested in what they call their 'competency,' which is the amount of agricultural income they need to live comfortably. But they want to live comfortably in the realm of the nascent consumer revolution of the eighteenth century. This means they need to get more and more from the land, the marshes, and the water.

"What begins to happen in the 1800s is the erosion of the sense of common land. When you're out in the middle of the river, that's a commons, but in terms of this land and marsh, that's all owned by somebody, and they begin to maintain and, for the first time, regulate their use."

People who control the fishery market and want to set up big permanent shad-netting schemes begin to complain about the small independent free blacks and poor farmers dipping the fish before they swim into the big fixed fish traps. At the same time the poor fishermen complain that the nets of the big landowners are restricting their access to their traditional fishing grounds.

Control even comes to the river proper. In 1812 Delaware passed a law limiting access to its oyster grounds to Delaware residents. (Elsewhere, inshore oyster beds were being wiped out quickly. A 1737 New York law stated that oyster beds off Staten Island were being "wasted and Destroyed by Strangers; the preventing of which will tend to the great Benefit of the poor People and others inhabiting the aforesaid Colony." A new law forbade anyone to take "any Oysters within this Colony, and put them on board any Canoe, Periauger, Flat, Scow, Boat or other vessel whatsoever, not wholly belonging to, and owned by, Persons who live within the aforesaid Colony.") In part, the ineffectiveness of these laws made Delaware oysters all the more valuable. By 1812 the oysters of New York and Raritan bays, and anywhere close to the coastal cities, had been nearly extirpated. In 1835 Delaware set a season for the oyster harvest along with controls on the size of the catch and the kinds of gear used. So began the development of the often arcane fishing and hunting regulations, designed to protect the proprietary interests of landholders against those who might make free use of ever more valuable natural resources.

"It's all tied together. What gave rise to these conflicts over open land and access to the marshes was that as people began to realize they could derive greater and greater levels of income from the land, they had to clear more and more of it. The more land they cleared, the less they could physically control it. Big marsh companies enclosed the wetlands with fences. In aerial and Landsat photos we can see evidence of fence patterns in the marshes. Some folks think they're plans of pirate forts—I love it. But they're far more prosaic."

The Swedes and Finns made few changes to the marshes along the river. Their first interest was the fur trade. They needed safe outposts, and so cleared land on the high ground. Coming from a forested land, they made their cabins, furniture, utensils, and tools of rough wood. They cleared and farmed only small plots of land. The Dutch had a different vision in mind. Arriving under the instigation of Peter Stuyvesant, who was bent on carrying the Old World war with the Swedes over to the New World (fat Printz and the hobbled Stuyvesant were well-matched adversaries, one as petty and cynical as the other). The Dutch knew how to drain and farm the rich lowlands. They built earthen dikes along the Delaware shore. Sluice gates in the dikes allowed water within the marsh to drain out while keeping tides or stream water from coming in. Wetlands became meadows, a word that originally meant a lowland used for the production of hay (so that New Jersey trappers like Marvin Rankin still refer to the marshes as meadows or, as they pronounce it, "meddahs," even where the dikes broke long ago and the land has long since flooded).

These dikes were maintained with difficulty. Spring runoff, high tides, and northeast storms washed them out. But by the end of the eighteenth century, successive wheat crops and erosive farming methods had worn out the thin upland soils. Wealthy gentlemen farmers who owned acres of marshland saw in its thick deposits of peat formed by centuries of decomposed vegetation a likely source of new farmland. On both sides of the river speculators formed marsh companies and appealed to state legislators for permission, as one colonial petition put it, to turn "a fruitless, loathsome waste into a healthful, fertile soil." One entrepreneur predicted lowlands worth a dollar an acre could become worth fifty. There would be no more "stagnated fogs and unwholesome vapours" plagued with "mosquitoes and putrefaction." In Delaware, writes University of Delaware archaeologist David Grettler, "improving marshes became a central tenet of agricultural improvement." The state gave the companies carte blanche—not only to dam, ditch, and drain where they would, but to tax landowners for the dredging and maintenance of those ditches that crossed their property—whether or not the landowner wanted the ditch dug or the marsh "improved."

The companies had their work cut out for them. The embankments had to be at least three feet higher than the average high tides—then, at least six to eight feet high. They were twelve feet wide at the base and three feet wide at the top, mud fortifications that, Grettler says, "had to be carefully maintained against storms, tidal erosion, and muskrats." A system of hand-dug ditches had to lower the marsh's water table at least eighteen inches. Feeder ditches nine feet wide by three feet deep ran to the main channels, twenty feet wide by five feet deep. And every drain had to be annually scoured of new growth and checked for debris from storms or tides.

For many poor, the diking of the marshes meant another loss of what they considered public domain for trapping, hunting, and fishing. Late-eighteenth-century fencing ordinances had already begun to restrict the tradition of letting animals, especially swine, out free to graze (cattle and swine could graze the marshes where horses and sheep were susceptible to hoof rot). "The havoc wrought by free-ranging hogs undermining fences, rooting up pasture, and snuffling about village streets," says Herman, "was antithetical to emerging sensibilities about privilege, property, and authority." And so, ran one ordinance,

> no swine shall be allowed to run at large (unless sufficiently ringed, to prevent them from rooting, and yoked, to prevent them from creeping or breaking through fences) on any of the unimproved lands, meadows, or marshes.

The poor protested. They could never fatten their pigs on the land they could afford. An angry demonstration in one town ended with shots fired and pigs lying dead in the street.

The poor also sought protection against the destruction of muskrat houses in the marshes. Many feared that rerouting streams away from the marshes would wash the loads of silt into the larger rivers. Runoff from cleared forests and farmlands had already begun to reduce the depth of these barely navigable tidal channels. Dams might also affect fishing grounds. Still, the ditching went forward. It brought no renaissance to Delaware agriculture. The state's landowners are still assessed for the ditches on their property, even as sea level rises and the land sinks, as the old embankments erode and the sluice gates fail, as the water tables rise again in the marshes and the shoreline falls away.

The organization of the countryside went on. Herman points out the thick hedges of Osage orange, a tree with twisting, intertwining limbs that still grows on the ridges and roadsides along the Delaware. They define the field boundaries from the 1800s, when the clearing of forests had made wooden fencing an extravagance, and colonists grew live fencing.

"Look, this is kind of awful."

I stop the car where the ruin of a barn lies in an empty field on a plain above the river.

"There was a great bank barn there which is illustrated in my book. But they knocked it down, the sons of—Pharisees. See the trees. In among them was a beautiful house from the 1830s. They kissed that good-bye without even applying for a permit to destroy it."

A house, begun in the 1760s, tells another story.

"A Dutch family builds an Anglo-American Georgian house sited in such a way that it presides over this landscape—there's Thousand Acre Marsh down through the trees—not only over the public road, but over the marshes and to the river beyond. This represents the incarnation of a new rural elite which comes to control both the agricultural and maritime landscapes and their whole range of trade."

The landscape is a patient on Herman's couch. Nothing is accidental. He analyzes every vista, every structure, and every conjunction of the two, as if they were images in a dream. Why here and not there? Why of stone and not wood? Why at a particular time and not before or later?

"You can see it all right here."

We are standing before a ruin. Ramshackle would be too kind a word to describe this wood frame house. The roof has caved in. We have to step over missing sections of floor. The inside is gray. Even on this damp, chilly day the house provides an extra chill, in part from the damp wood, in part from the sensation that any second the place might come down around our heads. Herman treads lightly, not, as I think at first, out of concern for falling through the floor, but out of respect for a place he clearly holds in some awe.

"You can see it all right here. To begin with, you have a mid-eighteenth-century, one-story, one-room, sawn-plank house. And it is so well built and tightly fitted that the joints are filled with oakum, the same pitch-and-plant-fiber compound used for caulking ships' holds."

The beams, which show through the fallen lath and plaster, show chamfered, beveled edges—workmanship meant at one time, Herman says, to be exposed.

"Around 1780 or so, they abut another building, a two-story structure, to this one. Now they have a Georgian plan. To make the two parts match, they raise another story on the first. It doesn't quite work, but it's there. Soon a shed is built off the back here—this was the front—and they reverse the orientation of the house to face the road rather than the marsh and river. But by the eighteen-teens this whole area is struck by an economic panic."

The War of 1812 had ended. The Louisiana Purchase had been completed. New land called farmers west. In his *History of the United States*, Henry Adams points out that between 1810 and 1820 the population of Delaware grew by only seventy-five people, from 72,674 to 72,749. All the Atlantic Coast states suffered. In 1815 a North Carolina legislative committee observed, "How many sad spectacles do her low-lands present of wasted and deserted fields, of dwellings abandoned by their proprietors, of churches in ruins!" They declared it "mortifying" that "thousands of our wealthy and respectable citizens are annually moving to the West . . . and that thousands of our poorer citizens follow them, being literally driven away by the prospect of poverty. In this state of things our agriculture is at a stand."

"What happens in the nineteenth century is that this whole landscape gets rebuilt. A new generation of landowners arises—folks from Philadelphia, from Virginia, knowledgeable in the literature of Europe, in a number of languages—who see agricultural improvement as a method of imposing a wonderful economic and social order. They want to reorganize not only the land but the entire social context.

"These new owners buy up failing farms and then let them to tenants. They develop a whole hierarchy of farm tenancy: landowner, tenants who farm, tenants who both farm and own their own land which they in turn tenant out to somebody else. Farm managers run the farms; beneath them, the nine-month laborers; beneath them, the day laborers; beneath them, the itinerant workers. We see these owners manumitting slaves—not because they're such good and enlightened folks, but because hiring workers for nine-month contracts is more cost-effective than maintaining slaves year-round.

"We tend to think of the early-to-middle-nineteenth century as a nation of landowners, everybody with a piece of the pie. Well, this place had moved to a level of inequity which was truly astonishing. By midcentury, eighty-five percent of the farms along the Delaware were tenanted. Now that's a pretty heavy blow to the myth of the Jeffersonian agricultural vision of a world of independent farmers.

"So what you see in this house—much of the building is gone, so I'm going to have to pantomime this for you—is this same wonderful progression. In the eighteen-forties or -fifties they rip off the attached shed and add on a new two-story service wing. Now the most formal room, the parlor, which is also the most public room in terms of its outlook, looks out not on the marsh or the river, but on the King's Highway—the road of commerce that runs down the north-south spine of the state toward Wilmington and Philadelphia. They've now created a situation in which the house becomes physically bigger while the rooms become conceptually narrower. You've gone from a period in which all of life's domestic functions can take place in one room that is situationally complex to an increasing number of specific spaces that are situationally simplified. These are folks who have basically begun to partition the world in ways that are sometimes sort of strange and arcane—in ways that are just like us.

"They develop a system of labor relations, develop elaborate rotational systems, and begin keeping leatherbound single-entry account books and itemized daybooks recording who cuts what, and what each crop yields."

Herman cites *The Farmer's Cabinet*, from 1836:

> *Let every farmer carry in his pocket paper and pencil, and as soon as anything requiring early attention occurs to him, which cannot be done immediately, let him make memorandum of it, and thus in a short time he will have a list of whatever is necessary to be done.*

Reform from the previously natural run of things took on an evangelical tone.

"The goal was maximizing the value of the land, and the means were good government, Christian living, applied science, and, most important, a consciously formulated sense of order: 'a separate place for each thing, and everything in its place.'

"They begin to experiment with new technology. They experiment with things like wheats that they judge not by their nutritional value, but on their ability to speed through a mechanized milling process. This is the beginning of the technologically viable crop," Herman says, "which will lead future farmers in search of a square tomato. They shift from plodding ox-drawn plows to horse-drawn plows which could cover twice as much acreage in a day. They buy horse-powered and sometimes steam-powered machinery in limited partnerships. In the mid-nineteenth century, this is the grain belt of the United States. And they market the grain not only up the river to Philadelphia, but down the coast to Virginia and the Chesapeake.

"By the time you get to the mid-1800s, with the railroads running inland, the Delaware is no longer a highway or an international route or even a regional route; it's become a subregional route, as it's continued to become, more and more. The trapping industry emerges. You see the fisheries develop. Not that they weren't there before. A shad galley attacked a British ship near Port Penn during the Revolution. But the railroads make it profitable to deal in highly perishable commodities like terrapin, oysters, shad, or peaches. So you see, this whole agricultural landscape relates to the river landscape behind us."

The oyster industry imitated the agricultural industry, even in its terminology, speaking of seeding, planting, cultivating, and harvesting oysters. (The use of the language of farmers may have been designed to cool the fever for what had become known as "white gold.") Tillered by captains with the temperaments of prospectors, hundreds of schooners sailed off toward every newly discovered bed. Delaware and New York ships jumped claims in the Chesapeake Bay. Pennsylvania vessels plundered New Jersey and Delaware beds at night or in fogs. A *Harper's Weekly* observer wrote:

> *A more peaceful and unexciting occupation than the pursuit of the dumb and unresisting oyster can hardly be imagined . . . yet there is engaged in this quiet waltz of life a class of as bloodthirsty pirates that ever drew a cutlass or hoisted the black flag.*

Working to gain control of what was becoming an armed fleet, the states began to protect their oyster banks. Delaware developed a system of "oyster plantations" by which the state leased oyster beds to oyster harvesters. The state acted as landlord, and the harvesting company as tenant. The companies hired captains the way tenant farmers hired farm managers. The captains might own their own vessels (or even their own oyster leases) or work on a monthly salary, but they would be in charge of hiring crew members who usually worked on short-term contracts and were called "month-lies" or "monthly men."

A system of rotating oyster beds developed, taking young "seed" oysters from the crowded natural beds in the brackish waters of the upper bay and planting them on prepared beds in the more saline lower bay, where the oysters grew faster and larger. As one author put it:

> *The character of the bottom determines the oyster's shape to some degree: on soft mud, in sedgy or crowded places, the oyster seeking room grows long, slender, crooked, and ill-shaped. But on uncrowded, hard, sandy bottoms furnished with clean food-laden water, it becomes well-shaped and fat.*

On the leased tracts, the oysters matured for anywhere from two to four years before they were harvested. In the meantime the acres of oyster beds—surveyed and staked like farmland—had also to be tended like a farm. Shells from the harvested and shucked oysters, called "culch," were taken out and dumped back on the growing beds. This kept the natural beds built up and the seed oysters from becoming covered with silt or mud, especially as clearing the forest and plowing the fields made the creeks and the river siltier and muddier. For oystermen now, like farmers, it was no longer enough simply to accept the natural cycles.

"Remodeling the world called for remodeling its buildings as well."

Herman brings us to a farm with a yard nearly enclosed by buildings, like a frontier fort. A group of sheds extend from a two-story barn, "a new barn with a little ramp so you can drive a wagon right up into it, with corncribs on either side and room for a mechanical sheller and hoists to keep separate grain bins on the second floor." Creatures below, haymows above: the totally organized farmstead, the Pennsylvania barn.

"This is one of the finest left—1885—framed without a nail."

And in the farm compound, the chicken coops, woodshed, carriage house, stable, piggery, and pigpen all under one roof carry out what Herman calls "the notion of consolidated function." This small shed, for instance, is "a combination privy-smokehouse—which must violate Leviticus in some kind of way."

The first thing you feel when you enter the farm compound is that the temperature goes up. The enclosure traps the warmth.

"Look around. This is like the house and the fields and the landscape all around. This compound is designed to contain all the functions of the farm: grain threshing, grain separation, creatures, the whole business. The design is published everywhere." It is the farm we all played with as children, placing our toy animals in their enclosures, the tractor in the barn, the hay bales in the loft, the chickens in the coops. This domesticated world, this well-ordered scheme of things, is not altogether so very old. But, as Herman says, "It becomes part of a national idiom—strictly American.

"We in the twentieth century speak of these as folk landscapes and folk architecture, almost in a pejorative sense. That somehow it was a more simple life. But nothing that we see here is designless. And because they were designed, they all have meaning. Our problem is just to unravel it in a responsible kind of way. And to say that this landscape of backcountry and watershed, of grain and shad and muskrat economies, were not integrated in very meaningful ways would be a real mistake. These simple folks are anything but. This is very much the modern world."

The Civil War ends. The completion of the railroads west brings western grain to eastern markets. Delaware farms worth $5,000 in 1850, $7,500 in 1860, and $10,000 in 1870 are suddenly worth $5,000 again in 1880. Tidal surges from a succession of October storms in the latter years of the century destroy the marsh fencing and wash out the ditches and dikes.

Items from the Dover Delawarean, *October 26, 1878, under the headline, "Terrible Wind Storm, Great Destruction of Property—Some Lives Lost":*

At Little Creek Landing the tide rose, in an hour's time, four feet above high water mark and rails, boxes, barrels, etc., were floating up the streets of the town. Twenty-four oyster boats were blown up on the marsh, some of them two miles from the creek. It was the highest tide ever known here.

At Mahon's River it is feared some lives are lost. All the outbuildings at the lighthouse are swept away and the keeper's horse and carriage swept away.

At Kitt's Hammock, the scene beggars description.

Along the Mispillion Creek the farmers have suffered severely in the loss of building, stock, corn, and hay.

At New Castle, a large break was made in the river bank and the marshes were all inundated. A schooner was blown through the break about a mile inshore.

In the wake of declining grain markets, farmers began to plant peach orchards. Within twenty years after the Civil War, Delaware was producing nearly all the country's peaches.

"Peaches, peaches everywhere," wrote Wilmington artist Howard Pyle in *Harper's* in 1879:

> *in baskets, in crates, in boxes, in wagons. . . . Along the roads in all directions rumble the peach wagons, each in a little cloud of dust, like a miniature thunder-storm, each wending its way and converging to a centre represented by the nearest railway station.*

"Now these Italianate houses we see on these farms are called, still called, 'peach houses,' " says Herman. "But these houses were built before the peach boom. These were really wheat houses and butter houses. So 'peach houses' is another wonderful historicism, an ironic one, because the houses are really a part of an older, much more stable, much more profitable mode of agriculture." But a risky replacement, for, unlike wheat, peaches were perishable and

couldn't be stored as a hedge against price changes. Peach blight—
"the yellows"—ruined the industry in a matter of a few years.

"In the 1880s, the building that had gone on for the past two
hundred years comes to a screeching halt. The area falls on hard
times that carry it right into the Great Depression. The farms that
survive are diversified truck farms. Machines replace farm animals
for plowing. To allow the machines to plow a long, straight row,
farmers take out many of the hedgerows. The runoff of soil is unbelievable."

Steamboats once plied the small creeks through the marshes to
take on grains and passengers at the small landings. In the 1920s,
oyster schooners still ran all the way up to Little Creek Landing.

"Now," says Herman, "you'd have problems rowing a *bateau* up
in there."

Gospill's Philadelphia Business Directory of 1874 listed 107 oyster dealers. By then the Delaware oyster industry had gone from
harvesting by hand tongs from the narrow decks of shallops to
running steam-powered dredges from the decks of schooners. The
harvest ranged from a million to three million bushels, as much as
25 million pounds of oysters a year. But by the end of the century
the harvests began to fluctuate sharply, and sometimes fail. The
industry clung dearly to declining profits during the Great Depression and survived and even began a recovery after the Second
World War. In 1950, however, the natural seedbeds began to fail,
and in 1957 oystermen working the planted beds hauled up dredge-
loads of nothing but dead oysters. Nothing like the sudden, massive kill had ever been seen before. Within two years more than half
the oysters in the Delaware died and no one knew why. Finally, in
1958, a Rutgers University parasitologist discovered a microscopic
organism, a single-celled parasite they could only call "multinucle-
ated sphere X." By 1960, MSX had reduced the annual oyster
harvest by 97 percent, to barely 25,000 bushels.

The parasite, apparently unique to oysters, infected beds along
the entire Atlantic Coast, but nowhere as badly as in the Delaware
and Chesapeake bays. Oddly, researchers were unable to infect un-
infected oysters directly with the parasite, leaving them to wonder

whether some other organism played host to the parasite until it came in contact with the oyster. The one identifiable factor in the spread of MSX is salinity. Young oysters on the seedbeds of the upper bay are rarely infected. But once moved down to the farmed beds, the parasite quickly infects the oyster's gills and eventually its entire body. The oyster stops feeding and within several weeks wastes away. As the salt line moves up the bay into the lower river—owing to the deeper shipping channel, reduced flow of fresh water from upstream from reservoirs and greater numbers of people drinking, washing, and flushing with the river water, and even the rise in sea level—the fear is that the parasite will gain more ground. ("Blow up the New York dams," Bob Beck told me. "Let the waters flow.") By any account, despite good beds of seed oysters and the ardent persistence of some oystermen in culching and tending their beds, the industry's been lost. A decades-long effort to create a hybrid oyster that resists the parasite has been difficult, if not altogether fruitless. Even if this can be done, however, the chances are slim of reestablishing anything but a cottage industry harvesting a kind of hothouse oyster, valued, like an orchid, less for its commercial value than for the art that went into its perfection. Along the Delaware the oyster, like the sturgeon before it, has become more of an icon than something to make a meal of.

Early in the twentieth century, oil and chemical companies that crowded the industrialized Philadelphia and Wilmington waterfronts began buying up the lower Delaware River shore marshes, filling them, raising great fields of oil tanks, and sprawling refineries whose lights give the impression of a great metropolis appearing along the river each night. (Herman calls them "the Emerald Cities.") An aggressive Delaware state plan to preserve the marshland, combined with the hard resistance of many farmers to oil company offers they really could barely afford to refuse, succeeded in holding a river frontier free of refineries and tank farms. But urban life had already sprawled southward, and in recent years suburbs began pushing the rural river life onto ever smaller preserves.

"Atomization," Herman declares.

We look across a field of winter wheat and see that in the fields around it, new housing developments have cropped up around paved cul-de-sacs.

"This is the crop. This is what the land now grows most profitably. And in terms of yield per acre, this is the way you've got to go—in the short term. Try to farm in an era of increased taxation and diminishing agricultural infrastructure? Hell, no. The problem is, we don't see the maintenance of the land as part of the long-term good. We ought to have learned that economies change, and crops fail after a time."

For the first time today he takes some pauses between his usually effortlessly connected thoughts.

"I can decry the loss of information, but I think it's historically significant, as significant as the impact of the Industrial Revolution on agriculture. We're in the process of it, whether we know it or not. But what its significance is—

"Let me ask you. What's the significance of this subdivision— Water's Edge—where they're building a pond because they don't have a water's edge to build on? I think to watch it happen is fascinating—but it's happening to our own culture, and so it's very difficult to respond to in ways that are not emotional." Which is all to say without compromising one's academic credentials, without taking it personally.

Out across the still-open, glistening marshland, out across the river toward the marshes on the opposite shore, "a shape intrudes" on the horizon, visible from nearly every point of land along this river shore, a great concrete cooling tower for the nuclear power plant on the very edge of the New Jersey shoreline, issuing a constant billow of white steam. As one scans the otherwise reliefless landscape, it draws the eye. Even aside from the issue of whether the plant, in drawing two million gallons of river water a minute to cool its condensers, at the same time traps and kills millions of fish a year in its screened intakes, the 512-foot tower with its steam plume rising fifteen hundred feet, and the transmission lines and towers that seem to hang over the marshes in the near distance like a string of Chinese characters, unquestionably destroy an ancient horizon upon which all the dream images of the landscape rest. The tower is a Magritte apple in the face—an exaggeration that obliterates the as-far-as-the-eye-can-see perspective of the coastal plain. It confines the vision. It is, Herman says quietly, taking it personally, with unacademic lack of restraint, like looking up some-one's ass.

"Let's put it this way. Imagine yourself a century into the future and looking at this landscape—at the development of subdivisions and the construction of the houses. It's all going to suggest some major transformation, not only in the organization of the landscape but in the consciousness people bring to the countryside. You see some sort of economic and cultural revolution taking place. I just don't know why it's changing the way it is. I can suspect certain things. But self-analysis is not my strong point."

We talk of the Quaker vision of the land, of their notions of silence and light and discourse with God. For the devout, this Delaware vista seemed divinely inspired. The Friends began hold-ing meetings in 1703 in the nearby village established on the banks of the Appoquinimink. The Odessa meeting house was eventually built there, and legend has it that it served as a station on the Underground Railroad. After the Civil War, attendance declined along with the remaining Quaker community. There had been a schism among the Quakers that reflected the changing agricultural landscape. The wealthier landholding Quakers wanted a more organized and worldly church. The Hicksites, mostly country Quakers, tenant farmers and working people, wanted to keep things simple, in tune with God's peaceable king-dom. Their leader, Elias Hicks, was himself a farmer who believed that city life was corrupt, and had nothing to do with preserving the inner light. The last congregant of the Appoquinimink Meet-ing was John Alston. In the years before his death at eighty, in 1871, Alston, a stubborn Hicksite, came regularly to the meeting house in Odessa and sat alone, in silent but dutiful communion with, I imagine, a landscape in his mind that even then was long since gone.

NUCLEAR FISHIN'

THE SHAD HAVE COME IN. HAVING SPENT THE LAST FIVE YEARS OF their lives at sea, wintering off the middle Atlantic Coast, summering in Canada's Bay of Fundy (during its lifetime a shad may log some ten to fifteen thousand miles on this route), they follow the rising spring water temperatures back to the rivers of their birth.

Few species of fish, perhaps one percent, make this kind of migration. Those that do may be in the process of evolving toward another way of life altogether. The relatives of the shad and striped bass, for instance, are mostly freshwater fish. These fish may well have begun migrating from freshwater streams out to sea in search of richer food reserves. While they now still return to fresh water to spawn, this anadromous phase may simply be an intermediate one, and they may eventually evolve into a completely saltwater species—that is, if they survive this precarious mid-evolutionary stage. As some see it, the diadromous fishes lead a precarious existence, for their survival depends on the health of not just one but at least two habitats: the places where they're born and return to spawn, and the places in which they grow.

"Imagine," writes the Canadian zoologist Mart R. Gross, "a 0.5 probability of habitat degradation by humans":

> *If the degradation of habitats is an independent event, and the time spent by fishes in each habitat is equal, then the probability that two habitats remain suitable is 0.5 × 0.5 = 0.25. However, since destruction of any one habitat may prevent successful reproduction and survival of a diadromous fish, we must calculate the probability that either one or the other is degraded. This probability is 0.75 or 1−(0.5 × 0.5). Thus, a fish using only one habitat has a 25% better chance of survival than one using two habitats.*

"Why do fish species become dependent upon multiple habitats when this decreases their long-term probability of survivorship? The answer is that neither 'foresight' nor 'group selection' is molding life history evolution in most fishes."

The Pacific Coast's sockeye salmon disappear from the Columbia River as the human corps of engineers dam its passage and loot its runoff for reservoirs and irrigation projects. And the striped bass, sturgeon, and shad on the Delaware, which live lives we all find so remarkable, have very nearly been extirpated. These diadromous fishes, possibly to compensate for their lower survival rates from these long journeys, lay three times as many eggs as their nonmigrating relations. Humans took this necessary natural abundance for their own plenty.

As the waters warm past forty degrees Fahrenheit, the shad move. They follow this warming isotherm up through the bay, into the tidal freshwater, up past the falls, and up the river. Here, where Rankin fishes, at the upper limit of the tidal saltwater, the fish are fat, silvery, with a greenish sheen. Most of these fish still have anywhere from another 150 to 250 miles to go before they reach their spawning grounds upriver. By the time they reach their most upstream destinations, they will be worn and wan, and most will not have the energy after spawning to make the return journey. They have not eaten the entire way; the energy expended on eating would have delayed them too long. Later in the summer these fish will be seen floating, whirling, circling miserably on their sides, fins waving weakly above the water as they try to return to the sea.

Now, however, they are fast. Even the females, each carrying up to a half a million eggs, move fifteen and more miles a day when conditions are right (by straight reckoning; no one knows how many turns or stops they make to keep on their course against tide and current). They didn't always have to make this long a journey. Only a hundred years ago, most shad on the Delaware River still spawned in the remaining coves, backwaters, and streams along the tidal freshwater shores between Trenton and Philadelphia. These were the river's major fishing grounds when the Delaware produced more shad than any other river on the East Coast. In 1896 some 15 million pounds of shad were caught along the Delaware: 4 million in the bay and 10 million in the tidal river, and some million in the river above the falls. During those years, shad fisheries lined each side of the river, boats and nets vying for water and shoreline. But those places are gone, replaced by docks and wharves, cities, industries, and refineries. The pollution along that fifty-mile stretch of river produced waters with virtually no oxygen. So at times, for years at a stretch, it was impassable to fish. They'd die on their way upstream or, if they made it upstream to spawn, the young died on their way back out to the sea. So the population of shad in the Delaware River is a fraction of what it once was.

Few colonial references give numbers of shad caught, but the fish were abundant enough to be disdained by many colonists as a fish for Indians, blacks, and the poor. The colonial English on the Connecticut River apparently thought as much:

> *The shad, which were very numerous, were despised and rejected by a large portion of the English for nearly one hundred years in the old towns of Connecticut, and for about seventy-five years in those Hampshire towns above the falls. It was discreditable for those who had a competency to eat shad, and it was disreputable to be destitute of salt-pork, and the eating of shad implies a deficiency of pork.*

One family, about to sit down to a shad dinner, heard a knock at the door and reportedly rushed to hide their fish under the bed.

(On the other hand, the English believed the herring, which were caught in the Delaware by the tens of millions on their spring spawning runs, to be "created in Heaven solely for their own benefit." Their migratory route, according to a 1750 account by a British writer, began somewhere by Greenland and crossed to Great Britain; then, guided by Providence, the fish crossed the Atlantic to provide for the British colonies.)

By the 1970s, bay and river fishermen together caught barely a hundred thousand pounds of shad. As the pollution has been cleaned up, the fish population has increased, enough to make it worthwhile for Rankin and some others to fish. But even if the Delaware waters were pristine, with the spawning places gone, the fish could never reinhabit their ancient grounds. Still, the situation is better than that on the Chesapeake, where the shad had so nearly vanished that fishing was banned completely. On the Delaware, the fish remain a part of the waterman's season. But there are fewer watermen.

Marvin Rankin and I hop into Clyde, whose cab now has the sweet, lingering smell of fish, no less lickerish than muskrat, and head over the flat blacktop toward the river. Rankin says he's sold all his muskrats, though he hated to do it. He averaged only a dollar thirty for the pelts, and even with the meats selling for a dollar sixty, and twenty-five dollars for a quart of glands, he still couldn't make up for the cost of the new traps he had to buy that winter at five dollars apiece. And, what with Easter and Passover coming at the same time this year, the holiday market was glutted and the price of shad was down. Before Easter the roe shad sold for seventy-five cents a pound, and the next week the price dropped by half.

Rankin may trap alone, but he's been fishing with Harry Duffield for the last fifteen (Duffy will say twenty) years. We find Duffield at his farm, holed up in his "skinnin' house," a low shed with a woodburning stove in the center and the shadowy feeling of a small, dimly lit circus tent. In front of the stove, as if in a center ring, is a little wooden pen, lit by a lamp, in which run a couple of dozen three-week-old ducklings. Duffy himself is a peppery guy, gray hair streaked with red, with the gait and squint of an old salt (squints his right eye nearly closed as he talks and his left, clearly blue, opens in the shadow of his cap's red brim). His face is ruddy and his front teeth missing. Duffy is as volatile as Rankin is reticent. Still, as we come in, he's huddled and fussing over his ducklings. Last night the temperature dropped and he didn't have his stove going.

"Welcome," he says, without turning, "to Goofy Duffield's Funny Farm." After a few seconds at the stove he cocks his head around, takes us in for a second, then pivots, stands, and offers his hand. I wouldn't have been surprised to see a parrot on his shoulder.

"I am what you call a diamond in the rough. In other words, I tell it like it is in plain English."

For example:

"I got little baby ducks in my skinnin' house there. I got two hundred little pullets that tall. I got a hundred pair of pigeons. I got ducks and chickens runnin' all around the yard. Now, the law says I can't trap raccoons after March fifteenth, but I'm trappin' 'em because they're so thick they got two ducks of mine this week, two of my chickens, and three or four of my pigeons. I've got to trap 'em to keep 'em out or I'm goin' to wind up with nothin'. But the do-gooders that live in the city don't see all this. They don't understand it. Trappin' is no good to them. But they're the people that's got all the money to throw around, and the power, and they get you into trouble. Where the common guy, you ain't got nothin' to work with, well, they're not going to pay any attention to you. So the first thing they cry is, 'Well, you ought to eat all vegetables.' Well, if all you eat is vegetables, why the hell did God put all the other stuff on earth? Just to take up space?"

We are near the end of the shad season, which has run from the second week in March, through the cold, blustery days on the river when often an extra hand is needed to haul the nets into the small boat, and now into the warming, calmer days of April. Both Duffield and Rankin have begun to think about the state of the vegetable seedlings in their little greenhouses, the peppers and tomatoes they'll raise during the summer. Last night's near frost was too close for comfort. When I arrived at Rankin's place that morning, he was out examining the small leaves for signs of damage.

Both men combine farming with fishing, trapping, eeling, crabbing, and occasional snappering. Duffy raises and sells chickens and ducks and pigeons. With the prices on muskrat down, eels, crabs, and shad have had to make up the difference. Thirty years ago that would have been difficult. The market for eels, once small, is now driven by exports to Europe, where many of the rivers have been so polluted the eels can no longer be eaten. The Japanese take shipments of live young Delaware River eels, fly them to Japan, and then rear them in their own tanks. Crabbing for blue-claw crabs was always pursued, but mostly for local consumption. Fishermen used trotlines, baited lines, rather than traps. With prices rising and the advent of refrigerated trucks, the pursuit increased. So, it seems, have the crabs, perhaps due to the salt water moving higher up in the bay. And thirty years ago shad barely seemed to be surviving in the river.

In any case, though their catch and profits have been increasing, Duffy and Rankin haven't seen fit to make any major investments. Fishermen who survive the cycles of boom and bust are usually those who don't get carried away making big expenditures, no matter how good things appear. Nature is just too unpredictable and they know it. But under any circumstances Duffy and Rankin remain far from overcapitalized. The boat has no Loran, no depth finder, no sonar. The only clock is a little battery-powered wall clock that lies in under the bow with the boots and rain gear and is still set on daylight savings time. They decided to make do with last year's net, its tears unmended. The dock they set off from is a makeshift arrangement of warped boards on tilted pilings.

Harry counts the boats tied up along the narrow channel and figures out how many of the other fishermen have already gone out. Some fourteen tie up at the little landing, and that represents only a few families. Here in Salem County the fishing is still passed on from fathers to sons and sons-in-law. Duffy explains, in his way, how it is.

"There's the F. family, they're the biggest. There's Donald, Nelson, Frankie, they're all brothers. Two of Frankie's boys are fishin' ['feeshin'] and crabbin' here. Another brother is Marty's father—my son-in-law. 'Course, some don't come back on high water, some don't catch the low water. My daughter works a crab boat and my sons can do it all."

On this bright day we can see clearly across the river to Delaware, looking across at Blackbird Creek. We will be fishing just downstream from the steaming cooling tower of the nuclear power plant. We even drift up on the New Jersey bay marker, the counterpart of the one at the Dukes' farm across the river, a stone obelisk bearing a bronze plaque that officially demarcates bay from river Delaware. Like the Dukes' marker, this one, too, was nearly washed away by tide rising over a sinking and receding shoreline.

"The sons of bitches were going to just let it fall into the mud," sputters Duffy. "The damn state. They don't fix anything that really needs fixin'. What the hell do they do with all the lottery money they get? The sales tax? Anyway, took three or four articles in the paper to get them to move the obelisk back, and they still didn't move it far enough. It's still washin' away. And they're supposed to have brains. They ain't got brains enough to pour piss out of a boot."

I hop off the bow onto the muddy shoreline and read: "Mouth of the Delaware River. A straight line drawn from the center of this monument to the center of a similar monument erected at Liston's Point on the Delaware shore is the dividing line between the Delaware River and Bay ascertained June 22, 1906, in pursuance of uniform acts of the United States."

"Nineteen-oh-five is when my father was born," offers Duffy, not conceding the last word on any matter.

Duffy and Rankin putter with the 2,400-foot net ("Say four hundred fathoms," says Harry, "sounds more professional."), "plan their strategy" as they put it, to keep their net from drifting into anyone else's, and then let the net run out from the boat, held high by its buoy line, a twelve-foot-deep net, flagged on either end, drifting downstream in some fifteen feet of water for the next two hours. Duffy, with the aplomb of a baseball manager explaining his winning game plan, puts it this way:

"We're going to set inshore where these guys is laid off out here. They're going to set out further, toward the channel. We don't want to get that deep water right now, but when we go out to get that high water, we go out down where them other boats are at. We try to lay the net off in the last tide so she comes right straight up here where you usually stop, right here at the dike. Because that's when we're hitting the most fish on that slack water. As soon as this net goes around this dike where she's up here all gobbledygunked, she'll start stretching herself out, because the tide'll be suckin' her here. When we get down here, she'll turn.

"Every day is different—every day. It never goes down the same way every day—never. It might be peaches and cream when you leave here, but when you get out here, it can get snotty. But we try to keep it where we think the most of the fish are. You don't always hit it, but that's what we're tryin' to do."

Duffy has signs he follows.

"When the sun crosses the Equinox, whatever way your prevailing winds are, that's about what your winter will be." Or: "Whatever Mother's Day is, that's when the horseshoe crabs will be up on the beach."

To get the most of drift-net fishing in tidal waters usually means drifting downstream on the two high tides each day. The fish are coming upstream while the net is coming down. So lives that run with the seasonal cycles now become tied to the lunar cycle. It means a lack of regular sleep, but most fishermen seem to like drift netting better than catching fish in nets anchored to the bottom. In either case, the fish are caught in the mesh of the nets as they try to swim through; their heads make it, but their gills are ensnared. The sooner the fish are removed from the net, the better condition they'll be in for sale. Drift netters drift and take the fish out immediately, while set netters often allow the fish to hang ensnared for as long as a whole passing tide.

These gill-net fisheries are especially productive when few fish are around. In the nineteenth century, when the waters seemed filled with passing fish, seine nets rowed out from shore drifted down and encircled so many fish at once they had to be hauled back in by windlasses.

One reason Marvin and Duffy want to fish close to shore is to avoid catching striped bass. Over the last thirty years the striper has gone from a valuable resource to near extirpation to a netter's nuisance. More striped bass than anyone can remember appear to be in the Delaware. (Hudson River shad fishermen have the same complaint.) Its numbers have increased, while the strict regulations about catching the fish remain in effect. Since the stripers migrate to spawn at nearly the same time as the shad, nets can become so loaded with striped bass that fishermen have been known to simply let the entire net, fish and all, just sink.

Marvin runs the boat, leaning his stomach against the wheel. The day is bright, and the broad vista of boats rocking after drifting nets is a peaceful one. Duffy barks and snarls from the stern over the noise of the engine and the fluttering of the breeze.

"Pollution—weedkillers, sprays, wastes—that is the main source of your problem that hurts you, and more than bein' overcatched or overtrapped. Some don't agree with it, but any stupid dummy been around long enough could tell that's one of our biggest problems. All those pollutants that get put in that ground, Mother Nature doesn't have time to dissolve it and spit it out. And it just goes in the dirt and just washes off into the river and the cricks. And then your little baby fish come along. . . ."

Duffy refers to Rankin as "Fluff," a schoolboy name that alluded to Rankin's head of tousled hair.

"We went down to pick up dead horseshoe crabs for eel bait and there's a couple of ladies down there sunnin' theirselves on the beach, and the next thing I know I'm pickin' up horseshoe crabs and Fluff is up there showin' the ladies the difference between a boy horseshoe crab and a girl."

Rankin smiles, pulls his orange watch cap rakishly down over his forehead, and leans into the bow as we come up on the net. With a makeshift gaff, a hook lashed to a wooden stake, he pulls the net up into the boat. We haul it hand over hand over the side. Shad—shining, silvery narrow heads, green-backed and hard-bodied—are jammed into the translucent purple nylon mesh. We pull them out any way we can; sometimes a tangle of net has to be stripped away like a tangled fishing line. Sometimes the fish fall hard onto the deck, but mostly we pull them from the net, hold them close, and lay them in the box. The net is full of tears but a fish is often found tangled in even a frayed section. "Damn," says Duffy, "if he wa'n't lookin' hard to find a piece of net to get into."

The action is steady, and through it all Duffy never stops talking: how he hunts, how he meets women, how he trains his dog, how he raises squab. He asserts that he is one of the last in the county to raise the birds, a dying art that in the 1930s was a major part of the local economy.

"I had pigeons all of my life. Since I was ten years old. It's like trappin' for muskrat. You get the mud between your toes and you never get it out. In 1950 I won the New Jersey state contest that they had for the most squabs raised out of six pair of pigeons. And it was publicized in this birdin' and pigeon journal that goes all over the world—Germany, England, Australia, New Zealand—every month. So I'm known the world over. Fluff ain't quite got that renown. Even though he was Mr. March."

"Yes," says Rankin, not lifting his head as he pulls up net, "I was Mr. March."

Seems the power company that runs the nuclear generating plant, whose tower smolders behind us as we fish, put out a combination calendar and plan of emergency evacuation that it illustrated with scenes of local trappers, farmers, hunters, and fishermen. Oddly enough, the cooling tower, which can barely be missed from anywhere in the county, doesn't show up to spoil any of the pictures. Still, March was Marvin Rankin walking the boardwalk out by his marsh with a string of muskrat pelts slung across his shoulders.

There is also included information "that area farmers should use in the event of a radiological emergency":

> *Sirens will sound. The signal is a steady 3 to 5 minute signal. It is not a wailing sound. . . . Close outside doors and windows. Turn off fans and air conditioners. This helps keep out radioactive material. Keep pets inside. If possible, shelter farm animals. . . . Radiation is a kind of energy. Heat, light, and radio waves are common types of radiation. Some kinds of radiation occur naturally. They have been here since the Earth began. . . . Other kinds of radiation are man-made. X-rays and radiation from nuclear plants are examples. . . . Radiation from nuclear plants is made by particles or rays which come*

from the centers of some kinds of atoms. There are three kinds.
Alpha particles . . . They can be stopped by a sheet of paper.
Beta particles . . . They can be stopped by an inch of wood.
Gamma rays . . . They can be stopped by lead or concrete. . . .
Low-level radiation is measured in a unit called a millirem.
The sun gives us 50 millirems a year. . . . The average person
gets about 125 millirems per year. People who live just outside
a nuclear power plant rarely get more than 1 additional milli-
rem a year. It would take 20 years to get as much radiation as
in a single dental X-ray. . . . How radiation affects us depends
upon: the kinds of particles or rays; the length of time of expo-
sure; how much of the body is exposed; how much radioactive
material stays in the body. . . . Learn more about nuclear power
. . . visit or call. . . .

The three-lane blacktop runs straight through the marsh. With
its painted lanes and overhead traffic signals it could be an interstate, but most of the time it sits empty, like an abandoned jungle
airstrip, for it leads only to and from the Salem generating stations.
The marsh spreads on either side; in the cool spring sun it's still a
golden brown expanse broken by pools of water shaken by a saltwater wind. Mad Horse Creek meanders through to the river. Starlings rise together, turn and swirl like schools of herring. There are
plenty of stick huts built by muskrats. Power lines overhead run in
toward the plant, a student's exercise in perspective. A billboard
with no evident sponsor cites Acts 16: BELIEVE ON THE LORD JESUS
CHRIST, AND THOU SHALT BE SAVED, AND THY HOUSE. An official
sign farther down the road instructs you to LEAVE CALMLY. At the
end of the road there is plenty of parking for an old restored ferry
docked on the riverfront and, in keeping with the apocalyptic mes-
sages revealed thus far, called the Second Sun Energy Information
Center. I would stand outside and admire the river view, but the
noise from the generating plant is like the drone of a hundred jet
engines, so one's eyes can't focus on the still undamaged vista across
the river.

Inside the boat is a little hall of radiation history, paying homage in photomontage to Dalton, Volta, Ampere, Watt, Faraday, Edison, Crookes, Mendeleev, Becquerel, Einstein, Rutherford, and Fermi. Captions provide life histories written in the style developed for television program guides: "Enrico Fermi, 1902—1954. In 1942, under the grandstand of the University of Chicago football field, Fermi's experiments led to the first controlled atomic chain reaction."

Next, a Hall of Energy History, beginning with a little diorama of Native Americans using fire to hollow out a log for a canoe. Then on to wind power, water power, steam, electric, coal, oil, gas, and solar. A group of schoolchildren pass me by quickly, heading toward the Hall of Nuclear Energy, which is a little arcade of flashing lights and electronic games.

"Split the Atoms and Start a Chain Reaction" has the kids aiming and shooting atomic particles.

"The uranium 235 atom becomes highly energized when struck by speeding neutrons and splits new atoms. This is nuclear fission. Other neutrons strike other atoms causing a chain reaction. As the atoms split they give off heat to the tune of $E = MC^2$."

At the end of the tour, everyone gets a sample fuel pellet, which is to impress the bearer with how small (the size of the head of a pushpin) it is. And, of course, the company assumes no one can conjure up the image of a million of these pellets, let alone seventeen million, let alone tons of them together, but here they are: seventeen million pellets of uranium fuel in a ceramic compound, sealed within thirteen-foot-long zirconium rods and sitting in water within a vessel forty feet high with steel walls eight and a half inches thick.

What are people afraid of? Not the risk of an accident—which is clearly small—but the risk if there is an accident, which could be substantial. The company will swear there's no cause for concern: "Nuclear reactors have accumulated over 2,000 reactor-years of operating experience." For most of us, radiation remains mysterious stuff. Not so mysterious, however, is the high-level radioactive waste the reactor produces, some ninety metric tons produced at Salem each year, which never leaves the site and sits on concrete, steel-lined, water-filled pools—what is euphemistically called temporary storage (the government has yet to find a permanent place in which something can be buried for the thousands of years it remains toxic)—that will keep accumulating until the reactor has to be scrapped, some thirty or forty years and a few thousand metric tons of radioactive waste down the road, when it, too, is a heap of radioactive junk awaiting disposal. (To create so much waste in such a brief lifetime—some of these fishermen and trappers will have their boats longer than forty years.) But while these things should cause the most concern, these contained fuels, these stored toxic wastes that can be neither smelled, felt, nor tasted—it's the cooling tower, both literally and figuratively, that takes all the heat. Unfortunately it's huge. A football stadium could sit in its base, and it can be seen from everywhere along the flat farm and marshland in two states. Its plume of pure white steam is constant. It has the presence of an icon, a hyperbolic cauldron of unnameable worries, and perhaps most unfortunate, its funnel shape and billowing cloud are the very image of an atomic explosion cast in concrete. This is a shame, when all that the tower should be blamed for is destroying the harmony of river, marsh, and sky.

"Well, at least the nuke plant is a clean industry," says Rankin, looking back to it as we drift. "I ain't afraid of it. Though I suppose it has the potential to wipe us all out. And I wouldn't doubt if somethin' happened and they could get away without tellin' me, they wouldn't tell me. But more people complained about the nuclear plant here than complain about the Du Pont chemical plant in Pennsville, which isn't required to have an evacuation plan, though I think of those people in Bhopal, India. When those people all woke up dead, I think it opened some people's eyes here." On the other hand, the nuke plant paid the county enough in assessments that Rankin's annual property tax bill went down eight hundred dollars.

"Before the nuke plant came in, the township had no tax base, no police department. Then millions started rolling in and we couldn't spend it fast enough. We built a senior citizens' complex for all the widow ['widda'] women on the old farms. Built a swimmin' pool.

Brought in buses for trips. There is a group of people down in Lower Alloway Creek who say that cooling tower's changed our weather, messed up the atmosphere, and caused this dry period. Well, whether it has or not, people can look up and see that cooling tower and right away it becomes the villain. Same way with the weakfish. They say the intake screens [which screen debris from entering the cooling system with the water drawn from the river] have killed all the weakfish. Well, when I was a young man there wasn't no weak-fish out here. You couldn't catch no weakfish out here, and there wasn't no nuclear plant, either. But I do hear they are killin' a lot of small fish and crabs and I do see a lot of gulls hangin' around there, and they must be there for a purpose. Still, the population of fish and crabs runs in cycles, so is it a cycle? Who knows?"

In fact, a bigger problem for the power plants than the fish caught on the screens are the fish eggs, larvae, and young that get sucked into the system. This is not a problem for nuclear power plants alone. All thermal electrical generating facilities produce heat to convert water into steam to drive the turbines that produce the electricity. To condense the steam, cooling water passes continuously through thin tubes. Power plants are placed along rivers because rivers provide a cheap source of water (and nuclear power plants use more water than most fossil-fuel plants). Aquatic organisms that aren't diverted from the system can be pinned on the intake screens by the force of the water. Those that pass through the mesh are in for a rough trip through the cooling system. The losses mount up. A report, long withheld, then finally released by the New Jersey Department of Environmental Protection, found that power company estimates of the losses of fish due to the Salem plants were far too low. The cooling systems at Salem may be killing the equivalent of 11 million weakfish a year, some 28 million pounds of fish, nearly four times the catch of the commercial and recreational weakfish fisheries combined. Worse, the killing of many more millions of bay anchovy, one of the primary foods of the weakfish, may account for more losses. (So, while the plant didn't do in the weakfish, it's not helping with their recovery.) The same report also estimated the loss of more than half a million herring, nearly five million Atlantic croaker, and 400,000 white perch. Shad were little affected since their eggs hatch and the young grow far upstream. "Continued operation of the Salem NGS, without modification to intake structures and/or operating practices, threatens the protection and propagation of balanced indigenous populations," said the report. One of the ways to use less river water, it concluded, would be to build another cooling tower.

The gulls flock over us as we head back into Mad Horse Creek. "You know," Marvin Rankin says, "people's eating habits change. I was thinkin' as Harry was talkin' about pigeons, I was thinkin' about rhubarb. You know how people—"

"Yeah," says Duffy, nodding.

"—used to raise—"

"Yeah."

"—that little field of rhubarb? And now people don't eat it."

"Yeah."

"You talk about the future here, and the past," Rankin continues. "We used to raise a lot of tomatoes for the canning factories like H.J. Heinz, Hunt's, Ritter's, Campbell's, and Del Monte, and then they moved all their canning industry away from here and that left the farmers to try and change."

"And now," Duffy jumps in, having had this repartee with his friend before, "now they double-crop the ground, all tryin' to get that extra dollar because the poor son of a bitch has paid eighty thousand for a combine or a tractor and he's got to make payments. So he puts all this weed killer on to kill the weeds. Then he puts bug killer on to kill the bugs. Then he gets stuff to spray on top of the tomatoes so they'll ripen up. Then, after they pick the tomatoes, they turn around and spray the vines to kill them. Instead of plowin' the cornstalks and the wheat stubble under, they spray stuff on it to dissolve it right on top of the ground, which is doin' no good because you've got to turn that stuff over to make humus and put that stuff back in the soil. Instead, they try to get the soybeans to come up through it, just bleeding the ground to death."

"A lot of farmers here," Rankin recalls, "used to have small herds of horses and cattle and they made a lot of manure and they spread this manure out on the fields and they used to spread hay out on the ground and it used to help the land. Now it's all chemical fertilizer, and you can't raise anything unless you put a ton of insecticide on it to keep off the bugs and disease. And I'm afraid it's all catchin' up to us. We look at the land—we can remember twenty-five to thirty years ago this was some of the best land in Lower Alloway Creek. Now it don't look like it would grow anything."

"Damn, Fluff, we're old. When I was ten years old I was in 4-H, back in 1945, I'd say, and I bought fertilizer off of Agway, which used to be GLF. Five-ten-ten was thirty-two dollars a ton. I sold wheat then for two, two and a quarter a bushel. This year just past I sold my wheat for two dollars and fifty cents a bushel. I paid a hundred and eighty dollars a ton for the five-ten-ten fertilizer. And I still got just the same amount of money for the wheat as I did when I was a kid back in the forties. Now you tell me what's wrong in the world."

On the way back I get a tour of the town of Canton, past the Melanovski house, "the Polish section of town," and past the little Methodist church, which, Marvin says seriously, "used to be a little rinky-dink, but now it's expanded." In a tree overhanging an abandoned farmhouse they point out a bald eagle's nest the size of a bathtub, in which rough, downy young can be seen from the road.

"Here," says Duffy, pointing out a woman working on her lawn, "here's one of Marvin's girlfriends. He'll blow the horn as we go by."

"Clyde's horn don't work."

"Well, she'll be real disappointed."

Recognizing the two, the woman raises a hand. "See," says Duffy, "she waved. I'm gonna tell his wife June on him. I'm gonna rat."

They point out the small "black cemetery."

"See," Rankin explains, "Salem County was founded by Quakers who didn't believe in slaves. So sometimes, when these rich Quakers died, they'd leave an inheritance to the black people that worked for them. That's where a lot of black people begin to own property here. And a lot of black people that we had down here were mixed-race people—they had Indian and white blood—"

"And they own a lot of ground," asserts Duffy.

"Down in Greenwich. Some white people tenant farm for black people. I farmed on shares for black people who owned the land. These people have been here a long time."

"Very wealthy and very influential."

Rankin nudges Duffy. "There's the mail lady."

"Don't worry about the mail lady, keep goin'. I once heard of a mail lady who fell in love with one of the guys on her route. But he was cheatin' on her, he had another girlfriend, and she seen this letter that his other girlfriend wrote him and she tore it up and throwed it away. The post office found out about it and fired ['farred'] her. Not for havin' a boyfriend on her route, but for tearin' up the U.S. mail."

Rankin smiles and shakes his head.

"They call us the odd couple," Duffy says. "Me, and Marvin the churchgoer."

"We had a Baptist minister on the boat once, and I thought Harry would burst from all the profanity just welled up inside of him."

When Rankin introduced me to eighty-six-year-old Lewis Fogg, he was polite and as sweet as honey, hat in hand, like a schoolboy meeting his old teacher. "Mr. Fogg," Rankin said, "I was telling Mr. Stutz about you and how you been farmin' here all your life and he asked if I would introduce you." Fogg, looking nowhere near his age, still square-jawed and with a steady gaze from behind gold-rimmed eyeglasses, sat up in the seat of his Allis-Chalmers tractor, nodded slowly, said he hoped he'd have somethin' to offer me, and climbed down as Rankin bowed out. Fogg gave my hand a brief but firm grip, and then strode in small steps, with a straight-kneed but steady gait, over to the open garage, where, in the entry, out of the sun, was a green upholstered Lazy Boy recliner. He sat—his green chinos shiny and creased—then offered me a wooden bench beside him. For a time we just stared out across the field to a marsh fire burning across the road. April is the month, has always been the month, to burn marsh or meadow. Trapping season is ended and the idea is to clear out the old cane to make way for the summer's growth. These days the hope is to get rid of some phragmites as well. The fires burn quickly, spread quickly, and smolder in long lines across fields on both sides of the river. They are hypnotic to watch, and burn so quickly I've been told you can stand within a flaming thicket and not get singed.

Farmland surrounds Fogg's eighteenth-century brick home. Salem County has a score of such homes, and few are surrounded by the suburban developments that have broken up the farmland on the other side of the river, for the ground is even lower and wetter here on this side of the river. Fogg, from his chair, likes to travel back and forth.

The story Mr. Rankin told me, I said, had to do with Prohibition—how rumrunners used to ship illegal whiskey up the Delaware to landings along the creeks in the Salem County marshes. A Mrs. Dukes, I said, on the other side of the river, someone about your age, also said the same thing. I wondered if you'd ever heard anything of it.

He squinted into the distance and shook his head.

"No. It was all legal stuff. It just come from Canada or Bermuda, but it was all legally made. Just wasn't legal to sell it here."

"Where did they bring it in?"

"Have you been to see the eagle's nest?"

"Yes, this morning."

Fogg tells me he and his wife raised their children there. Had a dairy farm. ("If you're milkin' fifty head of cows and you can't make a livin' on fifty head of cows, then you need somebody else to learn you how to take care of your finances.")

"Used to be a lot of eagles around in the thirties. But people thought they was eatin' the muskrats, so they did away with them. People say the eagles was done in by DDT. Maybe some, but I think around here lead did more damage than DDT. Look at that fire walk across that meadow, just running along on that reed. Yeah, we had some hot old times out there."

"On the creeks?"

"Yeah. You know, back in the thirties you never started shad fishin' until about the tenth of April. Now they're shad fishin' the twentieth of March. Now they're almost done. We never started till about the tenth of April. Before then we'd carp fish. My buddy and I—'course, he passed away long ago—he and I carp fished for better than twelve years. Always down at the creek here. Yes, we figured on catching a ton, ton and a half of carp a week—and get eight to ten cents a pound for it. Well, that wasn't too bad, you know. The average wage on a farm at the time was about twelve dollars a week, two dollars a day. And we'd generally wind up with forty or fifty dollars a week. Kind of spoiled us a little bit. Later on, we'd fish for shad. Then we'd have a floatin' cabin and we'd move down to the mouth of the creek and move the net stakes down so you could shake your net out every once in a while. We never caught as many shad as Marvin catches now. But we never had no trouble sellin' it. We caught sturgeon in our shad net every once in a while. They called them 'mamoose.' One time we caught a dolphin out there, but that was a shame because she drowned before we could get her out of the net. You'd stay there the whole week. And they have a boat come out from Hancock's Bridge every day and pick up the shad. Pick up the shad and give you a hunk of ice to keep your stuff cool. Man, them was the days.

"Let's see. I got out of high school in 1926. And then there was these trappin' cabins and we'd put up in them all during trappin' season. And, you know, that was nice. That was a part of my life I wouldn't want to miss. I'm glad I didn't miss it, either. Three or four trappers would get together, live there through the winter for three months, duck shootin', you know, and a lot of tarpon [snapper] proggin' in the wintertime when it wasn't froze up too hard.

"When I come out of high school my dad put me to followin' a walkin' plow in the spring of the year. Boy, I tell you, I wasn't happy at all. Go to high school, get twelve years of education, and then chase these damn team horses around. I'll tell you one thing, you ate. You had to eat to keep your strength. Now, that's been a day or two ago. My father, my grandfather, and his father was all farmers. All in Lower Alloway Creek, every one of them. This farm right here has been in the Fogg family since 1774. The original Foggs was Quakers that settled in Maine before they came here. I suppose the climate up there didn't exactly make them happy.

"We used to haul our grain to Alloway and put it on the freight train. Three box wagons and maybe two tons—you had to keep it down for those horses. You can't realize how small we used to operate years ago. Like this farm here was run with maybe four teams of horses and two hired men to help. Before the machines came in I'd have at least thirty people picking tomatoes ['tomaydas'] by hand for me. Sometimes you could get local help. But too many of them was winos and you'd go in after them and pick bushels of wine bottles. We had three or four families come up from the South. And they would pick maybe two or three thousand baskets a day. There was two fair-sized cannin' houses in Hancock's Bridge.

"Well, they sure improved upon tomatoes when they got those harvesters, let me tell you. If it wasn't for those tough little ol' plum tomatoes, you couldn't even use a harvester. The ones we handpicked were a bigger, softer tomato, but the harvester would mash 'em up. Now that old fair-sized tomato, as far as I'm concerned, he's the best tomato to put on the table to eat. Those plums are tough-skinned little buggers, you know.

"When the canning companies moved out of here, it was a diesaster, I'll tell you. That was a die-saster."

He stares out again at the fires.

"Would you like a highball?"

Though I would, I decline; I was up at four to meet Marvin and have a long drive home ahead of me. Fogg rises, goes to the refrigerator against the wall of the garage, takes out a pitcher, and pours himself a drink of something, looks like bourbon, into a paper cup, sits again and sips.

"So, during Prohibition I was twenty-one or twenty-two. That was a risky business, I tell you. And a lot of people involved in it, you know, who you'd never think would have anything to do with it. But the money, they needed the money, and if you had a place where a boat could tie up alongside of your land and you could get a truck there, there was a hundred dollars that you were gonna get. All you had to do is unload one night and a hundred-dollar bill is in your hand. It was just that easy. And a hundred dollars then would buy you something. It was nice money, you know, for unloading the stuff. Only about three of us left out of that bunch.

"At Christmastime you got all this fancy liquor from France, that high-priced stuff. But they'd never run that until November. See, they'd have a mother boat about fifteen to twenty miles off the Jersey shore and then they'd have speedboats that picked it up. Those boats were only about sixteen foot and they could fly, you know? They had Liberty motors in them, and I mean those gentlemen would move. They'd only carry about three hundred cases, which is just about what one of the small trucks would carry. I think at one time we had three or four boats run there in one night—that's twelve hundred cases—and they would generally run about three or four nights a month. They used to unload in the Cohansey, Stove Creek, Alloway Creek, and, of course, on the Delaware shore. They had certain times and certain spots accordin' to whether the Coast Guard got after them tight. Then they might change their minds about where they was going to unload. I don't think I ever seen one of them shot up too bad. But they'd get tough out there every once in a while and they'd cut it on to them rum boats."

Rankin had told me a story he'd been told by a guy who'd run one of the boats. The Coast Guard had been chasing them and shooting at them, so they'd turned off their lights. A shot came through the cabin, and suddenly the guy felt this warm stuff running down his arm, so he worked his way as best he could up into the creek—the Coast Guard vessels were too big to follow—and when he reached the dock he turned the cabin light on. When he did, he found that the can of oil they kept in the cabin had been shot through and the oil was running down his arm. And he thought he'd been bleeding to death the whole trip in.

Not everyone could be bought. When approached by a bootlegger to rent his creekside shed for storage, one old upright Hancock's Bridge farmer refused, even when offered about as much money as his whole farm was worth. But he did tell them that after they'd loaded the trucks with booze somewhere else, it would be all right with him if they stopped off to buy his potatoes to stack up in front of it.

There was local product as well, rye whiskey made from the grain of local farms.

"We had two makers," Fogg readily recalls. "One made pretty good whiskey and the other one, you fool with it long enough and you wind up you might be drunk and have a headache with it. Now, W——, who made the good stuff, he grew his own rye. You better not put his name in, he may still have some family here. But I'd say he was an asset to the township. He made whiskey—but somebody had to make it. So as far as I was concerned he was a decent man."

As we've talked, the traffic on the road that runs by his field has increased, most of it, he says, from the changing of shifts at the nuke. The whole idea of working by shifts seems appalling to him. No one had ever seen much of that around here. There was no day shift or night shift. There were things you did in the morning, things you did in the light, things you did in the dark. Things you did by season, things you did by tide.

"I used to love duck huntin' at night. The game wardens didn't like it. They didn't like it. But, well, you worked on the farm all day, so just about as it start to get dark the ducks would begin flyin' in toward the river. You'd get three or four ducks, and you'd eat them then. I used to have a friend of mine who was a doctor and we used to do an awful lot of duckin' in the fall of the year. We had a cabin down along the river shore. Beautiful place down there. Quiet. Ain't nothin' quiet around here anymore. Everything got upset when they put this nuclear plant down here. We got a lot of influx of new people and money. I think we got the highest-paid police force in the state of New Jersey. They got cooks down there at the senior citizens' center that get fourteen dollars an hour plus their health benefits. Have you ever heard of that kind of money? They have spent wild, wild, wild. And I'm afraid we disregard values."

If any further proof of this was needed, here was this line of traffic blocking his view of the wonderful fire still ablaze in the meadow beyond.

"The Negro Speaks of Rivers"

Mrs. Dukes had told me this:
"The country school was the Taylor's Bridge school. This was where I met my husband. We walked there and carried our lunchboxes. It was one room and eight grades. That was something for a teacher. Sometimes there would be as many as forty kids. But sometimes there'd be only half that. When the work got done on the farm, then the school would fill up with boys. Now, of course, there were white schools and black schools. The black school was down Route 9 aways. But there was only one black family that lived here right close."

"Was there always a white school and a black school?"

"Why, sure. You didn't go to school together. You didn't sit together. You didn't eat together. When you had help, you set a black table and a white table. We had a black fella that lived here with us when my boys were little. He was especially with us in the wintertime. My boys sat on his lap and he read stories to them many a times. We'd all sit there and talk together. But he sat at his table right there in the kitchen. That's just the way the custom was. He was here in winter to help with the trapping and he'd stay right up the kitchen stairs."

The little boy was sitting on Uncle Remus's knee, and he turned suddenly and looked into the weather-beaten face that had harbored so many smiles.

"We wear the mask that grins and lies," wrote Paul Laurence Dunbar in 1895, around the same time Joel Chandler Harris was writing his Uncle Remus stories. "It hides our cheeks and shades our eyes."

The Delaware River led two lives in slave times. In the early years it carried holds full of African captives bound for auction. Handbills and newspaper advertisements announced their arrival:

LIKELY NEW NEGROES,
AT FISHBOURNS' WHARFF, TO BE SOLD BY
WILLING, MORRIS, AND COMPANY.

Or:

. . . to be sold at auction at Front St. Paint business, tools for carrying on paint business, also a young Negro Wench, a new chair, and a good horse. . . .

But even as the evil business continued, the river would offer runaways their first northern refuge.

Africans had come up the river along with every other European import. Before 1750, most came as part of the West Indian trade. Philadelphia merchants shipped wheat, biscuits, and barrel staves to the Caribbean. Slaves, spirits, sugar, and spices sailed north, mostly coming ashore in Quaker Philadelphia. Many of these slaves were already creolized, born in the West Indies to an earlier generation of imported Africans. After 1750 the need for slaves grew as imported white indentured servants became more scarce, the poor being impressed at home to fight in the long European wars. The importers—Willing and Morris, George Meade, and Thomas Riche—began shipping directly from Africa. Warrants for runaways (and there were many runaways and many recaptures) describe them with scarified bodies, heads, and arms, filed teeth, and holes in their ears.

Shipments of Africans were referred to as "parcels." Handbills announced the arrival of "a parcel of Gold Coast Negroes," "a parcel of men, women, boys, and girls," and sometimes simply "a parcel of Negroe boys and girls." Between 1759 and 1765, at least a thousand slaves came up the Delaware River (the number smuggled in to avoid tariffs is unknown) and most landed in Philadelphia. In 1761 the City's Quaker conscience was stirred enough to get the Pennsylvania legislature to take action against the slave business. But with some very substantial merchants involved in the trade, the governors came up with a perfectly modern political measure: The colony would not ban the slave trade outright; rather, it would raise the import duty to ten pounds per soul. The slave trade might leave Philadelphia, but out of economic rather than moral concerns. The business simply moved south along the river.

On May 6, 1762, Willing, Morris and Company announced:

> *Just imported from the Coast of Africa in the Brigantine Nancy, William Clarke, Master; and to be sold at Wilmington, in New Castle County . . . One Hundred and Seventy five Gold Coast NEGROES. . . . In the West Indies, where slaves are best known, those of the Gold Coast are in much greater Esteem, and higher valued, than any others, on Account of their natural good Dispositions, and being better capable of hard Labour.*

Importers tried to bring the slaves in during warm weather because the cool temperatures of the middle Atlantic states could prove fatal to the ill-clothed and ill-fed Africans. By the time the schooner *Africa* arrived at Wilmington in 1763, thirty-three of its shipment of a hundred slaves had already died. Wrote slave dealer Thomas Riche:

> *What slaves is left are in bad order, five we have buried since they landed—&now ten at Lodgings under the Doct. Ceare, the weather is so cold—we Cannot move them about the Country for sale only four disposed of from 40 to 60 pounds a head it gives me Concearn, such a Consignment has fell in my hands at this season, as the Loss will be so Great. . . .*

More died after purchase.

Even while this slave trade persisted, manumitted slaves began establishing themselves in communities along the Delaware. Wilmington, with a population of four thousand at the end of the eighteenth century, had some 450 free blacks to 121 slaves. Slaves in the cities, especially the women and children, served mostly as domestic servants, but they might also be laborers and helpers for shopkeepers and teamsters. Along the river, some served apprenticeships with blacksmiths, coopers, ships' carpenters, and sailmakers. The few who had the chance worked their way to freedom (although there was apparently a pretty good business in kidnapping and selling free blacks back into slavery). Some, like Wilmington's black master shipbuilder Gabriel Jackson, made themselves financially independent. (These, though, might have to suffer the often condescending attention of the abolition societies who used them as examples of how blacks, once out of the primitive influence of the dark continent of their ancestors, might not only learn a trade, but learn to wheel and deal as well as any white.) Jackson worked his way from slave to apprentice to shipmaster, became the first black to buy land in Wilmington, and, wrote the Delaware Abolition Society in 1787, "erected two Tolerable Dwelling Houses Thereon." Along with his wife, Betty, "a colored woman of more than ordinary ability," who operated a confectionery shop on French Street, Jackson held "Considerable other property, which we Believe they Have Acquired by the dint of Industry and Ingenuity, and that they live in Good repute amongst their Neighbors." Even faint praise came with difficulty.

Wilmington, the first major city north of the slaveholding Chesapeake tidewater, became a hub of African-American activities. Archaeologist Wade Paul Catts excavated sites of eighteenth-century black dwellings in Wilmington, and found a diverse community of barbers, carters, blacksmiths, coopers, teachers, midwives, tanners, shoemakers, oystermen, spinners, ropemakers, and sea captains. But since, as Bernie Herman put it, the history of African-Americans in Delaware was too often systematically expunged—buildings and churches torn down indiscriminately in the name of urban renewal—archaeologists have to go digging to piece together a picture of a culture barely three hundred years old from the kinds of scant evidence usually used to study cultures much more remote. For instance, among the household debris in an excavated privy, Catts found shards of what archaeologists call Colono ware, an unglazed earthenware that is most like the ceramics used in West Africa and in America, made by slaves of the southern plantations. The Wilmington fragments, however, were of the same paste and temper as the ceramic used by the slaves of the West India sugar plantations. From them, Catts concluded, he could tie some eighteenth-century Wilmington African-American culture to roots in African-Caribbean culture. Even better, Catts could tie the ceramic to the story of a slave uprising that nearly succeeded, and which could not have fallen on deaf ears in eighteenth-century black Wilmington.

Here, after all, were French-speaking mulattoes, blacks, and their white masters, landing in Wilmington and Philadelphia with tales of barely escaping with their lives from St. Dominique (now Haiti), where the slaves, under Toussaint L'Ouverture, had rebelled and claimed, as free Frenchmen, the right of self-rule.

The flamboyant L'Ouverture must have been an especially appealing character. Though his father had been enslaved, L'Ouverture claimed royal Gold Coast blood. He flaunted his hard-won independence, calling himself "First of the Blacks," and "the Bonaparte of the Antilles." Napoleon considered L'Ouverture's antics a gross parody and referred to him as "the gilded African," but as Henry Adams observed in his *History*:

> In more respects than one [L'Ouverture's] character had a curious resemblance to that of Napoleon,—the same abnormal energy of body and mind; the same morbid lust for power, and indifference to means; the same craft and vehemence of temper; the same fatalism, love of display, reckless personal courage, and what was much more remarkable, the same occasional acts of moral cowardice . . . the parallelism roused Napoleon's an-

ger, and precipitated a conflict which had vast influence on human affairs.

In Wilmington, Catts suggests, the refugees mixed as best they could, the blacks probably better than the whites, who had hopes of returning, holding out until Napoleon, still involved with his wars on the Continent, might turn his troops against the rebellion's quixotic commander. A few taught fencing and French grammar to the Francophilic upper classes. One slave owner who'd lost his fortunes founded a town along the Delaware a couple of hundred miles upstream at the Delaware Water Gap.

The French finally reinvaded L'Ouverture's island, but only took L'Ouverture after the leader's own generals betrayed him. He surrendered on the promise of fair treatment—a promise he might have known better than to accept. The orders from France were unforgiving: "Rid us of these gilded Africans, and we shall have nothing more to wish." Wrote Adams:

> *Except for a few men who were in the secret, no one ever saw him. Plunged into a damp dungeon in the fortress of Joux, high in the Jura Mountains on the Swiss frontier, the cold and solitude of a single winter closed this tropical existence. April 7, 1803, he died forgotten, and his work died with him.*

Slavery returned to Haiti—not immediately, for the French realized the risk of, as its minister put it, suddenly breaking "that idol of liberty in whose name so much blood has flowed till now." Instead, he wrote,

> *For sometimes vigilance, order, a discipline at once rural and military, must take the place of the positive and pronounced slavery of the colored people of your colony. Especially the master's good usage must reattach them to his rule . . . then the moment will have arrived for making them return to their original condition, from which it has been so disastrous to have drawn them.*

The setback was only temporary. Haiti would soon be the first free African-American republic. In the meantime many landowners returned. Some with their slaves. But many of the mulattoes who had suffered the worst strains of dislocation had already dispersed into the Wilmington community. Catts found among the fragments evidence that, along the Delaware and in the nearby Christina, the West Indians had been able to pursue their long tradition of fishing. In the digs were far more fish remains than any other—bones of white and yellow perch, catfish, herring, snapper, shad, sturgeon, and crab, a cork net float and a lead sinker.

Blacks and the river have a long tradition. A Captain Cuffee of Wilmington was a merchantman who sailed with an all-black crew. Blacks piloted boats up the shipping channels. Blacks worked the oyster beds. Drawings from the nineteenth century show black crews hauling shad nets along the Delaware.

It was two freed Delaware slaves, Richard Allen and Absalom Jones, who began what W. E. B. Du Bois called the "great legacy of religious freedom," that made possible for African-Americans "the first wavering step of a people toward organized group life." In Philadelphia in 1787, Allen and Jones walked out of St. George's Methodist Episcopal in protest over the treatment of blacks and founded the Mother Bethel, the African Methodist Episcopal Church.

In 1813, Peter Spencer, himself an ex-slave, founded the Union Church of Africans in Wilmington. The following summer, on the last Sunday in August, Spencer held the country's first major black religious festival. Based on the annual Quaker meetings, Spencer's August Big Quarterly would be, for the next hundred and fifty years, a uniquely African-American religious pilgrimage and jubilee. It would make Wilmington, in the words of one newspaper account, "the Mecca of black people."

As historian Lewis Baldwin writes, the harvest was in, and both slaves and free blacks could travel to what one newspaper account called this "great swarming of the colored race."

> *Hundreds of slaves from Maryland, Virginia, and lower Delaware, bearing passes of identification and orders from their masters for articles of clothing, walked long distances and arrived in Wilmington footsore and dusty. Others came in hay wagons, in ox carts, and on the backs of mules.*

City folks came downriver from Philadelphia by steamboat and railroad:

> *All sizes, of both sexes, and all ages, and we might say all colors, for there was a sample from the jetty African to the almost white-faced mulatto, were present. The aged came with their gray heads and bowed forms, and little infant children were carried in the arms—some chuckling forth their pleasure, others squalling out their dissatisfaction. Some were clad in plain habiliments, others, both male and female, reached at the bon ton, and moustaches and imperials, bowed and smiled complacently at the side of full skirts and flounces.*

And all singing, dancing, clapping, feasting, preaching, and praying, as Baldwin describes it. The Methodists passed bread and water as they sang spirituals and embraced each other. Then came a sermon, perhaps from the fiery Spencer himself. "The words of consolation and hope that fell from the lips of those men," Baldwin writes, "lifted the spirits of a bruised and battered people into a transcendent moment." In a joyful exchange came shouts of "Amen" and "Alleluia."

At the same time one could attend the rites of immigrants hardly a generation out of Africa—huddling, swaying, urging one another, as one account had it, to "feats of gymnastic devotion," all the while chanting songs that would soon be heard no more.

There might be the "crooked sermons" as they became known, designed for preachment when local sheriffs or even U.S. marshals could be looking for evidence that the preacher was inciting rebellion. Paul Laurence Dunbar (whose wife, Alice Dunbar Nelson, taught in Wilmington's Howard High School in the 1920s

and 1930s) created a latter-day version, from which the following
verses come:

> *An' yo' enemies may 'sail you*
> *In de back an' in de front;*
> *But de Lawd is all aroun' you,*
> *Fu' to ba' de battle's brunt.*
> *Dey kin fo'ge yo' chains an' shackles*
> *F'om de mountains to de sea;*
> *But de Lawd will sen' some Moses*
> *Fu' to set his chillun free.*
>
> *An' de lan' shall hyeah his thundah,*
> *Lak a blas' f'om Gab'el's ho'n,*
> *Fu' de Lawd of hosts is mighty*
> *When he girds his ahmor on.*
> *But fu' feach some one mistakes me,*
> *I well pause right hyeah to say,*
> *Dat I'm still a-preachin' ancient,*
> *I an't talkin' 'bout to-day.*
>
> *But I tell you, fellah christuns,*
> *Things'll happen mighty strange;*
> *Now, de Lawd done dis fu' Isrul,*
> *An' his ways don't nevah change,*
> *An' de love he showed to Isrul*
> *Was n't all on Isrul spent;*
> *Now don't run an' tell yo' mastahs*
> *Dat I's preachin' discontent.*
>
> *Cause I is n't; I'se a-judgin'*
> *Bible people by deir ac's;*
> *I'se a-givin' you de Scriptuah,*
> *I'se a-handin' you de fac's.*
> *Cose ole Pher'oh b'lieved in slav'ry,*
> *But de Lawd he let him see,*
> *Dat de people he put bref in,—*
> *Evah mothah's son was free.*

The masters, sheriffs, and marshals had reason enough to worry. The Big Quarterly was growing from gatherings of hundreds to gatherings of thousands at the same time that Wilmington was becoming the Grand Central Station of the Underground Railroad. The route ran up along the Delaware from Ezekiel Jenkins's place in Camden through Dover, Smyrna, Blackbird, Middletown, and New Castle. Stations ran along the Delaware all the way to the Mount Gilead Methodist Church, north of Philadelphia, across the river and into New Jersey. Even farther north, Stroudsburg, along the Pennsylvania side of the Delaware, served as a station on the way to Canada. So, writes Baldwin, "despite being under the ever-watchful eyes of slave catchers [like the notorious Patty Cannon and Joe Johnson], overseers, black drivers, spies, and sometimes masters, slaves and free blacks mingled with some degree of freedom on the grounds of the Mother Union Church of Africans." The likes of Thomas Garrett and Harriet Tubman could work the crowd, and the Big Quarterly might prove the start of a big excursion to freedom.

Sometimes all it took was a night raft across the river. Springtown, New Jersey, ten miles from where the Delaware River meets the bay, was established before the Civil War by both manumitted slaves and slaves who had sprung to freedom across the river. There, many received odd lots of land from abolition-minded Quakers, and though the lands were often amid the woods and at the end of the rural dirt roads, these independent-minded folks built small farms and schools, and created for themselves a community where at last they might enjoy life at a distance from whites. The colored school, especially, became a place to learn African-American lessons—along with dignity and discipline.

Maria Boynton, a researcher who recorded conversations with longtime Springtown residents, found they would talk to her of everything—of their education, religion, and village—but rarely of the fact they often had to work as laborers on white farms, or shuckers in white oyster houses. Their pride, she wrote, was "in the life of Springtown and the elevation of black people, and not in the monotonous and continuous work in the white world."

So they rather talked of what they loved. Of singing (from the working chants of the shucking floors to the gospel quartets) and the art of recitation. Through the practiced art of someone like Springtown's Evelyn Lockman, Boynton found, a psalm or a poem became, in performance, "a careful, lofty thing."

> *Know ye that the Lord He IS*
> *God.*
> *It is HE that has made us*
> *And NOT we ourselves.*
> *We are his PEOPLE and the*
> *SHEEP OF HIS PASTURE . . .*
> *For the Lord IS good. . . .*

James Newton, trim beard and hair graying slightly, round eyes the focus of a round, deep brown face, cordial, thoughtful, intense, hands slowly lifting, turning, opening, dropping again as he speaks, recalls the country life along the river in southern New Jersey, the singing and the sermons, the street criers and crab sellers, the black kids peddling for the white fishermen, the white farms with the black pickers, selling greens and fruits for the white farmers. We sit in the faculty dining room of the University of Delaware, amid the curtains, crystal, and china of a restored Colonial, a place where black servants once most likely served. Newton teaches black studies at the school. Black rural life along the Delaware, anywhere, he says, was more than met the white eye.

In the effort to become self-sustaining, the families built a complicated economy, mixing farming and fishing with seasonal employment for glass companies or canneries. Everybody had a truck. With a truck and some hustle you could make a little extra hauling paper, rags, and trash. In the spring you picked vegetables, tomatoes or beans. Or you crated and boxed. There was something for everybody. And after the harvest, people out of work could qualify for assistance. The women did the cooking and preserving. Newton recalls his winter basement stacked with food: peaches, venison, corn. Nine children, everybody shucking, everybody with a job to do. Somebody had to pick up the coal by the railroad track. Tuesdays and Thursdays there were loaves of old bread at the bakery. Somebody was responsible for the fire. There was nothing much extra. Missing a chore made a difference. Sometimes you had to be creative. Newton delivered newspapers, but on his way collected blackberries down by the railroad track that divided the black and white sides of town. Then he'd sell the berries to the whites when he delivered the newspapers. "They called me Blackberry Jim.

"I remember me and a friend, DinDin, used to collect frogs out by the railroad tracks and bring them to Miss Mariana, a white lady in town. You know how patient and quick you have to be to catch frogs. Well, I'm just about to pounce on this one when DinDin whispers, 'You can't grab that frog.'

"I looked up.

" 'Why not?' "

" 'Because that's that white man's frog.' "

"Well, in those days there'd be a lot of hoboes riding the trains and when I looked over I saw one sitting picnicking nearby. I look at him, looked at DinDin, looked at the frog, and didn't know what to do. I thought, 'How could it be his frog?' But then at the same time, as a general rule in life, whites seemed to own most everything—the land, the boats, the corn, the fruits, the fish, the meat, why not the frogs? Anyway, I never knew what Miss Mariana was doing with all the frogs, and the day DinDin told me that she was eating their legs was the last day I ever brought them around to her."

In the spring and summer the men fished. They'd often pool their money in an informal cooperative to get a boat and gear. They'd catch white perch, catfish, and carp, and sell them to the white fish markets. The view from the outside was that these men were not working. It was the same view the Europeans took of the Indians who trapped and fished, pursuits that the white man reserved for idle hours. But in both cultures these men provided food for their own families, and maybe for several families. That they might go at it with such seeming insouciance simply showed how good they were at it.

This has not changed. After spending a morning working shad nets with a white Delaware fisherman, I asked him if he knew of any black commercial fishermen on the river.

He looked up. He thought. Then he shook his head.

"Why not?"

"Well," he demurred, "you know, this is hard, hard work."

I made a note.

Not ten minutes later, two black men drove up to his riverside dock in a pickup truck. They got out and from the bed took baskets full of freshly caught white perch. They loaded the fish on the scales, the netter paid them, and they drove off. My man never looked up at me. For him, these were not commercial fishermen, but just a couple of old black guys who brought him white perch. Maybe, I guess he thought, someday they'll get work. But until then they seemed to be doing pretty well just delivering the fish that jumped out of the creeks and into their baskets.

Newton does concede this much: "We lived in social isolation. We used to see the Fresh Air kiddies come down from Newark. We'd roll on the ground with laughter. These city kids had never seen a cow or a chicken. One of them would say to you, 'Give me a nickel.' And you'd just look at him as if to say, 'That kind of thing doesn't go here.' Or we'd go to Philly and watch the kids walking down the street, swaying in unison, and there we'd be, the country boys with orange clay on the sides of our shoes. That clay was from jumping and sliding in the sand pits around where we used to play.

"But people could live without worrying about living the way people thought they ought to live. They had things they valued and treasured. My grandfather lived off the land, he hunted and trapped, and being self-sustaining was important to him. The highest black I remember was a college-educated guy who was a grease monkey. But you could honor and respect the guy who shot a deer, the guy who provided for himself and protected his family and also got his children an "edumacation" as my father called it. Living like this made you able to make decisions based on the way things really are: the damn apples are either red or green. People were honest. People were up front. You knew the wooden nickels.

"There might have been more rewards to the rural natural life. All the people with character, where are they at? Like the fisherman. Like the ferryman who knows his life is all crossing. They know their business. To them life is not a riddle. In the quiet moments the fisherman gets to the essence of life and nature. How else is it that someone from the rustic corner of nowhere produces work that everybody admires? Why do we like to shop with the little guy? He gives you the personal connection you can't get with the bureaucracy. So we like to go to the guy in the funny hat whose truck won't start. But these little places are dying out. Gradually the rustic guys die off, the guys who sat around the barbershop in Smyrna. No one records them and they end up a forgotten culture. We move away from nature and fundamental things begin to change. How do I give my children that sense of day-to-day existence?"

As the rural economy goes, and people can't live off the land any longer, Newton fears the young blacks will be forced back into the serving class. When the canneries closed, many could no longer provide. Many moved to the cities. In towns where the oyster industry once provided work, I talked to young kids who were bused daily to work in Atlantic City casinos nearly two hours from their homes. "Is this," Newton asks, "what we offer our children?"

But along both shores of the Delaware the "little hamlets" as Newton calls them, are dying out. Gone, or nearly so, the small black enclaves of Delaware City, Middletown, Port Penn, Belltown, Star Hill, Buttonwood, New Discovery, and Andersonville.

This is what Newton tells kids when he goes to their high schools to lecture:

"We need 'high touch' as opposed to 'high tech.' This is not to go back. But don't let that past get lost."

It's a call for honesty that rings down from the lessons he learned in more turbulent days.

"Why do the kids, even the white kids, listen when I talk of Malcolm X? Because he was frank, candid, direct, whether you liked him or not. He was a man, like a fisherman, who depends upon his integrity for his livelihood. A man who goes out to praise the Lord for his food that day. We've got one foot in the millennium, but we can't walk away from all the insights of the old times. But those times are becoming very remote for young people now."

The day I go to meet with Harmon Carey, founder and president of the Afro-American Historical Society of Delaware, he shows me a newspaper article about a city council debate over the placement of a historic marker honoring African Methodist Episcopal Church founder Richard Allen. Originally placed on land the historical society believes was owned by Allen's slavemaster, the sign was destroyed.

"Not with graffiti," Carey says, "not bent, but busted up in little pieces. Delaware is a state of paradoxes. The first to ratify the Constitution. [It was so eager it ratified a draft copy.] It was last to ratify the Thirteenth Amendment that abolished slavery."

In Wilmington, Carey says, you were mostly left alone. Many blacks worked on the docks, and the longshoremen's union on the Wilmington waterfront was nearly a black local.

"Nobody came into your neighborhood, called you a nigger or a snowball. You had your own movies. You didn't grow up mad. You just accepted the way it was. Something more blatant might have been better for our attitudes."

Carey works to restore the history to the children. The characters in the society's pageant *Walk Together Children—A Story of Black Delawareans* include Peter Spencer, Richard Allen, Absalom Jones, Thomas Garrett, scenes at the August Quarterly, at the African Church, at the Wilmington race riots, and tributes to black school supporter Pierre S. duPont, Wilmington's Negro League baseball hall of famer William "Judy" Johnson, and a particular Carey favorite, jazz trumpeter Clifford Brown.

Peter Spencer died in 1843, and at every Quarterly afterward, writes Baldwin, "the pilgrims marched up the hill to the rear of the Mother Church on French Street and stood at the grave" and sang:

Father Spencer's body lies moldering in the clay,
Father Spencer's body lies moldering in the clay,
His Church is marching on.

After the Civil War the spirit and attendance at the Quarterlies reflected the changes in the African-American community. Intellectuals tended to consider it a forgettable reminder of slave days. Baldwin reports that even Alice Dunbar, who wished its demise, finally conceded that it was "too deeply rooted in the minds and hearts of the Negroes of the Eastern Shore of Maryland and Virginia, of Delaware and Southeastern Pennsylvania, to be broken up or rooted out by the mere disgust of a few intelligentsia."

During the 1960s, the attendance of civil rights leaders reinvigorated the Quarterly. But just as ministers during slave days had preached "crooked sermons" to appease white concerns, the president of the African Union Methodist Protestant Church felt it necessary in 1964 to offer reassurances that despite the presence of movement leaders, "We will only worship God this day, and honor the founder of our church. This day was never designed for any type of demonstration. There will be no civil rights demonstrations—there will be no racial demonstrations where this day is concerned."

In 1969 the Mother Church was moved from French Street to make way for urban renewal. "The faithful could no longer celebrate on the sacred ground," writes Baldwin. The link with the past was broken.

But Carey looks to revival, for a Quarterly to rededicate the community to its cause, for a link with the past restored.

"I've known rivers," wrote Langston Hughes in "The Negro Speaks of Rivers":

I bathed in the Euphrates when dawns were young.
I built my hut near the Congo and it lulled me to
  sleep.
I looked upon the Nile and raised the pyramids
  above it.

*I heard the singing of the Mississippi when Abe Lincoln
went down to New Orleans, and I've seen its muddy
    bosom turn all golden in the sunset.*

*I've known rivers:
Ancient, dusky rivers.*

My soul has grown deep like the rivers.

FRESH WATERS

FOR SOME FIFTY MILES, FROM CHESTER, PENNSYLVANIA, NORTH TO Trenton, New Jersey, the Delaware is a freshwater tidal river. The ocean tides, having pressed some hundred miles inland, now make their final push up the narrowing river channel. The Delaware tides are strong, owing to both the bay's broad mouth on the sea and the narrowing channel that constricts the flow upstream. The tide ranges six feet and more, three times that of the broader and shallower Chesapeake. Before shipyards, industries, and refineries built up the riverfronts of Wilmington, Camden, and Philadelphia with wharves, docks, bulkheads, and heaps of slag and spoil, the natural meeting of the twice-daily tides with the continuous flow from the two hundred miles of river above the fall line at Trenton made for a productive shoreline. The tide only made it to this reach of the river some 2,500 years ago. (If sea level continues to rise, this freshwater reach will become increasingly brackish.) But tidal mud flats and marshes can develop quickly. As the tides push the waters up the small tributary streams that meander through the lowlands, they overflow and flood; as their banks break down, they fill in. In the slowing waters the nutrients washed from the upstream soils, and the fine grains of sediment washed from the upstream ridges, in a constant swirl in the downstream currents, fall out and spread across the already silty muds of the river shore. (The Delaware has here fallen onto the coastal plain.) When the tide recedes, the outwash of enriched mud remains. Water, mud, and tide shape their own landscape: river channel, muddy shore, high bank, low marsh, high marsh, and patchwork of tidal ponds.

The water comes downstream full of oxygen. Dissolved nitrogen, phosphorus, and suspended silicates make it a highly fertile solution that, when stilled enough and sunlit, gives rise to a surface bloom of single-celled plant life—diatoms linked in chains that gleam under a microscope like diadems, and can impart a golden green glow to the water. These plants provide not only food but also oxygen for the many-legged and chitinous microscopic aquatic life upon which the river's fishes feed. An excess of nutrients from, say, sewage or farm runoff might lead to an overgrowth of plant life. Such an overabundance on the surface prevents light from penetrating. Too many plants die, and the bacteria that feed on them may quickly sap the water of its oxygen. Fish may not survive in such waters. When all goes well and the zooplankters graze happily on the phytoplankters, and fish can swim about freely feeding on both, the waters that come up into the marshes with the tide begin another cycle as they're soaked up by silty muds and plant roots.

But in fresh water there's no need for the complex molecular exchanges through cell walls that plants and animals in brackish or salt water need to survive. So these shores grow no great golden expanses of salt grasses or three-square that ripen like wheat for a fall harvest. Instead, the varied landscape can crowd in a diversity of plant life that keeps a freshwater tidal marsh in almost perpetual bloom: in among the stands of cattail and wild rice, water lilies and pickerelweed flower in the streams and ponds, bur-marigolds, jewelweed, and sweetflag (once used to flavor gin and candy) make fragrant, orange-dappled thickets on the high ground. These species dominate the view, but botanists along the Delaware have counted more than seven hundred plant species in a single freshwater tidal marsh and its adjacent uplands. Since few trees can survive in the flooded soils, the marsh is as open to the sun as the open sea. The plants photosynthesize at a tremendous rate, some growing inches a day, raising, in half a summer, stalks nine, ten, and twelve feet tall. And every runnel, hollow, or tussock seems to provide its own creature comforts. Fish, birds, turtles, and furbearers come seeking food and shelter, burrowing, roosting, nesting—some migrate, some reside, some summer, some overwinter. A good place to bear young. The shad, blueback herring, alewife, striped bass, and sturgeon come from the sea up the bay and into these fresh waters to spawn. (I once saw some young boys without a net lay a shopping cart on its side in a tidal creek; after the tide had come and gone their shopping cart was spilling over with silvery herring.) By the time the eggs hatch, most of the adults have departed, leaving the young less likely to be eaten and in a place with plenty of food to grow on. The harvest of plant life from a fresh-water tidal river and marsh can rival that of a tropical rain forest. And, as in a tropical forest, birds—hard to spot unless they call or fly up out of a thicket—nest and roost everywhere: red-winged blackbirds, swamp sparrows, goldfinches, and long-billed marsh wrens (now known simply as marsh wrens) the most evident, but perhaps some fifty more species nesting.

So figure fifty miles of this diverse shoreline habitat along the Delaware—fifty times two, figuring both shores; fifty times that, figuring the shoreline meanders; and that times all the little tidal creeks—and now only a few broken miles of it remain. The more common plants, such as wild rice, water hemp, and arrowhead, thrive where they can. A few of the rarer species disappear. Once a walk along the Delaware shores could bring river views of lusty masses of white-water buttercup and redhead pondweed. The last of most of these plants disappeared in the 1920s and 1930s. By then industry had had a good fifty-year reign along this section of the river. Much of the rich mud had been drained and built upon, and the waters that pushed up the creeks twice daily with the tides were contaminated with oil and sewage, and the silt carried particles of lead and industrial metals.

Richard Orson of Rutgers University reads the 2,500-year tidal history of the Delaware in the pollen and pollutants he identifies in deep cores dug out of the marsh. He found he could see when the tides finally broke through the old dike sluice gates and began flooding the lowlands by when heavy metals and contaminants begin to appear in the accumulated marsh sediments.

As we walk along the broad, muddy marsh at Woodbury Creek, south of Camden, New Jersey, he assures me of this: "In the sense of being unaffected by human intervention, nothing in these tidal marshes is 'natural.' They developed as the direct result of the cultural modifications since European settlement. So I'm groping, like a paleontologist looking at a collection of remains, for images, for stories of the past that fit the data." Orson sees this as the purpose of his work: before we rue what was lost, or try to fix what's there now, we ought to know how it came to be.

At Woodbury, 2,500 years before the present: the Delaware shore is oak forest down to the marshy edges of the stream channels, which are fringed with stands of hard-stemmed, spiky-topped sedges.

Fifteen hundred years before the present: rising sea level brings groundwater closer to the surface, and the oaks begin to die in the saturated soil; in the wettest ground, cattail grows in among the sedges while thickets of alder spread along the low meadow.

Five hundred years before the present: sea level rises farther, and groundwater soaks the upland. Now sedge marsh and meadow spread out from the streams, and the first tidal marshes begin to form along the streambanks.

Three hundred years before the present:

"In 1683 the John Wood family settled an area known as 'Pescozackasing,' Lenape for 'place of black burrs,' and renamed it for the family name and the parish, Bury, in England, from which they emigrated."

Giant ragweed in the pollen core shows that as the first Europeans settled the valley they created conditions that allowed this hardy, ten-foot-tall invader to thrive.

"What did these places look like to the colonists?" asks Orson. "Sedge meadows and the remnants of lowland forests—hummocky—you could walk carefully across them—with small streams running all through them."

The settlers, he says, began clear-cutting the forests for wood, then damming the streams and draining the meadows for farming and grazing. Although sea level continued to rise, the dikes prevented the tides from flooding the lowlands. A dam built at the mouth of Woodbury Creek in 1756 (which King George III officially sanctioned in 1760) remained until 1824 when an engineering report on the creek asserts that the dam was breached and that tidal waters from the Delaware were "let into Woodbury Creek as far as the town of Woodbury." A few years later, when the dam was removed completely, says Orson, "within one month five hundred acres of meadow was flooded." To protect the meadows, the farmers built dikes. But this section of the Woodbury where Orson has concentrated his research flooded once again in the 1930s, when the sluice gate of an earthen dike built in the early 1800s failed and allowed the tidewater to wash over the marsh. It was a classic case, asserts Orson: sea level rose outside the dike (owing in part to the dredging and deepening of the main river channel) while the water levels behind remained artificially low. When the dike was gone, the tidal waters and their sediments poured in and, in a matter of a few years, created a freshwater tidal marsh. While gradual flooding and silting may have accomplished the same thing, the colonization of the river valley had put a stop to the natural succession of tidal habitat.

This presents some new questions.

"How do you deal with changes on changes? They trapped and fished while they changed the habitat that produced those animals and what happened?

"Now, if we want to bring back those animals, do we dare disturb the system again to put it back the way it was? Can we do it?

"We have to start thinking of redefining what we consider 'natural habitat.' Is it precolonial? Preindustrial? Or is it what's there now?"

What's there now? Ecologists Mary Leck and Robert Simpson give me a tour of the Hamilton marshes, just downstream of the bend of the river at Trenton, the northern most freshwater tidal marshes on the river. Leck, small and lithe, and Simpson, a stocky man with a long stride, walk purposely through the marsh to sites where they have sampled the soils and plants for nearly twenty years. This day, Leck bends to a little transect of seedlings and calls out the species and their numbers. Simpson keeps the journal. Between the two they draw the natural world in a collection of detailed observations, accumulating years of field notes, until the life of the place and its species become clear.

Crosswicks and Watson's creeks meander across a broad wet plain, through a mile of marsh, and wind down toward the Delaware. The whole mosaic of habitats is here, but this is early spring and the marsh looks new-mown as it does every spring, since the most productive thing about the freshwater tidal marsh is the way the ten-foot-high stands of cattail, wild rice, and ragweed, the whole thickets of tearthumb, sweetflag, and jewelweed, die off in the fall and over the winter decompose to a layer of wrack and detritus. The detritus is the food of choice, the fuel that all the summer's synthesis of sunlight has produced. It caters to the needs of an entire unseen biota: bacteria, worms, snails, and insects. And these are the base of the Delaware's, of any river's—of the world's—food web. And by spring the litter of the last growing season is nearly gone.

The new season's roots have yet to spread, and so the ground offers little support for our feet except where the old cane lies scattered on higher, drier ground. It cracks underfoot. In the muck a deep bootprint fills quickly with water. We quickly spot seedling ragweed, spring cress, water hemp, jewelweed. But over the years, Leck and Simpson have continually added to their records from this marsh. ("Including uplands, we are now up to five hundred and fifty species!" Mary Leck informs me in a letter.) Like Orson's Woodbury, this is a much-altered place. Built up on an ancient meander of the Delaware with a fifty-foot bluff to the east, the Crosswicks floodplain has been traversed by railroad and canal, power transmission and gas pipelines. Areas have been drained, grazed, its mud dug up for making bricks, and used as a landfill. Still, it produces. And until the new highway cut across it, says Leck, it was a quiet and seemingly remote place to walk. She wishes, she says, she could have walked the Crosswicks a hundred years ago, when it was the purview of the cantankerous Charles Conrad Abbott, who, as he wrote in 1884, "never rambled elsewhere" than these, "my mucky meadows":

> *It too often happens that the sights best worth seeing come to you when in a bit of wet meadow. The swamp-sparrows, that are such sweet songsters; the king-rails and soras will not come to the dry ground at the edge of the meadow and sing and show themselves for your benefit. If you want to enjoy them, you must go to their haunts. . . .*

Abbott, Dr. Abbott—short and sturdy, red-haired but balding, thick-necked, stone-faced, with a brushy walrus mustache, a brusque little man with keen blue eyes—haunted the Crosswicks. Although he received his medical degree from the University of Pennsylvania at age twenty-two, Abbott was too irascible to bear his patients' complaints and too constrained by the academic and city life. In 1874 he and his wife quit Philadelphia and returned home to the Abbott family farm, Three Beeches, which stood on the terrace that overlooks the Crosswicks-Delaware floodplain. There, Abbott spent the better part of his next forty years "rambling," as he called it, the Delaware meadows, keeping and publishing rambling journals of long hours spent observing the fauna and flora of the marshland and writing, in the style of the day ("Live six months on the Delaware meadows and the recollection of that experience will not fade away, even though you mount the shoulders of a saint and peep into Paradise."), popular meditations on natural history.

Abbott did not set out to live a natural life, but a life that imitated what he considered nature's most valuable attributes. He would be as constant, as resilient, as forthright. He would walk out daily, regardless of the weather.

> *If I have seen something new, that day is pleasant, however the thermometer registers, or the winds blow.*

Although every indication favored rain, yet there was a chance that it might not, and these "chances" prove so often to be delightful days that I always take them. In the course of a year, I gain far more outings than I get soakings. Let it be borne in mind, too, that a rainy day in the woods is better than a fretful one in the house.

A good rule for one who walks in winter is, to forget that there are such things as thermometers, and never to look at one when leaving the door-step. Perhaps it is snowing. Well, the very creatures that the observant walker loves to see can not more readily dodge the snowstorm than he can; and is it not a sufficient incentive to learn what the birds and mammals are about when snowed up, to warrant a ramble over snow-clad fields and in the leafless woods? Who that has seen a cardinal grosbeak in the full glory of his crimson dress, perched upon a bare twig, with nothing but untrodden snow for a background, and heard his cheery whistle come ringing through the crisp air, can ever forget it? Such a sight is not to be witnessed from your sitting room windows. No, no, there is reason for rambling at all times, with perhaps one exception. In the noon of midsummer days it is proper to remain in-doors to rest, to keep cool, if happily you can. Nature herself, just then, is taking a nap.

Abbott observed many fewer charms in human nature, and this seemed to make him, when away from the Delaware, perpetually surly, especially toward the scientific establishment. Most scientists simply spent too much time locked up in dilettantish labors for his liking, and too little time out in the field. This iconoclasm did not serve Abbott well when he announced, in a paper published in 1872, that on the Abbott Farm on the Delaware he had found the first evidence of Stone Age humans in North America.

"Startling though the assertion may be," wrote Abbott, "it is safe to affirm that the Indian was preceded by an even ruder people."

Many in the archaeological establishment considered it simply a daft assertion. The American Indians might have been remnants of a now-extinct race, or even, as William Penn observed, of the lost ten tribes of Israel. But they were modern humans who had migrated to North America hundreds, not thousands of years ago. The stone hand axes from the Pleistocene Somme River terraces in France demonstrated that early humans had found refuge from the Ice Age glaciers in Europe, not in the New World, and certainly not in New Jersey.

Abbott contended his stone artifacts were of the same vintage as those of southern France. The archaeological establishment, still in turmoil from the publication of Darwin's *Descent of Man* just a few years before (many had still considered human history all of six thousand years old), quickly took sides in the Abbott case. Everybody wanted further proof. While the Smithsonian held its peace, Harvard's Peabody Museum of Archaeology and Ethnology deputized Abbott as a special field collector. For the next dozen years, New Jersey archaeologist Herbert Kraft writes, Abbott combed the Delaware River terraces and his own and his neighbors' farms, and even dug beneath the streets of Trenton. He collected more than thirty thousand artifacts that he claimed were clearly the rude implements of a New World Paleolithic culture more than ten thousand years old.

French archaeologist Gabrielle de Mortillet wrote Abbott that his finds made it "more probable that there was formerly a great bridge between America and Europe," perhaps "in the northern part of the ocean, in the latitude of Newfoundland." But many American collectors continued cool and sometimes overtly hostile, questioning the quality of Abbott's digs, and even the soundness of his judgment, scientific or otherwise. Abbott responded that too much of the science of the day was not only the result of "many men of many minds, but occasionally the same individual with numerous opinions." Intellectual progress in the field, he said, was weighed down "by the obstacles that ignorance, prejudice and hasty conclusions heaped about it." He was being hounded, he felt, by "disgraceful articles in pretentious periodicals, written by persons wholly ignorant of the subject. It is a blot upon American

Letters that editors should solicit from incompetency, however prominent politically, articles that their authors know are misleading. Unfortunately, the public cannot discriminate."

Were the Delaware paleo-people ancestors of the modern Indians, or a distinct culture perhaps more related to the Eskimos? How long ago had the last ice age receded—ten, twenty, sixty thousand years? Both archaeologists and geologists looked for some answers from Abbott's digs. In the meantime he lived an embattled existence. He had four children, and his few archaeological appointments paid little. The more embroiled he became in his cause, the less he wrote of his popular rambles. And his dauntless Delaware wanderings didn't help his chronic rheumatism and repeated bouts with malarial fever.

Abbott fought for the acceptance of ancient humans on his land, for he believed them to be part of his own ancestral heritage. Not his Quaker ancestors who came from Nottingham, England, who misunderstood, as he believed all the other Europeans misunderstood, the natives they met and the world they lived in. Abbott claimed to be embarrassed by that heritage. "Penn's thrifty followers," he wrote, "certainly knew little and cared less about their red-skinned predecessors." These were the people to whom the marshes were unwholesome places to be corrected, drained, diked. The kind of people who could alter the Indian names given to the land, or call both the bluffs and the stream at Crossweeksung simply "Crosswicks," had "no poetry in their souls."

> *The Indians were not content with such a paucity of names. One for the pretty hills at Crosswicks must not do duty for miles of meadow and a meandering stream that flowed for leagues through a wilderness of wasteland before lost in the Lenape-wihituck—now Delaware River—so they called the little river Mechentschiholens-sipu, Big Bend Creek.*

Abbott was determined that it be known that in this place humans had shared a long, harmonious history with nature, far longer than those who destroyed both the land and the people wished to acknowledge. In the marsh Abbott found refuge from an encroaching industrial age (and a scientific age growing impatient with raconteur-naturalists like himself), a place where he couldn't be hounded about his scientific or personal obligations or about paying his bills.

> One by one the birds in the thickets ceased their chirping; the titmice no longer whistled; the last marsh wren of the day sang a hurried roundelay and sought its nest in the reeds; the scattered hylas peeped complainingly, and a single fretful cat-bird was my sole companion. He soon grew tiresome and I longed for an owl to hoot or bittern to boom, but neither uttered a sound. There was an almost noiseless interim of half an hour and then the katydids were ready to begin their nightlong concert.

In the thousands of artifacts Abbott found support for his growing conviction that this same place had always offered humans food, shelter, solace, and personal allegory.

> These dusky-skinned natives were greatly attached to the neighborhood, and the abundance of their handiwork in stone still testifies to their prolonged occupancy of the country. Not only are there hundreds of their relics on every acre, but there is also a fragmentary tradition that, not far from my door-yard, Oconio-coco-coco-cadgi-cadgi-cadonko had his wigwam; and not far off, under an enormous white oak, fought, single-handed with the fiercest of cougars, long the terror of the neighborhood, and slew him with a flint knife. Oconio's grave is supposed to be quite near, but I have never sought to disturb his bones. . . .

But Abbott was wrong. His chipped-stone implements were nowhere near as old as the Stone Age. They were only eroded artifacts of far more recent vintage—maybe one to two thousand years old—but of a time during which his farm, bluff, creeks, and marsh on the Delaware were "the most extensive and intensely occupied" place in eastern North America. In that he had been right. And he was right because his reconstruction of ancient lives didn't depend upon the scholarly assemblage of found artifacts. He knew what the native world was. He had been out in it. At a time when most people wondered at how man might alter the natural order to suit himself, Abbott contemplated how nature fashioned cultures. There had been a Paleolithic people. There must have been. Nature provided for one.

Even as the glaciers receded north of the headwaters of the Delaware, fifteen, fourteen, thirteen thousand years ago, wanderers, hunters using fluted paleo-spearpoints, followed herds of caribou through forest and across tundra. To have survived at all in the cold, they would have had to be as adept at making clothing from skins as any Eskimo, scraping and tanning hides (in solutions made of animal brains or livers), fashioning boots and parkas and mittens, perhaps chewing the leather to soften it, oiling it to keep it waterproof, shaping knives and scrapers from chert and jasper, and designing awls and needles from antler and bone. Without many caves for shelter, they had to have been as resourceful, if not more so, as any Stone Age European cave dweller. These were distant relations of the people who'd crossed the Bering Strait land bridge perhaps ten or twenty thousand years before. As the climate changed and the northwoods look and habitat disappeared, the caribou no longer ranged as far south and the people who depended upon the animal's meat, marrow, innards, bones, and hides also stayed away.

As the world warmed, natives of the southeast coastal plains and the Appalachians began to move northward. As rising sea level inundated the coastal plains, the people could move inland and still find shellfish and, soon, migrating birds, among nascent oak woodlands with beech and hickory producing mast enough to feed turkey and passenger pigeons. Fish migrating to spawn in fresh water also moved farther upstream and inland. This migration took place over some six thousand years. Evidence of encampments along the river or anywhere in the valley during this long period of change are scarce. But there are the outlines of hearths and collections of fist-sized rocks that were scooped from the fires and piled into leather-

or bladder-lined holes for boiling water or gruel. There are carved stones called bannerstones, used to counterbalance the spear-throwing sticks known as atlatls. The spearpoints are smaller and no longer fluted—better for smaller game and the deer that grazed the spreading sedge meadows. Once the tide moved upstream to the edges of the new forests, the lure of such diversity became irresistible. But, in his time, neither Abbott nor any of those poring over the artifacts from the site would ever know this.

In 1914 Abbott's home on the bluff at Three Beeches and everything in it—his journals, manuscripts, and collections—burned to the ground. At seventy-one, Abbott had no money to rebuild. His sole support, the spirit of the place on the bluff, was gone. And when he died five years later, embittered and exhausted, archaeologists at the Smithsonian, Harvard, and the American Museum were, after forty years, still feuding over his fields. In the meantime, pothunters, irrepressible amateurs whose digs are often akin to lootings, scavenged the Abbott site. Many went right to the stone foundations of Abbott's house and dug up the potsherds and spearpoints that had been buried in Abbott's basement beneath the burned debris.

To get to the "farm" now, I have to park in the lot of a shopping center. Archaeologist Michael Stewart and I cross the street and hike into the scrubby second-growth woodland thick with vines. Abbott's Creek, described forty years ago as a narrow, shallow-banked stream, is now a rivulet in a four-foot-deep trough dug out by erosion from the silty outwash caused by surrounding development. (Large parking lots don't allow any water to seep into the ground; instead it runs off into streams not meant to carry such flows.) As we walk up toward the bluff the highway now intrudes through the trees, an incessant undrownable sound. We have to walk carefully, for pothunter digs are everywhere—some, by the looks of the soil and the condition of the beer cans strewn about it, no more than a couple of days old, if that. (That the Abbott Farm site is a National Landmark gives it no protection except that which the landowners themselves can offer. So the looting goes on.)

He bends to a hole and picks up a bit of a chert flake. The

pothunters dig down and, when they reach a layer of artifacts, tunnel to the side rather than dig down once again. The chert flake out of its soil horizon becomes meaningless.

"You could almost live with it—I can't live with it—if they wrote about it. But we'll never know what came out of the ground here. They're digging here with no thought as to where they're finding things in the ground. This is just . . . Look at this. A bunch of gophers.

"When you resharpened the edge of your tool with an antler tine you pushed off these chert flakes. But this kind of thing doesn't look good in a mount on your mantelpiece."

Stewart has been conducting the most recent digs down on Abbott's marsh. Nightmare digs, he calls them, for as he digs down the water seeps in, and as he pumps the water out, the sandy walls of the deep pit dry and crumble away. The weather has been below freezing, and frost forms on the soil. To protect the pit from the snow, he has to keep it covered with translucent plastic sheeting under which his crews work. So far, he says, the misery has proven worthwhile, or has at least given him some mysteries to solve. He is down nearly eight feet and still finding artifacts. He may, in fact, be making new discoveries from the still-obscure Archaic. It's no wonder the pothunters rankle him. For Stewart, the colored bands of soil in the pit walls are not only, like tree rings, a rudimentary key to the passage of time, but contain within them the very image of the time in which they were laid down. If one could decipher the soil record perfectly, one might know, from the seeds and pollen and the remains of plant cells, what grew and in what relative abundances. This would make a picture of the landscape and the climate that produced it. And from this one might construct in the mind a culture living in such a place. (Such an environmental-cultural stratigraphy is still a controversial reconstruction. As botanist Mary Leck has found out, it's not always possible to tell from the seeds in the ground what plants dominated the surface. The pollen record is affected by wind. The plants that produce more pollen can make it look as though they dominated the landscape.)

So Stewart still has to relate artifacts to depth and soil deposits. He digs in tenth-of-a-foot layers, and screens everything through a fine mesh. Standing in a pit eight feet below the present surface, he looks up from ancient ground. His green eyes sharpen in the gray winter light diffused beneath the plastic tent. He opens his hands toward the walls, like a museum guide about to explain a work, in this case a sand painting made over some eight thousand years.

"You look at these soil profiles; there are times when just a little soil is being dumped, times when a lot is being dumped. It all has to tie in with climate, vegetation, and what the streams are doing. And when you keep seeing the same patterns of lots and less repeated over and over, you start thinking that you're looking at something that's more than a local anomaly.

"These redder soils are made up of much finer particles than these lighter-color soils. This is basically a sandy silt, this is fine sand, and this is coarse sand. This tells us about the energy of the floods and where the river might have been. In order for a stream or floodwaters to carry soil of a particular particle size, they have to be of a particular strength. In this level, for instance, this red soil represents what was dumped during one flood episode. We have an artifact deposit that starts right at that level. We found pit features that originate at this line. So at one time the Indians were working and living on the surface represented by the top of this soil.

"The minute you anchor yourself in time, you're talking about fixed points with a range of environments and artifacts. People will talk about what drives climatic change, rotational shifts or cycles of solar activity. I don't care. I don't care whether the change has been episodic or gradual. I don't care if it's moon men driving the environment. I just want to know what it was like. Just tell me what it's like in 6000 B.C."

But even then he needs artifacts. A hearth site, a pit of fire-cracked pot-boiling stones.

"Part of our job is to figure out which of the disturbances are natural, from trees falling, animals burrowing, and which are Native Americans digging and doing things. Any time you dig into the ground, you can't put the soil back the same way, and it will show. An archaeologist who knows what he's doing can recognize disturbances in the natural soil. They show as dark stains against the lighter soil. This is not a figment of our imagination. The Indians would have cut a hole into the ground, built their fires in it. And when they were done and had moved on, these things gradually filled up. We clean out the fill until we hit natural soil. In here we found a collapsed pottery vessel made in a particular style that allows us to date it to no earlier than A.D. 1400 and a style that continues up into historic times.

"The neat thing is that none of the rock we find in this pit comes from anywhere on this site. As you'll see when we look at our deep holes over there, you have to really scrape just to find a pebble in this soil. So all of these rocks had to be trucked in. And it's always the same type of rock in them. The Indians were very particular about the kinds of stones they used in their hearths, especially about the kind of rocks they used to boil things—quartzite, very dense sandstone. One of the reasons you pick a rock like that is that you can heat it to a high degree without it exploding on you. And when it fractures, it doesn't fracture into a million pieces, and so you don't end up eating rock—although when you find the skulls of some of these folks, their teeth are worn down to nothing. Now I can walk up Watson's Creek where it meets the upland bluffs and find this rock. But they are not moving the fires to where the stones are, but the stones to where the fires are, so whatever they're doing here is more important."

Here, in the spring, came the herrings, striped bass, shad, and sturgeon to spawn, young eels feeding on their way upstream from their long migration from the Sargasso. Here on the marsh were cattails, wild rice, and arrowhead (known as Indian potato) to harvest, and plants for food and medicine. Here were turtles and frogs to eat. Here ranged beaver, muskrat, fox, rabbit, and otter. Deer browsed the sedges. In the fall were ripe acorns and beech and hickory nuts. Wildfowl migrated through for the killing. And between the game and the mast, and fishing through the ice, winter might be suffered through, for the abundance of the spring could

begin with the coming of the first herring by the end of March. And
for the next months the harvest of migrating fishes might be unre-
lenting: fishing with spears and oiled hempen nets, even at night by
torchlight. The natives blocked streams with brush weirs and
herded fish through to pens for slaughter. (Some devised a mixture
of mashed green walnuts, which, when tossed into the water, stu-
pefied the fish so that the Indians could simply scoop them up off
the surface.) While the fishing continued, the processing would
have required an even greater effort. The fish all had to be cleaned
and gutted. Hearths must have burned day and night, the smoke
from smoldering charcoal hanging over the marsh as fish were laid
up to dry on heated stone piles, hung from sticks, or strung on lines
to sun-dry in the haze. If the drying of the six-to-twelve-foot sturgeon was anything like the drying of salmon by the Northwest
Coast Indians, it was a labor-intensive operation. (Knife blades
from Abbott's Farm resemble those used by the Northwest Coast
Indians for butchering salmon. Digs at Abbott's produced thousands of these blades, many found in caches dug into the ground.)
As the fish cured, they had to be split and scored. The fires had to
be tended, and the fish, once dried, had to be packed away. Ceramic
pottery, which distinguished the prehistoric woodland Indian from
his archaic ancestors, was at Abbott's Farm shaped into large con-
tainers (many decorated with the impressions of fishing nets) that
were then buried to their necks into the ground, perhaps for the
storage of fish or fish oils. The number of artifacts and the large
scrap heaps uncovered may be evidence that clans gathered at
Crosswicks on the Delaware to work together processing the great
spring harvest.

Here the tidal marsh had spawned a tidal marsh culture of which,
in his time, only Abbott himself had been able to conceive.

The Indians looking out over the marsh saw not only a great
source of food but a great store of material and spiritual abundance.

According to Gladys Tantaquidgeon, a descendant of Delaware
Indians, who wrote frequently on the traditions of her people:

- *The bark growing on the east side of a tree is preferred for its greater strength-giving properties received from the morning sun.*

- *Rough roots on the plant mean the patient will be difficult to cure.*

- *If the crushed leaves sink in the stream, the patient will die.*

- *For an emetic, the water should be dipped from the stream with the current, the bark peeled upward from the tree; for a cathartic, it should be dipped against the current, the bark pulled downward.*

- *Black walnut sap reduces inflammation; the juice from the green hull of the fruit treats ringworm.*

- *Three chips from the east side of a sycamore steeped together with red oak bark and sweetflag root make a hot drink for colds.*

- *Ground chestnuts treat earache. A nut carried in the pocket relieves rheumatism.*

- *Sassafras purifies the blood.*

- *A white oak bark tea soothes a cough.*

- *Fox grape sap treats the hair.*

- *Elder flower tea treats infant colic.*

- *Peach leaf tea for pin worms.*

- *Ginseng is a potent general tonic, and a plant believed to have retreated from encroaching civilization.*

- *Goldenrod reduces fever.*

- *Blackberry treats dysentery.*

- *Golden aster quiets infants.*

- *Cardinal flower treats typhoid.*

- *Ragweed for blood poisoning.*

- *Wild carrot for diabetes.*

- *Yarrow for the kidneys.*

- *Sweet fern for blisters, and combined with mallow root, elder flower and dwarf elder for inflammation of the bladder.*

- *Cattail for kidney stone.*

- *Great mullein for coughs.*

- *Burdock as a stimulant.*

- *Skunk cabbage for whooping cough.*

- *Sweetflag for colds.*

- *May apple for a tonic.*

- *Dandelion for a laxative.*

Tantaquidgeon interviewed an old Delaware herbalist, Wi-tapanoxwe (Wee-tah-pah-NOKH-way), Walks with Daylight, who said disease came from the failure to obey the laws of nature.

> *In ancient times there was but little sickness among the Indi-ans. The Delaware were greatly blessed because we always kept up our ceremonies and observed the rules of right living. The Indian was healthy because he ate only clean, pure food and lived close to nature. Then came the new people with their strange ways and food, and dreadful diseases.*

Settlers early recognized the effectiveness of the native herbal-ists, mostly women, "who are in the habit of curing and healing diseases and wounds, by the simple application of natural remedies, without any mixture of superstition in the manner of preparing or administering them." They had, by another account, "consider-able knowledge of the virtue of roots and herbs, learned from the fathers, and who bring about relief." (There were men who prac-ticed, but by one account they differed from the women only "by their pretensions of a superior knowledge.")

To the herbalist, writes Tantaquidgeon, humans, plants, and an-imals alike were endowed with equally sensitive spiritual natures.

Wi-tapanoxwe offered prayers before he collected, prepared, or administered a plant. He cured the roots and plants in the sun, crushed them only in a stone basin or wooden mortar, and stirred his mixtures only from left to right. "One should never blow upon the concoction to cool it; to do so would represent an affront to the spirit of the plant."

While many herbalists worked on diseases, only a special few could deal with problems with wives, husbands, or lovers. The secrets of these potions were considered too important to be widely disseminated, for fear they might be used for ill. Evidently no one expected every herbalist to know it all, so the custom even then was "that a patient who has consulted an Indian and secured a medicine from him without, however, being benefited, will go immediately to another; if no relief is obtained through his advice, the patient goes to a third, a fourth, until he finds one whose medicine helps."

Not that spirits had nothing to do with healing. The Delaware natives had great faith in the spirit world, especially as it was revealed in dreams. The first cure the Delaware River Indians sought was the sweat lodge for the purpose of spiritual and physical purification. This was at least one thing they had in common with the Swedes and Finns, who also built their *badstus* and saunas by the river. The Swedes poured hot water over rocks to produce the steam, and the nude bathers then entered the hut and whipped their bodies with twigs to stimulate the circulation. Then, "glistening with perspiration, [they] dashed out and plunged into the cold creek water."

But from the viewpoint of Wi-tapanoxwe, writes Gladys Tantaquidgeon,

> *Like the wild game, the Delaware fled to more remote regions because their former environment had become so thoroughly contaminated. At this time, it is said, the dwarfs and other non-human folk had safety and seclusion in the rocky cliffs. Certain plants no longer reproduced and grew. Those Indians who clung tenaciously to the teachings of their elders were*

*greatly blessed by the Creator who guided them in visions as
of old.*

Stewart and I reach the stone foundations of the ruin of Three
Beeches, a sorry landmark if ever there was one, and walk on to the
edge of the bluff, where the paleo-vista ought to come into view.

"Literally," Stewart is saying, "you can go from one site to the
next along the edge of this bluff—"

Then: "Holy mackerel!"

He stands stock-still and stares out with a pained squint.

"I haven't seen this."

The vista is cut in two.

"That used to be tidal marsh just like that." But the southern
exposure is changed.

"It's gone! We had a site right there, and I used to walk down
the hill and over boardwalks to get out to the streambed. It was
all forested and wet marsh. I stared at that marsh for years and
years."

Now it's a dark swath of sand and dirt fill for a new interstate
interchange where I-295 will meet I-195 and Route 129.

"I remember when they started the bulldozers had to put mats in
front of them so they wouldn't sink away into the ground. And they
just crawled their way through. To see what they did to it in such
a hurry is quite a shock."

The site is buried, and will soon be beneath the highway. The
same fate awaits Stewart's present site. While the money to dig has
been provided by the Department of Transportation, so has the
sense of urgency and finality.

"You stand here and you realize they need the road and this is
progress and they have to deal with modern problems, but to watch
something that's been around so long go under so quickly is very
disturbing." (Mary Leck pointed out to me that when the roads
were planned, thirty years ago, the route across the wetlands
seemed the easiest and cheapest.)

This road, Stewart says, will allow traffic to bypass Trenton, the
state capital, and may make that city on the river no more than a

memory to many. "It's hanging on right now. When the government shuts down and the people go home, it's just a ghost town. Once these roads go through, that will be it."

The vista, the silence and the solitude of this, one of the last northern river marshes, will be gone as well. It will be impossible to get any real sense of the prehistoric vista, the kind of experience that inspired Abbott to distraction.

Stewart stares hard at the frozen ground of his site, where he's staked out a grid that describes the pattern of prehistoric settlement.

"The hearths with artifacts are surrounded by areas relatively free of artifacts, which I'm interpreting as living spaces in late prehistoric times.

"I could sit here and watch them shovel all day because any shovelful could have that one thing I'm waiting for that's going to make all this fall into place—some diagnostic spearhead that everyone else in the region is comfortable with.

"We've seen things here that are controversial. We've seen a knife style here that has never, ever been considered an early style, and unless I find something that everyone can agree on, I can't say, 'Look at all this new stuff.' I know our sequence starts sometime before 4000 B.C. but how much before I can't tell you, and where it stops I can't tell you. We're looking at something that's not well known here or in New Jersey. There isn't an archaeologist who wouldn't come stand in this hole here, look at the profile, and say, 'Jeez, you've got something early.' But until we know, we can't ask them to believe it. They can say whatever it is is out of place, came down a tree root.

"So I need to know how old or how young all of this is. I can tell you it's pre-4000 B.C. or as early as 6500 B.C. But I want something more precise, some radiocarbon date to work with. But something in the groundwater is affecting our radiocarbon dates, contaminating the charcoal and driving me crazy."

So he digs and tries to decipher the soil, taking Abbott's admonition very literally: "Sift the meadow mud through your fingers, and then search the underlying gravels; for not until this is done will you have read the story of the races, backward to the beginning."

There's no temple gold here. There's no temple.

"We're getting glimpses into the everyday life. It's not the glamour of the artifacts or how huge or complete they are, but just where things lie in the ground and what they're lying next to that helps us understand. What we're learning, piece by piece, is part of this story that binds us all together. We ought to at least preserve the knowledge of it before we pave it over. Once I pull these stakes, I can't come back. I have to get what I'm going to get right now."

Part Two

PHILADELPHIA

 WHEN OLD MAN FOGG, AFTERNOON TONIC IN HAND, recalled for me his days of rum running on the Delaware, he mentioned that river shores that once served as dropoffs were now underwater, eroded away. This being somewhat shaky evidence for sea level rise, I thought it might be useful to confirm his recollection with some records of busts and seized boats, and then return to the scenes of the crimes. But the librarian for the Bureau of Alcohol, Tobacco and Firearms told me that, much to her chagrin, no records remain of seizures, captures, or convictions during any of the years of Prohibition. When the Treasury Department transferred the whiskey policing duties to the BATF, all the pertinent archival material had been sealed up in boxes and promptly lost. My only hope, she offered, was to talk with some former T-men who might recall for me some of their own investigations. One, she thought, might be of particular help. His name was Ginn, like gin, Milton Ginn, and he'd been with the department in Philadelphia since the 1930s. Someone, she remembered, had called him "the Jewish Eliot Ness." I wrote Ginn immediately.

By the end of the nineteenth century the Delaware River between Trenton, New Jersey, and Wilmington, Delaware, was America's industrial heartland. All the best names in heavy industry were there, those who had made it or were about to: Roebling, Cooper and Hewitt, Disston, Du Pont, Baldwin, Nice, Cramp, Rohm & Haas, and Morse—steel, steel, saws, gunpowder, locomotives, bearings, ships, and chemicals respectively. There, also, were the industrially lighter-weight, but no less substantial names:

RCA's attentive dog could be seen atop the Camden studios where Caruso recorded, within range (Caruso's, perhaps) of the Atwater-Kent radio corporation across the river in Philadelphia. Camden had Campbell's Soup; Trenton had Lenox China; Philly could boast Tasty Kake, National (Jack Frost) Sugar, Fels Naphtha soap, Stetson hats, and A. J. Reach baseballs and sporting goods—for seventy-three years makers of the official baseball of the American League and "the only baseball endorsed by Philadelphia Athletics manager (1901—1950) Connie Mack."

By the time of the Civil War, Philadelphia, founded by William Penn to be a sylvan town of parklike greens, had become known as "the workshop of the world." Trenton, also an early Quaker outpost, emblazoned its somewhat surly device on the girders of a stone-and-steel bridge across the Delaware: "Trenton Makes, the World Takes."

Geology and the river had made all this possible. Trenton, Camden, Philadelphia, and Wilmington all sit on the border of two geologic regions: the Piedmont—the remains of an ancient Appalachian range (which paralleled the southwest-northeast diagonal of the present Appalachians)—and the coastal plain. The Piedmont is a mix of ancient rock, igneous as well as heat- and time-hardened crystalline sandstone and shale. The material of the coastal plain isn't rock at all, but sands and clays that years of rising and falling sea levels washed up around the crumpled ancient mountains. The border between the two, which extends all the way down to Georgia, is very distinct. In Trenton, for instance, Triassic rock meets Cretaceous sands somewhere around Calhoun Street, and crosses the river below the old Calhoun Street Bridge. And all along the divide, as rivers running southeast like trelliswork across the faces of the present-day Appalachians abruptly fall onto the coastal plain—the Delaware at Trenton, the Schuylkill at Philadelphia, the Susquehanna at Havre de Grace, the Potomac at Georgetown—they turn suddenly to flow southwest along the strike of the formation. This drop-off became familiar to colonists as the "falles" of these tidal rivers. It marked, in some cases in a dramatic display of rock and turbulent water, the farthest upstream reach of the

Atlantic, the head of the tide, and the end of navigable waters. By
the time the Europeans arrived, Native Americans had already
worn paths along the Delaware fall line, hugging the river to cross
by canoe below the falls at Trenton, at the place they called Sanck-
hickan. Since colonial schooners and shallops could go no farther
upstream, fall-line towns became transfer points for colonial goods
moving in from or out along the coast. The swift natural spill of
fall-line rivers made it easy to set up milling operations along their
banks.

"Ye ffalles of ye De La Warr," however, had its limitations.

Jasper Daenckaerts, a Dutch priest of a mystic sect known as
Labadists, passed through the barely year-old rough settlement of
Yorkshire Quakers nearby the Delaware falls in 1679. Neither the
falls nor the Quakers ("who live hereabouts in great numbers and
daily increase") impressed him:

> *We had supposed it was a place, where the water came tum-
> bling down in great quantity and force from a great height
> above, over a rock into an abyss, as the word falls would seem
> to imply, and as we had heard and read of the falls of the North
> River and other rivers. But these falls of the South River are
> nothing more than a place of about two English miles in length,
> or not so much, where the river is full of stones, almost across
> it, which are not very large, but in consequence of the shallow-
> ness, the water runs rapidly and breaks against them, causing
> some noise, but not very much, which place, if it were necessary
> could be made navigable on one side.*

Hardly worth the trip. Especially since he and his Quietist entou-
rage were forced to put up for the night in the cramped Quaker
quarters. "We had a fire . . . but the dwellings are so wretchedly
constructed"—he claims he could easily wedge all four of his fingers
between the ill-fitted clapboards—"that if you are not so close to
the fires as almost to burn yourself, you cannot keep warm, for the
wind blows through them everywhere." One would have thought a
priest of mystical leanings who had forsworn sensual pleasure would

have been more tolerant. But national jealousies ran high in those days, especially along the Delaware, where Dutch, Swede, and English laid conflicting claims to the unsurveyed land, and the postfeudal (but barely so) intrigue of foreign courts often made their way across the Atlantic. Daenckaerts predicted that Quaker Mahlon Stacy's humble gristmill on the Assunpink (where now South Broad Street in Trenton crosses the creek) as it ran toward the Delaware was so badly constructed it would pretty soon be a shambles.

But the Quakers were nothing if not tenacious. They had held on in England all through the changing religious whims of the seventeenth-century court, suffering continual censure and imprisonment only to become, in part through the aristocratic connections of William Penn, a recognized, if rarely appreciated, minority. Mahlon Stacy held on, eventually selling a share of his land to William Trent, a Philadelphia merchant who saw the economic possibilities of a river town on the westward route from New York that was also accessible to the farmers of the loamy fertile lowlands. But while Stacy and Trent came looking for commercial possibilities at the falls of the Delaware, Stacy's fellow Quaker across the river was dragged into the vigorous commercial nature of settlement at the end of the seventeenth century.

William Penn acquired his charter for land along the Delaware River in 1681 from Charles II—in part in recognition of Penn's father's military accomplishments (Penn the pacifist was a war-hero admiral's son)—in exchange for two beaver pelts a year. In his prospectus, Penn had promised his investors a New World suburbia along the Delaware: "creeks and small harbors" in a "greene country Towne" with each house "in ye middle of its platt" with "ground on each side for Gardens or Orchards, or fields." "A good and fruitful land" some six hundred miles "nearer the sun than England." The problem was he had never seen the place. When Penn's emissaries arrived, sent ahead to scout out the proprietor's claims to seventy miles of Delaware riverfront, they found that the river's most suitable landings at the mouths of the several navigable tributaries (at New Castle and Chester in particular) along with the best mill sites, had been taken, cleared, and settled at least forty years before by the Swedes and the Dutch.

The Swedes, early disappointed in their colonial adventure, continued to maintain their small farms in the wilderness even as jurisdiction over their lands changed from Swedish to Dutch to English with the fortunes of those European powers. Their humble log cabins seemed to crop up everywhere, yet Penn found their docility remarkable: "a plain, strong & industrious people; yet have made no great progress in their culture . . . as if they desired to have enough rather than plenty." Penn's surveyors, looking for a place to put his city, found that by 1681 "plantation followed plantation from stream to stream as far as the Falls of the Delaware." Penn's plans described for investors a suburb sprawling a mile back from the riverfront and eight miles to either side of the town's center. The reality was that Penn had sold thousands of acres of wilderness that had already been settled.

Penn's agents resolved to buy up enough property at an appropriate site to get things started. Forced to look upstream, they were north of the broad, marshy delta "fruitful in whortleberries" where the Delaware and Schuylkill rivers meet, before they saw any virgin woodland. The neck of land between the rivers was about two miles wide, high and heavily wooded, on the rising edge of the Piedmont. Streams ran east and west down the slope of a central ridge. The Schuylkill shore was mostly marsh, but the Delaware shore was sandy, with a thirty-foot embankment rising above the river. Most important, though the land was claimed, it was mostly unimproved and the Swedes and the few local Indians who lingered among the white settlers were ready to sell. ("Liquors for Treates," the surveyors reported, helped in making deals with the Indians.) It was enough land to lay out the new town's first streets "uniform down to the water from the country bounds" and set up a viable port along the Delaware, where a sandy cove provided a protected landing. The commercial district was of little interest to Penn. Pennsylvania had a higher purpose, to be a place where the embattled minority would have "the right and title of each to his own life, liberties, and estate; a voice in government; the right of trial by jury," and a piece of a "holy experiment."

Many of Penn's anxious investors, however, arrived before him, and not all were keen to compromise. "We are short our expectations," wrote Edward Jones, "by reason that ye Town is not to be builded at Upland" but "15 or 16 miles up ye River" at a place "called now Wicaco." The use of the Indian name for the land between the two rivers shows that the newcomers still regarded the place as a wilderness, full of Swedes and savages. "To the colonists' immediate physical need for adequate shelter against the elements," wrote historian Hannah Benner Roach, "was added their human compulsion, in the face of these realities, to maintain physical contact with their known friends, to keep within sight of, or within hailing distance of their own kind." (People may say they want to get away and commune with nature, a vacation-home developer told me, but those who know, know better. When night comes and no streetlights come on, a kind of panic often sets in among people used to the precise limits of city and suburban life.)

"I cannot make money without special concessions," Penn wrote in 1681. And his vision of an open, sylvan, broad-laned green country town along the Delaware began to fade. Penn clung to those visions that he could. The colony would remain steadfastly pacifist, even after the proprietor's departure, to the point of refusing British requests for a militia to help fight the French and Indian Wars. And though the two square miles between the Delaware and the Schuylkill established for the city of Philadelphia might be urban, its streets would still conform to Penn's ideals of order and symmetry.

This would not be easy. The delays in first finding, then surveying the land left the first settlers without staked lots. Many literally dug into the river shore, spending their first months in the New World in caves in the banks of the Delaware. When the surveyors still didn't arrive, and winter loomed, the cave dwellers decided to forgo any formal surveys of their allotted blocks and simply felled trees, cleared brush, and constructed log homes. For this work the Swedes came in handy. "They will build for you a house without any other implement than an axe," wrote one observer. "With the same implement they will cut down a tree and have it in pieces in less time than two other men would spend sawing it." A Swede, it was said, could clear your lot and build your house out of the felled trees for the price of nine pounds—including the cost of feeding him. Daenckaerts, who came glumly through Philadelphia after his uncomfortable stay with the Quakers at Trenton, was no less incredulous at the sight of the Swedes' housing, it "being nothing else than entire trees, split through the middle or somewhat squared out of the rough; these trees are laid in the form of a square upon each other as high as they wish to have the house; the ends of these timbers are let into each other, about a foot from the ends of them. So stands the whole building without a nail or spike." This was not the Federal Philadelphia of cobblestone streets and brick row homes.

It was not even too great a port, with its sandy landing (known as the Swamp but officially renamed the Dock) becoming silted in as the trees disappeared and the unconsolidated sands of the riverbanks eroded. The Dock very quickly became a polluted eyesore, a wrack-cluttered sewer. Very quickly, too, the vista of forest that had seemed at once so inviting and foreboding began to open up, not into a green country town, but into a spreading urban center. By the cold winter of 1684, settlers complained of the shortage of game, and Penn may have even begun to have difficulties covering his "peppercorn rent" of two beaver pelts a year. (The trapping had begun to decline even before Penn arrived, which may be why the Lenape, most of whom had moved west, so happily traded their lands away when Penn came solemnly seeking treaties.)

Philadelphia quickly became a haven for merchants and craftsmen: whitesmith George Guest, cordwainer John Test, the Irish cooper Archibald Mickle who arrived in time to make barrels for William Frampton's new brew and bake house. The deed and patent books, kept as meticulously as family Bibles, give brief outlines of New World lives: feltmaker Isaac Martin died before his land was surveyed, but his wife, Katherine, sold it to Patrick Robinson, who was living in Passayunk with a Negro servant by the

name of Robert Neverbegood. In two years Philadelphia grew to
some three thousand souls; a thousand came in the last couple of
months of 1684 alone. But these were craftsmen and merchants,
not farmers, and they had to depend upon the grain, meat, and
vegetables that came to the twice-weekly market. Since, by all accounts, the overland routes were barely passable, the Delaware
served as major transportation corridor, canoes coming from above
the falls, vessels ferrying downstream from Trenton, ships sailing
down the coast from New York and New England and then, along
with the English, French, and West Indian packets, turning up
into the bay to the river, and all "cluttering the harbor's already
overcrowded sandy shores." Most of the economy was barter, but
growing scarcities of fur and timber forced the Philadelphians to
use hard cash. One indication of the lack of goods to exchange was
the burgeoning counterfeiting operations with which Penn had to
contend. His "holy experiment," Hannah Roach concluded, had
become an urban real-estate development filled with the familiar
urban concerns of politics, taxes, litigation, and property disputes.
Penn, in an expression of pique, changed the street names from
those of friends to "things that spontaneously grow in the country": Vine, Sassafras, Mulberry, Chestnut, Walnut, Spruce, Pine,
Cedar, all most likely becoming rarer within the city itself, and to
the founder, as rare as the spiritual heart that led him across the
Atlantic in the first place. A disheartened Penn, a friend wrote,
seemed to feel that "the true Philadelphia and brother love is not to
be met with as freely in this our Philadelphia."

Still, Penn strove to make it a successful urban development. If
geography had got him a second-rate river port, farther from the
Atlantic than he would have liked and prone, in those days, to
freeze over in the winter (during which times "unemployment
soared, jails and workhouses filled to the bursting point and the
high-at-heart went skating") while New Castle, thirty miles downstream, remained free of ice, then the mercantile enthusiasms of his
settlers, though it compromised his sylvan ideal, might at least
sustain the still-unsteady settlement.

A measure of Penn's success in integrating the yeomen and

craftsmen of Philadelphia was the endless efforts of Lord Baltimore, who held the land grant south of Penn's, to claim jurisdiction over Pennsylvania. Throughout the first years of the colony, Baltimore and his cronies appear and reappear in Philadelphia like restless apparitions, warning the new settlers that they're holding lands that weren't Penn's to sell, and hadn't they better move south along the Chesapeake where things were warmer, for one, and a bit more secure? Penn was forced to return to England to defend his territory, and each time, as a Quaker who could not swear an oath (and perhaps worse, some said, a secret Catholic), his loyalty to the Crown came under scrutiny. Meanwhile, every time he left the colony, a Baltimore amanuensis would reappear, sowing doubt among the Philadelphians. Things weren't always the best at home in England, either. Penn's son Billie had become a well-known philanderer who rejected Quakerism and, when sent by Penn to America to mend his ways, came instead to head a ragtag Pennsylvania militia from whose clutches he had to be dragged, drunkenly, away. Penn, the admiral's son, had become a pacifist, and the pacifist's son a brawler.

To shore up the colony's economy, Penn made more deals. He allowed for the construction of new piers for landing larger vessels. Despite his initial desire to keep the waterfront public domain, he allowed pier owners to charge for their use. Penn bargained with the Swedes for the rest of his land, and especially a tract along the Quessinawomink, now the Frankford Creek, north of the city, where a mill already operated. The Delaware at Philadelphia drops only three feet each mile, not much of a gradient. When industries developed in the small riverfront settlements along the Delaware north of the city—Fishtown, Tacony, Frankford—they were, before steam, limited in size by this lack of water power, and a tradition developed of immigrant craftsmen working hand lathes and looms. Philadelphia became a workshop city. But when hard times came, the profits and the future were in mass-produced goods.

I do not get to meet Milton Ginn right away. But he is not shy and writes long letters, spinning for me, in a firm but rumpled longhand, his own Delaware River tales. And no matter what the story, or where it happens, Ginn's backdrop is always the same. It is Fishtown on the Delaware, a panorama in his mind's eye barely sixteen by sixteen blocks square, just a mile north of center-city Philadelphia, and including the working Delaware waterfront where the warehouses with tin facades stack up over the piers on Delaware Avenue, ships in dock pour bilge from their sides, and men heave lines in gray dawns and offload Central American bananas, coffee, and sugar cane from the "Great White Fleet" of the United Fruit Company. The cargo rises out of the holds from hands onto bent backs—a whole raucous, rolling, hoisting dockside carnival that no longer exists. Not, anyway, as Ginn remembers it from the time of the Great Depression, when the factories and mills that beat the great industrial beat of Fishtown began to slow, and when, all along the narrow row houses on the narrow Fishtown streets, families looked for relief. Ginn is a Fishtown native, a Fishtown student, a Fishtown graduate. Places rarely mean this much to anyone anymore.

"A lot of Fishtown families can thank God for the United Fruit Co.," Ginn wrote to me, "because a lot of them were able to get 2 days of work a week and were able to keep afloat. During that period there was 25 to 35 percent unemployment in the Fishtown area. I was fortunate in that I played a lot of semi-pro football at that time and the asst. mgr at Pier 9 was the business mgr for one of the teams I played with. He lived in Fishtown and offered me a job. Pier 9 at Delaware Ave & Race Sts was the location of the United Fruit Co. They imported bananas 2 days a week and about once a month, coffee beans.

"I worked there as a tallyman from 1933 to 1936. At 7 o'clock in the morning on ship days there would be a shape-up outside the pier. The stevedore bosses would come out and give out metal checks which allowed you to work for 65 cents an hour. They would hire certain regulars. The tallymen and riggers didn't have to wait in the shape-up. They walked right in. At about 8 o'clock they would have another shape-up. The stevedore bosses would stand there and throw the metal checks into the crowd. Sometimes the man who he was throwing the check to would drop it and then there would be a mad scramble with grown men fighting like dogs to get those metal checks.

"It was hard work for the stevedores. They carried bunches of bananas on their shoulders from a conveyor belt coming off the ship to freight cars or horse drawn wagons about 50 to 75 feet away. With the coffee ships, they carried 152 pound bags of coffee on their hump. And I remember discrimination even there. For instance, a half-dozen semi-pro football players from our neighborhood all had pencil-pushing jobs at the pier while a lot of older, slightly built guys did the brute work. Also, no blacks worked on the pier. Any of the blacks hired worked in the hold of the ship. This was terribly hard work. They loaded individual bunches of bananas onto a stage between decks and then two men on the stage lifted the bunches up over their heads to the next stage. These guys had to be relieved every hour.

"I was really fortunate, like I said. After my second week they put me in charge of the 6 tallymen in the aft end of the ship. I went to work an hour before everyone else and worked an hour after everyone else. The asst. mgr. also usually gave me a half dozen checks before the shape-up and I was able to give them to my relatives and neighbors. Like I said, I was lucky. I was making about 25 to 35 dollars for 2 and 1/2 days work, when the average married man with a family, lucky enough to have a job, was making $25 a week. Also, some of the chosen few were allowed to take several hands of bananas home.

"These days I hear many teenagers say they wouldn't take jobs at minimum wage at fast-food places or supermarkets etc. and I can picture about a hundred men, many with college degrees, many with families, standing on Delaware Ave for 2 or 3 hours out in the early morning cold, rain falling, or snow, hoping to get 5 or 6 hours work at 65 cents an hour."

Before those bad times, Fishtown had boomed. Fishtown by the Shackamaxon ("Place Where the Chiefs Meet"), where the Treaty Elm stood, under which Penn, if only in legend and portraiture, made his vaunted unsworn but dutifully maintained peace with the

Indians. Fishtown, with its broad tidal marsh and narrow creeks winding into the Delaware, had been, according to Penn himself, "one of the pleasantest situations upon the river." Spring runs of shad and herring had brought the Indians to its banks, and even well into the nineteenth century a thousand shad a day could be netted in the river nearby. Sturgeon were caught, pickled, and smoked. By the 1730s, as industry crowded the Philadelphia riverfront, the shipbuilders moved north, and along with them to Fishtown came the shipwrights, joiners, smiths, carpenters, ropemakers, mastmakers, caulkers, and wharf builders. The village of fishermen and farmers dispersed; streams became more valuable channeled for what power they might provide, and marshland more valuable filled than flooded. The coming of steam made even the dredged millraces superfluous, and the last vestiges of creeks like Gunner's Run eventually only flowed beneath the streets.

Steam had its first trial run in Fishtown when John Fitch launched his steam-powered paddlewheeler *Perseverence* from a Fishtown shipyard in 1786, crossing the Delaware to Burlington in two hours. While Fitch, Oliver Evans, and Robert Fulton all laid claims to the steam engine, it was Fitch who got to entertain the members of the 1787 Constitutional Convention with an excursion. But Fitch's venture never paid off and his investors, observed a writer at the time, were rendered

> *the subjects of ridicule and derision for their temerity and presumption in giving countenance as they said, to this wild projector and madman. The company, thereupon, gave up the ghost—the boat went to pieces—and Fitch became bankrupt and broken-hearted. Often I have seen him stalking about like a troubled spectre, with down-cast eye and lowering countenance; his coarse soiled linen peeping through the elbows of a tattered garment.*

Fitch, wrote Henry Adams, "made a deliberate attempt to end his life by drink; but the process proving too slow, he saved twelve opium pills from the physician's prescription, and was found one morning dead."

Steam wouldn't become viable for industry until coal was brought down from the mountains to power the factory lathes.

The weaving and glass-manufacturing industries brought skilled English immigrants. The immigrants went from working in shops to building their own businesses. In this, Fishtown along the Delaware reflected the growth of the age of the local capitalist, the one who developed and built his own industry and integrated it into the resources and industrial landscape of the place in which he lived. This Fishtown industrialist, while the very antithesis of the international capitalist, is also its first avatar. First Fishtown, then the world.

Take Martin Landenberger. An 1844 report on Philadelphia industry identified him as simply a "stockingmaker" employing twelve hands, perhaps all working in his home, hand-knitting hosiery. By 1850, with twenty-five men and one hundred women at a factory west of Fishtown, his status had risen to "hosiery manufacturer." In 1851 Landenberger put up the first of his factories on Frankford Avenue in Fishtown, a four-story building with "Italianate fenestration." In 1856, still, as it were, in woolen hosiery, Landenberger added on to the Frankford Avenue mill a four-story addition with a cast-iron facade, his name inscribed above the first story in a frieze supported by acanthus leaf and floral capitals. "For cleanliness and good arrangement," stated the industry report that year, "Mr. Landenberger's Kensington Woolen Hosiery manufactory cannot be exceeded and a visit to it is a bona fide entertainment." By 1860 Landenberger made not only hosiery, but opera hoods, comforters, shawls, and scarves. His works included a twelve-horsepower steam engine running 124 knitting machines and twenty-two sewing machines. These ran overtime during the Civil War, making hose and blankets for the Union Army. By 1874 he had added a fifteen-horsepower steam engine, ten twisting machines with four hundred spindles, a spinning department of eight jennies with 2,560 spindles, and fifteen power looms. His five hundred workers, mostly English and German immigrants, processed over 250,000 pounds of American wool a year. By 1880 two steam engines produced 160 horsepower and ran twelve machines with 5,800 spindles, 185 power knitters, 40 sewing machines, 209 power looms, and 155 knitting frames.

And all this time Fishtown was adding new immigrants, many of whom had lesser skills but could work in the increasingly mechanized factories or at the still-burgeoning shipyards. The riverfront was becoming the riverfront Ginn remembers: William Cramp & Sons, shipbuilders, which moved to Fishtown in 1830, and by 1895 employed six thousand workers; Reany and Neafie Penn Steam Engine & Boiler Works; Bancroft & Sellers machine tools; Henry H. Becker Knitting Mill; Morse Elevator Works, "favorably situated for shipping by both rail and water routes." These were not the times of industrial logos or initials; these were men known, as Penn himself liked to be known, as proprietors. So when Morse went mad, his elevator business could not hold together and was bought out by Otis, by then mostly owned by Roebling Steel. By the 1880s more than two hundred industries crowded this sixteen-block-square area. Bordered by the coal yards along the river, Fishtown had a brewery, three furniture makers, three glass houses, three brass and bronze smelters, five rolling mills, two iron shipbuilders, shipyards employing some twenty thousand, three iron foundries, one wire works, three sawmills, one sugar refinery, one wharf builder, and thirteen wrought-iron manufacturers. Day and night, Fishtown weavers spun carpets and cloth (loom sheds still stand in some backyards). The looms sang, "How dear to my heart is the song of the shuttle / As it flies through the webb in front of the lay."

Turn-of-the-century Fishtown: horse carts—ice vendors, horse-radish vendors—ambling along stone streets. Crowds shop at the Girard Avenue farmer's market or meet at Robinson and Crawford's, where the clerk gets your order for you, but soon will become Acme Markets, which will introduce the new self-service grocery. Hucksters cry through the streets "Fish!" each Friday. Cattle off-loaded at the river and herded along the street make "quite an excitement, the drovers with heavy sticks, belaboring the steaming sides of the frighten'd brutes" as they go from wharf to slaughter-house at Third and Girard (Steak 25 cents a pound, beef liver, 8 cents). Wild rice and reeds still rise bright green along the Delaware shore; reed birds and rail are still abundant for the fall shoot. Fish still run in the creek, turtles are still netted for Fishtown snapper soup. On good Sundays, families row the half-mile to Petty's Island in the Delaware for a picnic and fishing. Irish Fishtown barely survives the riots over their settling in the midst of the English millworkers. Polish Fishtown goes Sunday to buy herring at the smokehouse. Riding the ferries from the foot of Shackamaxon Street over to Camden, kids travel back and forth until the deck-hands chase them off.

"For two hours," Walt Whitman wrote in *Specimen Days*, "I cross'd and recross'd, merely for pleasure—for a still excitement" the ferry from Camden to Philadelphia.

> *What exhilaration, change, people, business, by day. What soothing, silent, wondrous hours, at night, crossing on the boat, most all to myself—pacing the deck, alone, forward or aft.*

To the north Whitman caught the view of the Fishtown water-front,

> *the long ribands of fleecy-white steam, or dingy-black smoke, stretching far, fan-shaped, slanting diagonally across from the Kensington or Richmond shores, in the west-by-south-west wind.*

Strikebound Fishtown: Unions organize the trolley and ship-yard workers. In 1922 the Frankford Avenue Elevated makes the run to center-city Philadelphia that was once only made along the river. Life moves into town. Saturday serials eleven cents at the Big J, the Jumbo movie theater at Front & Girard, with its elephant marquee.

Depression Fishtown: The era of the Fishtown capitalist begins to pass. After the First World War, shipbuilding slumps. Conglomeration comes. Local companies pass out of local hands—even A. J. Reach sells out. Here was a Fishtown original. Alfred James Reach, born in London in 1840, came to America and by 1865, after a few years with the Eckford team in Brooklyn, played second base and outfield well enough to become baseball's first professional—or at least distinguished enough to claim the title for himself—at twenty-five dollars a week. From 1865 to 1875 he played for the Philadelphia Athletics (which, through the late nineteenth century, was the name of just about every baseball team in Philadelphia), and then in 1876 bought himself the Philadelphia Phillies and began a small store on Tulip Street in Fishtown, which, along with being a gathering place for sportsmen, also sold sporting goods. He began publishing *Reach's Official Baseball Guide* and started a mail-order business in the 1880s, selling footballs, boxing gloves, twenty-one models of baseball gloves, and twenty different types of baseballs.

Reach made his name with his baseballs. He developed a winding machine to wind the string tightly around the cork center. Then, as now, the leather cover was stitched around the ball by hand, and in Fishtown, stitching A. J. Reach baseballs became a cottage industry, the company delivering the twine-wrapped cork centers to homes and picking up the completed baseballs. In 1901 the A. J. Reach baseball became the official baseball of the new American League. By 1916 Reach employed a thousand workers in Fishtown. But even by then the Reach baseball was "Reach" in name only, for the baseballer had sold out to a company begun by player A. G. Spalding. Spalding also claimed to have been the first paid player. His company bought out Reach in 1892, but continued to manufacture baseballs at the Reach plant and under the Reach name, even fostering the illusion that the two remained competitors, with the American League using the "Reach" ball through 1974 and the National League using the Spalding ball as it had since 1880. To Fishtowners the distinction was moot. Spalding closed the Reach Fishtown plant in 1934. In 1977 the contract for major-league baseballs went to the Rawlings Company. Rawlings baseballs were hand-sewn in Haiti.

Hard-times Fishtown: Kids hop the coal cars in the railyards and kick off chunks of coal as they ride along, then hop off, run back, and pick up the pieces to take home or sell. Dish nights and auction nights at the Jumbo seem to bring everyone out. The Brotherhood Mission of Russell H. Conwell of Temple University gave out flour, clothing, and food. But Fishtown was a working-class immigrant neighborhood. There had always been those in need. The Kensington Soup Kitchen was established in 1844 to give aid to the needy.

Everyone recalls a little steamship voyage to the place they called Soupy Island, down the Delaware from Fishtown to the river beach at Gloucester, New Jersey, across the river where kids and mothers (no fathers allowed) were given free soup and bread. People recall that the river stank—"the stinky Delaware River" the kids called it. It had a layer of coal oil on it. The shad tasted like kerosene.

"My wife and I, when we were kids, made that trip many times," Ginn wrote me. "And I venture to say that between about 1925 and 1935 so did 90% of the children in Fishtown. My wife attended the Penny Concerts at the East Baptist Church and today she is a Deaconess at that same church. My wife's mother worked at the A. J. Reach baseball factory for several years and during that time she brought baseballs home with her and my wife and her sisters helped her mom sew baseballs. As a New Yorker, I'll bet when you read this, you didn't realize that when Babe Ruth, Ty Cobb, Tris Speaker, et al, were hitting them out of the park, that one of those balls may have been sewn by my wife or her mother in Fishtown.

"About six months ago I paid a nostalgic visit to the Pier. They are storing some old boats there and it looks much smaller than I perceived it back in the 1930s. The United Fruit Co. stopped their operation at Pier 9 about 25 or 30 years ago. The old Pier is practically falling down, just like many of the Piers along the Delaware. Two of the adjoining Piers, Pier 3 and Pier 5, adjacent to the Penns Landing area have been remodeled into upscale expensive condominiums. I stood there and wondered what life would have had in store for me if I hadn't left United Fruit Co. in 1936."

We meet in Ginn's half of a narrow Fishtown row house on a street barely two cars wide. He is gnomish, bald, with large, active eyes behind thick, black-framed eyeglasses.

"I had taken a civil service examination for a messenger job with the government and I was hired to start on October twelfth, 1936. I remember this because I asked if I could start on October thirteenth, because October twelfth was a holiday at the pier and we were getting time and a half. They agreed, so I worked my last day and then went to work for Uncle Sam at one thousand eighty dollars a year."

From messenger, Ginn worked his way up to special agent, T-man, Alky-boy, busting the illegal stills and speakeasies that ran long after the repeal of Prohibition. While the Delaware had been an important route for traffic in untaxed liquor—produced legally outside the U.S. but illegally imported—its tributaries proved valuable in the local manufacture of moonshine.

"You needed water to run a still, so when you went looking for one, you began looking along the streams. In this area there were a lot of moonshine stills down in the marshes, from Tinicum to the Pinelands, to the farms in south Jersey. Sometimes they would dump the spent mash into the stream and you'd see it foaming up like beer suds."

The stills were run by local organized crime: Italian gangs, Jewish gangs, African-American gangs. In north Philadelphia the blacks ran most of the speakeasies.

"If it was a white speakeasy you'd go in undercover. If it was a black speakeasy you'd get friendly with a stew-bum, make sure he didn't have any whiskey on him, give him two dollars to go in and make a buy. Then you'd lean on the operator to tell you where he'd got the stuff. If I busted you I kept working you and working you, and you know the next time I bust you you'll really do big time." He pauses to lift his eyeglasses and peer at a couple of old newspaper clippings he's pulled out. One is from the *Philadelphia Record* of November 30, 1939: "T-men & State Agents Pose as Hoboes to Smash Illicit 'Alky' Ring." "They would," Ginn assured me, "come around."

In the fifties and the early sixties, before the suburban developments sprawled out to the rural river towns north of Philly, the woods could still harbor stills and safe houses, barns with built-in trap doors and hollow walls. To a writer for the *Philadelphia Daily News*, Ginn recalled busting Max Potnick's two-story joint in Bucks County. "Geechy Joe, a black guy, was doing the mechanic's work," running the mash through the still. "We had some agents surround the top and Ed Douglas and I went in the bottom. We pushed the door in, just like in the movies—out in the woods you didn't need a warrant. And Ed Douglas says, 'Okay, Geechy, you're through.' Ed's got his gun out"—Ginn points his finger and stretches out his arm to show me how—"and, never taking his eyes off Geechy Joe, Ed walks toward him." But, says Ginn, Ed got only a few steps before he fell right into the mash pit in the middle of the floor and came up swimming in a pool of yeasty slime. "The stink lasted a long time." Even Geechy Joe was allowed a grin.

Ginn often located an operation by smell alone. ("You could get a warrant based on an odor.") More often than not the distillery was a purely local concern, a soda or candy factory, say, that siphoned off sugar to a still. The sugar might come right from the Jack Frost refinery in Fishtown and the cracked corn from the feed store at Second and Spring Garden. Local gangs. Local outlets. Southern moonshine came in mason jars. In Pittsburgh it came in five-gallon glass jugs. In Philly it always came in five-gallon metal cans, 150 proof. Blacks drank it clear. Whites wanted it amber. Local color. Nothing shipped from Colombia. Little if any gunplay. (Ginn recalls having to fire once, a warning shot, in forty years, yet still he got on TV in 1951, as a guest on "You and Your Uncle Sam.")

"I never moved from Fishtown," he says, "and I did pretty well."

Fishtowners claim the statue of William Penn atop Philadelphia's City Hall points toward Fishtown, in particular toward Penn Treaty Park on the Delaware, where Penn supposedly made his peace with the Indians beneath the great, though no longer standing, Treaty Elm, a scene Edward Hicks commemorated repeatedly throughout his career, in one of the sixty-some variations of the Peaceable Kingdom he painted: Penn, Indians, and river, with Christ Child dignified in eighteenth-century swaddling looking on, escorted by peaceable lion and lamb. Nature, Savage, Beast, God, and Man in a repose made all the more peaceable by Hicks's primitive figures, fulfilling biblical prophecy on the shores of the New World.

It never happened. By the time Penn arrived, most of the natives had dispersed, most to the west, where they could still pursue the fur trade. But the place has become a landmark simply because it was so long mistaken for one. The park is a pleasant enough green where Fishtowners can still go to fish in the river for catfish or striped bass, one of the last open patches along a waterfront overloaded with wharves and buildings over which the highway swoops on its glide toward center city, a last gasp of grass in a square block of green in a city Penn founded to be more green than not. Fishtowners fought hard for it. Anyway, not much else of the seventeenth-century remains in Philadelphia.

When we met, Carmen Weber was the city's embattled archaeologist. Short, cherub-faced, tousle-haired, winsome in her sunny, Midwestern sort of way, and always exasperated by what she considers the too-often-commercial aspects of archaeological research. Some things, she feels, ought to be dug up and discovered whether or not they can be restored or turned into museum pieces. But the prevailing view of the past is not much different from Hicks's view of the Treaty Elm: simplified, idealized, lives that fit the frame. Unfortunately, such an approach to history sometimes gets in the way of Weber's more streetwise archaeology: life in the city has never been so simple. For Weber, the muck of the dig is redolent with the complexities of human and natural lives.

"To understand and feel a site you have to be there when it's opened. Riverfront sites, especially. They smell like nothing I can really describe to you—Techni-smell—murky, musky, the smell of the black gunky soil, the fishy river smell of a hot summer day, an old smell, with a patina of odors overlying it, like those that come from the boxwood plants in old colonial gardens."

Weber and I meet in a dilapidated parking lot on Delaware Avenue in Philadelphia. Above us the Benjamin Franklin suspension bridge swings out across the river toward Camden.

Delaware Avenue is four lanes wide and runs its potholed course along the riverfront. The lot is between Delaware Avenue and Water Street. But to get from the level of the parking lot to the level of Water Street, one would have to climb a steep stairway. The fronts of the brick houses on the river side of Water Street are four stories high, while the backs of these same homes are three stories.

"The difference between the fronts of those homes and the backs is the thirty-foot bluffs of the Delaware River, the riverbanks into which the first settlers dug their caves. Were we standing in the seventeenth century where we're standing now," says Weber, "we would be standing in the river."

History or archaeology?

"Right beneath us," she says, pointing to a gravel strip down the middle of the otherwise blacktopped lot, "I dug up a nineteenth-century boat slipway used to bring boats up out of the river for repair." Squared logs of white pine preserved because they had remained underwater. Next to them, a wharf, a three-sided log crib some eight feet deep, which, she says, shows what must have then been the rise in the tide—a strong tide—for the sand and fill used to hold the crib are clean, not at all like the harbor fill in Baltimore or New York, which yields centuries-old debris. (This same strength of tide may be the reason why so much of the pollution poured into the Delaware doesn't linger as it does in other rivers.) We picture the slipway and the wharf and Delaware Avenue not there, and walk up onto Front Street where Weber points out the downslope as it runs toward Dock Street, which, in the seventeenth century, was Dock Creek, Penn's first landing, where the Blue Anchor Tavern secured the high ground. Once the scum of tanneries and silt and debris had contaminated the creek, it was filled in and paved along its course, but the street still angles across the otherwise precise grid, the condominium towers of Society Hill rising (now on a slope exaggerated by developers' landscaping) above what was once the first industrial waterfront of the city.

"When I started work at the lot, I worked alone much of the time, and that made it mine. Archaeologists are always fighting that urge, yet some sites you become emotionally attached to. What attracted me to this place was just the absence of great numbers of artifacts. Here were just these wonderful huge timbers that had been set in place without machinery, by the muscle of men and animals, but which told me a great deal. People in general, as collectors and possessors of material objects, don't understand that archaeology tries to recover a culture, not just its objects, and that even the objects themselves have so much more value than their price on the worldwide black market we call the art world. The thought of this 1676 shipyard still being there was my time machine. And each day I was getting these views—and smells—of the past."

Preserving a place and its topography, Weber says, may be just as important as restoring a historic facade. Although sometimes the topography shows despite being buried. In northwest Philadelphia, early-twentieth-century developers filled in the wealth of streams that flowed from the high ground into the Schuylkill. They filled the streams with the fly ash from industry and built on the fill. Over the years the ash washed out, and several years ago many of the houses began sinking and finally sank so deeply into the buried but still-active streambeds that they had to be abandoned.

As for the landscape that Penn knew? Before being bulkheaded and built over and into the river on both shores, the Delaware must have appeared, especially to those in the small vessels of the time, a much broader river, sandy shores below forested slopes. Before being dredged for ship traffic, the river was shallower, perhaps swifter. Before the cutting of trees and the plowing of farmland led to floods of silt, the streams from the rises in Philadelphia must have been cool, rocky, cobble-bedded, lively with insect life, swarms of dragonflies, full of brook trout.

Wrote Penn, "The waters are generally good & springs frequent, for the Rivers & Brooks are mostly Gravilly & Stony at bottom &

in number hardly credible." Along their banks, black walnut, cedar, cyprus, chestnut, popler, gumwood, hickory, sassafras, ash, beech, and red, white, black, Spanish, chestnut, and swamp oaks. At their edges mulberry, strawberry, cranberry, whortleberry, and fox grape.

"Here are also Peaches, & very good & in great Quantitys; not an Indian plantation without them but whether naturall at first, I know not; however one May have them by bushells, for little. They make a pleasant drink."

And in the forests, "elck as bigg as a small ox; deer, bigger than ours, very plentiful deer, beaver, raccoon, Rabbits & Squirrills (& some eate young bear and commend it). Of foul, the Turky which is very great, the feasant, heathbirds pideons & Partridges in abundance."

Along the marshes, "Swan goos, white & gray, brants, duck teal, also the snipe and curloe, and that in great numbers; but the duck and teal excel, nor so good have I ever eat in other countrys.

"Of fish, there is the Sturgeon (Hering), Shad, catshead, Sheepshead, (smelt) perch, Rock; & in inland Rivers Trout, some say sturgeon above the fall of Delaware, of shellfish we have oysters, crabs, cockles & Mussles. Some Oysters four inches long and one sort of cockles as big as stewing oysters.

"The creatures (for profit only) that are natural to thes parts is, the wild catt (Panther) Otters, woolf fox (fishers) mincks, musk ratt, and of the water, the whale (for oyle) of which we have a good store."

But the ruin of this natural abundance lay in the Quaker's very belief that humans have a role in carving a peaceable kingdom out of the places where the wild beasts dwell.

"The Air is sweet and clear, the heavens serene, like the South Parts of France, rarely overcast & as the woods come by numbers of people to be cleared, that itselfe will refine."

Americans, one colonial journalist observed, seemed to "have an unconquerable aversion to trees."

The "refinement" of the forest quickly cost the colonists in scarce game and even scarcer fuel. By 1701, with the price of wood rising in direct relation to the distance from the city one had to go to find it, a "corder" was appointed in Philadelphia to make sure fuel dealers didn't shortchange citizens.

Weber and I drive north of the city, looking out for lost topography—a swing in a road where a bluff once rose, or a road beneath which once ran a stream. Whenever a road collapsed or a water pipe burst, Weber's job was to look down into the hole for evidence of things past. Old streambeds appear everywhere, mostly used for sewer conduits and covered over. We head into Bucks County, where Penn had a country home built along the Delaware at the bend in the river below the transverse of the fall line. This was Penn's peaceable place, his getaway from the commercial excesses of a growing Philadelphia. With the city left behind, I expect to find more trees, some marsh, and a more natural river shore. "You mean you've never been out here?" asks Weber, somewhat incredulously. And ahead of me, instead of a treeline leading down to the river, I see a kind of Colorado strip mine looming, or something like it: two bare mountains being molded by bulldozers, the bulldozers being followed by flocks of gulls. Following the dusty markers for Pennsbury Manor, we take the narrow, winding drives between these mountains of garbage that rise above great open lakes once mined for sand.

The wooden gateway leads into the shaded manor grounds where oaks, sycamores, and fruit trees create a dense cover and a screen from the landfill behind. Otherwise, the hill of garbage would make the best vantage for painting the pastoral scene below where sheep graze in the corralled yard, cows stand idly by the barn, geese cackle and scatter, and a peacock dashes across the field. The imposing manor house has been reproduced in great detail on the discovered foundations of the original and stands at riverside, its hedged gardens stepped along the slope to the shore. The river runs slowly and quietly here below the falls. The view across the water is of woods— thin, brushy, unimposing, but woods nonetheless.

This little landscape is what the Quaker proprietor of the Delaware had in mind, a peaceable meeting of land and water. It's what the Fishtowners wanted for Penn's park, treaty or no treaty—for the elements of the Peaceable Kingdom have become the artifacts of archaeological digs. As it's put in one study:

> *Interfaces of well-drained soils and low-lying marshes are considered to have been especially important throughout prehistory [as if they are not now] and would have also been among the areas most sensitive to environmental fluctuations. Deforestation concomitant with intensive agricultural development of the nearby uplands resulted in an episode of rapid sedimentation during the seventeenth century.*

What remains of many creeks must be seen through a pit in a collapsed street or, as the remnants of one stream are described, as "evidenced by discontinuous linear depressions in the fell surface and isolated stands of riparian vegetation."

The efforts to make the waterfront fit the needs of a port city on a tidal river came so very soon after Quaker settlement that Weber finds it difficult to fill in her view of precolonial Philadelphia along the Delaware only from her digs at the parking lot. Yet there was no time or money for more work, and now only that strip of gravel fill marks the spot. Still, she gives it a try:

"A kind of quay, a timber wall filled with earth and pitched with stone, was built against the street. Early proposals to turn Dock Creek into a protected anchorage were turned down in favor of a twenty-foot-wide channel from the Delaware River to Third Street for small craft.

"Front Street ran along a natural bank overlooking the river. A gully through this bluff at Vine Street, originally called Valley Street, afforded access from the river's shore into the interior. This provided a good location for the Penny Pot House and Landing, as well as for a shipyard. William Penn originally intended to maintain an open vista up and down the river along Front Street, with stairs providing access to the shore below the bank; however, property owners constructed storage vaults and eventually buildings along the bank. Early land grants on the Hertz Lot that encompassed the east side of the bank, the shoreline, and approximately one hundred fifty feet into the river reflect the compromising of Penn's plan." With little business to be done in the hinterland, everyone jammed up against the river, and when the river shore became too crowded they built out piers. Without the technology to drive piling, they used the same Swedish know-how that built their houses to construct log boxes as deep as the tide, into which they raked the shoreline. On top of these piers they built warehouses. By 1720 Philadelphia's waterfront already consisted of nothing but wharves jutting out into the river over the natural shore.

Philadelphia was the end of the line from the West Indies and Europe. Flour, lumber, corn, beef, bacon, maple syrup, pitch, turpentine, ship timber, bar iron, pig iron, deerskin and furs, and staves by the millions went out while rum, sugar, molasses, silver, salt, wine, linen, cash, and Negroes came in. (The Quakers came late to abolition, and many made a great deal of money on the slave trade before giving it up. Still, a free African-American community, one not yet segregated from pursuing life in the city's trades, developed early along South Street in Philadelphia.) All of this activity brought pirates. They say Blackbeard paid regular visits to the city, and that Captain Kidd buried treasure along the shores of the Delaware. But hollering "Pirates!" might explain any loss of merchandise in those days. Captain Kidd, for one, was never more than a paid mercenary of the British Crown and the East India Company, who, when he failed to catch pirates, was hanged for being one himself. Even the upright Penn was accused of granting blackguards safe harbor in Delaware Bay (a charge credited to the niggling Lord Baltimore).

Nonetheless, Philadelphia became second only to London in the value of goods coming into and out of its port. One of the first settlements unconcerned with raising fortifications or a militia, their pacifism allowed them to devote all their energy to commerce. The merchant elite made up Philadelphia society. Shipbuilders and draymen were the most common occupations, reflecting Penn's original belief that the strength of his colony would come from its "shipwrights, carpenters, sawyers, hewers, trunnel-makers [who made the wooden pegs for ships and wharves], joiners, slopsellers [who dealt in cheap sailors' clothing], drysalters [who sold drugs and dyes], iron-workers, the Eastland merchants [engaged in the Baltic trade], timber-sellers, and victualers, with many more trades which hang upon navigation," including the industrious husbandmen and day laborers, carpenters, masons, smiths, weavers, tailors, tanners, and shoemakers, all "men of universal spirit that have an eye to the good of posterity."

Such a spirited lot, Penn asserted, were no longer appreciated in England where men, in their corruption and luxury, had grown "to neglect their ancient discipline that maintained and rewarded virtue and industry, and addicted themselves to pleasure and effeminacy, they debased their spirits and debauched their morals, from whence ruin did never fail to follow to any people."

But when the British made New York their administrative capital for the colonies, Philadelphia began to lose trade. The Dutch in New York, an ambitious and inventive merchant elite, also instituted an innovative auction system at their docks. Shippers could sail into the harbor, dump their cargo to an auctioneer, take on new goods, and be quickly gone. By the 1790s, Philadelphia had already begun to decline as a maritime merchantile exchange. After the Revolution, protective tariffs imposed on imports kept domestic goods cheap to sell on the broadening frontier, but too costly to export. So the trading life turned inland, westward, leaving the river to become a conduit for the delivery of raw materials to the growing collection of waterfront manufactories.

Weber imagines more remains beneath the streets: "When they removed the gas tanks here in the parking lot, I found privy shafts and stone foundation walls still undisturbed." Somewhere lies the Penny Pot House Tavern and its landing, and nearby the James West shipyard.

All this from a look beneath the blacktop of a waterfront parking lot slated to be, as Weber puts it, "some kind of glitzy waterfront development":

"In the course of the two months I worked here, this meat wholesaler on the corner closed down his business. Across the street there were some really nice old buildings with Flemish bond brick, which means they were probably at least early nineteenth century if not older. They were torn down to make way for four condos. The house across the street, which was a sort of beautiful mid-nineteenth-century hotel, has been totally trashed into a modern house; the building over here, which was one of the last of the nineteenth-century brick warehouse buildings left on this part of Delaware Avenue, was bought by a firm in New York that was planning to put a massive office tower over the back of it."

But redevelopment plans fell on hard times, and now the city has little money for either digging up the past or setting new projects for the future. As I write this, the city employees who dig up the streets and repair the sewers and maintain the schools are working from paycheck to paycheck. So, after three hundred years, Philadelphia-on-the-Delaware is flat broke.

Wrote one colonial journalist:

"In a very little space everything in the country proved a staple commodity . . . wheat, rye, oats . . . timber, masts, tar, sope, plank-board, frames of houses, clabboard, and pipestave." Who could have imagined "that this Wilderness should turn a mart for Merchants in so short a space."

Below the falls at Trenton, commerce consumed the Delaware.

TACONY

DURHAM BOATS, THE LARGE BUT MANEUVERABLE SHALLOW-DRAFT vessels that brought Washington across the Delaware to Trenton on Christmas Eve, were designed and built at Durham Furnace on the Delaware to transport pig iron downriver to the foundries and shipyards below the falls. Some sixty feet long, eight feet wide, and forty-two inches deep, the flat-bottomed boats floated like shallow-draft boxcars. With a load of fifteen tons of iron they drew only twenty-eight inches of water, allowing them to run the falls. The Durham boat became the river standard. Pilots named rocks for the load a Durham boat might safely carry over them. With forty barrels of whiskey or flour on board, the boat might carry over the Forty Barrel Rock at Easton, or the Hundred Barrel Rock downstream at Wells Falls. There, past the Grass Rock and the Foamer, which spews froth at low water to warn away boaters, came Rodman's Rocks, where Captain Rodman wrecked his raft and drowned, then the Bake Iron and Buckwheat Ledge. Heading upstream, boaters might pause at the Dram Rock for "an invigorator from the whiskey jug." The even greater advantage of the Durham boat was that with a light load of two tons it drew barely five inches of water and so could be poled upriver.

The demand for wood—for fuel, for housing, for shipbuilding—was unabating. We were profligate woodburners, known to maintain blazing fires in fireplaces despite the cold drafts that such fires drew in from the rest of the house, leaving a man "scorch'd before while he's froze behind." Charcoal used in ironmaking required plantations of wood, some five hundred acres of forest cut and burned in the "insatiable maw of the furnace" to forge each thousand tons of pig iron. But iron made tools, iron made saws, iron made plate, iron made chains, rudders, spikes, and nails: "Through the thick sulphurous smoke, aided by the glare of light from the forge," the ironmaster might be seen "directing the strokes of a dozen hammermen, striking with sledges on a welding heat produced on an immense unfinished anchor, swinging from the forge to the anvil by a ponderous crane, he at the same time keeping his piercing iron voice above the din of the iron sound." "Iron," wrote Franklin, "is always sweet, and every way taken is wholesome and friendly to the human body—except in Weapons." In fifteen years a single forge could devour twenty thousand acres of forest. But the forests still seemed unlimited. The only concern seemed to be getting the ever-more-distant supply downstream.

Daniel Skinner claimed to be the first to run a raft of timber down the Delaware, perhaps the first such raft run on any river. In 1764, Skinner hammered together six pine trees seventy feet long to

be used for ship masts in Philadelphia and, with a companion identified as "a large Dutchman" by the name of Parks aboard,
launched into the river at Cochecton, Pennsylvania, some forty
miles upstream of Port Jervis, New York. When they reached Philadelphia some two hundred miles downstream, the men, the story
goes, were given the "freedom of the city" and Skinner was named
(or named himself) Lord High Admiral of the Delaware. (The title
has gone unfilled since Skinner's death, in 1813.) Reportedly, all
rafters owed him fealty and none could pass downstream without
paying tribute to the admiralty in the form of a bottle of appropriate spirits.

From Skinner's inspiration came spring flotillas of timber rafts of
white pine and hemlock, not only down the Delaware, but down
other East Coast rivers. And the rafts grew huge—one account of a
Delaware River raft recalls an entire family aboard with cabin,
stable, horse and cow all heading downriver to trade the timber
they'd just cleared off their land for goods needed to begin their
farm. Sometimes twenty or more rafts could be seen coming downriver at the same time. Rafts backed up two or three deep for a
half-mile along the riverbank awaiting sale at New Hope, New Jersey. The Delaware was declared a public highway. In the spring of
1828 some one thousand rafts containing 50 million feet of lumber
descended the river. Sometimes the traffic jams worked themselves
out: If one raft became hung up on the rocks, another might bump
it off. On the other hand, stranded and runaway rafts could thunder downstream and wreak havoc. Reportedly, so could the rafters
themselves ("hardy men" as most accounts have it) when they put
up for the night at one or another of the "Red Taverns" or "Old
Red Taverns" that sprung up along the river.

The season was short, lasting some four weeks after the first
spring freshets began. I have canoed the river during the high
spring runoff, and the waters can be shockingly cold. And since the
river meanders so, no matter what your direction of travel, somewhere along the way you'll find yourself with the wind in your face,
and when it gusts between the ridges of the upper river it can throw

up standing waves three and four feet high even in usually placid eddies. Ice often forms on the rocks at night, and I presume it coated the rafts as well. A hard rain added to the snowmelt can transform both the river and the shoreline, quickening the current and hiding rocks that otherwise serve as guides downstream. Men made a springtime salary along the river piloting rafts (at five dollar apiece) through the most hazardous rapids.

I imagine the end of the trip was the best part of it: the winter's cut of timber sold, cash in hand, a night on the town, and then the long hike, stage, or train back upstream just as the weather begins to break and the spring blossoms up the river valley.

The "ark" appeared in 1806. Built at Mauch Chunk, now Jim Thorpe, Pennsylvania, on the Lehigh River, it descended the Lehigh into the Delaware and the Delaware to Philadelphia, carrying three hundred bushels of anthracite coal. An ungainly vessel, some sixteen feet wide and twenty feet long, it was a coal crib set afloat, its heavy planks spiked together and caulked just enough to make it last downstream where the shippers unloaded the coal and sold the boat for timber, taking only the hardware that held it together back upstream. As coal demand and production increased, the arks grew sometimes to a hundred feet long. Still, it was said that in thirty minutes four men could build an ark big enough to hold twenty-five tons of coal. The vessels were also evidently enough of a curiosity to attract "pleasure parties of ladies and gentlemen" who would ride down some of the route, "seated in boxes for protection from the waves in the rough waters encountered on the way."

With the seagoing trade declining, the merchant elite of Philadelphia and New York invested in railroads and canals, maneuvering to control the transportation routes west across the Delaware. The competition was often less than met the eye. The Delaware and Raritan Canal Company incorporated in 1830, the very same day the Camden and Amboy Railroad and Transportation Company started business. Both were joined the next year, and in 1871 all their properties were leased by the Pennsylvania Railroad Company for a period of 999 years.

Canals ran down both sides of the river. The Lehigh Canal ran from the coal regions of central Pennsylvania, down the Lehigh valley to below the Delaware falls. The Delaware-Raritan Canal ran from the river just south of Trenton northeastward to the Raritan River at New Brunswick, where vessels could head for the bay and New York.

In 1837 the Reading Railroad bought up the river shoreline of Port Richmond north of Fishtown and spread over the marshland a maze of tracks and acres of anthracite storage. In another ten years hard coal would be king, its hundred-year reign-to-come heralded with blasting powder and supported on the backs of English, Welsh, Scottish, Irish, German, and Slavic immigrants. (The tyranny of the coal kingdoms gave the lie to the nineteenth century's much-touted concern for immigrant welfare.) Coal production grew from one and a half million tons in 1833 to over 20 million tons in 1860, coming downstream by canal boat and boxcar to feed the riverfront furnaces. Railroad and canal monopolies combined with those of coal, and by the end of the century the Reading, the Lehigh Valley, and the Delaware, Lackawanna & Western railroads controlled sixty percent of the anthracite and owned hundreds of thousands of acres of coal region land. By 1902 railroads controlled over ninety percent of the anthracite deposits. The canals and railroads put an end to the Durham boats, the arks, and eventually the rafts, but the raw materials continued to flow downriver.

Some of the costs went unrecognized. For every four tons of coal mined and shipped, nearly a full ton would wash away. The residue filtered from the anthracite, and, called "culm," rose in mountains upstream and washed into both the Lehigh and the Schuylkill, an estimated thirty million tons into the Schuylkill alone. The coal blackened the river bottoms and, despite long years of dredging and desilting, high water can still loosen buried veins of black silt, which rise and run downstream. The immediate effects of all the woodcutting were floods of soil washing off the land and into the creeks and rivers. This silt reached downriver and eventually began to fill in the shipping channel below the falls, stalling navigation between Trenton and Philadelphia. "The signs of artificial improvment," wrote farmer and naturalist George Perkins Marsh, "are mingled with the tokens of improvident waste." Any fair observer would call it our rain forest adventure—cutting the forest, killing the streams, and exploiting poor labor to extract the minerals. There were even assertions (now unquestionable) that the forest-clearing had already altered the climate, that winters were shorter and summers longer and warmer than those the very first settlers knew.

Soon enough, oil from the 1850s strikes in western Pennsylvania turned the Delaware riverfront from Philadelphia to Wilmington into the world's largest refining complex. And steam, Fitch's folly, began to power life along the river. The new age was now in the making, in the forging, in the crafting and the looming. Not that it didn't have its spiritual side: In 1847 the Churchmen's Missionary Association for Seamen of the Port of Philadelphia launched its Floating Church of the Redeemer, a permanent floating Gothic Revival cathedral on the Delaware.

The work of creating new goods fell to new immigrants. The Delaware grew into one great river village that went upstream to fetch the wood, fuel, and water to build its downstream industries. Local smiths sent iron to local shipyards; people lived where they worked and spent where they lived. The railroads brought coal, culm, and dust, but also Delaware peaches and Maurice River oysters. It was a world of local mills, local foods, local parades (everyone, everywhere, played baseball, white and black alike), of village philosophers and immigrant inventors with big ideas.

"This was a custom-made place of diverse manufacturing," Philadelphia historian Walter Licht tells me. "Very fine products made by small to medium-size firms making highly specialized custom goods. Even Baldwin never made two locomotive engines alike.

"It became so despite the fact that it didn't have a major waterfall like Paterson or the industries along the rivers in New England because it had good access to the hinterlands, good markets, and a good base of skilled labor which grew out of artisanal trades and was reinforced with the immigration of skilled German and British workers.

"The merchant elite had turned to investment banking or railroads and mines, and so capital resources for manufacturing grew organically from small, family-scale, highly specialized firms of thirty to eighty workers. Industry was local, with close ties between factory owners and employees, for the factory owners had themselves been apprentices and machinists, and so were close to the processes they developed into industries and personal fortunes. They felt their own fortunes tied up with those of their workers and, whether benignly or with paternal powers, remained close—Roebling lived in a home at his Trenton plant, Disston in Tacony.

"Disston made the finest saws imaginable, with brass bolts in applewood handles, but in the 1920s, firms in Toledo and the Midwest began stamping out saws and Disston, which had grown on its western market, lost out. Disston is a classic example of a Philadelphia firm."

Along the Delaware, 1840. Picture a twenty-one-year-old immigrant machinist's apprentice from Tewksbury, England, wheeling coal from the river wharf to his basement foundry. Over the years the apprentice refines the process, puts it in order, melds the crafts of sawmaking—hand-hewn and -finished aged beech and applewood handles, hammer-tempered, crucible-forged Sheffield steel—with the latest patents of the patent-happy steam age: belt-driven sanders, grinders, filers, and toothers cutting five hundred teeth a minute, "by which one man can toothe thirty dozen in the same time," or "toothe perfectly a sixty-inch circular saw in two minutes," which before would have taken two hours. By the end of the Civil War, Henry Disston's saw manufactory is the biggest in the world.

While other saw manufacturers import ingots of Sheffield steel, Disston brings over the Sheffield steelmakers themselves. To protect his growing enclave of craftsmen and apprentices (skilled steel smiths could command their own price in those years), he builds a town for them. Along the river at Tacony, a village of summer cottages several miles north of the center of Philadelphia, he intrudes with sixty-six acres of saw and steel manufactory, then builds on the slope above it a square-mile English village, complete with music hall and playing fields. He holds afternoon teas and sponsors a soccer club. And though in those days nothing more than open field and pasture surround Tacony, for the well-being of his community Disston creates a little park in the midst of his little rural town on the river.

Along the Delaware, 150 years later. Driving in a rattling school van with Tacony-born Harry Silcox, tall, lean, angular, Lincolnesque principal of Philadelphia's Lincoln High School. Once a basketball player and coach at Temple University, Silcox hardly talks but exhorts, always making it sound as if he's describing a game plan he's either stolen or hatching. The van belongs to the school's environmental lab, a program that Silcox initiated and got funded despite this being a time of crisis and despair in Philadelphia's city schools. Silcox is a gifted optimist who believes hometown is and ought to be destiny.

"We had a student by the name of Sylvester Stallone, whom we had to throw out of Lincoln. Believe me, he had earned it. But I wonder if the Rambo character that made him millions in movies wasn't named after John Rambo, a fellow who used to live off the land when there wasn't much of it left any longer, and was known to the kids at school as 'the wild man of Pennypack Creek.'" The name Rambo, in any case, had been in the area since before Penn's arrival, one of the many Swedes who claimed land in Penn's tract.

From center-city Philadelphia (Penn's statue, Silcox points out, faces not Fishtown, as a Fishtowner such as Milton Ginn might have told me, but Tacony, where it was forged, as any Taconyite knows) we drive north along Route 95, looking through the clouded van windows at the blocky formations of tar-roofed brick and concrete factories and warehouses along the waterfront below.

Jammed one against another, they jut out to the water's edge as permanent-looking as any geologic formation. For all their silent presence now, and but for an old brick steel mill painted yellow and now called Big Marty's Carpet Warehouse, they all might as well be rock.

We land in Tacony. The community remains, brick homes in neat blocks on a slight slope up from the river, but the industry upon which it was founded, Henry Disston's Keystone Saw Works, is gone—worse than gone, for the steelworks, the rolling mill, the file shop, the handle shop, the jobbing shop, all sixty-six acres still stand, cavernous and vacant, unhappy monuments to a past which still weigh on the Tacony mind. Just ask anyone in town about Henry Disston's saws, and aside from the fact that nearly everyone, or someone in his or her family, worked for Disston, it would be like inquiring about Stradivari in Cremona.

Tacony was one of the nineteenth century's most successful paternalistic industrial communities. Harmony reigned at Disston, Silcox says, at a time when the paternalistic order from the mills of Philadelphia to the mines of the coal region was being challenged, often violently, by the sundry knights of labor.

Pennsylvania's Secretary of Internal Affairs toured Disston in 1887 and found it a "well ordered healthful village." His advice to shaky industrialists?

> *Let the despairing go there if they wish to revive their hopes concerning the future of the working class. As demonstration is better than theory, study the history of Mr. Disston's enterprise and the vision of happier times will appear to you.*

Disston, Silcox says, pretty much thought of everything, from the *D* in the keystone logo on the factory facades to the music hall and free reading room and Washington Tea House to the fresh water piped in from the nearby Pennypack Creek (Disston was leery of the quality of the Delaware). Work and place were one and the same, and all belonged to Disston, whose ambitions for Tacony, says Silcox, were "authoritarian, hierarchical, organic, and pluralistic." The Disston family managed the plant. Henry's son, Jacob, was president of the Tacony Trust Company, which financed the homes that Disston built. The homes came with demanding deed restrictions:

> *No tavern or building for the sale or manufacture of Beer or Liquors of any kind or description and no court house, carpentry, blacksmith, currier or machine shop, livery stables, slaughter house, soap or glue boiling establishment or factory of any kind whatsoever where steam-power shall be used or occupied on the said lots, tracts or piece of land or any part thereof.*

Disston forbade bells in the church steeples in order to discourage the gathering of rowdy fire brigades and limit disruptions in the factory. No taverns, says Silcox, left men sober for work. No stables meant workers had to live near the factory. "Why a park in the center of Tacony," asks Silcox, when the land around was all field and forest? "Because if Tacony was to become a respectable, civilized community, it needed a park. The park symbolized orderliness and culture as opposed to the area's unorganized farms and the semi-wilderness around them."

The park's now a buffer from the city grown up all around. "With the coming of the trolley, urban life reached Tacony," says Silcox. "Tacony was only three miles from the center of the city, but the only connection had been by water. Now the workers could get out and go elsewhere. Life turned away from the river. My mother used to say, 'Don't go down to the river. It's dirty.' "

We walk down toward the river and the Keystone Saw Works.

"Disston took the money he made from making plate for Civil War ironclad ships, and with what he didn't spend on Atlantic City real estate, he bought Tacony."

His intentions in both purchases, claimed Disston, were better conditions for his workers: in Tacony, to get them out of the small row homes in an overcrowded Fishtown; in Atlantic City, to give the workers a modest seashore vacation resort. His son Hamilton, born to the wealth his father had earned (his father twice bought him discharges from Civil War duty), eschewed Atlantic City for more exotic terrain. After Ham inherited the company in 1878, he saw his own particular challenge in Florida and entered into a contract with the state giving him six million acres in exchange for his agreeing to drain the upper Everglades and create a passage across the peninsula from the Atlantic to the Gulf. When he finished the job, Disston would own nearly half the state. Florida would be his Tacony on a grand scale. He scratched out channels, raised sugar on reclaimed muck, founded whole towns, planned a model Disston City, and then, overextended as perhaps few men have ever been, went down with his empire in the depression of 1893. He returned to Philadelphia, retired to his bath, and shot himself in the head.

We step into the hundred-year-old mill and are awash in the murky amber light reflected off the well-oiled patina of the brick and wood. A few workers stand at posts, processing steel. They make up a skeleton crew running a small-scale saw operation for a company that's combined what was once sixty-six acres of manufactory into a single building. Silcox introduces the plant foreman, Roland Woehr, a large-framed, somber gentleman who was sent to Drexel University by the Disston family, and worked for the company to the end. He now oversees twenty employees in a plant that once employed twenty-five hundred. The process, he says, is no different. But a Disston hand saw took eighty-two steps, from pouring the crucible steel through furnace-hardening the flattened toothed blade to hand-hammering and angling the teeth.

We stand and stare into the fiery eye of the draw furnace—1,550 degrees Fahrenheit. From the furnace the blade is quenched in oil: "It gradually relieves the internal stress," says Woehr, whereas water-cooling might leave distortions in the saw. In the perpetual dusk of the high main work hall, with its row of angled skylights, the sunlight flashes off the finished steel and draws attention to one worker or another as they rotate and work their blades.

"Not much light on an overcast day, not much heat in winter, and not much relief in summer," Silcox intones. The ring of a hammer pounding steel cracks on the inside of the ears.

"He's pounding out depressions in the steel, the hammering actually raising the steel to level it. At one time fifty smiths worked in this building, each with an apprentice. It took a smith eight years to learn his trade."

A circular saw blade turns on the tooth cutter, the angled cutting blade carving out each tooth in a constant spurt of oil that runs, like water down an Escher waterfall, down a little flume around the machine, only to be pumped up to lubricate the cutter once again. The gears turn electrically; belts no longer connect the wheels to steam-powered turbines. In 1876, Disston bought all of the steam engines from the Centennial fair in Philadelphia, and these ran the plant until after World War II. All the grinding, cutting, filing, and sanding machines were connected to the mechanical clutter of the clerestory above them, the slanting light further filtered through a canopy of flapping belts along the length of the nave.

"These were dangerous operations," Silcox says. "Before a method was devised to float away the dust from the grinding machines, the sanders working at the sandstone grinders died at forty from silicosis." In Sheffield, England, the steel town most admired by the American steelmakers, stood a hospital for grinders and miners. The wheels started out at seven feet in diameter and were ground down to four. In Tacony, Disston constructed terraces of used grindstones. The Tacony Baptist Church is built of them—an unfortunate conjunction of spirit and commerce, considering the hundreds of workers who died in the shaping of the stones.

Silcox and I come out into the sun by the river, where some older boys who look like they should still be in school are fishing off the rocky bulkhead.

"Somewhere out there," Silcox tells me, "is a two-man chainsaw that Disston developed but couldn't perfect. To prevent anyone from stealing the idea, he rowed it out into the Delaware and dropped it over the side."

"I heard that story," says one of the boys as he takes a drink from a beer. "And I know all about these sandstones here." He shades the sun from his eyes and looks more closely at us. "And I know you, Harry! I used to go to Lincoln." Silcox smiles, and nods a knowing how-do-you-do. It was, he had to admit, a good clear day for being out of school.

Turns out a lot of people know Harry in Tacony. From Neil Rosenwald's Foodarama Delimart, where, owing to Disston's original deed restrictions, we can't get beer with our sandwiches, and all along the tree-lined streets of Tacony's Disston twinhomes. Bill Master comes out of his cluttered, aging home to greet us and repeats for Harry the story of his apprenticeship to Johnny Southwell, who started as a smith at Disston in 1880. "You had twenty hammers to choose from," says Master. "There's no way you could learn it by reading about it; you had to learn to feel it." "Smithing," Harry opines, the rhythm of the striking and the deafening clangor, "was a mystical thing."

Disston himself had had a simple, serious, workmanlike vision. "We all ought to live to make each other happy," he wrote to his employees in 1867:

> *God knows the greatest desire in my life is to see all that I am connected with happy. . . . The object of man and boss should be mutual, the boss to give all he can when times will permit, and the Men under close competition to be willing to help.*

"Disston never paid well," admits Harry. "But there was steady work and a protected life."

Master worked forty years at Disston, lost his hearing, retired on his pension. But after World War II, the firm's profits continued the long decline that had begun twenty years before. The family members holding the increasingly divided stock saw diminishing returns on their shares.

"After years of twenty-four-hour days, the factory was worn out," Harry says. "By 1951 the German factories had recovered and electric steel mills were working more efficiently, and in three years Disston accumulated four million dollars in debt. The banks began to worry. Then, in 1955, an acquisition game began, and a man by the name of Thomas Mellon Evans of H. K. Porter Company of Pittsburgh started buying up the stock. Once he had control of the company, one of his henchmen walked into the Disston office and told the foreman to get out of his chair.

"In 1955, Evans pays the Disston family twelve million dollars for the factory, then takes three million from the pension fund to help pay off the debt. In those days, since the company had created the pension fund, the company could dispose of it. Evans sells off everything. Half the community is out of work, and the workers, like Master, are left with nothing.

"With the company in the black and now into electric shears, Evans goes public with it and makes himself thirty-seven million. But it soon becomes obvious that it's just a shell moved around by a conglomerate."

When H. K. Porter died, in 1921, at the age of eighty-nine, the company he'd founded in 1866 with $20,000 his father had given him was making six hundred locomotives a year and was worth two million. When Thomas Mellon Evans joined the Pittsburgh firm at the age of twenty-nine in 1939, he found that "the founder's death, the changing economy, and an era of inventive progress, which saw steam locomotives give way to electric and then diesel, combined to effect a long decline. . . ." Over the next years, Evans transformed the company. In a 1955 address to a meeting of the Newcomen Society (which called for "a nobler Civilization" through "material progress") in New York City, Evans described how he brought the company back. The buyout of Disston was near but not yet complete.

"In searching for new products to manufacture to take the place of the dying locomotive business, we came to the conclusion that one of the quickest ways, and probably the most economical, was to add new products by the acquisition of good, going businesses. . . .

"So far," relates Evans, "we have found that it is easier and less expensive to buy a company and to develop its potential than to start something brand new. . . . The very obviousness of this evidently blinds people to its practicality. Think of the tremendous expense and effort if, for example, any of us today wished to start a new steel manufacturing concern. . . . It would take, no doubt, close to two years to build and put into operation such a plant, and then, of course, customers would have to be developed."

As if this had never been done.

"How much quicker and usually more economical it is to purchase a concern in a given field and thus secure overnight its engineering staff, technical knowledge, plant, products, and customers. . . ." All the things that it took the craftsmen founders like Disston some skill to create and devoted lifetimes to develop. Evans found these very firms particularly easy marks, for they were conservative, had no large corporate investors, and "as all of us know, there are major tax problems involved with inheritances and diversification of investments."

So:

In 1949 he acquired the seventy-year-old Quaker Rubber Corporation of Philadelphia. Started as a one-man distributing company in 1885, it became a supplier to industry from its plant on the Delaware River and the main line of the Pennsylvania Railroad. Quaker supplied the hoses that fought the fires at Pearl Harbor.

In 1950 he took over Delta-Star Electric of Chicago, which furnished transmission lines for Hoover Dam. Then Connors Steel in Birmingham, founded by George W. Connors, Sr., in Helena, Alabama.

In 1952 he took the Watson-Stillman Company, founded in 1848 by Eliphalet Lyon, who had built a small factory on Grand Street on New York's Lower East Side to make steam engines, hydraulic jacks, lever punches, and hydraulic presses that pressed oil from fish, cider from apples, and wine from grapes. (The capacity of each press was rated in terms of the thousands of fish it could press per hour.) Lyon died in 1883. The company engineered the diving bell used by Professor William Beebe in his 1930 descent to the bottom of the Atlantic.

In 1954, Evans purchased the A. Leschen & Sons Rope Company of St. Louis, which made wire rope for the Panama Canal; then Alloy Metal Wire of Philadelphia; then the McLain Fire Brick Company of Pittsburgh and the one-hundred-eleven-year-old Laclede-Christy Company of St. Louis, which developed fire brick in the late nineteenth century. Then Pioneer Rubber Mills of Pittsburgh and the Riverside Metal Company of New Jersey.

Disston would be next on Evans's buying spree.

In 1945, Evans told the meeting, the H. K. Porter Company was doing $10 million a year in locomotives. By 1955, under Evans's direction, it was doing $80 million a year in everything but. His agglomeration of small family businesses had the added advantage that if one division didn't make money, another would, and that "in an economy based on high corporate taxes, a losing division is presently more than fifty percent subsidized by the federal tax laws."

" 'What is your goal?' " he asks himself aloud. " 'Do you have a definite spot at which you are aiming?' The answer," he submits, "isn't simple. Today"—this is 1955—"in order to survive, we feel that a company must be relatively big to compete with the giant corporations. In this economic era, if you stand still you are actually falling back. If you go ahead slowly you are doing little more than standing still. With the tremendous resources in selling, research, planning, and manufacture of the very large organizations, smaller companies are faced with only two alternatives: growing, or remaining as they are, which we feel eventually means falling behind, if not finally going out of business.

"We feel that Porter is contributing something very important to our economy when we inject new life and very often new capital into an old established concern."

The saw company's new life was a short one. At least under Disston, says Harry, as if quoting economic scripture, Tacony's "life space and economic space were one." Under Evans, "capital became fluid and was simply drained from the business and the community." The steel mill was closed, the hand-saw operation moved to Danville, Virginia.

While businesses began to fear Evans's arrival at their door, his private life took on *Citizen Kane* dimensions. His first marriage ended in 1953—in the midst of his empire building—in a divorce that made daily headlines; Evans claimed his wife was using his money to feed steak to the dogs. Within a year of his divorce he married his second wife. That second marriage ended in a separation and his wife's suicide. The story goes around Tacony that Evans's second wife found him so relentless that when she decided on suicide she stabbed herself in twenty-two places and chose to bleed to death over her husband's favorite cashmere rug. Not true, though the reality was lurid enough. Distraught over his affections for another woman, his second wife went from room to room of their Virginia home, shooting herself with a shotgun. In any case, for those in Tacony, it was proof enough that Evans brought tragedy in his wake.

Harry cites the Victorian poet Robert Southey: "The greedy, grasping spirit of commercial and manufacturing ambition and avarice is the root of all our evils." Disston would not be Evans's last buyout on the Delaware.

In the Tacony music hall, with its burgundy crown, Disston started a scientific library. He was keen on scientific thought. And the original Tacony thinker was Frank Shuman. Shuman invented wire-reinforced glass to support the ever-larger panes being used in buildings at the end of the nineteenth century. He became wealthy on this and a concrete piling business, and tinkered on a large scale in his Tacony workshop. He developed a low-pressure steam engine that ran on solar power (in 1914 Shuman warned we would someday run out of fossil fuel). He sold the invention to the Egyptian government, which used it to power irrigation in the desert along the Nile. Now a wealthy and famous man—"an eccentric with a cane who had no horse and was unkind to everyone," Harry says— Shuman devised ever more incredible inventions, including a tank, or, more properly, a "land battleship" with a twenty-thousand-horsepower engine and two-hundred-foot-high wheels that could roll across the Delaware, raze Philadelphia in two hours, and end the war in Europe in two days. His idea for submarine design had enough ring of reality to bring the Secret Service to Tacony on the suspicion that Shuman was taking his unspecified invention to the Germans.

"Tacony went into the First World War almost as one," Harry

says. (To keep the factories running, Disston, like other companies, went into the rural South and brought up blacks to replace the white workers who had gone to war. Here, as elsewhere, when the war ended most of the blacks lost their jobs.)

"They had their own division in France. In those days you could enlist that way—if you were a coward then, everyone would know it—but they had a MASH unit and only eighteen people died in the whole war, and so all the rest came back heroes and were feted with annual parades."

From the porch of her house Mrs. Farley, ninety-four years old and, even on this warm day, draped in a long cotton dress and shawl, greets Harry and invites us in. "The inside of the house," Harry whispers, "has not changed since 1915." With a full bloom of a face, Mrs. Farley is in a jolly mood entertaining friends who are also in their nineties. She recalls the war and the peace, Frank Shuman and the parades, and stands leaning on her cane at the porch rail to see us off.

"Comes Vietnam," continues Harry, "when it's okay to be afraid or at least not eager to go to war, the lingering patriotic spirit—don't forget, every time there was a war Tacony had work—sends them off as before, but we lose some forty men in Vietnam. Few communities, few white communities, lost more.

"Suddenly they were uncertain. They were left with values that didn't fit the times. They lost their pensions and their sons in Vietnam, and now I find they're a very lonely people." Tacony has no more parades.

During World War I the shipyards boomed. At Hog Island on the Delaware, just south of center-city Philadelphia, a shipyard like no one had ever seen before was built in less than ten months on some nine hundred acres of marsh: fifty shipways, employing 35,000 workers. In two years of mass production they launched a fleet of Hog Islanders, 122 flat-bottomed, hard-chined, 7,500-deadweight-ton ships, and then closed down in January 1921. Chester, some several miles downstream, boomed as well in those days. But the emergency ended. Even Cramp's closed and the waterfront became a ghost town.

Something of a revival came to the shipyards during World War II, but thereafter the industrial decline that had begun in the thirties came more quickly. The shipyards that had employed some eighty thousand were gone, the coal gone, the mills gone. Hog Island was eventually wiped off the map, paved over by the runways of Philadelphia International Airport. The enduring legacy of the wartime shipyard may be the Philadelphia hoagie, an oversized sandwich on a long hard roll stuffed with cold cuts, peppers, tomatoes, and onions, and doused with olive oil, which one historian says may have originally been called the "hoggie" because it was eaten by the shipyard workers at Hog Island.

No transfer of commodities. Nothing doing on the Delaware. This is, historian Walter Licht professes, the history of American industry. See it here first. Soon the shutdowns and the buyouts begin.

The marsh by Hog Island must have been a wonderful place. In the July 1881 issue of *Scribner's*, both Thomas Eakins and Joseph Pennell provided sketches of the place for an article by Maurice Egan titled "A Day in the Ma'sh." (In subsequent issues the same year *Scribner's* published John Muir on the Sierra Nevada and John Burroughs's Pepacton elegy to the upper Delaware.) The area was then known as the Neck, or Frogtown, and had once been known as Southwark and

> *celebrated for its cabbages, its pits, its dogs, its dikes, its reed-birds, its inhabitants, and, above all, for its smells.*
>
> *The land is low, and high dikes, or banks, prevent the aggressions of the Delaware. These banks are fringed with wide spaces of bending reeds. . . .*
>
> *Green meadows stretch along the Delaware with here and there the relief of cows and horses grazing on this land, which was Ma'sh in the spring rains and which will be Ma'sh again in the winter thaws.*

Here live the "Neckers" in their patchwork shanties beyond the reach of the city, their backyards "oozy" with "green mire" and "dotted with oyster shells, bottles, a broken ladder, old bits of timber and parts of vehicles belonging to an older civilization." They are truck farmers, hunters, trappers, fishermen, the last of the "white Indians" able to live off what remains of the land so close to the city, raising ducks, pigs, and dogs that "look as if they enjoyed the right of suffrage in this village, and they receive you quietly and gravely, as becomes burghers who have the privilege of offering the freedom of the city to him who pleases them."

But this is 1881, and civilization is fast encroaching. A Pennell landscape shows an oil refinery looming behind the marsh. Continued Egan:

> In many places whole plantations of the primeval Jamestown-weed have been destroyed by the loads of refuse from the soap-factories that have been cast upon them. . . . The spatter-dock may disdain to show its spiky leaves in the rainbow-hued pools that surround the oil-refineries, but the scrub-willow grows in clumps and the Jamestown-weed, crushed to earth, raises its ribbed white bugle among heaps of rubbish, though it cannot follow the blue flag into the half-dry ditches by the road-side.

Still, Egan reported, the Neckers clung to their traditions:

> On New Year's Eve crowds of men and boys go dress themselves in fantastic costumes and roam through the Neck and lower part of the city all night. This custom, doubtless a remnant of the old English Christmas mumming grows year by year in Philadelphia, and the mummers, becoming bolder, penetrate as far north as Chestnut Street.

And at times they received visits from the outside:

> In the fall—on the first of September—sportsmen, boatmen, and "pushers," who propel the flat-bottomed skiffs through the

reeds, swarm into the Neck. Anybody who can beg, borrow, or steal a fowling piece sallies forth ... in search of the coveted reed-bird, (... which all true Philadelphians think and speak of with reverence—the bobolink of the New England summer, the rice-bird of the later season in North Carolina, the reed-bird of the Ma'sh ...) whose rich, juicy flavor resembles that of the ortolan, so famous in Europe. Toward sunset the reed-birds congregate in large flocks, and then the slaughter is great, and the noise is like that heard on an unusually jubilant Fourth of July.

A hundred years later the marsh, the wild rice, and the Philadelphia reed birds are gone. So are the hunters, with the exception of a stubborn soul or two. Frank Astemborski is one. Round, boyish face framed by the hood of his brown camouflage-cloth coat, he takes to the river each fall and winter when the recreational sailors and fishermen have gone. He faces into the fresh, cold air like a man relieved of his cares. In a light snow on a wintry fall morning we load up guns and boat and drive out in his pickup toward the river.

"If you never had it, you don't miss it. But I had a taste of it. I lived in the town of Riverside, and the marsh that ran along the Rancocas Creek that ran into the Delaware was right in my backyard. And I seen all the old-time gunners. Us kids used to follow them around, go down the street with them, and if I told them I'd carry the ducks out for them, sometimes I'd get to go out on the river. And then I'd just sit in the boat all day, and sometimes get to row and once in a while they'd let me have a shot and that was a big deal, you know. Then I'd help them carry their ducks home and we all used to say that's what we wanted to do when we got older."

There was always something going down on the winter marsh: fishermen with their nets hauling catfish, or trappers working muskrat. And on the landward edges, thousands and thousands of blackbirds flying and the men all lining up and shooting away at the rising flocks of birds and the kids running to pocket the empty shells and retrieve the fallen birds, filling their jackets and keeping their own for dinner. In the open fields there was rabbit and pheasant.

"You had towns, but between the towns was all farmland and along the river you had marshes. I was in the best of it. I was always out in a boat. I practically lived in a boat. I had so many duck boats and rowboats and canoes. And I was always walking out on the swamps. I'll never forget when my mother took me to Firestone and got me a pair of hip boots. I must have been just ten years old and they were so big on me. It was the middle of summer and there was this big marsh back there and I just walked around in it all day. I didn't know where I was goin' and the reed was so high I couldn't see, so every once in a while I'd find a dry spot and look over the tops of the reeds and say to myself, 'Yeah, I know where I am,' and go back in. Well, I didn't get back too soon, and by the time I did the mud was all stuck to me and I must have looked like a snappin' turtle just crawled out. And my mother said, 'Where the hell have you been?' And I was so happy to have my first pair of hip boots I just couldn't worry about where I'd been at all."

Out on the river the smoke-gray sky meets the iron-gray water. We are on the Pennsylvania shore, looking out over a small, sandy, treeless island known as Biddle Island, just fifty yards offshore from the house we'll launch from, which was once a Biddle house, one of a few great estate houses that stand along this shore of the Delaware.

"These were all prominent gunners," says Astemborski. "They had the best guns and the best boats—Heisler boats and decoys by John Blair and John English."

His reedy waterman's voice barely carries in the cold air.

"They all knew each other, poor guy and wealthy guy, and when they hunted together they'd respect each other and we'd all be friends, me and Charlie and Mercer and Catherine Biddle."

Railbird hunting was a rich man's sport. The hunter stood in the bow of the low, double-ended skiff, and the pusher poled him across the grassy marsh. There'd be yelling to flush the birds (as well as to let the other pushers know where you were, so you didn't get peppered with shot). The guides hollered, "Mark! Mark right!" or

"Mark ahead!" When flushed from the grasses, the small birds scattered up in every direction, like quail, but low, and landed with their wings raised, so they could be an elusive target even at close range. And what with the wind blowing the light boat and the current rocking it, the birds could be frustrating sport.

This late in the season the scull boats came out, like the one Astemborski unloads from his truck—low, kayak-like, but open and broader-beamed. The boat is powered and maneuvered by a single oar that fits out through a sleeve in the stern. The blade of the oar is sharply curved so that when turned in a kind of figure-eight motion, it churns away the water first to the left, then to the right, propelling the boat silently forward. Both the gunner in the bow and the sculler lie low and even pull some camouflage over them so that the boat, even as it moves up on the sitting ducks or geese, appears like nothing more than a drifting raft in the gray waters.

With the decoys set, Astemborski and I stand on the shore waiting for the birds, which have been flocking downstream and past us for the last cold hour, to set down on the water.

"Cloudy and cold," he whispers, "perfect for sculling."

The cloud cover has lowered, and a sycamore down the shore that I could see clearly when we arrived is now a hazy, wintry silhouette. The snow has begun to blow more steadily, coating the brown fronds of foxtail along the shore. Cardinals chip and jump in the thickets. Ducks and geese fly in and land among the decoys. Astemborski pushes off, lowers himself down into the boat, pulls a canvas over him, and begins to scull toward the raft of decoys. The boat is silent. There's no wake even as it moves upstream against both the current and the falling tide. It is a cat sneaking in on a bird.

Out of the fog now, a rusted freighter appears with a tug nursing at its side, both pushing upstream and driving a broad wake to either side. It now becomes a race between the scull boat and the freighter as to who will come up on the birds first. The ducks spook and fly. Astemborski stays down and sculls on toward the less flighty geese. Against the shadowy freighter he is a speck on the river. Before the larger vessel's wake can rock him, Astemborski rises and fires. As the boat passes upstream and back into the fog, Astemborski retrieves the birds and returns, once again a lone Eskimo moving out from a foreshortened horizon.

By the end of the nineteenth century, even the deeper Delaware channels near Trenton had begun to silt in, owing to the runoff from deforested river valleys upstream. The U.S. Army Corps of Engineers was charged with dredging, and as larger ships and tankers came to the steelyards and the refineries, the channel was made deeper and uncountable millions of tons of dredge spoil were dug up, sucked up, and dumped along the river shores. In 1910 the river channel was dredged to twelve feet deep. Now it's dredged to forty feet.

"That was all marsh there," Astemborski recalls. "And that was all marsh there." Now a golf course. Now a condominium. Now under a mountain of dredge spoil.

"I started hunting on my own on the river when I was fourteen years old. My father died at the Battle of the Bulge when I was about four years old, so I never had anyone to show me much, so I had to learn it myself. I saved my money for a scullin' rig, and some old-timer in the neighborhood gave me some beat-up old decoys. My mother was always worried about me. She didn't want me to have a gun. 'Your father got killed by a gun. You're going to drown.' So I had to sneak off sometimes. I used to go out to where the Delaware and Rancocas meet—there used to be a big marsh there called Ward's Flat—and on a Saturday you could see a dozen boats pushing at the same time. Ducks were so plentiful, rafts of black ducks, mallards, and pintails in every cove, you didn't even have to put out decoys to get your limit.

"I can still remember one day being out on Ward's Flat with the marsh and the woods around me, and I remember being so happy out there and thinking to myself, 'It's always going to be this way.' I'll never forget that moment. I didn't care if I got any ducks or not, because I knew I'd always be able to be out there doin' these things.

"And then they started dredging and filling the marshes, and in

a few years all the duck hunting and the rail bird shooting, all the
excitement come September—it was like you turned off a switch.
Guys quit gunnin' and sold their boats, put their decoys away. I
know this one decoy maker lived near me, made beautiful decoys—
detailed Delaware River decoys, hollowed out and the feathers
carved out and not just painted on—he threw away dozens. When
the wood got a little low in the fireplace, he'd just toss a decoy in
there.

"Here it had hit me when I was so young that it was always all
goin' to be there the rest of my life because it had been there thousands of years before. And now it was destroyed. It bothered me for
years. I'd just look down there at the river and say, 'Why'd they do
that?' "

After three centuries of hard use, the Delaware River below the
falls at Trenton and its bay was almost used up. Its shellfisheries
were in decline, its shad and sturgeon fisheries decimated, its shorelines often awash with human and industrial waste. Dying industries lined a wreck of a river. All the great stands of oak, hickory,
and pine, its tidewater swamps full of cedar, its marshes full of
roosting seabirds or flocks of migrating waterfowl all but gone.
"I have nowhere seen so many ducks together," said Jasper
Daenckaerts, describing a Delaware wetland in 1679.

> *The water was so black with them that it seemed when you
> looked from the land below upon the water, as if it were a mass
> of filth or turf, and when they flew up there was a rushing and
> vibration of the air like a great storm coming through the trees,
> and even like the rumbling of distant thunder.*

In the lower bay, towns by the name of Caviar, Shellpile, and
Bivalve had boasted of the productivity of the bay's waters. Schooners from as far north as Philadelphia worked the seemingly limit-
less oyster beds. Travelers in the upper Delaware Bay had written
of schools of leaping sturgeon that tipped small vessels. Even dol-
phins once schooled up the bay as far as Philadelphia. Shad made

spring runs to the freshwater reaches of all the bay's tributaries, but the main spawning had taken place in the waters just below the falls, where the streams had by now been channeled, silted in, or vanished altogether. According to an early history of Philadelphia, by 1884:

> *There have been great changes in the face of the country, in its levels and contour, and in the direction and beds of its water-courses since the days of the Swedes and the early Quakers. Some streams have disappeared, some have changed their direction, nearly all have been reduced in volume and depth by natural silt, the annual washing down of hills, by the demands of industry for water-power, the construction of mill-dams and mill-races and bridges, the emptying of manufacturing refuse from factories, saw-pits, and tan-yards, and by the grading and sewerage necessary in the building of a great city. In this process, old landmarks and ancient contours are not respected, the picturesque yields to utility, and the face of nature is transformed to meet the exigencies of uniform grades, levels, and drainage. The Board of Health, the Police Department, the City Commissioners, and the Department of Highways have no bowels of compassion for the antiquarian and the poet. They are slaves of order, of hygiene, of transportation, of progress.*

The effects of the transformation came slowly. Until well into the nineteenth century the fisheries still flourished. Packing houses daily shipped railcars full of oysters out from Port Norris along the lower New Jersey bay shore. Netters still caught sturgeon, stripped the roe, and dumped the carcasses back into the river. Many recall shorelines thick with dead and gutted sturgeon. Between 1896 and 1901, more shad were hauled up in nets along the Delaware River than in any other river along the Atlantic Coast. The catches almost made fishermen and scientists alike forget the decline only a few years before.

According to the 1895 report of the Pennsylvania Fish Commission:

The general impression among the fishermen is that the decrease in the catch during the past four springs is due to the increase of coal oil, gas and bone factories along the Delaware River. The obnoxious poisons and gasses are all turned into the river, killing the young fry; at least we believe that to be the main cause of destruction of millions of young shad.

While dams along the Susquehanna and other rivers early blocked the movement of shad upstream to their spawning grounds, the Delaware had remained mostly free of obstructions, and shad made spring runs as far north as Deposit, New York, some 350 miles from the mouth of the bay. But while the Delaware fish had no concrete impediments to their progress, they had another that eventually proved just as impassable.

"Regarding the pollution of the Delaware," began the Fish Commission research report,

the river below Philadelphia is so impregnated with coal oil that its peculiar flavor can be detected in the shad if they are detained long in the vicinity where the refuse from the coal oil factories is emptied into the water. Whether this is true or not, not one will deny that the discharge of waste into the river from the numerous refineries that are located only a short distance below Philadelphia fills the water with poisonous substances which would probably prevent shad from attempting the ascent of this stream except for the combined instincts of nativity and procreation—impulses so overmastering that nothing but death or impassable barriers will restrain them.

The reporter underestimated the cumulative effect of pollution from the shipyards, coalyards, the chemical factories and refineries. Further, the growing populations of the cities sent human and animal waste flowing out of the sewers and into the river and bay. The catch of shad, up to 15 million pounds for the bay and tidal rivers in 1896, was down to five million pounds in 1904. In 1921 the catch was barely a quarter of a million pounds and was to remain there as the commercial fisheries fast became losing propositions, declined, and nearly died out. The waters had become deadly. By the 1940s some 500 million gallons of raw sewage and untreated industrial waste were being dumped into the Delaware each year. Bacteria in the river, growing on the nutrients, used up the oxygen. Shad and herring attempting spring runs upriver were found dead by the thousands along the river shores of Philadelphia and Camden.

At Hog Island the smell of hydrogen sulfide gas felled shipyard workers. Wastes clogged ships' cooling systems; the waters, slick with greases and oils, corroded ships' hulls. In 1946 the U.S. Fish and Wildlife Service found twenty miles of the upper estuary anoxic from the surface to the bottom. The lack of dissolved oxygen in this stretch of river literally choked the adult fish returning to spawn in the spring. Those that made it through what became known as the "pollution block" to spawn in the cleaner upriver waters more often than not died on their return. And the young of the year, struggling downstream in the late summer to head to sea for the first time, often didn't make it out at all.

The river didn't live here anymore. It was a laughingstock. Ground controllers told pilots that the smell at five thousand feet was the Delaware.

Between 1925 and 1975, Philadelphia lost two-thirds of its industrial jobs. When the great firms went, they left the small firms, the jobbers and suppliers, without anyone to supply. Speculative buyouts brought hope, then the realization that for the most part it was little more than industrial scavenging. Jobs disappeared. The railroad yards shut down. The highways spread into sprawling suburbs. Those who came in on I-95 during the day, driving above the abandoned waterfront, flew off at dusk. It's no wonder the people remaining in Fishtown and Tacony fought the plans to land highway off-ramps in their laps. Why should they provide access to those who abandoned the neighborhood, school, playground, and park? Urban redevelopment, with its bulldozing social-welfare schemes and high-rise white hopes had not yet come. The row houses were still here. But everyone seemed to want a greener place with each house "in ye middle of its platt" with "ground on each side for Gardens or Orchards, or fields." Away from the city, "a good and fruitful land" perhaps a little "nearer the sun" than Philadelphia. So the highway comes anyway, a slash across the already disfigured waterfront.

TRENTON

NINETY-FOUR THOUSAND PEOPLE IN TRENTON, AND SEVEN MILES OF the city stretching along the shore of the Delaware, and on this warm summer night with a nearly full moon overhead, Clifford Zink and I appear to be the only ones on the riverfront. Zink, with a dark wave of hair, a narrow face, and a brooding look, strolls at a meditative pace, stopping at places where he's obviously stopped before, and standing to consider this particular meeting of riverfront, city, and history. His job is historic preservation, his aim to keep past and present in one working whole. But here he sees the elements in restless conjunction. To get here from the center of the Chambersburg section of the city, once the industrial heart, but now a hollow echo, of the vital three-shift-a-day Trenton, we have passed through a dimly lit section of town, lively with black silhouettes and cruising cars, then crossed a four-lane boulevard with a broad median, pulled into an empty parking lot for a hundred or so cars, lit with white and hidden from the highway by a grassy landscaped berm, and then walked beyond a dazzlingly lit mall past the curved facades of a group of four- or five-story office buildings with tinted glass skins. Behind the buildings, sculpted patios open onto a grassy terrace; below the terrace, a wooded slope; down the slope, the Delaware. And yet, as Zink points out, to get here from the dark neighborhood we just drove through, we had to cross highway, landscaped hillock, parking lot, and glass facade. And once here, to get over to the narrow grass path beyond the formal patios, where we can actually see the river running down below this steep, thickly wooded embankment, we have to pass a knee-high brick wall—a wall with no reason for being, but without a break for passage its entire length—so that anyone who wants a look at the river, or has the ambition to sit or stroll on the grass of the embankment, must step over this final embarrassing boundary. Zink marvels at the impediments the architects of Riverview Plaza were able to create between the people of the city and the nearby Delaware.

"I mean, just a bare quarter-mile away are people crowded on hot stoops and street corners, and here we are, in a city of ninety-four thousand people, the only two walking along this part of the river."

Why should they come here? How could they get here? Could kids cross the highway from their neighborhood to come here and fish? There's not even a path leading down the embankment—no steps, no place to launch a canoe, no place to cast a line. The patios themselves are so egregiously well lit that even the moonlight can't penetrate. The whole scene has a whitened pall to it. Neither we nor the buildings cast shadows.

"Look up at the buildings," Zink says. "Those windows facing the river don't even open. You couldn't catch a breeze from the river if you wanted."

Just you and me, Zink repeats. Two out of 94,000 on a hot evening in July. (A car pulls in. Zink and I watch as three teenagers get out, go to the bank's twenty-four-hour cash machine on the corner, make their transaction, pile back into the car, and speed off.)

Down the road, the one old gravel path to the river has been barred. Before that was done, Zink says, we could have driven down to the old wharf and watched the men fish, an old bait dealer standing by in his van and people having beer and coffee while stocking up on herrings to freeze or salt away—the flash of light silver scales in old grout buckets. In the spring the fishermen still come there, immigrant past and present, Italian-, African-, Hispanic-, Anglo-

Americans side by side partaking of the river's still-abundant natural life. But they don't come here to this fabricated "riverview" of
well-ordered elements, a modern, all too peaceable kingdom of
river terrace, office tower, and nearby cash machine, which, during
the day, separate those who only commute into Trenton to work
from those who live in the city and at night separate those who live
in the city from the Delaware. Once the industrial waterfronts
blocked the river. Now, even as ruined piers begin to weather into
natural formations (so much so that along the Hudson River in
New York City, even the fish found the old pilings at last suitable
habitat for feeding and wintering), the modern developer builds for
the "riverview" a "riverwalk" that has little connection with the
river's life, a life that tends to disappear in direct proportion to its
restoration. Cities can find plenty of developers eager to restore the
riverfront for new real estate. Many fewer are interested in restoring natural slopes and grasses along the river, sycamore, river birch,
and jewelweed, whose flowers dangle amidst the undergrowth of
the natural river shore like a crop of tiny Chinese lanterns. Let
developers give support to dragonflies, mayflies, peepers that
screech to distraction in the spring, turtles that bask in the morning
sun. Let developers restore the riverfront with slippery, algae-
covered rocks, driftwood, jetsam, and weedy wrack, a dead catfish
or two for heaving back out into the current—and then spend their
real money lighting the dilapidated schools and streets nearby.

Zink and I saw nothing like this. And Zink took this personally,
for he had in mind something more lively: as lively as the old immigrant men gathered on the pier fishing up herrings, as lively as
the waterfront of the three-shifts-a-day Trenton whose scattered
architectural remnants Zink conjures up into a romance of human
and machine, canal boat and railroad, steelyard and coal barge, a
jazz-age, eight-to-the-bar riverfront of immigrant muscle—African-American, Eastern European, English, German, Slavic, Irish,
Italian—a melting-pot Trenton pouring, molding, and drawing
steel, a Cooper-Hewitt and Roebling Trenton along a river that
would soon all but disappear beneath the shadows of smokestacks
from here to its mouth at Wilmington, a river glimpsed while cross-

ing a steel bridge or lit up under the acetylene spark of a shipyard torch, a river that served to quench the thirst of the mills' fiery maws, to receive the wastes that spilled back out.

We look into the vast, empty gut of the only remaining river-front building of the New Jersey Steel & Iron Company. Built in 1890, it was left standing next to the new glass-skinned office buildings leased to the state. ("In Trenton, architectural and urban planning feeds off the state," Zink asserts.) "This is what's left of the thirty-four-acre site built by Peter Cooper." His voice echoes up into the beams. "This was the machine shop." Within view, the nearly hundred-year-old stone-arched Pennsylvania Railroad Bridge. (Not far upstream is the steel bridge across the river on which is written, "Trenton Makes, The World Takes.") Now the developer of the site has plans to turn the old warehouse into a banquet hall with a waterfront view. Sometimes, Zink explains, to make an attractive public space, it's best to do less.

His face clouds as we turn back to the new buildings. "This," he says stonily, "is an example of thinking of the architect as inner-city savior. But it's architecture out of context." The design is suburban, and it stands in the moonlight white and uncomprehending against the darkening backdrop of a city many would rather not see.

Zink, from the loft of an old Trenton building, aims to help bring the city back into view.

"It is a country that produceth all things for the support and sustenance of man in a plentiful manner," wrote Mahlon Stacy in 1680:

> *It is my judgement, by what I have observed, that fruit trees in this country destroy themselves by the very weight of their fruit. . . .*
>
> *I have seen an apple tree, from a pippin-kernal, yield a barrel of curious cider; and peaches in such plenty that some people took their carts a peach gathering. . . .*

I have seen and known, this summer, forty bushels of cold wheat off one bushel sown. . . .

The cranberries are much like cherries for color and bigness, which may be kept till fruit come again; an excellent sauce is made of them for venison, turkeys and other great fowl, and they are better to make tarts than either gooseberries or cherries. We have them brought to our houses by the Indians in great plenty. . . .

As for venison and fowls, we have great plenty; we have brought home to our houses by the Indians, seven or eight fat bucks a day, and sometimes put by as many, having no occasion for them. . . .

My cousin Revell and I, with some of my men, went last third month into the river . . . to catch herrings, for at that time they came in great shoals into the shallows. . . . And then we began to haul them on shore, as fast as three or four of us could . . . and after this manner, in half an hour, we could have filled a three-bushel sack of as good, large herring as ever I saw. . . .

And though I speak of herrings only, lest any should think we have little of other sorts, we have great plenty of most sorts of fish that I ever saw in England, besides several other sorts that are not known there as rocks, catfish, shads, sheepsheads, sturgeons. . . .

For my part, I like it so well I never had the least thought of returning to England.

The falls of the Delaware were a temperate place, with well-drained loam over sandy clay, easily tilled; beds of Pleistocene clays for making brick and terra-cotta; and a broadleaf deciduous forest—chestnut, oak, poplar, walnut, hickory, black locust, and dogwood—for building materials and fuel.

Mahlon Stacy's enthusiasm brought new settlers, new mills alongside his own on the Assunpink, making iron from pig metal brought downstream from Pennsylvania mines; a toolworks and a smith's shop. John Fitch himself had a shop in Trenton where he repaired the muskets of Continental soldiers, a shop he had to abandon when the British and Hessian troops who occupied the city burned it to the ground, sending the luckless Fitch, now a fugitive, to Philadelphia.

Trenton on the river was at the geographic center of New Jersey, barely thirty-five miles from Raritan Bay, only sixty miles from New York and thirty from Philadelphia.

"The inhabitants of the place," wrote Peter Kalm in 1748, "carried on a small trade with the goods which they got from Philadelphia, but their chief gain consisted in the arrival of the numerous travelers between that city and New York," travelers and merchandise together, by ferry to Trenton, by wagon to New Brunswick and New York, "and both these conveniences belong to people of this town."

Trenton merchants stocked the exotic to provide for the well-heeled traveler—Jamaican spirits, West Indian rum, Madeira, Lisbon, and Tenerife wines, hyson and bohea teas, chintzes, cambrics, muslins, gauze handkerchiefs, black and brown lace, sugar by the box or barrel and, as everywhere, Negroes. Shops also stocked the necessities for a growing town: window glass, copper teakettles, pots and pans, padlocks, strap hinges, fire shovels, hammers, chisels, rat traps, pipe bar, cedar boards and shingles, dry goods, and Windsor chairs. By 1790, Trenton had two hosiers, two tailors, two staymakers, one shoemaker, two hatters, two gold- and silver-smiths, a gunsmith, a clock and watch maker, three blacksmiths, one doctor, a druggist, several lawyers, a hairdresser, a tobacconist, a bookbinder, and an auctioneer. The colonial legislature, citing the city's central location, made it the state capital.

In 1806 the first bridge, a thousand feet long and thirty-six feet wide, crossed the Delaware near the falls. In 1815 a wing dam built out into the river provided a lock large enough to convey the largest Durham boat. This diverted river traffic to the Trenton shore. Thus, more mills: flour mills, sawmills, paper mills, and soon cotton mills in a nascent textile industry along the lower Assunpink.

In 1830 the Delaware-Raritan Canal allowed cargo to make the trip to New Brunswick by water: forty-three miles long, seventy-five to eighty feet wide, seven to eight feet deep,

It begins at the confluence of the Crosswicks Creek and the Delaware, at Bordentown, and runs thence, through the city of Trenton and the valley of the Assunpink, crossing the creek by the noble stone culvert, to Lawrence's Meadows, whence it passes into the valley of Stony Brook; thence down the right side thereof, one mile S. of Princeton, to the junction of Stony Brook with the Millstone river; thence across the river by an aqueduct of eight arches, and by the right bank of the river to the Raritan River; thence along the right bank of the Raritan to New Brunswick, where it unites with the tide.

A feeder canal ran (and still runs) down along the Delaware from Lambertville. This network of waterways made it possible to route all the right raw materials—coal, timber, pig iron, flour—from New York and the upper Delaware Valley, from Philadelphia and from the west, into and out of Trenton. Factories set up shop along the canal and feeders, making their merchandise accessible for the world's taking. Only the lack of steady water power hampered the growth of larger industries, and so, to improve upon the ineffectual slope of the natural falls (which had so disappointed Jasper Daenckaerts), in 1831 the Trenton Delaware Falls Company began construction of the Trenton Water Power. A wing dam diverted water from Scudder's Falls, some seven miles upstream of the city, and sent it down along a riverbank millrace (sometimes used as a log flume for timber coming to mill) across the Assunpink by aqueduct and then through downtown Trenton in several raceways before emptying again into the Delaware. New mills built along the artificial falls finally brought heavy industry to the Delaware riverfront. The Eagle Anvil Works, for example, the first anvil manufacturer in the country, came down from Newport, Maine, in 1849 and over the next years increased its production from one thousand to fifteen thousand anvils a year.

Two years before, at the Delaware waterfront on South Warren Street, near the end of the Water Power, Peter Cooper, flush with capital, had established the Trenton Iron Company, which became the New Jersey Steel and Iron Company (the nation's largest), making wrought-iron beams (which still hold up New York City's Cooper Union and the Capitol dome in Washington, D.C.) and cast-iron building facades. Cooper, intrigued by the wire cable work of immigrant German engineer John A. Roebling, recommended that Roebling bring his western Pennsylvania cable works to Trenton. Cooper and his son-in-law and partner Abraham Hewitt planned to supply the steel wire which Roebling would twist into cable. In 1849, Roebling set up shop where South Broad Street crossed the canal and railroad. By 1864 coal could travel by rail down from the upper Lehigh River valley across the Delaware to Trenton, providing fuel even when the canals froze.

In 1890 Trenton had forty ironworking industries, fifteen cotton and woolen industries, fifty-nine clay and brick works, and thirty woodworking industries. The entrepreneurs, the "civic capitalists" as Trenton historian John Cumbler calls them, the steelmakers, the china makers (Lenox himself, for one), textile and rubber manufacturers, ran their industries as well as the city banks, school board, libraries, YMCA, and the Trenton Country Club. The Roeblings not only made steel cable and bridges, but also owned the Trenton Traction Company, which carried commuters around the city.

Ferdinand Roebling, John Roebling's financier son, was a director of the Trenton Hall and Building Association, the New Jersey Wire Cloth Company, the Otis Elevator Company, the United Power and Transportation Company, the Trenton Brass & Machine Company, the Inter-State Railways Company, the Public Service Corporation of New Jersey, the National Copper Bank of New York, the Mechanics & Metals Bank, and the Mechanics National Bank of Trenton. He was trustee and first president of the Trenton Free Public Library. Ferdinand's brother, Charles, the melancholy engineer whose son died on the *Titanic*, was the largest stockholder in the Pennsylvania Railroad, which passed by the

Roebling's front door, and which held the 999-year lease on the canal lands.

The workers of Trenton—English, German, Irish, Italian, Jewish, Slovakian, Magyar, African-American—established their own immigrant villages within walking distance of the factory doors: church, school, corner bar, corner grocer, social club—Ancient Order of Hibernians, Sons of Italy, Garibaldi Society, Dante Lyceum, Moose, Elks, and Odd Fellows—and union hall: Central Labor Union, American Federation of Labor, Knights of Labor, and Amalgamated Rubber Workers. Trenton was a union town with an unwavering faith that what was good for Trenton workers was good for Trenton. Who bought the row homes that surrounded the factories, spent in Trenton shops, drank up in Trenton bars? Between 1860 and 1890, Trenton's population grew from 17,000 to 57,000. Manufacturers and workers alike became starstruck by the city's expanding industrial universe. And nowhere more than in the area of Trenton known as Chambersburg, near the terminus of the canal, around the expanding Roebling plant. By 1920, some twenty percent of Trenton's workers worked for John Roebling's Sons.

It was, as one author of the period has it, the wire age:

> *wire mattresses, trolley lines, bonding wire between rails, telephone, telegraph, wire rope for elevators, wire in locks, wire in garters, airplane frames strung with wire, wire rope for coal mining, wire to bale and bind the broom, cooking pots, baby's toys, mother's corset, hairpins and needles and safety pins. . . . Modern life, in all its intricate bearings, runs on wire. Wire everywhere; in the heavens above, the earth beneath and the waters under the earth. In all the legerdemain of science, which has put nature in bondage, wire is the indispensable agent.*

Cancel all the orders for wire tomorrow, "and the world would stop stockstill," for "wire holds the world together." And Roebling was synonymous with wire "in every language under the sun."

Six thousand people lived in Trenton when Roebling arrived, but it had a river, a canal, and a railroad. Roebling installed a twelve-horsepower steam engine and a railway to draw the strands of wire. The accounting was simple: for the first year of operation, ending June 1, 1850, Roebling's balance sheet looked like this:

Invested in Real and Personal Estate:	*$20,000*
Raw material used, including fuel:	
300 tons Iron	*$35,000*
400 tons Coal	*$1,200*
Employees:	*20 males; no females*
Average monthly cost of labor:	*$500*
Annual product:	
250 tons wire rope, valued at	*$40,000*

Like Disston or any of the other Fishtown, Assunpink, or Delaware industrialists, Roebling's fortunes began with his understanding of the materials—the chemistry of the hearth, the physics of the cable—with which he worked. Industry was more than simply the nature of capital. John Roebling had made the first wire rope in 1841 to replace the hemp hawsers that then drew canal boats near his home in western Pennsylvania. Roebling developed the machinery to twist the wire strands into a rope that would not wear out. His first major suspension bridge spanned the Monongahela in 1846, and he built four suspension aqueducts along the Delaware and Hudson Canal in 1848. He designed his own work and wrote careful analyses of the work of others. He even prided himself on his humorless disposition, blaming it on his Hegelian leanings (he claimed, although there is doubt about it, to have attended Hegel's lectures while a student in Germany). He considered himself as much a metaphysician as an engineer, who, his son Washington recounts, had written "Roebling's Theory of the Universe" in an age of universal theories, when the raw materials and the spirit that shaped them were presumed to be of one and the same nature. In 1848, Edgar Allan Poe began his *Eureka* in order to speak of the "Physical, Metaphysical and Mathematical—of the Material and Spiritual Universe:—of its Essence, its Origin, its Creation, its

Present Condition and its Destiny." To Roebling, the suspension bridge might be all of these things.

The Roebling production grew steadily. By manufacturing his own steel wire he became one of Cooper's thornier competitors. The 1870 accounts, a year after John Roebling's death, showed a 250-horsepower steam engine and

2,500 tons Coal	*$17,000*
800 tons Iron	*$88,000*
50,000 feet Lumber	*$1,250*
20,000 acids	*$800*
Employees:	*75 males over 16 years old*
	10 children and youths
Total annual wages:	*$52,000*
Production:	
700 tons wire rope, valued at	*$250,000*

The sons, Washington, Charles, and Ferdinand, took over the business, and with bridge work and new contracts for telegraph wire and cable-car wire, the Chambersburg works grew to twenty-five acres. Washington, who completed the Brooklyn Bridge work, was more of his father's temperament, an engineer deeply involved with the development of his craft and recording, with sometimes greater pride than accuracy, the Roebling history. In his later years he became a fixture in Trenton, living in his house on West State Street until he died at eighty-nine in 1926. And though Roebling and Trenton had thrived, much of the metaphysics had begun to go out of steelmaking. "In 1898," wrote Washington Roebling, "the United States Steel began its career by buying up all the cheap steel properties that were lying around for sale on account of the hard times." U.S. Steel was one of the companies shaped by J. P. Morgan and Andrew Carnegie, the dons of conglomeration at the end of the century. Cooper's son, Edward, sold out to them in 1904. Roebling's Sons, by dint of disagreements among the brothers themselves, had refused more than one buyout offer. But with U.S.

Steel ready to squeeze them on the price of steel, the Roeblings realized that the only way to keep ahead was to control the entire process themselves. Without enough room in Trenton, Charles, who brother Washington wrote "had to do the actual work of creating the realities," in 1904 bought 250 acres of farmland with two miles of Delaware riverfront some ten miles south of Trenton. On this rise above the Delaware, Roebling proceeded to build an industrial Xanadu, a state-of-the-art, fully integrated facility: open-hearth steel furnaces to mold ingots, and mills to roll the ingots into smaller billets, the billets into rods, and to pull the rods into wires. The railroad line that ran through the nearby rural Kinkora station was brought in to the site, connecting each mill and process. ("The Pennsylvania Railroad people were delighted with the prospect of a real business in place of peaches and potatoes.") While the Trenton works had grown without any plan, at Kinkora, wrote Washington, "everything proceeded in a quiet, orderly manner."

All that was needed were workers. So, along with the new furnaces, mills, and rail sidings, Charles built houses, a general store, a bakery, a drugstore, and a hotel. (To those who objected to a bar in the hotel, Charles, the realist, replied that there was "no use in trying to make a mollycoddle out of a mill man." Whiskey "not gilt-edged but decent" would be served.) The Roeblings provided water, gas, electricity, sewers, drainage, streets, watchmen, policemen, doctors, a jail, a theater (with a Brooklyn Bridge curtain across the stage), a public school, and, of course, a park. "The man who owns a town," lamented Washington, "often wishes he had never been born." Kinkora became known as Roebling-on-the-Delaware.

This was no noble experiment. As one early Roebling biographer put it, "No utopian plans were cherished. There was no thought of establishing a model town or making a philanthropic experiment. The project was viewed purely from a commercial standpoint and apart from sentiment." Separated from Trenton, labor strife seemed more distant than ten miles. Workers were less apt to kick up when their boss was also their landlord. From all reports, Roebling was a spirited place with a waiting list of those eager to move from Chambersburg.

But in 1931, despite a contract for the George Washington Bridge, the wire age seemed about to close, and rising wages met depressed markets. Production slowed. The huge plants needed work to survive. There were layoffs. But just when an offer from one conglomerate or another might have been welcome, war production, as it had at Tacony and Philadelphia, revived the wire business, or at least arrested the decline. Roebling, in the 1940s, built up its largest workforce since World War I, more than eight thousand, and Chambersburg—Italian, Polish, Magyar, and Romanian—worked a marvelous three shifts a day.

But not for long. Another few years of running the factories at full capacity made the need for recapitalization even more obvious. What was state of the art in 1904 was inefficient by 1950. The Trenton steel, pottery, rubber, and textile works were also aging, but neither profits nor the markets recommended retooling. And the Assunpink entrepreneurs who founded the businesses had begun leaving them to their offspring as heavily taxed, cash-poor legacies. In 1952 the Roebling family sold out to the Colorado Fuel and Iron Company. Like an old car, however, the company was worth more in parts than whole, and gradually Colorado Fuel found ways to take from Roebling what it needed and sell off the rest. With cheap land available outside the cities, and the river no longer needed for transportation, new owners with no sentiment attached to the places in which the companies grew up simply saw no reason not to close them down. This was the Thomas Mellon Evans school: maximize your short-term profits instead of regearing. This, says Zink, was the ultimate betrayal of the workers.

Evans himself had been circling Trenton. The H. K. Porter Company bought Trenton's largest rubber industry, only to close the Trenton operation and sell it off to finance a new Ohio plant. By 1968, Colorado Fuel closed down the shell that was now Trenton Roebling. In 1972, the Crane Company took over Colorado Fuel and, with it, the Roebling facility on the Delaware. Crane had suffered its own bitter takeover battle, a battle it had lost in 1959 to

H. K. Porter chairman Thomas Mellon Evans. (And for almost the next thirty years, Evans chaired both companies. In 1980, *Fortune* magazine named him one of America's ten toughest bosses, "a genius" who "has his own ideas and pursues them." One executive called him a "corporate Jaws.") In 1973, a year after selling off Disston, Evans, this time as chairman of Crane, closed down the wire rope plant at Roebling, leaving a company town without a company and abandoning what Zink calls "an unparalleled industrial landscape—a kind of museum of the last hundred years of industrial design."

Crafts Creek runs north toward the Delaware, winding through the broad marsh east of Roebling. The river has made its turn beyond the falls, and the land is sandy plain. In building the town:

> *The whole tract, originally little more than an arid waste of sand, has been gradually transformed into a fertile and pleasing prospect. The sand dunes have been levelled, the ground graded, new soil introduced and shade trees planted. The mills were completed first and occupy a space in the eastern section of some hundred acres, about twenty feet above the level of the river, while the city proper is built to the west of the mills upon a hill about twice as high. To the north of the town a park has been laid out which commands a pleasing view of the river in both directions for several miles.*

Acres of marsh were filled in (some million cubic yards of fill altogether, says Zink). The river supplied water—at one point Roebling used more water for its operations than all the rest of Trenton combined—and the riverfront was used for the dumping of slag and ashes.

At the chained gate to the plant, a few cars are parked outside the guard's gatehouse. The scene is not much different than at many of the abandoned industrial sites along the river where suspicious guards offer cagey greetings to let you know immediately that they have no information that would be of any use to you. At Roebling, however, a sign speaks for itself:

ROEBLING STEEL CO. SUPERFUND SITE
HAZARDOUS SUBSTANCES PRESENT

I had made official entreaties to the government agencies in charge, but my requests for a tour of the site were not so much denied as officially and peremptorily ignored. Zink, hired to do an assessment of the industrial architecture, had seen the whole place—after a course in hazardous-waste training. Technicians in sterile white suits were taking samples of the air and water from the unmarked barrels and lagoons of unidentified sludges.

"It's incredibly intact," says Zink. In some buildings it looks as if the workers left after their last shift and they closed the doors and sealed the plant." Desks, files, and drawers are still full. "It's been frozen in time."

The grasses have grown so tall that from where we stand we can only see the tops of buildings: the sawtoothed roof of the wire mill, the machine shop under the water tower.

While Roebling had left twenty acres of slag heaps twenty feet high in place of the marsh and sand dunes along the Delaware (the town is just across and downstream of Penn's Manor), Colorado Fuel brought in new processes and upped the industrial ante, spilling copper, zinc, and cadmium wastes, acid solutions, sludges, oil, solvents, and baghouse dust—the contaminated soot from electric-arc steel furnaces—into the river. Ordered in 1968 by the New Jersey Department of Health to cease polluting the Delaware and construct a plant to treat its 15 million gallons a day of wastewater, Colorado Fuel continued to work for the next four years without the new plant in operation.

New investigations of the site found unlined sludge lagoons, contaminated groundwater, and illegal storage of hazardous wastes. In 1979, with Colorado Fuel gone, the business reopened with financial assistance from federal and state economic development agencies; the New Jersey Department of Environmental Protection and the Delaware River Basin Commission gave their blessing to an updated waste-water treatment plant. The plant was never operated or monitored properly. Only a year later the site was named one of the most hazardous in New Jersey. The state's requests that the new company clean up the site went unheeded and it, too, soon shut down. In 1982 Roebling made the National Priorities List of most contaminated sites in the country, and since then some $15 million has been spent on studies and small cleanups. The major work has yet to begin, and according to the U.S. Environmental Protection Agency, "No potentially responsible party [known to the government lawyers as PRPs] accepted responsibility or liability for hazardous substances at the Roebling Steel site"—not for the 757 drums, 106 rusting tanks, 183 transformers with PCB-contaminated oil, the fifty-two railroad cars of slag and dry sludge, the pits and sumps, the chemical piles and lagoons, and the baghouse dust contaminated with cadmium, chromium, and lead that has already contaminated the soil in and around the site and, worse, the soil of the playground at Roebling Park.

The road around the plant perimeter leads into the town, the warning signs posted at several places along the way. Gate number one, the main entrance to the plant, looks like an old railroad ticket office, and the town itself—the small two-family houses in neat rows on straight and level tree-lined streets—looks like it was laid out on a train board. The small front yards are well groomed, and planters of flowers hang in the small enclosed porches. It is a clean, quiet town with little traffic—only a couple of streets lead into or out of town—but as close as it is to the river, it has little relation to it. The town didn't begin at the waterfront and build back from it; the slope to the river is too steep. And while the people of Roebling may take umbrage, I mean it as a compliment to say the little town, with its pleasant town green and Roebling pharmacy, general store and old savings and loan, its Hungarian bakery, its Roebling assembly hall and theater (which still has the Brooklyn Bridge curtain), its Roebling Athletic Field and Scout camp and Roebling School and VFW, its still-unshakable pride at being descended from the Roebling that built the Brooklyn Bridge and cabled the

Golden Gate, could be, all of it, a wonderful small Trenton neighborhood. But, as Zink points out, it was a neighborhood apart, and so never experienced the changes that came to Chambersburg.

"Imagine," says Zink, "going down the canal in the 1880s, with the steam engines going by and the black smoke rising out of all the stacks of these buildings and the white steam out of the factory steam heads and thousands of people working—every shop working." Hard to imagine in these leaner times in Trenton.

The railroad tracks still run by the front gate of the Roebling works in Trenton. The Belgian block paving of the millyard shows through the blistered asphalt drive. Grass and purple vetch have pushed through the cracks. Down between the formidable brick facades runs the old canal, filled in by the WPA in 1936 and now overgrown with high grasses and littered with old tires. Zink and I walk along South Broad Street by the low sheds of the old Cooper Trenton Iron Company. While Roebling invested in new buildings to house expanding operations, U.S. Steel never modernized its Cooper plants. What's preserved is of an older vintage, with a craftsmen's village look to it. At the corner of Hamilton Avenue are the 1853 pattern shop, wire mill, and warehouse by which the railroad spur passes.

On Hamilton Avenue still stands the long, two-story, 1871 wire mill, with Palladian details, brick pilasters, and arches along the front. Next to it, the wood-framed 1860 power house, and the 1879 main office with its High Victorian detail in the brick eaves and the decorative turnbuckles. We stand alone in a nineteenth-century landscape. One can look around and not see a sight less than a hundred years old. "This is the finest industrial streetscape in the city," says Zink. "We want to save it."

For whom? We have not seen a soul on our walk along this whole derelict street. We might as well be on a Hollywood set.

"Thousands and thousands of immigrants established themselves here," Zink says as we continue to Clark Street and walk past the Roebling's Sons wire rope shops, the steel-framed buildings with concrete walls, flat roofs, and sawtoothed skylights.

"They worked hard. These were dangerous jobs and there was little compensation for losses, even of lives. But they bought houses, raised families, and dedicated themselves to the education of their children."

With each new bridge contract (after the Brooklyn Bridge came the wire work for the Williamsburg and Manhattan bridges, the George Washington and the Golden Gate) Roebling invested in new buildings. Housing the massive machinery, the engines and the railworks, called for a new kind of architecture, but what seemed to come to mind was Greek temple or basilica church in masonry and red brick—archway, gabled roof with monitor clerestories and sturdying pilasters. For the makers, these machine shops were buildings of high purpose. Red brick on brownstone foundations with bluestone sills, the bluestone brought down from the upper Delaware, where once the trees were cleared the ridges were quarried, and the stone sent off on the canals to make New York City sidewalks or Roebling sillwork.

We enter the 1890 machine shop. Inside, it is the classic cathedral of industry with its long, two-story nave and overhead traveling cranes. A 1901 addition tripled its size, making it a city block long and the city's largest machine shop. Around the corner, Zink points toward a bank of tall windows and talks about the marvelous invention within. Built in 1893 by Charles Roebling, it is a four-story, eighty-ton machine designed to lay one-and-a-half-inch wire rope for cable cars, turning out ropes thirty thousand feet long without a splice. Although the Trenton Roebling Community Development Corporation got the National Society of Mechanical Engineers to designate the machine a National Engineering Landmark, Zink won't be satisfied until it's open for viewing and inspiring a new Trenton generation. Here is his vision:

Nine o'clock. Bright banners snap in the breeze while in a yellow schoolbus drives into the cobblestone millyard. . . . The large doors swing open and the children enter "the Invention Factory." It is a place like none they have seen before. . . .

On the other side of the Discovery Courtyard, merchants open-ing their shops put out pots of flowers, merchandise, carts, and displays. . . .

When lunchtime arrives, office workers, local residents shop-ping in the complex, and visitors fill the Brooklyn Bridge Res-taurant. . . .

A staff member relaxes on a bench, watching the color, move-ment, and action . . . the diversity of the people . . . a busy, happy, abundant place."

Zink would bring people back to Trenton. Not to come in during the day and leave in the evening, but to stay, to spend, to live. He'd preserve Trenton Roebling, create an industrial museum, office space, shops. . . . From the new highway that follows the path of the old canal, Zink envisions people seeing a vital new village. "This is not pie in the sky," he assures me with a trace of indignation when I seem skeptical. "This is grounded in the current reality."

"Trenton is a livable place, a livable place on a livable scale. We can't keep moving on. We have to stay and rebuild."

Zink's plan, for instance, includes a supermarket, which would hardly seem revolutionary, except that the city of Trenton, the capital of the state of New Jersey, doesn't even have a major supermarket—or bookstore. In 1890, Trenton had 104 wholesale and heavy retail goods dealers, thirty-six dry-goods dealers, forty-seven bakers, fifty-four butchers, five fishmongers, forty-eight gro-cers, twenty-two milk dealers, and twenty-three produce and fruit markets. It also had three booksellers, two bookbinders, three en-gravers, thirteen printers and publishers, thirty-five tailors, thirty-three dressmakers, seventeen milliners, eighty-five barbers, and seventy-two boot- and shoemakers. Trenton residents now have to drive out of the city to the suburban shopping plazas. Zink cites a study that found Trenton residents spent over a hundred million dollars shopping in suburban food stores alone. (As the highways sprawl, new shopping plazas open up, leaving older plazas wanting for tenants, renting to adult book shops and karate academies.)

At a small symposium on the future of the city, historian John Cumbler and the city's director of housing and development talk of rebuilding small, of forgetting the hope of returning to the industrial Trenton of the past. Trenton, says Cumbler, will no longer make for the world to take. Industrial corporations sabotaged the city. Neither hand-wringing nor wishful thinking will bring them back. The efforts to revive the city must come from within. Cumbler's message was: face facts—no computer giant or Japanese automaker is coming in to redeem Trenton. Rebuild a green Trenton, he says, build a botanic garden, farm vegetables and flowers on vacant lots.

"Trenton's population is for the most part poorly trained," says Cumbler. "They need jobs which will put food on the table and pay the rent; it would be nice if they could earn enough to live above the poverty level, and that is the kind of target that the city should be aiming at."

A hard fall for a proud city. Cumbler draws fire from Jack Washington, a Trenton teacher and writer of a history of the city's African-American community, and himself the only African-American in the small audience. He calls Cumbler's vision "chicken-little." Are Trenton's students, mostly African-American, going to be inspired by botanic gardens, by farming vacant lots, greening the city? "Is it a self-fulfilling prophecy to say that's all we can do? Can we move into the computer-chip industry by building gardens?"

In 1867 Trenton's African-Americans held a Negro Sufferage Convention "pledging ourselves to the eradication of the word white from the Constitution of New Jersey by every legal and honorable means." It was a fiercely political community and like many other city wards had its share of singular characters, like the dapper newspaper editor R. Henri Herbert, who ran a baseball team for white youths, and Theodore "King Poke" Hutchins, who hosted thirteenth-ward politics out of his saloon and gambling house on Belvidere Street until he let one too many white women drink at his bar. Trenton was home to the Cuban Giants, one of the best African-American baseball teams in the country, which drew fans by the thousands to its Chambersburg grounds. But African-Americans had hardly had the chance to participate in the rise of Trenton. Were they now being asked to accept the limited horizons of a Trenton that so many whites had abandoned?

Here at the ClinMott Inn, at the corner of Mott and South Clinton, across the street from the red brick complex of the Roebling works, they used to serve nightcaps to the workers coming off and eye-openers to those coming on, and they finally had to install a circular bar to accommodate the crowds standing four to five deep at the shift changes. No more. The little tavern sits in the shadow of forty-five monumental acres of abandoned manufactory (twenty-five Roebling's and twenty Cooper's). There are still signs of life at the edge of Roebling's defunct universe: Italian restaurants on one side, a new Liberian-American restaurant on the other.

The scale of this side of Trenton is still of a river town. Small two-story row houses clustered between factory and church: in south Trenton, St. Stephen's Hungarian Catholic Church; Magyar Reformed; Holy Cross Polish Catholic, with its attached school and convent, nearby the Pozca Market; the Romanian Reformed Church; St. Mary's Greek Catholic Church, school, and convent. Outside, women in housedresses sit on lawn chairs in tidy postage-stamp yards where plots of sunflowers dominate.

In Chambersburg, next to the ClinMott as dusk falls, we talk with a family on their front porch, which faces a brick facade with a fading Roebling name. They sit on the small porch in lawn chairs, smoking cigarettes and tamping them out into an empty coffee can. They are proud of the Italians, like themselves, who have stayed. But they see themselves as the end of the line. They tell us how they harass the hookers who have recently begun to stand on South Clinton in the evening, and they ask who in their right mind would return.

They treat Zink with gentle bemusement. Why keep all this? Tear it all down. This is 1990. Put up something new.

Over a bottle of the red wine in the little dining room at the back of the ClinMott, Tony Bosso, whose father opened the place in

1943, says the same thing. "Tear it down. Will whatever you're making bring me business?"

Zink says that in time it will. Bosso says he's out of time. He's selling the place. As he walks off into the kitchen, Zink assures me that Bosso's been selling the place since he's known him. He survives, and other places nearby still thrive, on the people who stay, who return, who feel that what Trenton had to offer can be had nowhere else. We have fine pasta and blue crabs, more wine and bread, and close down the little dining room. Out in the warm air we bid Bosso a good night. The streets are empty. We drive off to find the river.

Part Three

LAST HAUL

 FERDINAND ROEBLING, JR., BORN IN 1878, BECAME president of John A. Roebling's Sons Company in 1926 after the death of his long-lived uncle Washington. His sister, Augusta Henrietta, born in 1875, married William Townsend White on February 4, 1903. They had two children, Margaret Roebling White and Ferdinand Roebling White. Ferdinand was born in 1907, graduated Princeton University in the class of 1931, and became vice-president of the Union Mills Paper Manufacturing Company and the Universal Paper Bag Company on the Delaware River north of Trenton, in the village of New Hope, Pennsylvania. In the years following the decline of traffic on the Delaware-Raritan Canal, whose paths and feeders ran through New Hope and Lambertville, twin towns across the river from each other, the Union Mill became the sole support of many families.

As Fred Lewis, who worked his whole working life at the mill, recalls it, Mrs. Augusta White had sworn that as long as she lived the mill would never close. Then, "on the eighteenth of December, 1970, Ferdy called the fella who was production superintendent and said 'put up the notice that we're closin' down for Christmas vacation, but change it so it says we're closin' down indefinitely.' And it was only a week after that we found out they closed it up to get a tax write-off to settle Mrs. White's estate."

Lewis's father, William, began working at the mill in 1918. Lewis joined him in 1936. And then there had been all the other families of Mechanic Street in Lambertville: Pete Eisler—Donny's dad— and the Everts, each family with some dozen children.

"Christ," blurts Donny Eisler, "that was when New Hope had charm. That was when we'd all swim bare-assed and on Halloween you upset everybody's outhouse, and put their gates up on their roof and rang the school bell.''

It was a time when, come April first, the Lewises and many of the other men of New Hope and Lambertville took ten weeks off from their work at the mill to fish the Delaware for shad. Camps of fishermen crowded each shore. They used long nets called haul seines. With one end harnessed to a horse on shore, and the rest stacked into the stern of a three-oared wooden boat, they rowed out into the river, paying out net. When they reached two-thirds of the way across the river, they began to drift downstream with the current—this is above the falls at Trenton, so there's no longer any tide—the moving wall of net turning back the upstream-moving fish. A net's length downstream from the start of their drift they turned back to shore and began to row hard, hoping to reach shore and close the net around the fish before they could fall back downstream and out of range. As the boat came in, the horse holding the shore end of the net walked down to meet it. If the set was right, the fish would be trapped in a slowly closing impoundment that formed a U whose top ends met on shore.

A reporter for *Harper's New Monthly Magazine* in 1872 described the final moments of a haul:

> *The half-moon area of the water inside the line of corks now begins to show an agitated appearance. At first occasional irregular waves and dull movements of patches of water, and later, little quick swirls and ruffled wavelets, cover the surface. Now and then a large fish makes a rapid curve shoreward, and out again. Soon the splashing begins, and increases as the mass of fish is pulled and crowded on the beach, until spray obscures them, and whoever ventures too near is sprinkled with flying drops, and spangled with adhering scales.*

The number of fish in a haul could be two, or could be a thousand. At the Lewis fishery in Lambertville the men might make a dozen or more hauls in a day.

"The longest day I ever had on the river,'' a still-lean and lively

Fred Lewis recalls, "was in 1933. It began at midnight on Sunday and lasted until four o'clock Wednesday morning. We caught thirty thousand pounds of shad."

The men crated the fish, always sold by the hundred—"plus twenty-five jiffins," or small males called "buck" shad, thrown in—and got it onto the 4:00 P.M. train for New York's Fulton Fish Market. The price might be as high as forty cents a pound for roe shad and twenty cents a pound for bucks. But the prices could fall quickly. By the end of April the shad runs in the Hudson and Connecticut rivers glutted the Fulton market and the price might be cut in half, or the market might simply accept no more fish.

The log of the Lewis fishery, kept to exacting standards since 1926 by the diminutive Mrs. Lewis, records the decline of the Delaware that began at the turn of the century. The numbers of fish always fluctuate, from several hundred in a year to a few thousand, but then the river fishery fails utterly:

1947	*1,258 shad*
1948	*43 shad*
1949	*3 shad*
1950	*9 shad*
1951	*25 shad*
1952	*27 shad*
1953	*0 shad*

During the war, Lewis recalls, the shad bore the effects of munitions manufacturing and wartime production from the upstream mines. "You knew when you got a high river out of the Lehigh. It was black. The whole river was black. In fact, we used to go down there below the mill where they fished and pick the coal out of the gravel that came down the river."

But Lewis continued to haul out the net, if only to make a few dozen passes each season to see if he might conjure up some fish.

In the meantime, the first faltering pollution-fighting efforts—this was twenty years before the passage of the Federal Water Pollution Control Act—began to break up the pollution block on the tidal river. At least at times in the early spring the river might have enough oxygen for the adult shad to make it upstream past Philadelphia to their spawning grounds. When, in the early sixties, Fred Lewis began to catch shad once more, no one knew where these surviving fish had found safe haven. But it soon became evident that the fish that spawned farthest upstream had the greatest chance of surviving and that Hancock, New York, some three hundred miles upstream, at the confluence of the two major streams that meet to form the Delaware, had become the shad's last best spawning grounds. Their young reached the tidal river in the late fall, when cooler weather and fall rains had washed out enough of the pollution to allow them passage out to the bay and ocean.

How quickly did the clean-up efforts become apparent? Between 1958 and 1983 the depletion of oxygen in the tidal fresh waters of the river was cut in half. Here's the Lewis log:

1959	*27 shad*
1960	*6 shad*
1961	*90 shad*
1962	*250 shad*
1963	*3,983 shad!*
1964	*1,646 shad*

More important, the number of shad per haul at Lewis's beach increased through the 1970s to more than twice that of most years since 1925. By 1980, 147 hauls landed 1,910 fish. In 1928 it took Lewis and his father more than five hundred hauls to catch that same number of fish.

This is considered a great victory. But it took half a century to comprehend the problems of development and human and industrial waste on the river and decide to deal with them. Then it took practically another half-century to get the damage halfway cleaned up. Over that time it cost some one and a half billion dollars to increase the dissolved oxygen level in the Delaware River at Philadelphia by barely two milligrams per liter, the minimum needed for fish to breathe.

Now New Hope and Lambertville are changed places. The trains no longer run to New York City. The Union Mill's been converted into riverfront condominium apartments. The workingman's town of large families and kids skinny-dipping in the creeks has become a village for tourists. Not many children play on Mechanic Street these days; it's mainly curio shops. Factory outlet shopping has moved in. And Fred Lewis is the last commercial fisherman left on the Delaware River north of the falls at Trenton.

During the spring I worked on this book and spent some time fishing with the Lewis crew, I learned that if I wanted to get anything else done, I had to stay away from Fred Lewis's little island. For it was the only way I could stay out of my fishing boots and rubber jacket, and deny myself the pleasures of standing waist deep in the river amid the flashing spray of silver "spangled and adhering scales." It made no difference whether it was a great, musky, warming, smell-of-greening, red-sun-setting spring dusk or a cool, misting-rain, dark-river evening in which we worked in a haze of hatching gnats, one hated to leave the place after the hauls were through. Between sets, and after, the crew—which had its core of Terry Fletcher, Norton Hartpence, Johnny Eisler, Fred's nephew Donnie Lewis, and Fred's grandson Steve Meserve—stomped up the red stairs of little white wood-framed fishing shack with "F. Lewis" carved into a wood board on the door and sat by the woodstove having a beer that came from a tap on the side of the little refrigerator. The work, the company, and the beer would also be generously shared with some like myself, biologists such as Art Lupine, John O'Herron, and Mark Chittendon, who had a special interest in the river and the shad and came looking for a feel of the art of the net.

"Oh, when we get done fishin' I may not see the rest of them for a year," Fred says. "But when I call them, they'll be ready."

Who would not be? With the forsythia and daffodils in bloom around the shack, warblers in the budding trees, mallards paddling in the shallow creek that separates the little oak- and sycamore-shaded island from the mainland, watching the oarsmen push off, row the net out into the river—one of the crew now holds it harnessed to the shore and walks the well-worn horse path—the setting sun behind them swimming in a roseate glow, a Hart Benton life and sky, turning by the swim rock as they call it, drifting, then rowing again into shore. And every evening a little audience crosses the wooden bridge and comes down to the beach to see the haul come in. And as they reach shore and grab the lead line and begin to haul, hand over hand,

> *As the bunt of the seine nears the shore, silence prevails, partly because it is a critical moment, and the orders with regard to handling the net must be promptly obeyed, and partly from the common hope that it may be a great haul of fish. This hope that the next haul may be the fortunate one is long sustained, and as often revived as each disappointment is met. The fisherman's imagination populates the waters with wandering shoals of fishes, which may at any moment crowd into the seine berth and reward the hopes which the fortune of the season as not before fulfilled.*

Such hopes, as the *Harper's* reporter put it, not only belong to the fishermen. On Lewis's island the people press in as close as they can get, and as the net closes, and the thrashing of the waters begins, it never fails to bring a great rising murmur of excitement. And each silvery fish we pull out of the net is greeted with a cheer, as if, like firemen who had arrived on the scene in our boots and coats, we had just pulled another kitten to safety. But the cheering was for the fish, not for us, and mostly for this irresistibly uplifting glittering show of abundance.

Lewis himself likes the show, and plays the part for the reporters and television crews who come out each spring to view the unchanging tableau and to report on the great strides made in cleaning up the once-ruined river and Lewis's part in it. For many years Lewis tagged and released half the fish caught on his shore so that they might continue their spawning runs and provide scientists with clues to the fish's migrations. But for a man who respects his place, respects the tradition, remembers the fishing as it was, or remembers being told of it, with the river rife with nets and crews and boats, when New Hope and the little river towns had that bare-assed rural charm, and the rooms overlooking the river weren't in condominiums that sold for half a million apiece, the show can wear a bit thin. Fishermen may fight it terribly, but they can be realists. And Lewis knows that although he's catching more fish, he is the only one left fishing. And he only fishes four hauls a day, not a dozen or more. Even the biologists agree there's not a chance the shad could ever be as abundant as a hundred years ago, or support a greatly intensified fishery—even if the waters were pristine. For the most productive freshwater reaches of their spawning streams, in some cases even the streams themselves, along the tidal river, are long gone.

"You saw the sign out there the state put up?" Fred asks me.

Lewis Island Fishery, Holcombe Island, Lambertville, N.J. Richard Holcombe began this historical American shad fishery circa 1771. In 1888, William Lewis assumed the responsibility of the fishery and after his passing, his son, Fred Lewis, and crew have continued the tradition of seining for shad.

"They say this is the last commercial fishery, but not really. This is not really fishing." He does not say this cruelly, or cynically. It is a matter of fact. No one should accept the appearance of abundance for the real thing.

More Ancient Lives

LISTENING TO FRANK CARLE AS WE DROVE UP ALONG THE RIVER WAS A great joy because he often forgot I was there and transported himself in his mind across continents and millennia, which is what a great understanding of nature ought to do.

"Anisozygoptera. It's one group a lot of people don't know of. They know dragonflies and damselflies, but not the Anisozygoptera. The name is sort of a combination of Anisopteran and Zygopteran, which is what the bug is. Like an extremely primitive Anisopteran. As if you took a damselfly and crossed it with a dragonfly. Two species worldwide: one in Japan, one in the Himalayas. Really neat, right? Something you want to go and study, right? Their nymphs apparently suck on to rocks sort of limpet-like in fast currents. I'll get you to come with me and collect these things. They're so neat. They spend a lot of their last nymphal instar crawling around in these moist little terrestrial environments around mountain streams. And they've got these little stridulating organs. Can you believe that? On a dragonfly? Where they can rub their legs on the sides of their abdomen and make these little sounds. Hey, they're really neat. Totally different. And their mechanism for copulation is totally different. And I was the first one to realize that some of the fossil dragonflies they found in the Solnhofen slate in Germany, like back in the eighteen hundreds, before the Anisozygopterans were even known, also had the same type of genitalia. These guys are like relics left over from a hundred and twenty million years ago. Obviously there must have been one in eastern North America. But because the mountains aren't high enough, or I don't know what, they aren't found here anymore. Hey, but you know what? It may turn out that someone will turn them up somewhere else. It's not unreasonable that they might turn up in the Andes. When you really get into dragonflies, it's really interesting. And their reproductive mechanisms—a kind of lock and key—can get really outlandish! Not only does it involve the male terminalia but also the dorsal and ventral surface of the male abdomen, the female thorax, the female head—really ornate structures with hooks and all kinds of weird stuff. Like Archaeogomphus, for example, all kinds of hooks sticking out of the male, I mean, they're not positive how these things hook together—and females with horns sticking out of their heads. And, of course, they're very beautiful insects. They have fantastic sight, and because of that you find each species with its own color patterns on the wings and body. Everyone knows they're beautiful, but people have no idea of the diversity around the world.

"Like the Petalurids, for example, which are very, very ancient dragonflies, a small group of semiterrestrial dragonflies, if you can believe that, whose nymphs don't live in water like those of normal dragonflies, but tunnel and burrow down to the level of groundwater, where there's the constant flow of spring seeps. And you have like maybe five species in Australia, one in New Zealand, one in Japan, one in Chile, one in western North America, and one in eastern North America. And our species, the one once found in New Jersey, New York's Central Park, and Philly, seems to be the most ancient of all of them. It's like North America pulled a lot of things through whatever the extinction event was. This was a very important place before so much of the diversity was lost. You find a lot of ancient things here: here and in southern China and in Japan. Like horseshoe crabs, giant salamanders, and bald cypress. I mean, there's no dragonflies left over from the Carboniferous, I mean all those are gone, but dragonflies have been different from everything else for at least three hundred and fifty million years. And they're still here.

"I mean, you've got tropical dragonflies whose nymphs live in bromeliads, which are the largest dragonflies living. Things with wingspans of like ten inches. Damselflies, right? With an abdomen, right, that is like half the diameter of a straw, but eight inches long! Like great big knitting needles flying around! 'Oh, my goodness,' they say, 'I didn't have any idea!'

"Unfortunately, birds get better coverage in magazines. There's probably about the same number of species, eight thousand, as dragonflies. But at least twenty percent of the dragonflies are still undescribed. We're going to beat out the birds, I think. And we go so much farther back into time. I mean, some birds are neat. You get flightless birds and swimming birds. But dragonflies—holy mackerel! You get such diversity!"

Dr. Carle has an outlaw look: thick dark hair, long sideburns, and goatee. An entomologist of international reputation, he hasn't taken a full-time position teaching at a university because it might give him an agenda other than his own—swallow him up, as he puts it—and keep him from doing the kind of thing that we're doing today: driving out along the river and checking the shores for evidence of insect, especially Odonatan life. So he works as a mechanical engineer during the day and studies his dragonflies at night. He and his wife must also devote their time to educating their own children, who they feel will learn more from them in home schooling than in public school. I couldn't imagine a better teacher; Carle holds nothing back. Over the course of a long day along the river, we talk, or Carle talks, about everything from taxonomy to politics, and all seem somehow easily related.

"People wonder, 'Why do you care so much about dragonflies?' Well, it's the entire habitat: all the plants and everything else that's found there. You destroy their homes and that's it. You're not going to find them anymore. Look what we're doing. We're destroying this biological diversity. We're pushing these widely distributed species into little places, and the species that only have little places left we're driving to extinction. And so you lose the patterns of distribution—where a species occurs tells both its own history as well as the history of the place and of related species. I mean, you look at the Delaware River in relation to glacial events and obviously it was a very important refugial river for northern forms. It's the most northern major river in eastern North America that wasn't a total wipeout, that wasn't lost totally beneath the ice. But a lot of things are missing."

Dragonflies can be extremely sensitive to pollution. They live long lives in the water, most one or two years, but some as long as six years. During this time the wingless dragonfly larvae use their "fantastic eyes" to stalk everything from worms to mosquito larvae to fish and tadpoles. They feed voraciously and grow to two inches or more, passing through some dozen or more stages of development, called *instars*. This same appetite stays with them as flying adults, when they'll stake out a territory and prey on flies, midges, and especially mosquitoes. Pollution at any time during those years in the water, an oil or chemical spill, even a heavy wash of silt into a stream, can kill off the insects (which is the absurdity,

Carle points out, of claiming that a stream is clean "most of the time"). In its final larval instar the dragonfly climbs out of the water, takes a perch on a plant or rock, and slowly emerges as a winged adult, leaving behind its larval skeleton. This pale, hollow shell from which the adult has flown is called an *exuvia*, and to Carle each is sufficiently distinct to make an identification of a species. To know if a species lives along any section of the river then, all we had to do was find its exuvia. So we spent the day climbing rocky bulkheads, putting on our boots, traipsing mud flats, taking off our boots, driving, hiking through brush and poison ivy, examining the river shorelines from Camden to Belvidere.

Along the Delaware, as along many other eastern rivers these days, the negative data—the things once there but no longer there—is collected as often as the records of the things that still exist. This, says Carle, is not the case everywhere.

"My father had a twenty-five-square-mile lease in Quebec and I was managing the camp and it was amazing. I mean, to see the dragonflies flying around eating the mosquitoes and the black flies. . . . And you'd say, 'Wow! Look at these dragonflies. They're everywhere!' And I think within a half-mile of the main camp I collected something like fifty species. I've never been able to do that anywhere in the eastern United States. Then you really get an appreciation for what's happened—mankind, you know, and what we've done. There has just been a tremendous suppression of the natural diversity and you don't notice it until you see the way things really are supposed to be. And most people do not have any idea—we've been numbed to what it really should be like. Like people from the city on their first night in the bush, gazing up in amazement at all the stars. I mean, dragonflies—had I never seen them like that, I don't think it would ever have occurred to me to collect them."

He collects them everywhere.

"I was collecting in Florida. A lot of neat things in Florida. And my parents, they had to go to Disney World, right? I don't want to go there. Are you crazy? So I said, 'It might be an experience, but I'm not going in.' You know, they destroyed a big chunk of Florida

with that garbage. So we get there. And we're in this huge parking
lot and I say, 'I'll stay with the camper, you guys go in.' So I sat in
there for a while and finally I got sick and tired of doing nothing, so
I said, 'Oh, I'll take my net out and see what's living in those
trenches they made between the parked cars.' So I'm walking
around, and I'm catching some common species of things that will
live anywhere, I mean, like on rooftops. And this guard comes over
and says to me, 'You can't collect here. We don't allow the killing
of animals anywhere on our property.' And I'm thinking, 'Holy
shit!' I mean it's like central Florida has been hit by an ecological
time bomb and Disney World is like ground zero. Now these same
people who make dummy animals for people to watch are telling
me not to collect some insects to at least have a scientific record of
what was once here. I said, 'Okay, whatever you say. But, oh,
man!' "

But there are refugia as well.

"There is a place I know in Virginia where the dragonflies were so
abundant that as you walked through the woods and kicked up
insects, the dragonflies just came out and grabbed them. If you've
ever been into the woods when the lepidopterans, you know, the
caterpillars, are really chomping away, you can hear the frass falling? Well, here you could actually hear the frass falling from dragonflies! Yeah, I know. It was weird! But I was never bitten by a
mosquito or blackfly in that place. We definitely have a problem
with the use of pesticides and draining of wetlands. I mean everywhere, anytime anyone saw standing water and got bit by a mosquito, it was 'Yeah, let's spray it. Let's drain it.' And it only ends
up magnifying the problem. The mosquitoes are an 'R' species: fast
turnover, large number of young. You're never going to wipe them
out. Dragonflies are 'K' species: long generation time, relatively
small number of young. But then, you can't make money on dragonflies like you can on ditching, draining, and spraying pesticides."

Along the tidal freshwater river we were having little luck. In the
town of Burlington we walk out onto a metal dock to inspect the
bulkhead wall—no exuviae.

"There is no insect life here at all," Carle pronounces.

Dragonflies have evolved an acrobatic mating display that Carle believes came about to keep the female from eating the male as they came together. He wrote it out for me so I wouldn't get it wrong:

> *All flying insects except the dragonflies mate by transferring sperm directly between the primary genitalia located on abdominal segment 9. The Odonate reproductive process is so unique that its evolution can best be explained by comparison to the archaic wingless insects which place spermatophores nearby and then guide the females to them. Dragonfly males simply place sperm on their own abdominal segment 2 where a secondary penis and hooks have developed. From here, it's transferred to the female primary genitalia during establishment of the familiar 'copulatory wheel.' This system probably developed because males had to establish the tandem hold on the female— male terminalia to female neck region—to avoid being eaten while guiding females to the spermatophores. And this has led to an even more odd revelation: male dragonflies spend most of the time during copulation using the highly specialized plunger-like or hook-covered apical penis segment to remove previously deposited sperm from the female!*

Once mated, the female hovers over the water, dipping her tail to the surface to lay her eggs. Some dragonfly eggs are adhesive, some have hooks attached, some lay strings of eggs in ponds, and in one species several females will lay in the same place, leaving a kind of fungicide in the water that protects the eggs. Along a river they'll deposit the eggs at the head of a riffle so that as they're tossed about on their way down, they'll be spread across the stream, getting as many chances as they can to sink into safe places to develop. Once safely ensconced between rock and bottom, they hatch, burrow down, and begin feeding.

We walk along the washline of river wrack along an abandoned railroad track south of Trenton.

"To be honest with you, we should be picking up stuff here. I mean we're getting no Ephemeropteran exuviae; no Odonate exuviae; not even any Plecopteran exuviae. What happened? You know, people will look out there and say, 'Well, the river looks good to me. But it's dead here. Man, I'll tell you what. This is bad. There's nothing. Nothing. I hate to say that. I mean, the emerging adults love to hide themselves in weeds like these so the birds can't find them. It takes about an hour or two for a dragonfly to come out and harden up. So they like to find a place—an area of grass close to water—where they can hide."

Carle promises better hunting along the tributaries—along the Flatbrook, along the Pequest—and along the Delaware north of Trenton.

"In temperate North America we have some three hundred and fifty species of dragonflies. In New Jersey, somewhere around a hundred and eighty, and it's almost the same for Plecoptera, the stoneflies, and I would guess for Ephemeroptera, the mayflies, it's less, probably around a hundred species. Pretty good diversity. If you had that diversity of mammals you'd be absolutely tickled."

But here, nothing. A chunk of old jukebox, an alternator. A pile of car batteries.

On the shoreline upstream of the falls at Trenton, Carle spots a clubtail dragonfly flying out across the river and pronounces "a tremendous change right here." In short order we make a find: an exuvia of what could be a rare Gomphurus. Carle crawls down into the brush to photograph it before he pockets it in one of the small cellophane envelopes he carries with him. The find makes him yearn for remembered scenes of abundance.

"Oh, if we were on the Penobscot, you wouldn't believe what you'd see."

By the rapids at New Hope we find in the brush the wing of a *Gomphurus* that must have been eaten by a bird as it emerged. The wing is glassine-like, with a map of fine, dark veins. Dragonfly wings are fluted, fanlike, and twist and bend on tiny membranous joints. They can rotate independently and bend on tiny membranes, allowing the insect to hover as well as maneuver—back up, spin, and turn quickly. Military aircraft designers study their mechanics. So do biologists like himself, says Carle, not only to explain how the animal moves, but how it lives, so that the wing patterns become keys to identification, and their structure "the key to survival." Dragonflies were the first insects, the first animals, in fact, to take flight. Fossils from the Carboniferous show them with two-and-a-half-foot wingspans. Carle believes it was competition with birds that allowed only the best of the dragonfly flyers to survive.

"If this is *Gomphurus vastus*, it is a state record. And if that guy is here, we could find a lot of good stuff."

And we do find more—and more each several miles up the river. And by Bull's Island we find groups of exuviae on sycamores close to the river, on bridge pilings, on rocks.

"When I get people started looking, they get hooked. They're so ancient. And friendly. Bold. A lot of these old ancient dragonflies tend to be surprisingly bold. Little bosses, you know, that will land right on your shirt, on your shoulder, and stay. You don't have to set up anything or tell people much about it. Just say, look at this dragonfly and it's 'Wow! It's from the Triassic!' "

We pass up the industrialized waterfronts of Easton and Phillipsburg because Carle is anxious to get up to the wooded shorelines.

By Belvidere, where fishermen fish for shad from boats and the river shore, we're finding even more. But the light is getting too low to see the exuviae among the weeds. At dusk we see yellow swallowtails by the dozens come to the wooded river shore to drink.

For dinner, Carle directs me to his favorite spot, a few miles east of the river at Belvidere along Route 46. It's a little hot dog stand marked by a hand-painted sign in the shape of a twenty-foot-long hot dog lying atop its bun like a log atop a canoe and awash with a wave of yellow mustard. This is Hot Dog Johnny's, and it's been here since 1944. Aside from its food, two things recommend it to Carle: it has survived nearly unchanged in a world much changed since its founding, and it sits on the bank of the Pequest, one of Carle's favorite dragonfly streams. In his enthusiasm for the place, Carle evidently forgets the diet he told me he was on and orders three hot dogs, two with ketchup, one with mustard, and a cellophane-wrapped Tasty Kake coffee cake. Johnny's sells only hot dogs. Hot dogs, french fries, birch beer in frosted mugs, and buttermilk. Why buttermilk? Hot Dog Johnny Kovalsky's daughter, Pat Fotopoulos, who now runs the stand, told me that when her father opened up, there were so many farms around here that buttermilk was just too available not to offer.

Now most of the farms are gone. Before the eight-lane interstate, I-80, was built, this winding Route 46, two blacktop lanes, was the only route for Sunday drivers coming from Newark, Jersey City, and New York on their way to the Delaware Water Gap. In those days that could be a three-hour trip, and the folks were probably just about ready for lunch by the time they reached Johnny's; or they stopped for a last bite before making the long drive back home.

Now the trip to the Water Gap takes an hour and twenty minutes, or even less, along the interstate. But the road cuts straight across the ridge and valley, ignoring the terrain (much of it now screened by high wooden or concrete barriers from the growing numbers of housing developments on either side) as much as the old road had to abide by it. Route 46 still winds through the mountains and so close along the Pequest that out the car window you can see the waters rushing. Traveling such a river road, when you can find one, is almost as good as traveling the river itself. It meanders, tree-lined, shaded, dappled, and imparts an identity to the world through which one is traveling. You might stop along the way at the Indian Moccasin Trading Post, Cliff's Ice Cream, or the Dover Dairy Maid. Or pull off the road to take a drink or fill a water jug from a spring spilling out of a rock embankment.

All of this comforts a man like Carle, who enjoys traveling back and forth through time.

"Just think," he begins somewhat wistfully, while opening his third hot dog. "If we didn't have birds, in another ten million years we might have dragonflies like we used to."

VIEWS OF THE WATER GAP

I

SUFFICE IT TO SAY THAT AT THE DELAWARE WATER GAP, OVER THE course of the last hundred and fifty million years, the river cut down through the ancient rock of an Appalachian ridge until it now runs through a steep, rock-faced ravine some sixteen hundred feet deep. That the scene defies description is evident in the number of attempts made to describe it. The *New York Commercial Advertiser*, for example, on Tuesday, September 17, 1839:

> *We had only been able to survey the outlines of the mountains that had been cleft in the mighty convulsion which had enabled the river to pierce its sinuous course between them, while the spike rocks hanging upon their sides, and the irregularities of their conformation, had remained comparatively undistinguishable. Now, before yet the sun had gilded their tops, the whole mountain structure of the entrance to the pass from above—for the most part, on the western shore, clothed with wood to their summits, including a huge naked cliff on the Jersey side, beyond the first winding of the river below, which seemed to lift its grey crest above the others, was distinctly in view, gloomy from the yet unretreating shade, disclosing all the irregularities incident to the freshness of nature, and wild and grand beyond description.*

Or *The New York Times*, May 21, 1877:

> *Nature presents herself here in so many phases of gentle beauty and wild savagery that even scant justice would hardly be possible in attempting a description of the scenery of the Gap without more fullness of detail than circumstances permit. Imagine to the north a double valley, divided by a mountain with pointed*

base and rounded top. Down from the right ripples the broad, shallow Delaware River, now 150 miles on its way to the ocean. A succession of mountain bases gives it direction, but at the junction of the valleys a part of the saucy stream escapes and a number of low, sandy islands are formed, some with only a trace of shrubbery to hide their nakedness. The river's freedom is of short duration, however. The stern mountains rush together, and the stream, suddenly abandoning its pranks, moves silently between, a submissive captive.

The natives called the ridge, which is a part of a geological formation that runs from New York to Alabama, the Kittatinny, which means "endless mountain." In its conjunction of natural forms—mountain, forest, and alluvial plain—Edward Hicks saw yet another peaceable kingdom, a promised landscape of plenty against the background of a geologic wonder. That scientists, and nearly anyone else who passed through, puzzled over its origins is also evident.

2

THE WATER GAP, WROTE SAMUEL PRESTON IN 1828, WAS BROUGHT about by a huge eruption at some remote period of time, which released the waters of a great lake that had been dammed behind the once-unbroken wall of the Kittatinny Ridge. Part of his evidence, he wrote, was that the area was known by the Indians as Minisink, meaning "where the water is gone."

How long ago did this occur?

Nicholas Scull was esteemed a first rate man of his day as to science and general knowledge. Ninety-eight years ago (1730) he was on Dupuis' Island and from the vast size of two hollow trees, a buttonwood and an apple, he concluded that the water "must have been gone" one thousand years or more for trees to have grown to such an uncommon size.

The fact was that Minisink meant "the land of the Munsee (or Minsi)," the Indians who lived north of the Water Gap, and that Munsee meant something like "people of the stony country"—a way to distinguish them from the Unami or "downriver" Indians. The distinction was made by and for the benefit of the Europeans, most of whom considered them all "Delaware" or "river Indians." The natives themselves were distinct enough cultures that a Munsee would need a translator to speak to an Unami.

Preston would not let any of this spoil his narrative. A Pennsylvania surveyor, he had taken a working trip through the Gap in 1787. In 1828, at age seventy-two, he began what one historian called "a frenzy of writing that ranged over the early history of northeastern Pennsylvania." That Preston had no scientific credentials and that his articles had no basis in what was even then scientific fact, seemed to make no difference to the editor of the upstart Philadelphia journal, *Hazard's Register*, that published, without reservation, all Preston's correspondence. The narrative, in one form or another, was repeated as gospel for the next hundred years. Sometimes it was embellished. Based on Preston's theory, tall, thin, large-nosed, temperance-minded Luke Brodhead, one of the Water Gap's nineteenth-century hotel entrepreneurs, contended that the "great convulsion" of a thousand years ago had blown out some 8,451,600,000 cubic feet of earth. This, he concluded, was "a sufficiency of matter to overwhelm a township of ordinary size to the depth of five feet."

Such "great geological transformations" and "the constant mutations still continuing, together with our own wasting lives," wrote Brodhead, ought to "admonish us of the instability of all sublunary things, and that ere long 'The great globe itself,/Yea, all which it inherit, shall dissolve,/And, like this unsubstantial pageant fade,/Leave not a rack behind.'"

Not your usual hosteler. Although he does then remind his readers that he happens to offer tours to the best spots from which to view God's handiwork.

3

THE MODERN GEOLOGIST WOULD SAY THAT SOME 350 MILLION YEARS ago all of the Pocono and Appalachian plateau from the Kittatinny west to Pittsburgh was beneath a great, warm, shallow Devonian sea in which horseshoe crabs, or their trilobite-like ancestors, swam among a crowded ancient sea-floor forest of sponges, corals, jellyfish, and worms, a sea life far more varied than any today. Over the next hundred million years, streams filled the sea with silt, and the sediments, layered some four thousand feet thick, were compressed into shales and slates and sandstones. Southwest of the Kittatinny lies the Pennsylvania slate belt, where rare, flat, unflawed, billiard-table-quality slate is still mined. The compressed vegetation of the ancient sea's swampier shores—tree ferns a hundred feet high, among which must have flown some of those giant Odonata (no birds had evolved yet)—formed the nearby Pennsylvania coal deposits.

Then, as continents moved in their own slow pageant across the globe, what was to become the western coast of Africa pressed into what was to become the East Coast of North America. The crush of these continental plates over the next 50 million years raised up an ancient range of Appalachians, which may have looked much like the present-day Himalayas and which may have harbored even more of Carle's ancient Anisozygopterans. (At the same time a great extinction took place. Over the next 20 million years the world, now one huge continent surrounded by a single ocean, would lose some eighty percent of all its forms of life—a diversity never to be seen again.) About 200 million years ago, this continent began to pull apart, and the Atlantic Ocean began to form between what is now the northwest coast of Africa and the northeast coast of North America. The ancient progenitors of the Delaware and other East Coast rivers now began to carry the sediments of the eroding mountains eastward out into the new sea and, combined with the sands washed up by the new sea itself, thickening the continental shelf and creating the vast coastal plain across which the ancient Delaware flowed. Seventy million years ago, what remained of those ancient Appalachians began being pressured upward once more. As the ridges, the modern Appalachians, lifted, the rivers cut deeper into the hard rock and secured their permanent courses. All in all, an unimaginably slow process that would never have pleased the readers of *Hazard's Register* as much as did Preston's far less remote cataclysm.

4

THE MUNSEE RIVER VILLAGE MIGHT HAVE A FEW SMALL BARK-COVERED huts surrounding a larger longhouse a hundred feet long by twenty feet wide. Farming plots lay nearby, on the fertile, well-drained, muddy soils close to the river. They planted with a stick dibble and cultivated with stone or deer-bone hoes. They planted corn that grew only four-inch ears that bore only eight rows of kernels (from which came its Spanish name, *maíz de ocho*). They grew beans and squashes, but did not, points out archaeologist Herbert Kraft, who did the most complete of the Minisink excavations, use fish for fertilizer. Fish was more valuable for food, and once a field was no longer fertile, the natives simply cleared and planted another. These were, after all, not very big plots. Nonetheless, writes Kraft, "the practice of gardening had a profound effect upon the lives of the Late Woodland people. They settled in small towns, built more durable houses, developed religious and ceremonial practices, and made their lives more comfortable."

They lived here year-round, and combined farming with fishing, hunting, and gathering. They shaped pottery and jewelry. They committed their dead to graves facing west so that their souls might follow the sun. (The Unami, on the other hand, buried their dead facing east.) Their agrarian comfort lasted for some seven hundred years—until the Europeans came to the upper Delaware valley. Within less than seventy-five years after that, the Munsees found themselves exiles from the Minisink.

5

IN THE EARLY 1700S, SETTLERS MOVING INTO THE UPPER DELAWARE valley, many coming south from New York, seemed to have no idea the land was part of William Penn's original grant. In 1684 Penn had returned to England to face up to a crush of debts. His colony had proved a disappointment both morally and financially. At one point he asked a hundred Philadelphia citizens to loan him a hundred pounds a piece for four years to cover his debts, and was refused. Little was left of the green lands he had planned. He saw a city not altogether unlike the London he so abhorred. He finally tried to sell his rights to Pennsylvania back to England, first for forty, then for twenty, finally for twelve thousand pounds. In 1712, before he could finalize the sale, he suffered a stroke. For the next six years he clung weakly to an increasingly despairing existence.

In the meantime his agents in Pennsylvania continued to make more land transactions. One was a 1686 option on land north of Bucks County along the Delaware, land that extended west "as far as a man could go in a day and a half," and then defined by a line drawn from that point to the Delaware River. These vague terms were not unusual at a time when a deed might specify "as far as a man can ride in two days with a horse," or release all lands claimed "from the beginning of the world."

When Penn died, his son Billy, who would die only two years later, received what remained of Penn's Irish estates, and John, Thomas, and Richard, his sons from his second marriage, shared the Pennsylvania proprietorship. When Thomas came to Pennsylvania in 1732, he realized he needed to reestablish authority over the upper Delaware lands. He made treaties with the Iroquois, who held lands to the north and west of the Munsee, and in 1737 he looked to exercise his options under the 1686 treaty. The Indians then living in the area just north of Bucks County, which lands the treaty involved, had not been there in 1686. They had moved into Pennsylvania from New Jersey, and so knew nothing about the original deed. Nonetheless, since they were the only Indians there, they took to the bargaining table with Penn and agreed to the land sale. If they thought they might make some gain out of lands they had never owned in the first place, Penn went them one better. Since the transaction called for a distance that a man could "go" in a day and a half, Penn found three of the best runners he could, and offered cash and land to the one who could go farthest. By the end of the day and a half, one of the runners had dropped out, and one lay near dead from exhaustion, but Edward Marshall had gone some sixty-five miles, enabling Penn to draw a line north to the upper Delaware River and thereby enclose all the Munsee lands. When the Munsee refused to leave, Penn drew on his friendship with the powerful Iroquois to enforce the Walking Purchase and the Munsee's final exile.

6

IN THE NEXT YEARS CAME A FRENZY OF TRANSACTIONS AND TREATIES. The whites wanted to secure their leases and appease new settlers. The Indians seemed to want to make the best of it while they could. Some whites seemed so anxious to make sure they had a written contract for every property that they often bought them twice or even more, from different groups of natives who claimed to live on them.

As with the fur trade, the whites found it difficult to buy land from these chiefless egalitarian bands. They pressed the Indians to appoint agents to negotiate and to put their mark to the transactions. Sometimes the whites addressed these agents as chiefs, sachems, or kings of the Delaware. Tamamend, Sassoonan, Nutimus, Teedyuscung, and Netawatwees became familiar treaty signatories. But the nature of the natives' lives, and their relationship with the lands they sold, made the very idea of a sale itself, to the Indians, a European's delusion. When the settlers were few and far between, so were the conflicts. But the Indians soon came to realize the whites really believed these transactions gave them ownership not only of the land but of everything that grew or lived on it.

With the French encouraging them with arms and promises of better treatment, the Indians went to war in the 1750s, and wreaked some measure of bloody revenge on the Minisink settlers. The conflict was sporadic and short-lived, sparked by raids and counter-raids, and real and reported massacres, one in which the runner Edward Marshall was wounded, his wife scalped, and his daughter killed. But at the Treaty of Easton in 1758, all Delaware Indians quit all claims to Delaware lands, and tribes and fragments of tribes—southern tribes, northern tribes, well-traveled Shawnee, downriver Nanticoke, Miami, Conoy, New York Iroquois, Philadelphia Lenape, and Minisink—found themselves scattering across the mountains west of the river, all on the same disheartening retreat. Many Munsee moved north into Wisconsin and Ontario, where they still live today. Other "Delaware" became accomplished horseback riders, buffalo-hunting Plains Indians. By 1846, Francis Parkman could report that the Delawares living around Fort Leavenworth, Kansas, on the Oregon Trail, were considered "the most adventurous and dreaded warriors upon the prairies." But within twenty years what remained of even these warrior Delaware had been coerced by successive treaties to remote outposts in Oklahoma.

7

SAMUEL PRESTON'S FABULOUS CORRESPONDENCES WERE THE SOURCE OF yet another persistent piece of Water Gap lore: that in the middle of the 1600s the Dutch mined the hills at Pahaquarry, north of the Water Gap, and took from them wagonloads of copper ore up to Kingston, New York, along what "must undoubtedly be the first good road of that extent ever made in any part of the United States."

According to historian F. J. Stephens, the mine and the road both were fictions: "If viewed in the light of mining practices in vogue in the seventeenth century, Pahaquarry would have been an exercise in futility."

There were no tungsten carbide bits. Mining was done with hand picks, wood buckets, iron gads, hammers, and wooden wedges. Gunpowder was not introduced to mining until late in the seventeenth century, and even black powder for mining would not have been available until the eighteenth century.

"The tough Kittatinny quartzites withstood the grindings and the abrasions of four glacial onslaughts," writes Stephens. Any man who, "with his puny pick, shovel and gad attempted to encroach upon and excavate the equally hard sandstone" would be a fool, especially for the low-grade ore of Pahaquarry.

And what about the much-vaunted Old Mine Road from the Water Gap to Kingston?

"All evidence militates against the premises of there ever being or having been, a one-hundred-mile road built by the Dutch exclusively for the purpose of hauling copper ore from Pahaquarry to Kingston."

"In 1658," says Stephens, "there were seventy-five able-bodied male residents in Esopus (Kingston). It is not to be supposed that such a handful of men had hewn their way through a hundred miles of forest infested with savages." And, in fact, during the period the Dutch were supposed to be building the road, the Esopus natives were on the warpath, for the Dutch had developed among the Indians a well-deserved reputation for exceptional brutality.

In 1643, for example, according to a contemporary account:

> *When it was day the soldiers returned to the fort, having massacred or murdered eighty Indians, and considering they had done a deed of Roman valor, in murdering so many in their sleep; where infants were torn from their mother's breasts, and hacked to pieces in the presence of their parents, and the pieces thrown into the fire and in the water, and other sucklings, being bound to small boards, were cut, stuck, and pierced, and miserably massacred in a manner to move a heart of stone. Some were thrown into the river, and when the fathers and mothers endeavored to save them, the soldiers would not let them come on land but made both parents and children drown—children*

from five to six years of age, and also some old and decrepit persons. Those who fled from this onslaught, and concealed themselves in the neighboring sedge, and when it was morning, came out to beg a piece of bread, and to be permitted to warm themselves, were murdered in cold blood and tossed into the fire or the water. Some came to our people in the country with their hands, some with their legs cut off, and some holding their entrails in their arms, and others had such horrible cuts and gashes, that worse than they were could never happen.

The next day, writes Herbert Kraft, Cornilius van Tienhoven's mother-in-law "amused herself, it is stated, in kicking about the heads of the dead men which had been brought in, as bloody trophies of that midnight slaughter."

No, Stephens concludes, as far as the mine and the road are concerned, "anyone who really looked into it found the story wanting. Those that wanted it, didn't." But Stephens is up against legend. The mine and road remain part of every travel guide to the Water Gap — as does the legend of the Water Gap's Lover's Leap.

8

THE LENAPE PRINCESS WINONA FALLS FOR THE DUTCHMAN HENdrick Van Allen, "a gentleman of fine accomplishments, pleasing address, and fair exterior, full of adventure," who has come from Holland to work the copper mines at Pahaquarry and build the wagon road along the Delaware up the Neversink to the Hudson at Kingston, New York.

Winona, child of nature, has things to teach the European "of the wealth of her nation in unbounded forests, plains, and rivers." She even tells him "of the old tradition of this beautiful valley having once been a deep sea of water, and the bursting asunder of the mountains at the will of the Great Spirit." These stories hold him spellbound, "although she [feels], at the same time, the meagerness of the intellectual repast she [is] furnishing to him whom it would be her highest ambition and enjoyment to please." Hendrick claims he has only ever seen the famous Water Gap from the New Jersey mines. And so they decide that when they next meet they will climb to the summit.

> *She appeared lovelier than ever before . . . dressed mostly after the custom of her white lady friends, through whom she had ordered from abroad a habit of rich crimson cloth, trimmed with gold lace, made somewhat after the style, which in modern days has vainly struggled for supremacy, known as the Bloomer. She wore her long hair in plaits reaching near her feet. Her head, usually adorned with a wreath made from the gay plumage of birds was now crowned with wild flowers.*

A necklace of beads of quartz crystal and jasper complete the Pre-Raphaelite ensemble.

They go off in her canoe. They climb Mount Minsi, the Pennsylvania side of the Gap. But now he shows her a letter that tells of the English victory over the Dutch. His mission is ended. He has been called home. Though it is written in Dutch, she reads the letter and, her love somehow conquering the temptation to cheer the defeat of the slaughterers of her people, recites, in English blank verse: "Farewell, brother!/Tutor! lover!/Winona's sun has set forever."

"In a moment, she disappeared from view. Hendrick ran to the cliff, caught her in his arms; they reeled on the precipice, and—"

At this point on the cliff, a nineteenth-century travel writer found, "is now a little booth, where lemonade and birch beer regale the fatigued but less despairing lovers of today. Had lemonade been sold here in the days of the fair Winona," he writes, "her fate might have been different."

"There are fifty Lover's Leaps long the Mississippi from whose summit disappointed Indian girls have jumped," Mark Twain reported in *Life on the Mississippi*. But instead of dying in her fall from the cliff, Twain's maiden (named, as chance would have it, We-no-na), lands on her parents, dashing them to pieces. She and her lover go off to live happily ever after. "The only jump in the lot," wrote Twain, "that turned out in the right."

9

*B*AEDEKER INCLUDED THE DELAWARE WATER GAP AMONG THE FIF-teen scenic marvels of the U.S. By the 1870s, so great was the demand for summer accommodations in the Water Gap, *The New York Times* said, that

> *antiquated wayside inns and village taverns, whose former pa-tronage was mainly derived from the frequent visits of the brawl-ing out prodigal raftman, or the periodic influx of the resident of the backwoods districts to attend sessions of the county courts— have grown into commodious modern hotels, each catering to the comforts of hundreds of people from New York and Philadel-phia.*

Not that raftsmen weren't welcome, or could be kept out even if they weren't. The Gap marked the end of the first leg of the trip downriver, and often the place where rafts would receive new pi-lots. Sometimes five hundred raftsmen landed along the shores of the Water Gap on a single night.

Luke Brodhead was not the first to put up guests at the Water Gap. His father had bought the Kittatinny House in 1851 from a Frenchman, Anthony Dutot.

In 1828, Maximilian, Prince of Wied, a world-traveling German writer, came through the Gap and met Dutot:

> *A poor old man entered, who was the first person that had settled in this part of the country; his name was Dutot, and the village was called after him. He was formerly a wealthy planter in St. Domingo, and possessed 150 slaves; but, being obliged to fly during the revolution, had purchased a considerable piece of land here on the Delaware, and commenced building Dutots-*

*burg. He had previously lost part of his property by the capture
of ships, and his speculations here too seem to have failed. The
property melted away and the last remnant of his possessions
was sold. He had built houses and sold them, so that he might be
called the founder of the whole Dutotsburg; yet, after all this, he
is reduced to a state of great poverty, and his situation excites
the compassion of travellers who pass that way.*

Dutot founded the Kittatinny House in 1820, but his temperament, perhaps sensitized by his long streak of bad luck, was unsuited for hostelry. A German neighbor, Ulrick Hauser, who made an ungenerous remark regarding Dutot's little developing "ceete," quickly paid the price. As Dutot told the court at Easton:

"Mr. Hauser, he von grand, what you call him—he no tell ze true; he call my lettle ceete Hard Scrab (Hard Scrabble); then I say, Zounds! Mr. Hauser, you be von Hard Scrab yourself! Then Mr. Hauser, he put his fist in his hand and strike me, then I lift my foot and I strike Mr. Hauser."

The grand jury didn't buy his story, and indicted Dutot for assault and battery.

There were eight Brodhead sons, and most were over six feet tall. Their mother reportedly boasted that she had "over forty-eight feet of sons." Luke Brodhead designed his 1872 mountainside Water Gap House without a bar, but he began to popularize the resort among a better class of tourists by appealing "to the good taste of a true lover of the beautiful in nature."

The railroad put the Water Gap within reach of New York and Philadelphia. A ticket from New York to the Water Gap was $2.55 in 1895. The Delaware, Lackawanna & Western Railroad ran excursions from New York to the Water Gap (round trip fare $3.40) and extolled the virtues of clean-burning blue Pennsylvania coal in the person of Phoebe Snow, a cupid-lipped, auburn-haired creation of the railroad's advertising department, whose white dress, accented by a corsage of delicate violets, remained always unsoiled by coal soot.

The Wondrous sight of mountain height
At Water Gap bring such delight
She must alight to walk a mite
Beside the Road of Anthracite.

Miss Phoebe's there, don't you know where?
Why, Water Gap on the Delaware.
Good sport in sight, both day and night,
Go by the Road of Anthracite.

(Mark Twain, after a trip on the DL&W in 1899, sent a telegram to the company: "Left New York on Lackawanna Railroad this A.M. in white duck suit, and it's white yet.")

By 1908 a passenger could board the "Delaware Water Gap Limited" at Chestnut Hill in Philadelphia at nine-thirty in the morning and, after traveling by the Slate Belt Electric Railway Company, and then riding on the Bangor & Portland Traction Company, or the Stroudsburg, Water Gap, & Portland Railway with its open, screen-sided, lemon-yellow cars, reach the Gap a mere six hours and forty minutes later.

Brodhead knew the whims of the wealthy at the turn of the century:

The healthful influence of the climate of the Delaware Water Gap has been well tested and it is known that numbers of invalids from various causes are from season to season cured or benefited by a sojourn here. The air is dry and invigorating. The winds, whether from the east or the west, follow a long range of wooded hills and mountains, with their constantly purifying influence and those from the north across a succession of forest clad mountain and valley. As the location would indicate, it is entirely exempt from anything like malarial influence. The water is the purest and best in the country, and is supplied to the principal hotels from mountain springs.

Doctor F. Wilson Hurd declared the Gap's waters worthy of his Wesley Water Cure and opened his health resort, The Water Cure of Experiment Mills (later the Water Gap Sanitarium) in 1873.

By 1877 the Kittatinny House boasted electric lights, elevators, steam heat, private baths, and running mountain spring water in rooms, a telegraph office, a full-time orchestra, and "golf, tennis, bowling, shuffleboard, boating, fishing, driving, bathing, livery, and garage."

Visitors to the Gap could read about themselves in *The Mountain Echo*, the resort newspaper, which "came into bloom with the rhododendron and went out with the goldenrod."

"Saratoga," wrote its columnist in 1881, "has an army of genteel loafers who haunt the front of the hotels and are not above insulting ladies. The worst of it is that they appear to be on friendly terms with the local policeman."

In 1908 the Water Gap House advertised itself as "A MOUNTAIN PARADISE; highest altitude, coolest location, always a breeze, no humidity . . . Now THE FINEST EQUIPPED, BEST APPOINTED, AND LARGEST HOTEL IN THIS REGION, entertaining refined, high-class patronage." Brodhead could offer golf to women in long dresses and straw hats, and men in knickers, ties, sport coats, and caps on the Caldeno nine-hole golf course at the Water Gap House, laid out by Charles C. Worthington around 1897.

The hotels of the Water Gap could ply a strictly limited trade. "No Hebrews or Consumptives," was how many resorts at the time put it.

"We prefer," stated the Croasdale Farm brochure, "not to entertain Hebrews." The resort was later struck by lightning and burned to the ground.

Visitors took burro rides along the mountains, carriage drives to the famous falls at Bushkill or Winona, or hiked the steep Water Gap trails to the overlooks at Rebecca's Bath, Eureka Falls, Cooper Cliff, Table Rock, Caldeno Falls, or Lover's Leap, where an Indian maiden . . .

It was still not to everyone's taste. "What a most wonderful place would be the Delaware Water Gap," a woman remarked to Brodhead, "if Niagara Falls were here."

10

*I*T'S A LITTLE DRIZZLY WHEN MY ELEVEN-YEAR-OLD SON, BENJAMIN, and I pull off Interstate 80 into the parking lot at the trailhead of the path that leads up to the top of Mount Tammany on the New Jersey side of the river. The highway now bridges the Gap, crossing the river like a concrete flume nearly always flowing with cars and eighteen-wheelers. (The Gap deserved something more monumental or Roebling-esque than this straight prefab concrete beam.) But this highway has made the Poconos accessible to commuters who can live more cheaply in Pennsylvania while continuing to work in New York City or New Jersey. Below the cliffs that once marked the end of the road are now rush-hour traffic tie-ups. Not until we've climbed a few hundred feet up into the woods does the sound of the trucks begin to fade.

Benjamin's just about the right age for his first trip up the mountain. It's a short hike, but rocky and steep, and when the going gets hard I recall for him the view from the peak. It's a wet day, but warm. Small streams of water cascade over the slate ledges and make the going often slippery. Hikers who come to the Kittatinny, even those who have hiked much of the rest of the Appalachian Trail, always remark on its rockiness. The glaciers dragged rocks along for hundreds of miles and left the crumbled, ankle-twisting debris behind.

As we near the overlook, the weather, rather than clearing, begins to close in. By now I know that when we reach the top we won't be able to see a thing. Soon, in fact, it is difficult to make out the trail only twenty feet ahead. Now the trees become more scarce, and high ground gives way at fifteen hundred feet to a swamp full of snags. In the fog they appear as narrow dark figures barely sketched in to the gray surroundings. It would be a time to see a bear, for this is a weekday and the parking lot was empty, and we seem to be the only ones on the trail. We have hiked up into a cloud, and the mist clings to our clothes and faces. This was fine as long as it was warm, but up at the top of the ridge a wind comes straight on, as if blowing across a tabletop. It leaves a chill in its wake. We have reached the overlook but can't even see the edge. If you didn't know it was out there, you might well walk off it and over the ledge. Usually, I tell Benjamin, the view is out over a seemingly distant river threading its way around narrow, wooded islands. Turkey vultures and, occasionally, osprey soar on the updrafts between the slopes. Across the canyon is Mount Minsi, whose northward-facing slope grows thick stands of rhododendron, but whose xeric upper ledges have a desert climate where prickly pear and pitch pine sprout and copperheads and timber rattlesnakes find warm rock shelters.

The hotels are gone. Most burned to the ground early in the century. But with the coming of the automobile the Gap seemed to become a day's drive from everywhere. The rich could take planes to more remote and exclusive resorts.

We sit and have our sandwiches, staring into the soundless fog. Benjamin asks if I think I'll be able to find the trail back, and I say, "Sure." But I'm looking out into the hazy silhouettes of bare trees and hoping the wind calms, or that as we come around the ridge and down the mountain, we'll be out of its reach.

A Munsee father might leave his child of twelve or thirteen out here in the forest, in Mesingw's realm, so that the child, after days of fasting, might, in a vision, find his guardian spirit. It might be a snake or a bird. It could be as seemingly insignificant as an ant or as great as the sun or moon. But this *manitto* would identify itself to the weakened boy, befriend him, and then inform him of the new powers he would possess.

An old man in a gray beard may have appeared and said in soothing tone, "Do not fear, I am a rock and thou shalt call me by this name. I am the Lord of the whole earth and of every living creature therein, of the air and of wind and weather. No

one dare oppose me and I will give thee the same power. No one
shall do thee hard and thou needest not fear any man."

Benjamin's manitto might have been the mushrooms we picked, or the pileated woodpecker we first heard and then followed on its erratic flight through the trees, or the newt, or the red shale of the mountain itself. Perhaps it would fly in on this wind, or appear on the way down, as the fog cleared.

Benjamin says nothing. I listen. We walk. The wind dies but the rain comes harder, and soon we give up trying to keep dry and splash our way through the little growing rivulets that stream down the slope toward the creek that runs along its base and into the river. Instead of taking the bridge across the creek, we wade through it, sloshing amid the rocks. The rain stops, but now we're so happy with our soaking clothes that we look for any opportunity to muddy ourselves more. Suddenly, in the near distance, we see what appears to be a very white light through the forest. We come closer, and awash in the flood of light is a young white-tailed deer, standing stock-still. We stop and look a moment, then approach uncertainly.

A young man, tousle-haired, comes out to greet us.

"Can you hold here for a moment?" he whispers.

I look ahead. I try to recall where I am. Ahead of us is a Japanese film crew busily hustling cameras and sound gear through the forest.

"What is it?" I ask.

"A Japanese television commercial. For IBM."

The deer, he explains, is from an animal farm and it's fenced in.

"In the commercial, an American boy is writing to his friend in Japan about how he was in the woods with his new shotgun and spotted a deer. He lay down and took aim and had the deer in his sights—they'll show a shot of the deer through the sight of the gun—but the boy decides the animal is too beautiful to kill."

"What's that got to do with IBM?"

"He's writing the letter on an IBM computer."

We are allowed to pass through the little on-location set and then can barely find our car in the lot now crowded with motor coaches.

Wet and cold, I wonder what this end to our day means to Benjamin? Was our whole little hike through the manitto-rich woods a spiritual washout? What can the river and its wooded ridges mean when a camera crew can bust in on Kishelemukong himself, "who creates us by his thoughts."

Feeling like we had been yanked up from a dream, we agree to head for the comfort of Hot Dog Johnny's.

"Will you write about this in the book?" he asks.

"Sure."

"What will you say?"

"When a boy," Wi-tapanoxwe told Gladys Tantaquidgeon,

> *my grandfather always went swimming every morning before sun-up, even when there was a thin coating of ice on the river. One time he dreamed of going down to the ice-covered stream very early to bathe as usual. When he jumped into the water the echo could be heard down the river. Then suddenly he heard a voice saying to him, "I am going to make you a strong man. You will be able to go under the water as I do." He did not see anyone around, but there close by was a teal.*

And after that, said Wi-tapanoxwe, his grandfather had the power to stay underwater for several hours at a time. He had many times located the bodies of people who drowned in the rivers of Kansas, and once even rescued a whole team of horses that had broken through the ice. But, Wi-tapanoxwe had to admit, his grandfather may have been the last of the Delawares to possess such powers.

LISTEN UP!

MIDSUMMER, EARLY COAL-BLUE POCONO MORNING. 5:30 A.M. WE pile into the yellow schoolbus, wave good-bye to Chef Bud, a lanky silhouette in the doorway of his brightly lit camp kitchen who doffs his red cap and waves us out the drive.

To the river. Thirty-two of us: twenty-six campers nine to fifteen years old, and counselors. Too early for song. Heads press up to heads' reflections on cool windows as we wind down the narrow mountain road along Marshall's Creek. The mist drifts off the forest floor. By the time we get to the river at Dingman's Ferry an hour later, the mist begins to lift. Warmed by the still-unseen sun, it swirls and drifts above the slow current of the broad eddy at Dingman's, some twenty-six miles north of the Water Gap. Swallows break through, skim the water, and disappear back up into the mist. The last few days have been hot. The water is warm. The kids, anxious to get started (the trip marks the end of their week's stay at the county conservation camp), stand by their aluminum canoes with their chosen partners, leaning on aluminum paddles, life vests slung about their shoulders.

"Listen up!" begins Monroe County naturalist Roger Spotts. "There are a couple of questions that I am always asked that I would like to clear up right away. First, we will be going that way—downstream. The Delaware River does not go in a circle. We will not end up back where we started. Second, this side of the river is Pennsylvania, and that side of the river is what?"

"New Jersey!"

"Right. New Jersey. It will always be New Jersey. I hope no one asks me about that again. Third, you each have a life jacket and you must wear it at all times—buckled.

"Last, inside each canoe is a green plastic garbage bag for each of you. Your rental fee is a full bag of river litter. If you don't fill up your bag, your trip will cost you two hundred dollars. Per day."

Some moaning.

"I promise you, you'll have no trouble filling them up. Any questions? No one said to get in your canoes yet. Listen up. There will be some rapids. None of them are very bad. But when we go through them you spread out and follow single file behind me. All right? Then let's go."

General clamor of aluminum canoes being climbed into, dragged along the gravelly shore, pushed off, banged into one another.

"Listen up!" Roger yells above the din. "It's going to be hot. In another hour it will be sizzle city. We have twenty-six miles of river to cover in two days, which is not a lot. We are in no hurry. Don't wear yourselves out. If you don't race and splash, but just look and listen, there will be all kinds of possibilities. Animals from bears to eagles to otters. All right? Let's go."

Roger and I go off ahead to get a little quiet paddling in before they've figured out their bow and stern strokes and are up on us.

Cedar waxwings and swallows swoop from the shores. On the New Jersey side, pine and hemlock shade the steep stone outcroppings. On the Pennsylvania side, oak and maple crowd gentler slopes, the narrow strip between the river and the first ridge of the Pocono plateau where the land was once farmed. Green pervades the river shores and hillsides. Anyone visiting the Delaware from the West or Southwest is astonished by the green. For even in the deeper shadows of the trees the forest is full of the leathery green of rhododendron and mountain laurel, and beneath these the jagged and lighter greens of ferns and mosses.

The sun breaks through. We see carp, heavy-bodied and golden, sunning themselves in the shallows. Silhouettes of fat-headed suckers in twos and threes hover over the bottom. The water is very clear, as it is on the whole upper Delaware. Clear enough to snorkle in, to spear fish and eels, to catch crayfish by hand if you're quick enough. A young great blue heron leans out from the riverbank, looking impatient for a strike. We see smallmouth bass and eels rush out from the shadow of the canoe. In the bow, I take out my spinning rod and begin to cast a little silver minnow lure toward the pebbled shore. Too late. The flotilla's upon us. The fish scatter. The heron takes off. The kids begin to overtake us, each having by now established his or her own makeshift paddling rhythm—two strokes on the left, one on the right, or, bow and stern together, four strokes on the left, then together four strokes on the right—rhythms that will remain and sometimes plague them the rest of the trip.

As Regina would recall in her required river essay:

After an hour my arms felt like they were gonna fall off. But we kept moving on. When we made our first stop about two

*hours later I wanted to kiss the ground. We were on this island,
I don't remember the name. We went searching for different
kinds of bugs. That was pretty cool though, cause afterward we
went swimming. That was great!!! My whole body wanted to
thank me.*

Buck's Bar. The great load of material that washes down the
Delaware makes for the formation of many islands. A fallen sycamore snag may begin the process, dragged out from the shore by
the winter ice and sent downstream, where it may jam in rocky
shallows. Drifting brush, debris, and silt begin to build up in its
backwater. The obstruction grows, teardrop in shape, broadening
on the downstream side. Soon grasses take root in the silt, and the
low, spreading, narrow-leaved river willow. On such islands—
Mashipacong, Minisink, Shawnee—the Lenape encamped each
spring to set out nets and weirs for spawning runs of shad and
sturgeon.

Buck's Bar is still not much more than a rugged little brushy
shoal around which the water rushes in a frothing fall. The river
willow is in purple and white bloom. Twisted sycamore and river
birch have begun to grow where the soil has built up above the
water. The kids find deer tracks, a deer skull. Plenty of plastic
trash, which also finds its way downriver and lies in the lee of the
currents. Once the kids have cleaned up a bit, Roger sends us all out
into the water.

"Listen up." All stand ankle deep in the current that rushes
around the narrow tip of the island, over the rocky shallows whose
brown gravels catch the gleam of the morning sun. Roger is holding
a small hoop of wire netting. "Without insects," he says, "there are
no fish."

"This was cool," Troy would write, "because I never even
thought about it that insects are all over almost everything in the
water."

If there's nothing else one ever learns about what to do when one
comes upon a stream, one at least ought to know that the first thing
to do is bend down, lift a rock, and inspect the damp, dark under-

side for signs of insect life. This is like lifting the hood of a car one is about to buy, or putting a melon up to one's nose. The first thing this does is put you right into the experience, be it car- or melon-buying or stream living. And to most of us, what we find under a rock in a stream is surely as mysterious as what we find under the hood of a car.

Insects find streams to their liking or not because of the amount of oxygen the flow of a stream brings to them. They lay their eggs on the water, and the flow of the stream sets the eggs into the crevices of the rocks. The eggs hatch and the often ungainly-appearing nymphs, with their thick heads, large gilled undersides, and gnarled limbs, displaying the best of paleozoic ergonomics, will then live for weeks or months in among the currents—far longer than the lifespan of the adults whose limited terrestrial lives allow them barely enough time to mate and set out their eggs on the surface of the water. The nymphs are the ancient predators on the stream's smallest drifting inhabitants, the basis for the food web of the stream.

For the general consumer, the caddis fly larva, in its little home-made trumpet-shaped case the size of a match head, is a good sign. It is ubiquitous in good streams. Find stone fly nymphs with their two little hindmost whiskers, and the stream is a bit better. Find the mayfly with its three hind whiskers, and the stream is probably even better. For the stream entomologist (a field dominated by fly fishermen), this may be a little too simplistic a guide. Some stone flies and mayflies do better than others in polluted streams. Some are more sensitive. There are degrees of good streams, and the changes in their quality can be discovered pretty quickly by a good look at the insects. What most are sensitive to is the amount of unconsolidated silt running downstream, too much will clog the flow between the rocks and cut off the good supply of oxygen.

There are certain rules to oxygen content: moving water accumulates oxygen better than slow-moving water does. Cold water holds more than does warm water. During the day, photosynthesizing and respiring plants enrich the water. At night, or even on cloudy days, the oxygen levels decline, and on a warm summer night a stream that may appear to hold enough oxygen during the day to supply its insects and fish may be unable to support any but the most adaptable organisms.

In the case of streams, the survival of the most adaptable is not always the most encouraging sign. Some insect lives go on under the foulest circumstances, thriving in streams polluted with sewage. Such life is of little value to fish, since finding them in a stream means very little else can survive the anoxic conditions. So in a natural system one first checks for diversity; if the life in the stream is not diverse, then conditions are too extreme in one way or another.

Following Roger, the kids wade in up to their chests where they can barely stand in place in the strong current that sweeps around the small island. Working in pairs, one lifts a rock out of the river, and as the water rushes around them, the other holds the net near, trying to catch whatever washes downstream: specks of black debris that upon closer examination turn out to be alive—nymphs of caddis flies, stone flies, mayflies.

Turning rocks. In the spring along the river shore, when the water recedes, looking beneath rocks close to the waterline will reveal dobsonfly larvae, called hellgrammites, dug into little sand nests. They are the size of caterpillars, black, and with grasping pincers at their heads, one of the fiercest stream predators and the best bass bait.

Then the kids themselves go drifting and swimming, cooling off, learning firsthand about flow and life on the river.

Troy's journey:

> *As we went along you gained trust with your partner and got to get used to the canoe. When it came time for the rapids I got butterflies in my stomach but when we got through them, I felt proud. I noticed a lot of insects and Jack and I had a lot of arguments but I was always in the wrong, so I adjusted to him. I don't have many complaints because we were fed well.*

Lunch! Nine loaves of white bread. Five jars of peanut butter. Jelly, turkey and mayo, carrot and celery sticks, somebody's pickled eggs in an institutional-sized Hellman's jar. Chips and bug juice: Chef Bud's best cherry-red. Set up sandwich assembly line. Take a picture of Chris with five pairs of sunglasses on his head. Save your paper cups. Who wants the last sandwich? Only one oatmeal cookie each. Police the area. Listen up! Let's go.

A couple of miles downstream the Bushkill Creek makes a swift confluence with the Delaware, spreading a delta of fine cobble out into midstream. We run our canoes up onto the gravel bar and the kids clamor out and wade into the cooler tributary, now prospecting on their own for insect life, as much for the bugs ("I got a stone fly." "Let's see it, dude.") as for the splash when they heave the cursorily inspected rocks back into the river. Moving rocks, damming rivulets and even whole creeks, is the most intense child's play. In the city we'd dam up streaming gutters with gravel, stick, and leaf dams. On the beach we built moats against the rising tide. A running stream of water is a tireless playmate that has its own singleminded way of behaving, and a kind of wit that any child understands, but that those adults who build dams seem unable to appreciate. They dredge, channel, and dam, and always seem surprised at the resulting ecological twists—the dying lakes, ruined backwaters, lost spawning and nursery grounds—when all they had to do to know better was to stand in a stream and turn a couple of rocks. Just listen up—*Henry IV*, Part I, act three, scene one:

> *Hotspur. See how this river comes me cranking in,*
> *And cuts me from the best of all my land*
> *A huge half-moon, a monstrous cantle out.*
> *I'll have the current in this place dammed up,*
> *And here the smug and silver Trent shall run*
> *In a new channel, fair and evenly.*
> *It shall not wind with such a deep indent,*
> *To rob me of so rich a bottom here.*

> *Glendower. Not wind? it shall, it must. You see it doth.*

"Listen up!" Roger begins. "Does anyone notice anything about the water here?"

"It's cooler."

"Yes, it's cooler. It's cooler because it's running faster and its banks are more shaded. What else? Anything else?" No one's getting it. "Look at the color."

"It's brown."

"It's brown. It's orange-brown."

An amberous current that can be traced out into the main stream.

"Why? Where does the Bushkill come from? Anyone remember?"

"From the top of the Poconos."

"From the top of the Poconos," Roger repeats. "And what's at the top of the Poconos that would make this water brown?"

Everyone squints hard to show they know it but just can't seem to say it—everyone except two boys who have found a large leech attached to one of the stones.

"What's at the top of the Poconos?"

Finally, a thrust: "Fogs!"

"Fogs!"

"Not fogs—bogs." And his explanation goes like this: The top of the Poconos are high plateaus, and on top of the plateaus are bogs, and the watery soil in the bogs is peat, and the plants that grow in the peat produce tannin, and the creeks that run through the bogs carry off the tannin, and the tannin colors the creeks. It is the remaining tannin in fallen leaves that colors them brown when their reds and golds have gone. It was the tannin in the bark of the hemlock and oak that the nineteenth century used to tan leather. They stripped the trees bare for the bark, dried it, milled it, and soaked out the tannin. Hides that had been soaked in lime to loosen the fat and hair—lime cooked out of the limestone from the hard sedimentary rock of the Delaware ridges—were scraped and then stored for months in vats of tanning solution. Tanners felled whole hillsides of deep green Pocono and Catskill hemlock and oak forest—a cord of bark for every ten hides—and burned the logs or left them to rot. The deforestation left the Pocono streams unshaded for the first time in ten thousand years, since the glaciers had passed and leveled the ridges. The streams became too silty for the native insects to survive. Too warm for the native brook trout. As the forests returned, the streams regained some coolness and clarity, and insects and trout—if not the native species, at least the more tolerant sorts—ran again in the amber shallows.

A scream goes up. The boys have displayed their succulent find to two of the girls, who rush out of the water, the boys behind them all the way, assuring them, "It's just a leech," until they can hardly bear it any longer. Roger intervenes and attempts to calm the static of panic in the air, with some scientific detachment.

He plucks the thing from the rock. Observe, please, the leech. They crowd in to watch it curl around Roger's finger. "I want to talk about this leech . . . good camouflage . . . flat and streamlined . . . sucks fast . . . the water runs off it and can't pull it from its perch. . . ." At the back of the crowd, two of the girls are making a pact not to swim again ever, the rest of the trip.

Back in the canoes we begin the first loop of the Walpack Bend where the river winds along an **S**-shaped cut in the Walpack Ridge that runs northeast/southwest parallel to the higher Kittatinny ridge to its east. The first loop takes us northeast around the base of the wooded hill to our left, and a mile later the second loop takes us back south around the rounded rocky rise on our right known as "the five loaves of bread." The water is slow and deep; the name Walpack may come from the native word *walpeek,* for "deep water" (although a whirlpool in the Big Flatbrook Creek, which enters the Delaware here, was known by the natives as *wahlpeck*). The stillness may reflect the peace of the broad, rolling, ghostly valley of the Flatbrook, its vista unchanged for more than two hundred years, lying nestled—truly nestled—between the Walpack and Kittatinny ridges.

Little green herons stab at fish in the shallows; damselflies in a copulatory circus perform on drifting watergrasses and willow. Along the riverbank, deep groves of sycamore, silver maple, and river birch grow in the thick glacial silt. Whirligig beetles spill across the surface. River shiners school below. Narrow-headed mergansers preen on the shore, exposing breast feathers to the hot afternoon sun, a sun that has shifted from shoulder to shoulder as we maneuvered the bend. If the kids had thought about it, it would have seemed as if we had just gone in a circle. But the kids were wearying and busy slapping at dragonflies with their paddles until I showed them a couple of blue-faced dragonflies riding along harmlessly on my arm and explained that the dragonflies, despite the look in their large eyes, had no taste for human flesh and, in fact, devoured thousands of mosquitoes. They quickly became great fans and fierce protectors of the Odonata, and quickly and sharply admonished the kids who had been out of earshot of my lesson for doing what they themselves had been doing only a minute before. The commotion scared off everything, even a previously pretty tolerant great blue heron—"that bird again" as one boy put it, assuming, I guess, that there was only one on the entire river—that had been crouched on the Pennsylvania shore.

Late afternoon, a clearing on the high bank above the river. "Listen up! Cabin one, get rocks for the fire ring. Cabin two, get wood." The woods come alive with exploring campers. The ring is formed. The fire is started. Hot dogs are broken out and skewered on sticks. Ears of corn are wrapped in aluminum foil and tossed into the fire. Tents are pitched. Clothes are changed. Wet sneakers are set up on rocks or dangled on sticks near the fire to dry. Sometimes there's the smell of burning rubber as a stick falters and a shoe falls.

"Hey," someone will call, "I think that's your shoe."

"Well, get it!"

Dusk falls—as long as I can remember, always the best time of day—not only out on the river but even where I grew up in Pennsylvania where the kids all played outside on summer evenings until we could barely see the ball any longer and you tried to trace the path of its silhouette in the dark and catch its ghost as it came out to you, anticipating my father coming home and knowing that ten minutes after he walked in the door I'd get my first call to come in for dinner. And the bats came out from their limestone caverns nearby, scattering over our heads in the wondrous light of the summer dusk. (The bats, of course, are nearly gone now, the victims of suburban sprawl.) Only a few streetlights came on in those days.

Mostly it was just porch lights or the glow pouring out through living room windows. So the coming of dusk in the woods where, unlike in the city and the suburbs now, no lights shine, was always pleasant to me. But then my feelings changed somewhat when I met a man by a campfire once who had fought in Korea, and who sat stiffly by the fire and told me, to ease his own mind, that the fall of dusk in the woods by the river always brought him a chill of fear—"like the world starts to close in on me and I keep looking out, trying to see." And I sometimes wish he hadn't come out of the blue like some Ancient Mariner who told me that, for every fireside dusk I wonder when I'll pass his story on to my own children.

Nine P.M.

"Listen up! Flashlights off!"

Roger is all business again.

"We're going to go out in the dark. Flashlights off, whoever that is. Why? Because the nighttime is a big part of the day, and we always miss it. Tonight we're going to be night animals."

Roars and hoots.

"Listen up. Now I know you've heard people say they're night people. Well, you might be a night person, but that doesn't mean you're a night animal. Now you're going to be a night animal— which means that since you can't see, you're going to have to use your ears, your nose, and your sense of touch. No flashlights. Line up single file and follow me. Let's go."

We walk out of the glow of the campfire and thrash through the high grasses of the path cleared by the electric power company to maintain their lines. A blond girl's hair, bleached by the day's sun, shines in the starlight. We walk on into the blue. Heat lightning flares silently in the near distance.

Roger speaks in a stage whisper.

"As you look across this open field you hear crickets, katydids. There are bats eating insects, insects eating you. When mosquitoes see twenty-six campers in shorts and T-shirts, they've found a smorgasbord. Mosquitoes, bats, crickets—no bears, no coyotes— nothing out here to be afraid of.

"Now, as we walk up this hill I'm going to send you off by yourselves to alternate sides of the trail. I want you to walk into the woods thirty to forty feet and just stand or sit for ten minutes. That's your time. I just want you to relax. Something crawls up your arm, it isn't going to bite you. You're not going to die. Just listen, quietly, to the night."

And one by one they go off out into the dark. And now they have all vanished from the trail. All twenty-six of them.

And as my own senses adjust to the starlight I identify the smell as oregano-like, minty, bee-balmy, and the stand of trees as cedar. I think of gilia flowers of the Southwest, which pollinate after the bees have gone by, growing white flowers that attract moths. The hum overhead is from the electric company's transmission lines. In the sky, as high as the stars and just as silent, the blinking red lights of an arcing airliner. Barely three minutes pass before the campers begin to lose their composure and the silence begins to break down. One coughs. One whimpers. One whispers. One gives a low whistle. Two sit cross-legged on opposite sides of the trail, idly tossing up bits of grass and stone. A few others join them.

"I think I fell into a thorn bush," one whispers.

"I feel like I'm in a dream," says another.

Roger appears and calls hoarsely for everyone to come out. We have a head count and find we're missing two who think the game is hide-and-seek. Finally convinced it's not, they join the rest.

The sky darker, the air dampened, the campers getting weary, the walk back to the campsite seems longer. Back at the fire the kids wrap Bisquick dough on sticks, bake it over the fire, and serve it wrapped around melted marshmallows, a treat in which there's more pleasure in the making than in the eating. The kids finally straggle off to bed, the sounds from their tents fading with the fire.

I recalled being their age and lying awake in the tent listening to the adults in conversation around the fading fire. The tents were old army-navy issue, and drowsiness mingled with the musk of damp canvas. I remember especially the *tup-tup* of rain when it fell on the tents, and how running a finger along the inside wall released a rivulet of rainwater that left a long, damp stain on the green canvas. Outside, in the dark, the woods and the dark itself beyond the fire seemed endless, though a paved road might be a bare quarter mile away. I remember camping in the snow, a troop of us digging through to the ground to lay tarps and pitch tents in a freezing winter camp. And then, when we were all settled, with a fire begun, warming water for cocoa from a stick tripod, another group pulled up in an aluminum-sided camper with humming generator, and risked exposure only when hanging their corrugated awning. Still, we slept trustingly in the chill, in the belief that our troop leaders wouldn't let us freeze to death. And none of us did, although one of the troop leaders came down the mountain with frostbitten fingers.

These were American adventures in the 1950s for us, descendants of European immigrants whose families had come in a quick two generations from the crowded tenements of Manhattan to the suburbs and now to camping in the great outdoors, an experience so far removed from that of my great-grandparents that they probably would have thought there was something suspicious and even vaguely fascistic about it. And, in fact, I found out that just being in the great American outdoors didn't automatically raise anyone's moral outlook—something I guess the Native Americans could have told me. I remember waking up one morning in a summer Boy Scout encampment to find that overnight our tents had been painted with swastikas. Since every troop was sponsored by one or another church, it had not been difficult to figure out who was what, and that we were the only Jewish troop in the camp. It was also not difficult for us to find out the harassment was the work of a group of scouts camped nearby. The morning was spent washing the tents and planning the strategy of our *jihad*, how we'd pick off the Christians as they scattered in retreat and one by one drop them into the latrines. The drama got to a pretty intense pitch before an apology of sorts was forced out and we were told, weakly, that the kids didn't know what the swastikas meant (in fact we weren't too certain ourselves), and an uneasy peace reigned for the rest of the week. But a whole forest of prejudice had been revealed that I had not known before.

Camping was the outdoors. But when I think back on it, we

never were given the chance to see very much nature. We scouts were still taught to tame the wild as best we could: get out into the woods and do something—clear your camp, set up your tent, gather your firewood, make your meals. No one ever gave us a net and said go out and turn over rocks. And so my meeting up with nature was usually unplanned. I remember a canoe trip on the Delaware— water clear, bright sun overhead—turning back to see, about a mile behind our group of canoes, a curtain of black cloud coming down the river like a sky-high locomotive. I could hardly believe I could so clearly see two such opposite worlds at once. Needless to say, when I pointed out the storm bearing down on us, it was once again time to do something, and my transcendent moment was gone in a pounding of aluminum canoes as everyone made great haste for shore. I had gone into a kind of reverie, however, at least as much of a reverie as a twelve-year-old could muster. I resolved to let the storm overtake me. I would weather it. My partner in the bow was more given to panic. He pleaded with me to paddle. I couldn't. I had rapture of the deep. At one point I swear I saw him in sunlight, while I was engulfed in the dark. And as we touched shore the rain came in a warm, drenching wash that blurred all distinction between shore, sky, and river.

The wonders of nature on film, and the expensive illusions of nature in modern zoos notwithstanding, all the money and effort would be better spent preserving the nature itself and taking kids to see it wherever it is. No one has to see lions to appreciate nature. A kid who appreciates leeches will appreciate lions. Roger and his group gave the kids as much as they could: they paddled, waded, and floated; they turned rocks, held frogs, mayflies, and leeches, and stood alone at night in a dark cedar wood. They were told of the Native Americans who lived here, and of the fishermen, trappers, loggers, rafters, and what wildlife had once been along the river: flocks of passenger pigeons that darkened the skies; osprey, eagle, elk, black bear, otter, beaver, brook trout in cool, stony streams; so many rattlesnakes no pioneer went out without his leather leggings; mountains of hemlock, oak, and chestnut; riverbanks bright with the scarlet blossoms of cardinal flower. And they were told of the dam that was planned that would change everything.

Roger asked them to think about the future. "What do you think things will be like a hundred years from now?"

"I think we'll probably be living on the moon by then."

We run by a couple of larger Delaware islands—Depew and Poxono—and now move along the base of the Kittatinny Ridge, which rises steeply to our left. Known as the Shawangunk in New York and Blue Mountain in Pennsylvania, this quartzite ridge is a feature of the land clear to Alabama. The river actually met up with the Kittatinny thirty-five miles upstream at Port Jervis, where it turned from its eastward course to run southwest along the strike of this last ridge of the folded ridge-and-valley formations of northern New Jersey. Across the Delaware in Pennsylvania lies the Pocono Plateau. South of the Kittatinny is rolling Piedmont farmland. It is a hard ridge that has weathered the glacial surges that wore away the land around it. As steep as the slope sometimes is, the ridge—some fifteen hundred feet high—is everywhere thickly wooded with hemlock, hardwood, and rhododendron shading a trelliswork of narrow streams that cut craggy channels through the rocks, which, during rains, often spout falls from the side of the mountain into the river.

The river and Pennsylvania floodplain broaden. We're only a few miles from the Water Gap, where the river cuts through the ridge, narrowing to barely three hundred feet in a slow, deep channel between two steep mountainsides. It's where the trip ends—just as the kids seem to have got to know their strokes and move more surely—and weave less—than before. They even get annoyed at the wakes of the motorboats that run this stretch of river and rock them off their quiet course. At the northern end of the long, narrow Tocks Island, we're called to meet.

"Gunnel up!"

Sixteen canoes pull together into a broad raft. After a brief rain shower a warm haze has formed that is tinted by the hues of the reflecting light: gold from the sun, green on the riverbanks, and blue off the Kittatinny Ridge.

"Listen up!"

This time it's Craig Todd, director of the County Conservation District, an ecologist with the gaze and demeanor of a hard-boiled private eye. He stands in his canoe and leans on his paddle.

"What's this dam thing all about?"

The kids listen up.

"We've been canoeing the last two days on the longest remaining stretch of undammed river in the East. What's that mean to you?"

Todd conducts a calm interrogation; he gives his charges time to think, as if to say, "We've got all day, so we'll get this right."

"A dam was once planned for this small island. A dam that would back up the river here and make a lake thirty-five miles long. Why?"

He shifts on his paddle.

"Water is becoming very precious. And everybody is looking at the Delaware and everybody is thinking of having a part of it. People need it for drinking, washing their dishes, brushing their teeth, flushing their toilets.

"This is called a drought-prone river. It is called that because so many people rely on it for their water.

"How would they build it? What would happen? All of what we've seen in the last two days would be underwater."

I think of the grasses bending under the current suddenly straightening as the dam stops the flow.

"When I was born, the world had two billion people, now it has five. More people need more water and more power. How long will this river be allowed to continue to exist?"

The kids are blank-faced, serious and silent.

"I feel a dam would be the ultimate abuse. But this is just one thing you will have to think about. That's why we stop here and float together by Tocks Island. We'll just stay hooked up here and drift."

And we do. And they are silent. No sound but the breeze. Damselflies hovering, flying into the wind like seabirds. Fish crows bleating like sheep on the island shore. Reflections of ourselves off the shallow, gravelly bottom, reflections in thick mats of flowing grass.

Interstate 80 crosses the river at the Water Gap, and as we pass beneath the highway the kids signal to the trucks to pull their air horns. Civilization at last. We beach the canoes, dump wet clothing, and await the bus.

Joe B.:

> *The river trip was graet. I had a lot of fun. I liked the water. I liked the part on the animals. We saw alot of people on the river. I lost a lot of stuff. The graet Delaware is nice. But I don't like writing. I was awake on the river for a while, but the river like put me at easse. I hated canoeing at first. But it got better. I saw alot of fish. I saw alot of fishermen. I saw alot of places on the river. We ate, sleep, and swam on the river. We had ok food. But it was not a graet feast. I think I had fun on the river trip.*

Tom I.:

> *I thought going down the river was great. In the begining it was a Drag Because we were moving slow and the Fishing wasne't so hot. But then, on the other Hand once we got Moving, it was Fun. I and my canoeing budie, Scott, had a ball going in and out of the Rapieds and crashing into other boats.*
>
> *After we got to our camp grounds We Set tents I slept all by my SELF in a small green milatary tent. I was succesful when it dident Fall Down. We had a campfire and cooked wienneies & corn. We went on a night walk to test our night vision. We got to sleep later then usually the next morning I slept Fine. and the Fox Fire which I collected Was still glowing a bright blue.*
>
> *The courent wasn't extremly fast but it look Like a storm was going to hit us But it missed so I'm glad about that. I and Scott got going and also got stuck in a current that woudent let us go. But thanks to the help of my counsular we managed to get out and down the stream. Once we saw the Delaware Water Gap*

brige Mike wanted to spit on it, But I wanted to feel it so we just went Past it and that was our Fun Filled camp trip.

Dell P.:

The river trip was Boring but I learnd alot. I learned about the out doors Like Don't forget Suntan loashion and thoes little bugs that grow on them rockes and I don't think I'll come to camp ever agin because I thought you could Do what ever you wanted and Not be in grops. I thought the Bathrooms would be better and bigger and you could take a warm shower. Thats all I have to say. Don't mine my hand writing I'm Just tired!

Joey W.:

I will be 92 yrs. old with no hair and I still will not believe that we (Eric & I) actually picked up out of the river an automobile tire and a lawn chair. How does our "civilization" justify theirselves for these wrongdoings which have been inflicted upon nature? They don't because the people here now don't care about the people here 100 yrs. from now.

We must learn to keep what we've got, and clean what has been dirtied. I feel this trip has taken me a large step towards being the ideal conservationist.

Back at camp, Chef Bud is waiting with baked ham, candied carrots, applesauce, peas, and macaroni and cheese.

I WILL REMEMBER YOU

SOME OF THE NUMBERS, ANNOUNCED IN 1961, WERE THESE: BASED ON a two-year, $2-million, eleven-volume study, the U.S. Army Corps of Engineers proposed a fifty-year, $591-million program of fifty-eight water projects including nineteen reservoirs along the Delaware and its tributaries for a cost of $437 million. The 160-

foot-high earth and rock dam at Tocks Island would cost some $150 million and create a 250-billion-gallon, 12,300-acre lake, thirty-seven miles long, that would reach up to the Delaware's confluence with the Neversink in New York. The reservoir would be surrounded by fifty thousand acres of land and be "the greatest inland resort in the Northeastern area," serving the 20 million people who lived within seventy-five miles of Tocks Island, the 30 million who live within one hundred miles of Tocks Island, an estimated ten million visitors a year, bringing some $30 million to the region's economy. To accommodate the traffic, some two hundred miles of highway would have to be built or improved in New Jersey and Pennsylvania at a cost of some $700 million. A new sewage system—565 miles of trunk lines and 275 pumping stations—would cost $190 million.

According to *The New York Times*, "The park service said in its report that relocation of families and businessmen in the Tocks Island area would be minimal since about 75 percent of the land to be inundated was now forested."

"Our farm," begins Nancy Shukaitis in a measured, soft-spoken manner, which, combined with her clear green-blue eyes had, I'd heard, brought calm and common sense to an edgy assembly or two, "was about one mile north of Tocks Island. It had been in the family since the first Michael came here in 1754 from Germany. George Michael was thirty years old. He was the third owner of the land after William Penn, and that's in an old sheepskin deed down in the Northampton County courthouse. That's how we have this cider-press screw, which probably dates from the first settlers. I was born in 1925, which makes me either the sixth or seventh generation. Not so many years, really."

The cider-press screw is eight feet tall and carved out of larch—big enough, Shukaitis says, to run an eighty-bushel press. It looks like a giant's corkscrew within the otherwise modest scale of her home, with its corner cupboards and long wood trestle table and ladderback chairs. An embroidered sampler above a small stop organ bears the following verse:

Time Endears
but cannot fade
the memories
that love has made.

"My dad grew potatoes, corn, and melons, and we sold them along the road. We had a thousand-tree apple orchard and a three-hundred-tree peach orchard. We had a summer boarding house, and in the years when the river was the main rafting route, the rafters would stay overnight. It was a small farm resort: Michael's Farm. We had boats for rent, though mostly no one paid—my dad was a good-natured guy.

"We had oil lamps. I remember cleaning the globes. We didn't have electricity in the valley until '36. And before the power company would come in, you had to cut the trees yourself. In those years we had doctors, lawyers, some very wealthy guests from the city. They came every year for two weeks, some of them, or the wife and the children would stay all summer and the husband would just come weekends on the train. The Water Gap was thriving on tourists then, until the automobile came and the trains stopped running and the hotels fell into disrepair. The people who came to us were those who wanted a farm vacation instead of a fancy resort, who loved the idea that there was a garden and they could see you picking the vegetables or getting eggs out from the chicken house, who wanted to be near the river.

"In those days the river was loaded with shad, and we'd fish for them with fykes. Then we'd salt down the catch to preserve it. I lived my first twenty-one years there, and I knew and I know the river like a book. People either respect rivers or they don't.

"My dad knew that. I mean, in his view you just didn't take a pristine valley and turn it into a water tank. He used to say that would be like taking Miss America and using her for scientific research. He also knew you cannot bungle up a river any more than you can tie tourniquets up and down your arm and survive. When you block it, it can't function. He said he could see making the river and the land around it into a park. He'd be willing to give up his

land to share it. He'd given free use of it for years to hunters, archaeologists, and hikers. I mean, if the valley could remain the way
it was, that would have been perfect. But that wasn't going to be,
because people die and their kids don't care about the land the
same way they did, so you can't guarantee what happens after
you're gone. He knew that and he saw the development coming.
That was something unique about my dad. He was against the
Vietnam War before I ever heard very much about it. I don't know
how he knew. But when you live long enough and pay attention, I
think you begin to read between the lines of events."

But no one in the valley had figured on the singlemindedness of
the dam builders. Had the dam been built, the river would have
ended not far downstream from here at Mashipacong, where I sit in
a house on the river and watch the swift current of a midwinter
thaw flow by. It is deep blue, wide, lit by the sun, roiled by the
wind, rushing to its own lilt and bounce. I assume it would have
been difficult to imagine, after living two hundred years on the
river, that someone would want to, or could, just stop the whole
thing, letting go all the life it has by dint of its movement and
making all the upstream currents only an illusion of a river. (The
river is even now partly illusion. While the claim is often made—
and often too much protested—that the Delaware is the last undammed river on the East Coast, this is not really the case. At
Milford, Pennsylvania, sits the River Master—an office of the U.S.
Geological Survey—whose charge is to maintain the flow of the
Delaware River past his instruments at 1,750 cubic feet per second.
If lack of rain causes the flow to fall short, the River Master, like a
tenant banging on the pipes for more heat, must call for the release
of water from one or another of the reservoirs on the tributaries
upstream. The major reservoirs on the East and West branches of
the Delaware belong to New York City, which early in the century
claimed its rights to the upper Delaware waters, rights confirmed
by the U.S. Supreme Court in 1931.)

For Shukaitis the issue of Tocks Island was a moral one: "Right
in this little neck of the woods these were people," she reminds me,
"who'd fled Germany for religious purposes"—who, before the

church was built, held services in someone's home or in the barn or, in fine weather, out of doors. Her father had been named for the man who came from France to show them how to make the bricks out of which they built the church. The U.S. Army Corps of Engineers may have had the will, the know-how, but it had no moral vision. And if the search for water was not a spiritual matter, what was? If she knew this, why didn't the Corps of Engineers, and the Congress which passed the Tocks legislation and the Presidents— Kennedy and Johnson—who signed it?

"I mean, droughts are cyclical, just like floods and ice. Our spring would go dry and I can remember washing the sheets in the river. I can remember walking all the cattle down to drink out of the river. I think this serves a good purpose because it teaches people to be resourceful and not to take everything for granted. In those days you didn't waste anything. You didn't hire someone to haul away the stones you plowed up out of the field, you made stone rows. You didn't put your house up in the center of the flats and use up the good, productive land. You put it on the sidehill, out of the way and with a view to the water. You didn't waste. That was an ethic. Of course, you can't tell that to the Corps of Engineers or Congress or big business—they'll think you're an idiot."

Her patient manner notwithstanding, it is Nancy Shukaitis's Shavian temperament, her insistence (which some consider naive) upon integrity in just about everything, that makes her just the kind of woman one would be glad to be able to escort just about anywhere, but especially to a public hearing, say, or to a meeting of commissioners.

The Shukaitis mission was to bring religion to the dam builders. With the same aplomb that inspired her organ playing in church, she would take her seat, eyes sparkling blue as if the river were running sunlit behind them, as if she were herself thrilled to be a part of this event, and she would play and everyone would listen up—even, she hoped, in Washington.

"I started testifying in 1964. When I first went down, there were thirty organizations testifying for the dam and then there was me, a housewife. And I kept thinking, 'Oh, I bet I'll hear something here today that I didn't know. And then I'm going to feel stupid and it's going to be in the papers that I was mistaken.' But I began seeing the flaws in their presentations.

"There was another housewife—from a New Jersey PTA—who said we needed that recreation area because the city people had nowhere to go. And she had a very well prepared statement, which I'm sure was written for her by one of the public relations firms hired to work on the project, describing all the things up in the valley. And when she finished there was just one question from the chairman. He said to her, 'Have you ever been up in this proposed recreation area?' She said no. And I thought to myself, 'You have a hell of a nerve. You'll take forty miles of private property, uproot thousands of people, ruin a good river, and you don't even know what it's like. Maybe it's a hole. Maybe it's a pigpen.'

"Well, they had said we were part of Appalachia. I mean, this part of Pennsylvania in the 1960s was like Vermont in the 1940s. We were a world that had not yet woken up. We were not aware of a lot of things. We were rural and we had a number of poor people, a number of what you might call backwoods people, but I really think that the people sitting with the Army Corps or the Park Service in Denver said, 'Oh, it's a rural area, so we'll put the dam and park right there.' They're like little boys with their train table at Christmas, moving water and roads and buildings, whole towns full of people, wherever they think they'd like them to go.

"And then they go get the support of the locals. Well, anyone in politics knows how to get support for building anything. You type up a neat resolution that tells all the great things that will happen when you sign it. Then you take it around to every living organization—the chambers of commerce, the tourist bureaus, the service clubs, the miners, the farmers—all you can think of—and it's like *The Music Man*—you whip 'em into a nice froth, they sign it, and you take it to Washington."

No one was immune to dam fever. (Almost no one. A December 1965 editorial in the *Blairstown* [New Jersey] *Press* stated that "only about twenty-five people turned out here last Friday night to hear the economist from the Water Resources Association of the

Delaware River Basin talk about plans for the proposed Tocks Island development. We like to think it was the bad weather that kept so many away.") The Boy Scouts, however, caught the very spirit of the development and announced that they had worked out a deal with a pair of amusement entrepreneurs who promised the scouts ten percent of the gross receipts from a cable car running from the scout camp at the base of Mount Tammany to the Water Gap overlook at its peak. They reckoned the scouts would clear fifteen thousand dollars a year. And lest anyone suspect the scouts' motives, they told the newspaper, "The many men involved in the making of these decisions are among the most outstanding civic leaders in the counties and they are, without exception, dedicated scouters."

Needless to say, the scouts drew more attention than the water resources economist. "No one will dispute the fact that the men on the scout council and its executive board are outstanding civic leaders," wrote one outraged local citizen. "But, on the other hand, the world—even the local communities—is filled with mistakes made by outstanding civic leaders."

The scouts, for their part, contended that the traffic the dam and reservoir would draw would ruin the solitude and isolation of their camp, so why not at least profit from the parade, and perhaps make enough to support a more remote retreat? Besides, why "restrict the breathtaking view to those who are young and able to climb the rugged mountain?"

"I hope," wrote another protestor, "I never see a cable car filled with weak-kneed Americans clanging its way to the top of Mount Tammany." The consensus was that the scouts were only in it for the money.

They were not alone. After the announcement of the dam and recreation area plans, some property values in one neighboring county went from one hundred to five thousand dollars an acre in five years.

"The first question they ask you down in Washington is, 'Who do you represent?' So I sat down and asked myself, 'Who do I have to be?' All I wanted was a hearing to be held up here, in the valley, among the people. And I asked them, 'Do you need a petition?' And they couldn't say no. They gave me five days. Well, I quick came back and got a petition circulated, leaving copies in stores and hotels from here all the way to the upper end of the valley. In five days I had it back to Washington with well over a thousand signatures."

In the meantime the Corps of Engineers began to buy up the land. Homes, farms, whole communities were being bought. The Corps, Shukaitis says, had underestimated the cost of buying the land in order to get the project approved. Now the difference between the estimated cost and the real value had to come from somewhere, and it was going to come from the landowners. The Corps would make its offer, and the only choice the landowner had was to settle up or face a long and expensive legal battle. It was, by any account, an exile of a culture that had been two hundred years in the making.

"They found people first who didn't know the value of their land and would pay low and then try to make you feel like a heel when you asked for more, like you were trying to rob the federal government. They would come and appraise your place when you weren't there. They would call you and say they wanted to talk with you about buying your land. And you'd say, 'But nobody's appraised it.' And they say, 'Oh, yes, we have it right here. It was appraised on July 22.'

"Well, the government had sent out letters saying, 'Your land is going to be acquired in this fiscal year.' But they had not yet been authorized the money. So we decided to sue. My husband and a couple of residents combed the mountains to get powers of attorney. And we got 604—many from people we had never met. Our promise was that we would take the case all the way to the Supreme Court. That is what their twenty-five dollars lifetime dues in the Delaware Valley Conservation Association would get them.

"Well, the government couldn't be sued unless it consented to be sued, and of course it didn't consent. In the federal court in Scranton they said you can't have the Congress passing things and the people suing them for it. And the three-judge appeals court in Philadelphia pretty much felt this water was for Philadelphia and turned us down as well. Our attorney then told us it would take eight thousand dollars to appeal to the Supreme Court, and our chances of winning were nil.

"I said, 'Yes, but we promised.' "

At this point she suddenly lowered her voice, as if someone might be listening in on us. "I said, 'Can a citizen file to the Supreme Court?' He said, 'No, it's never done.' I called the Supreme Court and I got the clerk and I asked, 'Can a citizen file a suit?' And he said, 'Any citizen of sound mind can file a suit in the Supreme Court.' And I wrote that down—because I could just hear what would be said about that later.

"So they sent me the Book of Rules, and it was like learning to play Parcheesi. A retired attorney who someone knew helped me out, and one Saturday morning I flew to Washington—the appeal had to be there by Monday, and the Supreme Court closed at noon on Saturday—and raced from the airport with this suitcase full of papers I had spent all night putting into those blue-backed things with the clasps. And the clerk says to me, 'These should have been printed by a printer.' And I said, 'Oh, but we don't have the money for that.' And he said, 'Well, then you have to file a writ of pauperis.' And I stood there blinking and then he said, 'Do you have a stipulation?' And I said, 'What would it look like?' And he said, 'It could be a single sheet of paper or several boxes full that would have come from the Philadelphia court.' I said there was something on the dining room table at home but I didn't know if that was it, could I use the phone?

"So I called my daughter Alice who was only fifteen, and she answered and I said, 'Alice, this is very important. On the dining room table is a piece of paper. Read what it says on top.' I said, 'Okay, get an envelope'—all this in front of the clerk of the Supreme Court—'put it in the mail right now.' She mailed it and they got it in time.

"Our case was denied, but what fun! I put the letter right into a frame: 'From the Supreme Court of the United States: Dear Mrs.

Shukaitis, your writ of pauperis is hereby approved, your writ of certiorari is hereby denied.' "

The story left me brightened and still more amazed at how she could make the most quixotic choices seem the most practical. And she was practical—practical, canny, and politically astute. Part of her success was undeniably her ability to keep opponents off guard. I mean, she might be driving toward some political point and suddenly remember she had to play the piano at the nursing home that afternoon.

"Do you play the piano, by any chance? I know this is crazy, but I play at two o'clock at a nursing home, and last month a lady there from New York City asked if I would play 'New York, New York.' I said, 'How about next month?' Well, the truth is that I can play it but I can never get it to end, you know what I mean? It just keeps going. Maybe a waitress will just drop a tray."

This kind of openness drove even experienced political hands to distraction. For as charming as she was, her grasp of the details was keen and Shukaitis could be a relentless examiner. Her view, for instance, concerning a local real-estate developer: "They called him 'Snake Eyes' because he put a glaze over his eyes when something got to him. If he were looking at you right now, he'd be thinking how you could be beneficial to him. If you couldn't be beneficial to him, you'd know that he had an appointment somewhere else.

"That's so foreign to the way I was raised that I have to dismiss him from my mind. Because I can't fathom that kind of person. It's a very different ethic. Instead of being based on the value of people, it's based on the value of the land. Tumbleweed. You know they don't have roots. They probably never will, because their roots are in money."

Well aware of her abilities and encouraged by local support ("I was always mindful of the question, 'Who do you represent?' "), she ran for county commissioner and won a seat she'd hold for the next sixteen years.

"At least when I wrote to my congressman on the county letterhead, I got an answer."

And she got her local congressional hearings on the Tocks Island Dam project.

"Some of the most glorious things happened in those hearings. And to see those congressmen sit there, who never had to think of more than what's for lunch, and have biologist Larry Rymon sit there with his glasses and in his serious way read off the list of animals which would be lost if the dam were built and the valley were flooded—thousands of skunks, deer, and raccoons—I want a copy of that testimony buried with me when I die.

"Some things were so great. People who came out of the blue to say the most eloquent"—she holds it out with a long *e* and the accent on the *o*—"eloquent things. There was one boy with long dark hair, one of the squatters who had moved into the homes the Corps had bought and the owners had abandoned. He was in a plaid shirt, but was not a country kid but a kid from the city, and so he wasn't afraid and he just sat there with nothing in writing and just said, 'I get religion from the river.' And it gave me chills, because I thought, 'That's true, but you can't say that, you can't sell that.' If I had said that, they would have thought, 'Well, this is it, she's finally gone.' But he asked the congressmen to come out and stay with him along the river for just five days and just sit on the riverbank and fish or whatever they wanted. And he would guarantee that they would never dam it.

"And it was so beautiful because it was straight out and he looked them right in the face and he didn't have any buddies back there tittering, so you knew it was real."

With the sun setting, the light over the river changes again, the contrast now great between the flat gleam of the open areas and the greener gray in the shadows. I realize that the sound of it must also have its effect, and that loss could not be made up either. One ought to think now and again about how far one would have to travel to sit alone and listen to the sound of a running river, and to what lengths one would go to preserve it.

Shukaitis took her father's case to court. The government had started out offering $85,000 for the hundred and twenty acres with the sand beach and the thousand-tree apple orchard and the three-hundred-tree peach orchard and the twenty-six-room farmhouse and the mammoth barn. The federal court in Scranton allowed that the farm was worth $120,000, less attorney and appraisal fees.

"In court," she explained to me, "they used another farm on the Brodhead Creek for comparison. And our attorney said, 'Well, this is on the Delaware. You can't even take a boat out on the Brodhead, it's all rocks.' And this McKee, the attorney from Washington—the cutest little guy who looked like a little doll—he went like this: 'Well, I mean a slow-moving boat.' Well, you can't even take out a toy sailboat on Brodhead Creek."

Her father worked the farm until the government condemned it in 1971. Even though the dam was not nearly ready to build, the government refused to allow people to remain in their homes. The contents of Michael's Farm went up for auction, but the auction had to be stopped because of rain.

"It was the day after Thanksgiving. The people were leaving. The auctioneer locked the door of the barn and we left. They told my dad that day they wouldn't demolish the barn—it was immense, forty-five by seventy-five feet and pegged together. But they bulldozed it the following March—before he had been paid a thing for it. To this day no one knows what became of all his farm tools and equipment.

"I know you're wondering how I even stand to talk about it. Well, if you take care of a person who's sick and they die, you can accept it more readily than if you were away and you came home and there they are. I did everything I could to save it. Many people did. And it is saved. The homes are gone, but the valley and the river are still there. And I rejoice that it's there. And I think knowing that someone like you still gives a damn and will get others to listen makes people like me able to stand it."

And so, one winter morning, we take a trip up along the river where the farms and communities once stood that are now overgrown woodlands beneath which bare, ruined foundations sit, disconnected stone walls and steps that lead nowhere, old places fallen into disrepair becoming part of the undergrowth. This did not take a hundred years to happen. These were thriving farms and communities until twenty years ago, when the government decided it wanted to stop the river. And as often as I have found myself on my trips along the river lamenting the encroachment of people into wilderness, here I found myself lamenting, with Shukaitis, the return of this place to wilderness. The culture that was here was very much suited to its place. Had it not been stopped in time, of course—knowing the way we destroy a landscape—it would not have lasted, so perhaps this is the only way we can have a place like this, as legend, as a reminiscence.

The riverbanks are white and frozen.

"All the farms in the valley were cut so that you had riverfront, flats for your crops, the plateau for your orchard, and hillside woodlands for your timber. The whole valley was cut into slices on both sides. It's really neat to go up the mountains even now and through the trees see all the old stone rows that go right up the slopes. As more and more people arrived in the valley and the land was claimed—the choicest first—the new settlers must have been told, 'Well, you can't stay here, but you can move up the hill.'

"The fields were cleared and open for grazing. They took pride in their woodland because they needed it. My father's most popular crop was his cantaloupes and watermelons. And my uncle had a great melon business as well. They sold to all the resorts.

"The barns were right in there. And the crops stored right in there. There's where we used to make maple syrup. Now it doesn't look at all as it looked when I was a child. We used to have all these maples from down where the property line starts all the way up here. When you drive around and see all the maple trees, people say they were planted for shade. Shade, my foot! No one had time to sit in the shade. They were planted for syrup. We made thousands of gallons of maple syrup. Tap the tree, boil the sap, and plug the tree. If you were on a farm you'd say it was time to gather walnuts, or if the sap was running, 'We're going to make syrup.' This was the way you lived. The actual part of making things like syrup or sausage or scrapple was a family event. Everybody had a chance to turn the grinders or stir the giant kettles.

"So we would take the peaches into town and go from house to house with the old open Buick, you know, and people bought and you were called a huckster, which has a different connotation now. But that's what we were," and she smiles, "isn't that awful?"

The car Nancy's driving now also happens to be a Buick, not made for the hard bumps when we go off the winding blacktop river road to try to see some stone foundation or old springhouse hidden beneath the underbrush. The new growth of brush and forest has sprung up quickly in the abandoned farmlands and grazing lands, and the orchards thick with brambles among the withering fruit trees.

"While my father was still alive he said to me, 'You know, some of the peaches ought to be ripe. Why don't you get some?' He was eighty-one and I went and I could hardly walk in there for the tangle of brush. The peaches were like little prunes. I got lost. And these were the hillsides which had been completely cleared because the cows would eat everything except the blackberry bushes. We had wonderful blackberry bushes." But these, too, are so overgrown with brush that the sun no longer reaches the fruit.

"When I was a young girl I used to go up on the mountain with the cattle to let them graze all day and to make sure they didn't get into someone else's field. Although there were fences up there, I stayed with them because I was the youngest and was sort of excess baggage anyway. But it was such fun. I remember one day I sat down on a huge rock and when I went to put my hand down, this black snake was there. It began to uncoil as much as to say, 'Well, if you're going to sit here, I'm going.' But it took its time unwinding. I saw so many snakes up there, I began to like them. They were about the only creatures I'd see up there, and we became like friends, along with the deer. I mean the deer would come right up to you. Because we didn't wear jeans in those days—I'd be wearing a bright-colored cotton dress, and a deer doesn't know what you are. And they would come up closer and closer to me and I used to think, 'My God!' because daddy had said they could attack. But I remember thinking, 'I'll sit here. I am not afraid.' And then I gulped because I was afraid, and the doe heard me and whirled away."

As we drive now, Nancy has a vision in her mind of a landscape that no longer exists. All along the river, the original land grants had been devised to arrange the land in strips from the riverbank inland, giving each landowner a piece of lowland and upland. In the woods the stone boundary walls are everywhere submerged in the undergrowth—the only clues to the patchwork of fields that once spread across these now densely wooded hills. The woods are peaceful and full of birds and wildlife, but for Nancy the life of these hills is inseparable from the vista: the tapestry of farmland and grazing land, orchard and river, and the people who farmed it. The Minisink and Walpack valleys were the very models of a Jeffersonian agricultural vista. Allowing the forest to grow up and cover this scene is not a return to nature as the National Park Service likes to claim, but, Shukaitis says, a result of ignorance and neglect, as if to say that the people who farmed here didn't lead natural lives, when to Nancy no life could be more natural.

She leads me down stone stairways to the rear of homes that no longer exist, to show me where the stone springhouses still stand over gurgling springs. In the pools, watercress grows, even in this cold, for the water at the spring remains at a nearly constant temperature. "You'd keep anything in such a place—milk, cakes of butter, fresh fruit, meat—and the cold water would keep it fresh. At our farm we had a cave dug right into the mountainside with a door on it about a foot thick."

Here is where Reuben Treible made boats and rented them out. He used to take his daughter trapping. She died in a car accident coming home from bowling. "I keep telling her daughter," Nancy says, "how great she was. An outdoorswoman." Below, hardly visible through the trees now, is Poxono Island, which was called Chauncy's Island because a man named Chauncy DePew owned it and farmed it. Nearby she points out an inlet on the river where she would go to spot muskrat. Although her father refused to trap anything but foxes that were getting the chickens. Anyway, he didn't have much luck at it.

She recalls a place known as the Turn farm, where her grandmother worked as housekeeper to a man she only knew as a wealthy industrialist. The farm was greater than any she could recall, with outbuildings and a view down a long, broad slope toward the river. Gone. All that remains is a weaving house and the icehouse and an open well. The Turn farm was also the site of some great finds of Native American pottery.

"I remember the wedding there of one of Mr. Turn's daughters. That was when the whole place was alive."

We traipse on hard-packed snow. "You see up there? There's a neat little wagon road along which they used to haul wood." And I notice, which I had never noticed before, that the woods had several trails that could be made out if one looked carefully—more than trails, roads still passable and probably not much changed since the wagons traveled them.

"And here's a real work of art." A great stone hearth built into a steep, wooded slope. "I keep coming back here. This was a lime kiln. And it was made of big round river stones placed together. The farmers would come here for the lime for their fields." But vandals have dismantled some of the kiln and stolen some of the stones, just as others raided old cemeteries for headstones, mostly those of infants, since these stones were lightest and easiest to carry away.

The DeWitt farm springhouse, 1827: "This was another beautiful farm. The house was an adorable clapboard white frame house by the road, and the big barn was back there.

"There were houses all through—wherever you see pillars. There was a little community in through there. You can see by the way the contours of the land are, by the way the roads run up that led to the homes. I used to ride my bike in here—selling war bonds—so these are my old haunts.

"Back there, by that arborvitae tree, was an old stone schoolhouse.

"Here was a place that was called Shangri-la, that was owned by a relative of the mayor of Hoboken, I think. They were the nicest people. Their mirrored coffee table was right in front of the window and you could see the river reflected in it. The living room had a balcony around it, and they had wallpaper that went all the way up to the top. She was an artist and had painted roses on the lamp-shades to match the roses on the wallpaper. I was completely taken with it. And here was a stairway going down to the river.

"One day I met a woman living back here who must not have seen anyone for months. She began talking about her husband being stationed at Pearl Harbor, and she wanted to tell me all about the bombing. I was all ears because I had never heard about it in such detail. I stayed till dark and had to push my bike home."

And as we drove, Nancy would recall this camp or that home. "Look at these big buttonwoods. When I was a child I always wondered why they needed such big trees to just make buttons." But then, in the middle of another house tour, she would simply stop: "I keep forgetting the houses are gone and there's nothing to show you."

If the loss of the homes weren't so tragic, the scenario that led up to their destruction might be laughable, combining all the best of governmental blundering. Once having decided the valley would be dammed, the dam goal was pursued at all costs and without the least comprehension of the natural or human costs. The Corps of Engineers, to borrow a phrase coined by Churchill, is a bull that carries its own china shop around with it. As Richard Albert describes it in his book *Damming the Delaware:*

> *As more and more land fell into government hands, new problems arose. The area became increasingly desolate, with declining road care, police, and fire protection. As a result, many of the newly emptied houses were occupied by squatters or picked over by scavengers and vandalized. Arson became a widespread fear. Between June 1970 and June 1972, for example, about three dozen buildings in the valley were burned. Trespassing also increased because it was no longer possible to tell government land from private property. Adding to the fear were several cases in which government demolition teams accidentally destroyed the wrong house. The remaining residents, many of them elderly, became afraid to leave their homes for fear that something would happen in their absence. Many no*

longer had nearby neighbors. . . . Many of these properties had been in the same family for many generations or represented the culmination of a life-long dream.

By mid-1969, the Corps had accumulated a collection of empty houses and other buildings near the Tocks Island Dam site. The Corps offered these buildings for rent by advertising in various newspapers, including New York City's Village Voice. *The leases were supposed to be temporary since the Corps believed that dam construction would soon start.*

Instead, the environmental fight over the dam continued, and the Corps found itself landlords to a counterculture of squatters and hippies who—and I doubt the Corps caught any of the irony in this—professed to be seeking a special communion with the land and river. They wanted to be farmers, to live off the land. As one told Albert, "It was an outpost, a settlement in the middle of a wilderness." Never mind the fact that the Walpack Valley had not been a wilderness for three hundred years or that its present ruinous state had been brought about by the Corps. "It was a chance of a lifetime," one of the squatters said, "to live on a beautiful river with no neighbors, miles and miles of land, anybody around was just friends. You could try out all your dreams of the time."

Not only wouldn't the squatters leave; they, too, began to protest the building of the dam that would now flood them out of the valley. Three times the government sent in police and federal marshals to evict them, the last time in February 1974. According to Albert:

Ninety marshals were brought in from the Midwest, and a backup force of dozens of Pennsylvania state police was readied. In paramilitary fashion, the marshals swept into the sleeping squatter community on the bitterly cold morning of February 24, 1974. The marshals were armed with tear gas and pistols and were wearing bulletproof vests. . . . State police first sealed off the area to prevent access by the news media.

To keep anyone from coming back into the valley, the Corps speeded up its demolition schedule, demolishing nearly anything in sight—historic buildings burned, and the Zion Lutheran Church was stripped of its floors, windows, and woodwork. "After the church was gutted," wrote Albert, "Nancy Shukaitis, the Delaware Valley Conservation Association, the Sierra Club, and the New Jersey Public Interest Research Group obtained a restraining order stopping all further demolitions." New environmental studies showed that the amount of nutrients coming downstream into the reservoir would pollute it. Studies of the geology of the Tocks Island area brought up questions of whether an earthen dam would hold. The U.S. Fish and Wildlife Service claimed that holding back that much fresh water would increase the salinity in the bay and destroy the $4-million oyster industry. The cost of the dam itself had more than doubled.

Second thoughts brought about new dissenters. The Tocks Island Regional Advisory Council, made up of representatives from all counties surrounding the planned reservoir and recreation area (Shukaitis for one), began squabbling among themselves, pulling out of the council county by county over whether or not to support the dam. Attendance at their annual dinners, featuring programs such as "Law Enforcement in a Rapidly Expanding Region," drew less-than-enthusiastic crowds. After all, by this time the dam was supposed to have been nearly complete. The Corps remained relentless.

"I remember it was near Ash Wednesday," says Shukaitis. "The squatters had refused to leave, and there were rumors of a cache of guns and explosives somewhere in the valley. The government tried to paint the picture that these were very dangerous people—

"Here," she interrupts herself, "there was another community in through here.

"Up in this hillside, incidentally, there are Indian skeletons and caves, but we don't tell anyone about them because we figure someone would ravage them and take them out to some museum. So I told the young man who told me about them that I was just going to forget about it.

"The valley is full of Indian burial grounds. We had one in our garden. My grandfather came upon it accidentally one day, human bones and some trinkets, and he demanded that no one remove any of it, even though there were people who wanted to take it out. 'Do you want that done to you when you're gone?' he said. 'Well, then, we're not going to do that to anyone else.'

"It was military intelligence—an attempt at psychological warfare. They used the squatters as a ruse. First of all, they wanted to make those of us who remained as uncomfortable as they could. I mean, we had local people who were eager to rent these houses, but they instead chose people from outside the area—

"None of these trees were here when I was a child. It was all clear fields with grazing cattle and sheep. It looked like Scotland. There was wonderful watercress and elderberry. And across the way was the Kittatinny Ridge, where we used to hike with the kids.

"During the time of the squatters, it seemed every Saturday night another place mysteriously burned to the ground. Once the fire companies had been sent to burn down the wrong place, and the people who were still living there came out and saw their little shed burning and all these firemen standing around doing nothing about it—talk about a nightmare—and the guy says, 'What are you doing?' And the fireman says, 'We're burning this place down.' And the guy says, 'But this is mine. I own it.' I mean, it was a nightmare. Time and again, I would be driving down Shawnee Hill and the sky would be red."

It had become an undeclared war in the Minisink valley. Each time the Corps took a village—Bushkill, Dingman's—it flattened it—school, stores, gas station, hotel evacuated, bulldozed, burned—and saw to it that no one would move back in. When questioned about the continuing demolitions, a National Park Service spokesperson said that its position was that "lands within the authorized boundaries of the recreation area are devoid of cultural remains associated with historical events of national significance. There are no great battles to be remembered, few personalities of other than local significance, and no broad events with impact felt much beyond the narrow confines of the valley."

"And when they finally turned this valley into a National Recreation Area," says Shukaitis, "President Johnson said, 'We will have reclaimed a wilderness.' And I just had to laugh. Did they think the squirrels laid up all those stone rows? And who are those tombstones for? So I wrote him a letter explaining to him it wasn't his fault, some speechwriter wrote that for him, but we were paying taxes, all of us, all those years. And the definition of wilderness in the Wilderness Act is a place where man has never set his foot. Well, you could hardly say that for much of the valley except for a few rattlesnake ledges where it wouldn't be too smart to set your foot. But our congressman at the time, named Rooney, said, 'Oh, even the pioneers came here for recreation.' I thought, 'Oh, God, he thinks those people were fishing and hunting here for the fun of it.' That was how we kept alive. These things have to make you laugh.

"Then I heard a man on the radio say that the Indians were not the first ones to live here. They weren't natives, he said, they were transient tribes. And I said to my husband, 'I bet you could prove in law that a place from which you leave but intend to go back to is your home.'

"Now," Nancy says, "you drive through and you hardly even know the river's there because the farmers who kept the brush cut are gone. But when I go down Shawnee Hill I can smell the river. I can feel the coolness. When you've grown up with that, you know it's there."

I drive back along the road we just traveled. A gray winter dusk has fallen. The river itself is frozen and snow-covered, giving its meanderings new forms. I think that Nancy's tour of the valley might have been a ghost story when she was young. Marley's ghost, this being near Christmas, come to show some local Scrooge what greed could make of a vital landscape: your homes burned, collapsing in on themselves, gone, even your gravesites abandoned. I stopped and pulled over where I thought we had seen the springhouse and watercress, to see whether the shingles of the springhouse were pine or cedar. Somehow I couldn't find it again. And in looking I lost my way. Without her, the landscape she painted disappeared.

I am a little angry with myself for not having paid better attention, but I have to smile when I think of our parting conversation.

Had I ever written any music? she asked. No, I hadn't.

"When we were kids," she recalled, "the minister at the church taught my cousin and me to play so he'd have an organist. He taught us the basics of composition, but we listened to Nashville on the radio and imagined we were ranchers, big cattle ranchers. Now lately I've tried writing songs. Country-western songs. And it's fun. I've just written one for *Billboard* magazine's songwriting contest."

What was it called?

" 'I Will Remember You.' "

April 22, 1974

Senators:

The creation of a lake behind the Tocks Island Dam would cause the loss of ten thousand acres of wildlife habitat.

The immediate or eventual losses in wildlife numbers due to construction of the Tocks Island Dam are as follows: five thousand white-tailed deer, six thousand five hundred raccoons, six thousand possums, five hundred foxes, two thousand gray squirrels, five hundred red squirrels, twenty thousand cottontail rabbits, five thousand woodchucks, five bobcats, one thousand five hundred skunks, four thousand muskrat, four hundred mink, four otters, eighty-five wild turkeys, one thousand two hundred weasels, two thousand five hundred ruffed grouse, one thousand five hundred ringneck pheasants, twenty-five thousand amphibians and reptiles, ten to the x number of invertebrates, one hundred and fifty birds of prey, and nesting habitat for two hundred and forty thousand passerine birds.

Is this nation so desperate for water and energy that we will sacrifice one of the last open river valleys in the East? Are we to tell our children's grandchildren that we decided to extirpate one of the last vestiges of our national heritage in the interest of technology that they will consider to be obsolete?

*Millions of tons of productive topsoil, millions of trees and
shrubs, hundreds of thousands of animals, and countless hours
of man's identification with his past will all be lost beneath a
thirty-seven-mile-long lake. We have the power to accomplish
this; do we also have the will?*

L. M. RYMON, PH.D.

The Tocks Island Dam has not yet been built.

THE OSPREY

AT A HUNDRED METERS THE BRIGHT GOLDEN EYE OF THE OSPREY FILLS
the eyepiece of the Questar. The large bird perches on the
edge of the stick nest some thirty feet above the river, the white of
his breast and eagle-like head catching the ambient light on a bright
but showery day. The eye has cat's-eye clarity, but is as large as the
whole side of the bird's head. It not only sees far but focuses far—
distinguishing, from a height of some 150 feet above the river, a
six-inch fish from a floating stick—and then adjusting its focus as
the bird dives or, more properly, drops, head and then feet first
toward the water. No blind dive: the fish nearly always comes up in
the hooked talons head-forward, eliminating drag as the large bird
lifts off. This bird has just delivered a fish to the brooding female,
who tears at it, takes a piece herself, then lets the next piece fall to
the ruffled chick whose head and already distinctly hooked beak
barely show above the twined nest walls. A camper with its side
door open is our blind. Larry Rymon, a man with a small, angular
face framed by a wispy red chin-beard and an unruly cascade of
long red hair, has already spent many hours over many years studying these birds and so is patient as I toy with the close-up lens. As
I focus and refocus, he paints for me the broader picture, as he has
come to see it, of ospreys, the river, and the land.

"When I was a kid in the forties I had seen a few eagles. The only osprey I had seen was in Florida, when I went to visit my grandfather in the winter. In fact, he lived very near a place called Osprey, Florida. But when I was ten I was fishing near here for smallmouth bass and walleye in a cove on the New Jersey side of the river called Bruce's Eddy, and I saw the classic thing: I saw the osprey with the fish, and then an eagle come by out of the Water Gap and take a swing at him. The osprey held on. I was awestruck. That happened within a hundred fifty yards of this very place. But I didn't see any more eagles or ospreys here after that."

The bird disappears from the scope. I look up. The female is alone. She is slightly larger than the male, and has a broad band of brown feathers across her breast.

"Now he's gone off over the river. He's swinging around and will probably come back onto one of those snags behind the nest. He's got so many fish on that nest now . . . But I get paranoid. The other day he went out and chased another bird over the river; I followed him with the binoculars and he went way out over the Water Gap. She was hungry. The rain was coming. I was afraid he wouldn't come back to feed her. He will not tolerate another nesting male. I thought at one time I might have two or three pairs nesting here, but he drives them all away. If one came now, he'd drop his fish and just climb like a World War II fighter plane up to intercept him and then just pound the devil out of him. At one time there used to be fifty turkey vultures that would come in here every night and roost on these high-tension towers. For years they would go between New Jersey and here, foraging in the day, coming back at sundown to roost, sun themselves in the morning, then go back out. He just started to come along and nip them off like a strafing fighter plane, and they haven't come back here since."

We hear a distant, high-pitched *cheereepcheereepcheereep*.

"A warning call. Fishermen along the river. In the early spring the farmer disturbed the birds with his plowing, and then, as soon as the field was plowed and it rained, the field would be crawling with artifact hunters poking around with their sticks. Then very shortly shad season would start and the fishermen would come in."

A distant squeal. Now Rymon goes to the scope.

"Looks like he's got another fish. Boy! He's just hauling fish in like crazy. This one little bird is so chock full, his crop is stuck out like a tennis ball."

Now we can see the bird coming through the riverbank oaks. My turn at the scope. The bird delivers the fish and is off again.

"I grew up—I was born in this little river town. Portland had an American store and an A&P, two butcher shops, two car dealerships, a private hospital, two active railroad stations—freight and passenger—a pharmacy, two hotels, several active churches, a dentist, two physicians, and an undertaker. A telephone exchange. A newsstand. A silk mill, a pencil factory, an aluminum window factory. A sandlot league. A haberdashery run by Max Effross. And a bank. A little town where farmers came to do shopping and buy autos. Mostly Fords. And Effross had a clothing club where you bought tickets and then made payments until you got the clothes. A&P, Acme—convenience, but not self-serve. The people who needed credit couldn't shop at chain stores, so the local general stores survived by giving credit. There was the Hercules Corporation in Belvidere, which made gunpowder in World War II. The haberdashery burned down after Effross's son Irving took it over. It couldn't compete with the K mart anyway.

"This was the day of the black and white fifteen-cent soda. People didn't have ice cream at home. There were no home freezers. You'd have to go to the soda fountain—a shy little country boy coming up to the counter to eat—mind your manners. I remember old Doc Ott, with his big wad of money, and Doctor Rushin, whose brother was the dentist. And ancient old Doc Morgan the veterinarian, who drove a prewar—a 1930 blue Dodge or something like it—a five-window coupe with little windowshade pulls and spoke wheels and all his medicines in the back that smelled so strong. He was a horse doctor. And I was going to be a veterinarian. And Doc Morgan always took me around and he never drove over twenty miles per hour. That's how I got interested in biology. Even though I ended up in the Merchant Marine Academy."

The osprey returned, but with only a stick.

"Nest-building goes on through the season. It's part of the pair-bonding, to always bring something back to the nest: a stub of fish, a stick, a Whitman's Sampler. They began building this nest in March." He pages through a little diary he's picked up from the dashboard of the van. "Last year, March eighteenth, was the earliest ever. This year, not until March twenty-sixth, Easter Sunday. She was on the nest on the twenty-seventh, but he hadn't come back yet. The literature says the male precedes the female, but not always.

"They rebuild the nest, repair, copulate, then lay eggs in early April. Incubation is for thirty-three to forty days, and then eight weeks of nest attendance until the young are fledged. Their development goes: out of an egg the size of a duck egg. . . ." (Whitish brown eggs with brown to rosy red spots, the pride of European collectors—"minor barons and royalty," says Rymon—who helped wipe out the ospreys of the British Isles. Here, birds feeding on fish contaminated by pesticides, especially DDT, laid eggs with shells so thin they caved in during incubation.)

"The young are helpless, naked and altricial, their first coat of down replaced by a second at about two weeks. Still downy at four weeks, they begin to pinfeather out and at six weeks look like young adults. But they're still standing on their whole foot. But they are a toe-walking bird and can't control or tear up their food until they're up on their toes, which is about seven weeks. When we hacked birds, raising them from young we brought from the Chesapeake Bay, feeding became a lot easier when we could just throw them chunks that they could tear up by themselves. One year I must have cut up a ton and a half of shad into little strips, which I fed to the birds on sticks.

"The first year, upon fledging, they fly south in September or October and spend their first winter in the American tropics. They go to the Amazon or to other places, spend the winter, the entire next summer, and the next winter. They don't start to return to their natal sites until they're two, and that is generally an exploratory trip. Their first real breeding is at age three. Fifty percent will breed at age three. Thirty percent will breed at age four. And the remainder don't breed until age five, and now we're beginning to suspect it might be more like six years before some start.

"Technically, statistically, factoring in juvenile mortality, ospreys only have a life expectancy in the wild of four-point-seven years, but they can live to be twenty-five. So the South American situation is important to us, but the Amazon and all its tributaries is a huge area. The one band I had recovered from down there came from Iquitos, in Peru, three thousand miles to the south of us. That bird was shot and eaten by Amazon natives. How prevalent that is, I don't know—some tribe might be using our bands as ornaments. But the osprey is pretty vulnerable here as well. Anywhere near man. For a twenty-first-century osprey to survive, we have to balance habituation to man's disturbance with keeping out of rifle range." This was not always the concern.

"When I grew up, this area of the river was the end of the road. But after the war, when gas rationing went off, you began to see, around the late forties, early fifties, people coming out from Jersey City, Newark, and the Philadelphia-Camden area to visit the Poconos. They didn't go very far, and there wasn't very far to go. You got to the Delaware Water Gap here and didn't go beyond.

"Imagine a 1947 Chevrolet. Here's father-knows-best driving. To Otto's Gap View. To the Bear Stop, where there were bears in cages with rubber tires. To Indian Head Overlook, where they sold souvenirs right at the point of the Gap with the famous natural rock profile of an Indian. And the Cold Air Cave—'A Decidedly Natural Curiosity'—a crack in the mountains where the air that comes out is fifty degrees in summer or winter, where an enterprising person, and I can't tell you exactly what year, built a restaurant and could control the air conditioning in the summer by opening and closing the door to the cave. And everyone stood out there with their Brownie cameras and their Kodaks, taking pictures with the family firmly posed against the rocks. On up a little ways in the Water Gap itself, on the left-hand side, where the water drains down, was a waterfall where people would stop to fill water jugs from the freshwater spring. I think there was a little refreshment stand there called Child's Arbor, where you squeezed over against the rocks, stopped the car, and ran in for a cold buttermilk or soda or ice cream or hot dog.

"These people had come along through Hackettstown at thirty-five miles per hour over the mountain on Route 46, and on a Sunday drive this was about as far as they could get. And they were blue-collar, mom and dad both working five and a half days a week in Jersey City or Newark, and they brought the family up for a picnic, which consisted of some hand-wrapped sandwiches, which they ate on a log in the woods. And along the way it was all enterprise: diners, locals selling baby blankets and bittersweet in the fall, farmers bringing out the produce, souvenir stands selling maple candy from Maine and little Indian hatchets carved from spruce trees somewhere by the Cherokee Indians, which cost you thirty-five to forty cents. Go feed french fries to the bear or the deer. And all of it contributed to the economy, I suppose, which was then only dairy farming. The biggest raw product here was milk, raw milk which went in tank cars from here to pasteurization plants. The biggest concern of the farmers in this area was their milk check. That was their paycheck. One of the local resources was horse urine from pregnant mares. Farmers collected it in twenty-gallon jugs and sent it out to Baker Chemical in Easton for hormone refining.

"Coal trucks used to come up and down this route toward Newark and Jersey City with coal from Scranton—blue coal, burning coal—over the Mine Hill through Dover and down, and the drivers would stop at the diner here for coffee and food and fill up with diesel fuel if they had to. And peanuts came from the Planter's Peanut Company in Wilkes-Barre, and this town was on their route.

"And everybody talked about the days when the Water Gap had the old hotels, and recalled the day—August second, 1910—Teddy Roosevelt came, and the streetcar extension that ran all the way from the Lehigh Valley. The days of the old grand hotels, the lemonade, the croquet, the wicker chairs."

The vacationers fished for trout in stocked lakes and streams, for brown and rainbow trout, not the native brook trout (which is not a trout at all, but a char), which was lost as the lumber industry exposed shaded streams, and as sawmills, paper mills, and tanneries loaded them with industrial residues. Browns and rainbows could bear warmer temperatures and muddier waters. "All the streams in the vicinity of Water Gap," wrote Luke Brodhead, "are more or less plentifully stocked with trout, and during the months of May, June, and July great quantities of them are taken with both fly and bait." There were shad and striped bass and, as Brodhead writes, a fish new to the Delaware:

> *Several years ago the Delaware River was stocked by the State Commissioners with Black Bass, and these have increased in number so that in the fall of 1875 a great many were caught with hook, line and rod from row boats anchored in the stream. These fish weighed from one to three pounds each, and being lively game fish, produced great sport in the catching; they have also a fine flavor, and the quiet, deep water in the Gap will undoubtedly contain them in such quantities and of such increased size as to make it an attractive spot for the disciples of Isaac Walton.*

Brown trout, rainbow trout, black bass, carp, and muskellunge are not native to the Delaware River or its tributaries. The Lenape would have never seen them. Their livelihoods depended on shad, striped bass, and sturgeon, which then ran even north of the Water Gap.

"By the end of World War II," says Rymon, "the resorts had mostly gone, many burned. The wealthy moved on. The local people fished for suckers because the shad and striped bass weren't running, blocked by the pollution downstream. With the advent of the automobile the Water Gap became reachable by a more egalitarian crowd.

"Summer camps sprang up everywhere, where the local kids earned extra money. Down on the beach on the river below the Gap was Ernie Oshefsky's Kittatinny Inn. Ruth Jones is Ernie's daughter, and she acts more and more like her dad every day. He was a wonderful one-man string band, a man who ate raw hamburger and

popped nitroglycerine tablets. His wife was a workaholic. This was
the only swimming beach of any merit on the river. Right up from
there was Camp Karamac, a summer camp for girls. Not wayward
girls, but stenographers and secretaries. This was the place for the
local boys to go for dates. It was about three-to-one, four-to-one
girls, so the local boys used to go out and hang around the shuffleboard, and if you were too young to drink, you had a little something in the car and entertained the girls swimming or by the
jukebox.

"Then Frank Jones, Ruthie's husband, started taking some of
these people upstream with canoes, and when they came down
they'd come in and drink beer. It was a great concession. They sold
alcohol, and beach-blanket bingo and convenient cabins were available. They were the first real chandlers of canoes on the river, and
it grew into Kittatinny Canoes. And now the canoe industry may
have grown too much. I've counted as many as two hundred canoes
come past the osprey nests without a break.

"I came back here from Oregon in 1968, and started teaching at
East Stroudsburg with the intention that in two or three years I'd
be back out west. . . . The fishermen are out of your view, but if
they get much closer the birds will be disturbed. I don't like too
much disturbance when they're breeding because the young can't
thermoregulate. Now . . . she's settling over the young . . . looking
alert to something. Oh God, here I go. At one early stage of this
whole business, this female had laid eggs and we got a freak April
hailstorm. I went home and I ran into the house, threw open the
refrigerator, grabbed an egg, and ran out and set it down in the
yard. Then I covered my head and sat and watched it. And my wife
said, 'What are you doing?' And I said, 'I'm just watching these
hailstones bounce off this hen egg.' And she said, 'Have you gone
mad?' And I told her I was afraid that the storm might spook the
young mother off her nest and the eggs would be cracked by the
hail. But after I made my test and the egg didn't crack, I came back
and the bird had never left the nest. She just stayed and got pum-
meled by the hailstones.

"I raised these birds here. The male in 1982. He appeared back in

August of 1984 and left again in September. During the time he was
here, he interacted with the birds we were hacking that year. He
flew with them, called, and they flew with him as if he were a par-
ent. In '85 I decided, 'Well, he'll be three, I best get some nest poles
up.' And he came back in April. And she came back, this female,
and they started to keep company. And they built a nest and they
copulated and it looked like action was going to happen, but then
some excavating began in the field and she got spooked away. She
wouldn't return to the nest pole and finally abandoned. But he
stayed and kept attending the pole. And I thought, 'Oh man, I've
got a golden opportunity. If I can just hold him on the nest, maybe
when the new birds I'm raising fledge, he'll foster them.'

"So I went to the museum at school and I got some osprey eggs
and I duplicated them in plaster and painted them and lacquered
them. And I put them in the nest, hoping he would attend them.
Well, he really didn't, but he stayed in the area until the young
fledged, and just looked at them flying around, coming back to be
fed, and then one day I saw four of them on his nest pole. He flew
overhead and began courting them with a fish, 'cheep cheep cheep,'
because he was still trying to attract a female. They responded to
his courting call by turning their heads and giving the juvenile
begging call: 'cheepcheepcheepcheep.' And in one split second his
neurons turned around from courtship to paternal behavior, and
instead of courting with the fish, he flew to the nest and gave it to
them.

"Eventually, I had nine of them that would go to the nest, and it
really was comedic to see them all up there clamoring over the nest.
It got so bad that he would come in on eight-minute intervals with
a fish and just drop it like a World War II torpedo into the nest and
keep going. He didn't want to get into the clamor and furor of these
squawking, hungry chicks. This was the first record of a hacked
bird fostering a whole bunch of young.

"She came back in '86. I was here when they met. It was in April,
a foggy, cold, early-April morning. He was on that perch with a
large fish. I was hoping she would come, and then, through the
valley fog I hear, 'cheep cheep cheep' and then she came through,

and she was carrying a stick. I mean, he's a slow courter, this guy—if birds didn't have individual personalities, the study of behavior would not be very much fun, but they're as genetically different as we are. So she just came right over to him with the stick and dropped it, almost hit him with it. And then they flew to that pole and their courtship began. It was like a Jimmy Dean movie—I mean, anthropomorphizing—she was looking out at the river, he was looking out at the river, they hardly seemed to be paying attention to each other, but then, a brief flirtation and they were over here nest-building and copulating. And they produced two young. The first osprey produced in Pennsylvania in fifty years."

Now, with some two dozen of the hundred birds Rymon has raised already returning to the river, along with the birds that migrate through the river valley on their way north, it's rare to be out a day on the Delaware without seeing an osprey. In early spring, while I fished for shad from the riverbank with a few other fishermen, braving the cold, fishing in woolen gloves, I saw an osprey take a single swing over the river, and on its return make a low pass that brought it down onto the water for a second, where it seemed to skid and falter but suddenly recover and come up with a trout in its talons.

"Fish hawk," muttered the man next to me in a not-too-admiring tone. Many osprey had been shot by anglers who believed the birds took too many fish.

In summer I have seen pairs of ospreys circling high, working the river. Even my kids have seen them enough to recognize the M-shaped seabird profile, the bright, mottled underbelly, and by now they even recognize the cheereeping call and take their time about looking up when they hear it. At ages seven and eleven they have seen more ospreys take fish than Rymon ever did.

And yet the bird's revival is still an uncertain one. From the Water Gap south along the Delaware, as far as the bay and Cape May, only seventeen other pairs of osprey have been spotted. Fifteen of these pairs nest near Salem, New Jersey, and two others along the Maurice River. This number of birds has not changed in fifteen years. The number of new clutches seems to be declining,

and tests show that pesticides, including DDT, may still be working their way through the system. The Delaware is a shallow river
and bay for most of its length, and chemical-laden silt may linger in
the shallows where young fish hatch and develop—fish upon which
ospreys feed.

For the birds to succeed, says Rymon, we need to secure habitat.
"But human history has been to come in and break up the habitat,
and whatever coexists with it is gone." The pre-Columbian forest
was endless, and full of beech and chestnut which fed flocks of passenger pigeons. As described by Stevenson Whitcomb Fletcher in
his book *Pennsylvania Agriculture and Country Life 1640—1840:*

> *"They flew over Philadelphia," says an eye-witness, "in flocks
> which obscured the sun for two or three hours and were killed by
> the hundred by people using sticks on the tops of homes." Crève-
> coeur relates his experience at Carlisle about 1770: "I caught
> fourteen dozen at one time in nets. As many as a man could
> carry home were sold for a penny. Every farmer kept a tamed
> wild pigeon in a cage at the door ready to be used at any time to
> decoy the wild ones as they approached."*

> *The reminiscences of Charles Miner of Wilkes-Barre contain
> this description of pigeon flights: "The whole heavens were
> dark with them, the cloud of wings continuing to pass for an
> hour or more and cloud succeeding cloud. There were not mil-
> lions but myriads. . . . Towns were built by them for five or six
> miles in length along the Meshoppen—every branch and
> bough of every tree holding a rude nest."*

The passenger pigeon, according to Fletcher, was the most important meat-producing bird of colonial Pennsylvania. In Lan-
caster County in the spring of 1846, "a dense mass of pigeons
extended to the eastern horizon and as far north and south as the
eye could reach and was continuous from about 12:30 to 4:30 P.M."

> *The seemingly inexhaustible supply of pigeons was quickly
> decimated by wholesale slaughter, mainly by market hunters.*

In May 1851 the Elk Advocate reported, "The American Express Company carried in one day over the New York and Erie Railroad over seven tons of pigeons to the New York market."

The slaughter, combined with the cutting of the trees in which the birds nested and which produced the mast crops on which they fed, brought the birds to extinction, the last flocks being seen on the Delaware in 1900.

This loss of forest affected more than the pigeons. Wild turkeys, once so abundant that thirty-to-forty-pound birds sold for a shilling, were lost. The deer, which Fletcher calls "the most prized wild animal" of the frontier, was also running out of food and habitat. Bears, whose meat was fatter than venison and so could be preserved better, along with providing oil for cooking and lighting, were hunted out of the hills, in part for food, in part because they preyed on the settlers' free-ranging swine.

Rymon: "The gray squirrel was so abundant that there wasn't much sense in shooting deer. The accurate rifled barrel of the Kentucky rifle was developed by the Germans in Pennsylvania in order to shoot squirrels. It was the rifle that won the Revolution. Here were these British soldiers with their blunderbusses standing there getting hit between the eyes by a sniper firing from behind a wall two hundred yards away."

Fletcher:

Unlike other wildlife, squirrels seemed to increase rather than decrease after settlement began, since farm crops added to their bill of fare. The General Assembly authorized counties to offer a bounty of three pence a head but this did little to check them. In 1749 the sum of £8000 Pennsylvania currency was expended as bounties on more that 64,000 squirrels. This exhausted the treasuries of a number of counties. The minutes of the General Assembly for 1750 record, "The farmers complained this year that the bounty given for squirrels had tended to their injury, for the labourers, instead of helping them with

their harvest, had taken up their guns and gone to hunt squir-
rels, as they could make more by squirrel scalps than by wages
at day labour."

"At one time," says Rymon, "when mast crops failed, forest
squirrels were seen swimming en masse west across the Susquehanna, going like lemmings from one forest to another."

Bounties were offered on anything that became a nuisance. A
crow or a dozen blackbirds brought threepence. Rattlesnakes were
slaughtered by the thousands as lumbermen clear-cut the high
ledges on which snakes denned. As deer disappeared, packs of
wolves preyed on sheep and calves. Fletcher cites a ruling by the
Swedish court at Chester in 1682 that if anyone "shall kill a dog-
wolf hee shall have ten shillings, and if a bitch-wolf, fifteen shillings, if slain by a white man; if by an Indian, five shillings and the
skin for his pains."

In 1840 the General Assembly passed "An Act to Encourage
more Effectively the Destruction of Wolves and Panthers," offering bounties of twenty-five dollars on a full-grown wolf, sixteen
dollars on a full-grown panther, and half the bounty on a puppy of
either one. "In wolf drives a large area, perhaps half a township,
was surrounded by hunters. At a given signal all advanced toward
the center, making an outlandish noise. Few wolves within the cor-
don escaped." By 1860 both wolves and wildcats were nearly ex-
terminated. (A hundred years later the state of New Jersey would
begin trying to undo the damage by reintroducing the wildcat into
the state.)

As the deep forest disappeared, so did the woodpeckers, grouse,
and warblers. "I'm sure," Rymon says, "you would have had a
problem finding even an American robin or woodchuck in any great
numbers. At one time there was even an East Coast population of
whooping cranes that ranged from Quebec to Florida."

With the National Park Service now holding the Delaware corridor, the hills from the Water Gap and a hundred miles upstream
have once again become wooded and once again filled with deer,
bear, and wild turkey. Beaver and otter share streambeds. But

humans have begun to intrude once again—this time fragmenting the forests with suburban development rather than farms.

"At one time," Rymon says, "in back of the bakery at Belvidere there were black ducks and wood ducks, hooded mergansers and great blue herons. No more. And in the past few years one of my hottest spring warbler spots was taken over by a retirement condominium, and the bird life has been reduced to starlings, robins, and blue jays."

We sit in a booth in a small Portland diner, the rain now falling steadily outside. Seems like everyone passing gives Rymon a pleasant greeting.

"No hooded warblers, no ovenbirds, no nothing."

Jukebox plays country music. Rymon looks down shyly into his coffee cup.

"So I ran for township supervisor."

Then, almost apologetically, in order to explain somehow the connection between warblers and politics, he follows with a poignant political exegesis.

"We were all concerned with the lack of zoning, with garbage, with sewage, with a master plan that called for eleven nuclear power plants along the Delaware. We had a group that felt they needed to protect the area.

"The wetlands that used to recharge the tributaries were being destroyed. They may tell you they are saving wetlands, but they save some and lose some, and the result is a wetland fragmented—too small to function properly either hydrologically or biologically. And when all the fields and woods become rooftops and shopping-mall parking lots, the rainwater can't be absorbed and the runoff bounces the small streams out of their banks. They flood on every spring freshet. In excavated areas every raindrop lifts soil, muddying streams. Mud has a completely different fauna than stone. And then the streams go from flood to drought.

"The complexion of the place was changing. Farmers could sell two lots and make what they used to make on a year's worth of milk checks.

"I mean you've got a farm, let's say my parents' farm. Eighty-five acres in New Jersey, near Hope. In 1943 that eighty-five-acre farm with buildings—no livestock—sold for ten thousand dollars. It's in a valley, it's picturesque—it's where I grew up. But now it's five minutes from Interstate 80. It's subdividable. It looks like it's dying to become a Quiet Valley subdivision. What do you think it's worth in 1990? Per acre. Plenty of drainage. Plenty of water. I mean, we're talking quarter-acre lots at thirty-five thousand dollars, right?

"Now, let's say my father hadn't sold it for ten thousand. Let's say he decided to work the farm. That is, if he could have kept his son who's been to Rutgers and a daughter-in-law who's been to Vassar and wants to raise Norwegian horses or something. He may take in forty-five thousand net from his milk check on what is now, say, a five-, six-, seven-, or eight-million-dollar investment. But now comes the offer from the developer, the ticket to sell out. Here's his Del Ray Beach or Santa Monica condo. Move out to where his son-in-law is working for North American Aircraft. Why not? He's worked all his life on what was a dirt farm with a few cows and chickens during the Depression. He traded eggs for groceries to stay alive. What does he owe it now?

"So the farmers get old and get out. Now he's in Florida as a malcontent, and the developer has the land. But somewhere the ethic of the land is lost. Suburbia encroaches. All that survives are fragmented fields and woodlots, some gray squirrels and garden-variety birds. Even where the total number of birds may increase, the diversity index plummets. The biomass is high, but it's monotonous. Little woodland ponds are lost where salamanders survived for thousands of years; where toads and snakes, which can't move easily from one place to another, are holed up in small refuges. No gene flow. We tend to think in a broader way about more conspicuous species. But even if millions of individuals aren't endangered, diversity is. Birds need vertical as well as horizontal habitat. Migrating birds lose out to permanent edge-happy resident birds. The environment becomes more homogeneous. The people do, too. The diversity and age structure in the population change, and the richness of the social fabric fades. Now the guy in the trailer with the few chickens—for all his crudeness, the guy who pulled your ears before he gave you a piece of candy, the hillbilly who had a sense of place from which he took sustenance and well-being—is the last Indian. These people, these stump-sitters and checker-players, are now fast gone. The spirit of the region gone with the depersonalization of the land." I recall Bernie Herman's lament for land and people of the lower Delaware, and James Newton's lost African-American world along the New Jersey river shore.

"The group needed someone with local roots who could go out and talk to people," says Rymon. "I was swept in by a few dozen votes."

He served his couple of years as the "hippie mayor," merging natural lives and modern times. When he left office he continued teaching and studying his ospreys. Many of his students follow Rymon's own example and do their work in the places in which they live. I have met them banding eagles on the Delaware, tagging otters, and prosecuting polluters in the Poconos. I ran across Rymon and students at a hunter check-in station, inspecting the teeth of killed deer in order to find out the age range of the overextended deer population. On a plane back to New York from an international conference on the environment held in Miami Beach, I met a Mexican student whom I recognized from one of the sessions. His name was Xicotencatl Vega and he was from a small village an eight-hour drive north of Puerto Vallarta. His ambition was to finish school and return to his home to set up a preserve for migrating raptors. What school? East Stroudsburg; Rymon was his adviser.

Rymon will take credit only for the return of the osprey.

"Maybe it's true that my one great-grandfather was half Indian and me one-sixteenth."

We stand outside the diner in a cool spring mist, finding it difficult to part company. I want to hear more; he seems to enjoy the telling.

"I know when I stand in this valley and take in its mood—when I see an osprey—I believe that the Great Spirit knows appreciators of his work and when the Great Spirit sees appreciators of his work, he puts on the big show. He often does that for me.

"Ospreys have been here for fifteen million years. They haven't evolved much over all that time. Long before we primates ever put our foot down on the ground, these birds were nesting up and down these river valleys through all the glaciers and geologic changes. So when I see an osprey circling the Delaware now—and this pair has produced seven young in four years—it gives me a lot of satisfaction."

NOW THE LIGHTS COME THROUGH THE TREES

*W*ROTE LUKE BRODHEAD:

The surroundings of Lake Utsayantha are said to be very wild and picturesque—a mirror of beauty in a wilderness of woods, so secluded that few save the red men have ever gazed upon it in its solitary serenity. This is said to be the source of the river.

The source of the Delaware River is no mystery. The river can be followed by car as easily as a finger can trace its winding path on a map. There is an East Branch Delaware and a West Branch Delaware, shallow mountain streams that flow southwesterly across the Catskills, parallel to each other and separated by ten to twenty miles of scalloped, wooded slopes nearly three thousand feet high (parallel, too, to the nascent Susquehanna, flowing to the west of them both). These streams each flow into and out of reservoirs that send their water to New York City, and then run down to meet below Point Mountain at Hancock, New York. As lacking in romance as this may sound, it should serve to make a point about a river: its "source" is not only one source, for its waters come from uncountable sources over a wide area known as a watershed. In the case of the Delaware River, this watershed covers some 13,500 square miles in four states. Fifty percent lies in Pennsylvania, twenty-three percent in New Jersey, nineteen percent in New York, and eight percent in Delaware. Along the way it takes in the waters of three major rivers: the Lackawaxen at the town of Lackawaxen, the Lehigh at Easton, and the Schuylkill at Philadelphia. But it also takes in the waters of some two dozen good-sized streams and uncountable smaller ones along its long, undammed main stretch, the longest length of undammed river on the East Coast. The watershed averages forty-five inches of rain a year, and up to twenty-eight inches of that rain runs off into these streams and to the river. But these days runoff not only flows out of hidden mountain springs and clear streams, but comes down in acidic rainfall and then, over all those square miles, runs off every rooftop, erodes treeless slopes, runs with the fertilizers and pesticides from every farm, orchard, lawn, and garden, the oil from every highway and parking lot, the animal wastes from every street, the drainage from every septic system, and the discharge from every treatment plant. All of these are the sources of the river.

In some places, where development has been great, the amount of waste water discharged into a tributary from a sewage treatment plant can be two, three, or more times greater than the stream's natural flow. In the worst cases the stronger current erodes the streambank. It keeps the diatomaceous plants that energize the food web with oxygen from establishing their thin golden brown and green slicks on the stream rocks. It drowns out the algae and mosses, washes out the insects, leaves neither nesting place nor food for fish, and sends silt downstream into the river. A rainfall of a couple of inches may overwhelm the capacity of a sewage plant, and the sewage runs out without treatment. To make up for the septic overflow, a treatment plant may add an extra dose of chlorine that can scour out the good with the bad. Over the course of a year the plant and the state testing agencies may claim they've maintained a good average water quality. But averages mean little when the stream life can't survive the extremes.

For example, with biologist Don Baylor, I go down to a creek in Stroudsburg, Pennsylvania, that runs just along the edges of two large shopping plazas: a common enough sight in any town, a stream-bed littered with old shopping carts and discarded beer bottles. Baylor, whose career as a specialist in aquatic insects began with a love for fly fishing, dips a long-handled cloth net into the stream. He scoops up a gray-brown muck, and in the muck we see some small, red, threadlike worms jerking to escape the light of day—nothing more. We are a couple of hundred yards down from the shopping mall's sewage treatment plant, which, Baylor knows, has had problems in the past. This swift little run is so beset with silt and sewage flocculent that nothing can live in it but these worms, which are the larvae of midge flies. And the only reason they survive, and the reason for their blood red color, is that they contain hemoglobin, the substance in our own red blood cells, which enables them to produce their own oxygen. Baylor recalls that when he was a boy, before the shopping centers were built, he used to fish the then-shaded stream for trout. It was just such trout streams—the Brodhead, McMichael's, Saw Kill, Tunkhanna, Tobyhanna, and Little Bushkill—that first drew visitors to the cool Pennsylvania hills west of the Delaware.

These Delaware tributaries flow down steep rock ridges from the fifteen-hundred-to-two-thousand-foot summits of what's known as the Pocono Mountains. Made up of the same Devonian sediments as the Kittatinny, the Poconos (like the Catskills) never folded into steep ridges; instead, the layers of rock remained horizontal as they lifted to create a high, broad, flat plateau. During the million or more years of ice ages, mile-high glaciers ground back and forth across the plateau. When they retreated, some fifteen thousand years ago, they left behind ravines and river gorges, boulder fields, deep holes, lakes, waterfalls, and swift, cold trout streams.

During the same latter years of the nineteenth century when fishermen were slaughtering the sturgeon, and plainsmen the buffalo, tanners and timbermen came to the Pocono hemlock forests. They exacted no less a toll. The denuded slopes left lakes and streams that had been shaded for twelve thousand years exposed to the sun. Warm water can't hold as much oxygen as cool water—the streams lost their glacial fuel. A forested slope retains some eighty-five percent of rain that falls on it; the treeless hillsides eroded and the mud washed downstream. The mud clogged the swift, stony glacial courses and left the stream insects without their substrate retreats. The prized brook trout began to disappear.

In 1889, worried less over the disappearance of the trout than over the possibility of losing the growing trout-fishing carriage trade, the state of Pennsylvania introduced hardier European brown trout to the Pocono streams. This seemed to satisfy the wealthy Philadelphia and New York lawyers and industrialists, men who used two initials rather than first names, and who had become obsessed by fishing with lures delicately modeled of hair and feathers to imitate the stream insects upon which the trout fed. This made catching fish an effete and scientific enough business that it might not be construed as being completely without redeeming social value. The Henryville House resort along the Brodhead Creek gained the status of a shrine among these fly fishermen. Soon celebrities of the day joined them. The actor Joseph Jefferson and the boxer John L. Sullivan, Theodore Roosevelt and Gifford Pinchot, Buffalo Bill Cody and Annie Oakley all fished the Brodhead from the Henryville House. (So enthusiastic was the response to the introductions of both the black bass and the brown trout that in 1890 the Pennsylvania Fish Commissioners brought Atlantic salmon to the Delaware from the Penobscot in Maine. Despite great fanfare—"THE FISH COMMISSIONERS TAKE GREAT PLEASURE IN ANNOUNCING the almost certainty that their efforts to stock the Delaware river with Atlantic salmon have been successful"—none survived. Ichthyologists seem to agree that neither the Delaware nor the Hudson ever had native salmon runs. But should anyone think that today, a hundred years later, a state might be more concerned with preserving existing streams and fish than with spending the time and money importing exotic species, it happens that the state of New Jersey, in perhaps the spirit of the woman who suggested the Water Gap would be a better place if Niagara Falls were there, now plans to plant Pacific salmon into the Delaware.)

The great flood after the August hurricane of 1955 left the Brodhead and many other Pocono streams in ruins. Frank Carle finds that that year many species of dragonfly vanished along the Delaware. Don Baylor found the same along the Brodhead. But to make matters worse, the Army Corps of Engineers diked and channelized the Brodhead, straightening it into a shallow flume. The old guard of fishermen went elsewhere, many to the still-unspoiled streams of the Catskills, upper Delaware tributaries like the Beaverkill. The young lions of industry went deep-sea fishing for marlin and tuna. The remaining fellowship of Pocono fishermen retreated to small, privately owned stretches of stream. Baylor brings me to one fishing club's section of McMichael's Creek only a few miles from its headwaters. The stream, in this October rain, gushes over a rocky stretch of riffles, swirls around a bend, and rushes off into deep woods. Baylor dips his net and brings it up full of a river mud alive with scuttling and burrowing insect larvae. Taking a plug of the mud across his palm, he quickly identifies four different species of mayfly, three of caddis fly, four of stone fly. Most of these, he says, are species with little tolerance for disturbed waters. Their filamentous gills can't cope with fouling silt or oxygen-poor water. On a tolerance scale of zero to ten, he says, those shopping-center midge larvae rank ten, and these, zero to one. And he guarantees that in the spring we'd find at least twenty-five different species in a single dip of the net, and that along the bend where the water pools, he'd bet on at least a dozen bright little brook trout.

Walter Burkhart won't despair. He was a cop too long—a Fish Commission cop—a man who tangled in the wilds with poachers and polluters. He's a big man with an invincible stare, invaluable unblinking blue eyes, and a large, ruddy, but still firm-chinned face that barely moves a muscle even as he's talking or chewing gum. "When I first came here," Burkhart recalls, "this place was so rural that you couldn't just go someplace and get a sandwich. There was places I'd be you'd have to drive thirty miles to get something to eat. So I used to carry my fly rod in my car. And I always had my little one-burner Coleman and my cooking kit and so forth, and if

I was working certain areas of the county I'd go up some little brook trout stream, catch three or four, clean 'em, come back to the stream, dip some water out for coffee, make my coffee, fry my brook trout, and that's my lunch. And that's what I liked to do. But you can't do that today. I know of no stream that truthfully I would drink from without some kind of treatment. This is terrible. This is a disgrace. To have to buy water? In the Poconos?"

So he thinks people ought to just take this all more seriously than they do.

"I was never the kind of person who tolerates being ignored. They paid attention to me because if they didn't do something, I'd arrest them and it could get real expensive. They could get fined a thousand dollars a day. That got their attention. The way it is now, if you don't operate a sewage treatment plant properly, the DER (Pennsylvania Department of Environmental Resources) will come to talk to you for five years, for ten years, tell you how you've been a bad boy, and make a report and say, 'Now, you have to do this and this.' But they won't take the next step and say, 'Hey you're going before the county judge and it's going to cost you thirty-five thousand a day and that's going to go on forever until we put you right out of business.' Then, by God, they'd start to do something."

A septic system works like this. Sewage and wastewater flow from the house into a watertight tank sunk into the ground. The solid stuff settles out in the tank and the remaining liquid flows out to a drainfield where it's purified as it percolates through the soil.

The problem for Pocono developers was that beneath the stony gray glacial soil was solid Devonian rock. Five feet of soil was the minimum required for proper treatment of sewage wastewater and in some places in the Poconos there was not even two. In many places, wastewater barely percolated at all before hitting the impervious rock layer and running out over the ground.

But with a lot of land sold to hopeful second home owners, a solution, of sorts, was found. The developer provided the extra percolation depth by building a raised mound of sand into which the wastewater would drain. The state DER bought the notion, despite warnings that those mounds might only have a limited working life before they had to be removed and rebuilt. Now, when one drives through the Poconos, one sees houses off in the woods and next to each is a mound, not unlike some Native American burial mounds, some four feet high by ten feet wide, some twenty feet long, taking up a great deal of the yard. The people who live in these houses don't even always know what the mound is for, or don't care, for many have placed their picnic tables and chairs atop them, or planted shrubbery around them although the roots will eventually choke the wastepipes within the mound. But without these mounds, much of the Pocono plateau might still be the retreat it once was.

While the Pocono resort brochures now tout suites that would "befit a Roman Emperor or Empress" each with a lipstick-red heart-shaped whirlpool bath and "an enticing custom round bed encircled with roman pillars, mirrored ceilings and walls and a romantic log-burning fireplace, a forty-five-inch color cable television with bedside remote control," all of which give

Privacy—when you need it
Excitement—when you want it
Luxury—that bubbles over like uncorked champagne,

the Poconos had far humbler beginnings.

Two Pocono resorts, Unity House and Tamiment, for example, began as retreats for New York City socialists and labor unionists. These mostly Jewish immigrants had come from Lithuania and Eastern Europe at the turn of the century. They worked in sweatshops during the day (my grandmother, then a teenager, took the train daily from her tenement on the Lower East Side of New York City to Yonkers to sew in a clothing factory), and at night studied English and labor organization. Unity House was the retreat of the International Ladies Garment Workers Union. Adjacent to it, under the sponsorship of the Rand School of Social Science, was the People's Educational Camp Society, better known as Camp Tamiment.

The Rand School was founded in 1906 as a place of study for immigrants, a training school for shop stewards, a lecture hall for socialist thinkers, and a music hall for choral and theatrical presentations. When Camp Tamiment opened in the Poconos in 1921, it was designed "to diffuse a general knowledge of literature, art and science through the medium of lectures, publications, and dramatic performances," an educational, cultural, and recreational retreat from the difficult conditions of city tenement life. The officers and directors were serious men who, in their papers of incorporation, referred to one another as "comrade" and wrote their birthplaces and the dates of their naturalization as citizens next to their names: "Jacob Blaufarb, president. Bialystock, Russia. Naturalized 1910. Alexander Kahn, v.p. Smolensk, Russia. Naturalized 1903. Adolph Held, Treasurer. Bouplaw, Poland. Naturalized 1902." At Tamiment these workers installed a sawmill and built their own cabins, kitchens, and social hall.

Soon, however, the center of activity became the Tamiment playhouse. Beginning with guests writing and performing their own musical and comedy shows, Tamiment became a place where young performers and writers, many of them the children of immigrant parents, could meet and develop their talents. By 1927 the camp was making money on its paying guests, and the Rand School was living on the camp's income. Under the leadership of Ben Josephson, "a master of the picturesque expletive," the camp became more and more profitable. But Josephson, it was contended, "had long ceased to be a socialist," and the camp suffered a split with the school. By the end of World War II, Tamiment had dropped all but the tax-exempt status of an educational institution (although it *was* training entertainers like Woody Allen, Carol Burnett, and Danny Kaye). In 1947 the camp opened the "Skyline" golf course, designed by Robert Trent Jones, and Josephson reported that Tamiment was "a summer resort that has attained top rank in the field, outranking by far many of the privately owned vacation places both in beauty and in business." This boast would prove the camp's downfall, for it would reach the ears of the Internal Revenue Service.

In the meantime the resort business everywhere in the Poconos boomed.

In 1945, Rudolf Von Hoevenberg opened Farm on the Hill in the Poconos, a collection of rustic cabins in which newlyweds spent a rugged week of country living. The wives made the beds and kept the cabins clean, and their husbands waited on tables. This cut down a lot on Von Hoevenberg's expenses. Nevertheless, and despite—or because of—his allowing White Anglo-Saxons only, his cabins reportedly always had a waiting list of about-to-be-marrieds. This was not the first anyone had heard of the honeymoon vacation business; in 1914 a film called "A Honeymoon Trip to Delaware Water Gap" portrayed newlyweds on the new Liberty Bell Limited from Allentown, Pennsylvania, to the Delaware River resorts. But after World War II there were brides and grooms to spare, and by the 1950s the marriage trade had become a mainstay of the Pocono lodges. Their repute reached a pinnacle of sorts in 1959, when Morris Wilkins of the Cove Haven resort introduced the first heart-shaped bathtub. Photos of the tub ran in *Life* magazine, and the Pocono Mountains began billing itself the Honeymoon Capital of the World. (The Wilkins tub remained pretty much the state of the art for the next thirty years until the recent introduction of a clear acrylic bath in the shape of a champagne glass.) The nature of the mountains, of course, became secondary to the poolside lounges and cabanas, tennis courts, nightclubs, and dining rooms. The ideal resort was a cruise ship at anchor in a sea of mountain greenery. It was all good fun. No one worried about the percolation capacity of the podzolic Pocono soils. So it was a honeymoon period in more ways than one.

Over the next years the new parents brought their children to see the falls at Winona, or to Bushkill, the Niagara of the East. I can remember trips to Winona, where a ticket bought you a long walk through the dim grottoes of the five falls where the Saw Creek drops from the Pocono plateau, falling across fractured slate terraces in hemlock-shaded ravines. The spray raised a continuous mist, and the wooden bridges across the falls seemed, to a nine-year-old, so flimsy they might have been made of thread. They were nervous crossings over what were, to my mind, fearsome drops. But I don't think I ever saw all the falls, because in the distance, even through the constant rush of water, one could always hear—or at least so I remember it—the noise of the little Winona amusement park with its bumper cars and Wild West shooting galleries and smell the caramel corn and cotton candy.

The Poconos were as exotic to me as the cobras within the wooden confines of the Pocono Snake Farm. I don't think we actually ever walked into the woods, at least not without a ticket, but it seemed a wild enough place. The cars drove slowly and the stops were few and far between. The gas stations were small country stores. We always stopped at the same silver diner. And there always seemed to be enticing glimpses of streams or lakes through the trees. We spent most of the time in the car because we had many miles to cover before dark.

In the 1960s, many of the family-owned resorts fell on hard times. The tourist industry spread to more remote climes. Honeymooners could go to the Caribbean. A campaign was begun to legalize gambling in the Poconos. There was speculation of resort takeovers by entertainers like Frank Sinatra and Wayne Newton. Organized crime was rumored to be setting up shop in the Poconos; the mountains had always been rumored to be gangland's vacationland. A referendum on the issue sent the gambling proposal down to defeat. Then, in takeovers reminiscent of industrial buyouts, corporate entities, land development companies, moved in. Many resorts found that the only way to survive was to develop more of their open, "unused" land. They sold it off, or built vacation homes, or crowded the land with rows of attached town houses. The idea for these last was called time-sharing: one owned a vacation house with many buyers, each of whom had bought the right to use it for a specified amount of time each year. This was great business for the realtors and lenders, who could sell the same house over and over again. They built golf courses and ski slopes that gave way to golf course and slope-side developments.

The IRS won its battle with Tamiment. The resort was sold. Now the once-wooded hillsides around the old wooden bungalows have been cut into lots for new homes.

Saw Creek estates, on the adjacent ridge, is the same story: the woods are cut by a winding maze of roads and glutted with large new second homes. Driving, disheartened, out the gate and down the steep slope toward the river, I see an old parking lot off to the left, the macadam broken up by weeds. I turn in to investigate. The lot slopes toward a little entrance gate. At the gate I recognize the place, even in its ruin, for it's the little Winona amusement park. The bumper cars sit parked in silent disarray on their metal floor, the shooting gallery and all the Wild West facades—Post Office, Opry House, Last Chance Saloon—all stand shuttered. The little midway was so small, I can't imagine how it entertained us. But now, with the amusements silenced, I could hear the falls and I walked the path with no ticket. They were smaller than I remembered, the bridges lower, but all was still embowered in fern and rhododendron, the ledges slick and the mosses sparkling from the spray. But above the falls now I could hear the hammering on the new houses on the ridge.

When big-time real-estate development came to the Poconos, it came to rural counties and small towns that believed they saw new sources of revenue that would ask for little in return. These were vacation developments, after all, and so they would not increase the needs for schools or roads, but they would be paying taxes just the same.

"Now the townships all run their own affairs," says Burkhart, "and I know a couple of the supervisors who never went past the fourth grade. They were able to take care of the roads, but they have no understanding of the larger problems of development. These are not people who should be supervisors in this day and age. But people like them, and they're good bullshitters, and they take care of the roads. One in particular, a good friend of mine, I asked, 'How can you authorize these developments when you know that two feet underground is solid rock?'

" 'Well,' he says, 'I rely on an engineer.'

"I said, 'Well, how do you know he's telling the truth?'

" 'Well, we pay him.'

"And that makes him truthful? The guy is a friend of mine and he's a nice fella and he's only got another three years before he can retire and get his pension. So he depends on a piss-poor engineer. The engineer is in cahoots with the builder!"

Soon the vacation homes became permanent homes. In the last ten years Monroe and Pike counties, along the west shore of the Delaware River, have been the two fastest-growing counties in the state of Pennsylvania, two of the fastest-growing counties in the nation. Pike County to the north grew by nearly fifty percent, and Monroe by thirty-five percent. And while this still only means some thirty thousand residents in Pike and ninety-five thousand in Monroe, the effects of such change have been the beginning of the end of the rural lives these counties could, up until ten years ago, say they enjoyed. For instance, in 1970, Monroe County had an average of one house per eighteen acres; in 1980, one house per ten acres; and in 1990, one house per five and a half acres.

"When I first moved to where I live," says Burkhart, "I could not see another home from my home. The closest was a half-mile away. Now I'm pretty much surrounded, and when it becomes dark, you can see all the lights come through the trees."

Tamiment has applied to increase its sewage treatment plant from 250,000 gallons a day to 1,150,000. Concerned that this upstream sewage plant threatened the quality of their waters, the owners of Bushkill Falls, downstream of Tamiment, filed official protest with the state. The falls, family-owned since 1904, when Charles Peters suspended a swinging bridge over one and began charging admission for visitors to cross, attract some 250,000 paying customers a year "to enjoy the spectacular scenery, as well as the birds, air, bear and trout in abundance." They had already seen parts of their Niagara of the East, the family said, run green with eutrophic effluent. The National Park Service, which owns the land adjacent to Tamiment, became concerned as well, not only for the little Pond Run Creek into which Tamiment would discharge its treated water, but for the Bushkill Creek into which Pond Run

Creek flows, and for the Delaware itself, only four more miles down-stream.

In the near future, all the concern over how fast the Poconos grew may seem quaint. As the straight-talking Craig Todd puts it, if nothing changes, in another decade people may be amazed to hear that anyone ever came to the Poconos for a vacation. Todd, the embattled conservation officer of Monroe County, is, as someone told me, the man with his finger in the dike, trying to keep the several hundred square miles of natural Pocono watershed from being overwhelmed by land development. This is not a job for the fainthearted. "Last night," he tells me, "I was called Hitler and a buffalo chip." But it is also a lousy beat for someone who spent much of his youth yearning to be a hermit, and most of his reluctant-undergrad days hiking and hunting. "Now I just go to construction sites. I don't even know what a damned tree looks like."

He explains himself as a hard case and conducts himself with the demeanor of a Hammett private eye: Don't talk to me about it, just get the job done. His office has the look of a hard-up detective bureau. Bag lunches perch on the corners of beat-up old desks; when a visitor comes in, someone has to give up his or her chair. Todd's staff all look young, bright, and underfed. Todd himself is just thirty-six (his wife is expecting their first child any day), but he's developed a skeptical look that makes him appear older than he is. County maps cluttered with red- and blue-capped pushpins paper the aging walls. Tacked to one, a yellowed cartoon of a ravaged woman registering at a rape counseling center: "The name's Nature," she says, "Mother Nature." Taped on Todd's gooseneck desk lamp, the following: "If you ain't paranoid, you ain't paying attention."

For all the county's growth, things at the conservation office are tough. Todd's budget is slim. His staff of three has not grown since 1983, when the county had only thirty-eight site inspections and forty-three site reviews. In 1988 the group had 336 site inspections, 495 reviews, and one thousand cases in which they provided technical assistance to help developers comply with environmental regulations. His technicians, as he calls his assistants, with five years of college, make barely seventeen thousand dollars a year. To help meet their budget, everybody sells seedlings and birdseed.

The local anti-litter campaign fared better. Within two years of being established with great fanfare, it had as many employees as Todd had to protect the county's wetlands.

"Now, I'm anti-litter," he assures me with a somewhat garrulous drawl, "but I'm not necessarily in favor of picking up after adults. I think my anti-litter campaign would be, 'Okay, nobody picks up litter.' That's it. Then, after three years, everybody would be able to see what hogs they are. You know, when you pick up after a kid, it's only there again the next day. Litter is a symptom of growth. It's always easy to get money to treat the symptoms."

Meanwhile, left untreated, often undiagnosed, the health of water, wetlands, and wildlife suffers.

For instance, says Todd, where wetland laws may protect the water resource, they may shortchange the rest of the system.

"If you can still develop right up to a wetland edge, that does the wildlife absolutely no good at all. At some point in their lives the majority of the wildlife in the Poconos depend upon either wetlands or the equally important associated uplands. Those aren't being protected. And you can understand why they'd be extremely difficult to protect. A developer may agree not to develop on an acre of wetland because it's going to be a pain to go in there anyhow. 'Okay,' he says, 'I'll go along with that. I'll use the land for a park or add it to another lot and double the price of that lot.' But when you tell a developer he can't get within three hundred feet of a wetland because it's required to protect associated upland habitat—that gets real tough. You known what I mean?

"It's very hard for people who live in subdivisions to understand their impact upon wildlife. Because some of these areas actually become sanctuaries for wildlife. You get state game lands surrounded by huge, sprawling subdivisions, and after the first day of hunting season every deer that was in the game lands is in the subdivision. There's a garbage source there for the black bears. So these people are seeing wildlife all the time, and their general attitude is, 'Hell, there's more deer here than before.' It's very hard for them to perceive the impact because they're not seeing the whole picture.

"You take somebody who's lived in a row house all their life and they see a tree on a lawn and they think they're in the middle of Alaska. Now, I have seen guys out here with sidearms. As soon as they get out here, they put their pistol on. You'd think they were in the bush. So wilderness is a relative thing. One of the problems is that all of their lives some people turned on faucets and flushed toilets and ate food and they had no idea where it was coming from or where it was ending up. You know what I'm saying? Now they come out here and they've got this sand mound in their backyard and it's the only grass they have and they put a picnic table on it and some chairs around it, and they mow it and it's like their lawn, and they don't even know it's their septic system. They don't know how to maintain it. They know their water comes from a well, but they really don't have any concept of what a well is. And they certainly aren't attuned to the life-support systems around them. So it's a long way to go before they realize the impact they make.

"Traffic, roads deteriorate: our roads can't handle it now, and most of the projects that have been begun over the last three years aren't anywhere near built out. Storm water problems, wells drying up or contaminated, septic systems failing—we probably have more on-lot septic systems than any county in the state, and definitely more sand mounds. But our soils are terrible. We're on steep slopes. I mean, one of the functions these wetlands perform is to soak up the high spring flows and slowly release them during the summer into the tributaries.

"So you try to educate everyone. But often, during the education process, the whole thing breaks down. When you build in the Poconos you have to look. Where are your steep slopes? Where are your agricultural soils? Where are your wetlands? All right? You decide where you can pack 'em in, and where you can't, okay? One obvious solution to me is that maybe the rate of development here

is too much for the natural systems to handle. You know what I'm
sayin'? Ultimately you come to the situation where you've got to
determine what the carrying capacity of a certain geographical area
is, and what happens there has to hew to that, or your quality of life
goes down the tubes. People seem to somehow recognize that, because someone will come over the bridge, buy a house here, and
within six months hate everyone else who's coming across. I'm a
firm believer that if we're going to continue to procreate the way we
are, then put a hundred people on three acres, okay? You have less
infrastructure, and you keep the rest open. Keep the wetlands open,
keep the slope areas untouched. Have a buffer around a stream for
wildlife. Okay? That's what I believe in. But I don't think we've
gotten to that point yet. So we keep making more regulations. And
you need regulations because people don't behave. What I hear is
that it's always somebody else's responsibility, the state's, or the
Feds', or the county's, and they say it's the developer's. Now I
don't buy that, because if I live here and somebody else isn't going
to take care of it, then I'm going to take care of it. But then, I'm an
old coot.

"I bought a place in the borough with central sewer and water. I
don't necessarily like a neighbor ten feet from me, but I felt that
given what's happening, that's probably the best place to be. The
place will look the same thirty years from now: central water, point-
source discharge, trash pickup. I recycle. I have a compost heap in
the garden. The problems that I see going to happen out there in
the next ten years if we continue this way are just—*A* to *Z*, I'd
rather not deal with them. I felt that intelligently, though it goes
totally against my grain, and I sometimes literally feel like a wild
animal in a cage, I felt that intelligently it was the best move—
which, when you think about it, is crazy."

Like its cool trout streams, the Poconos' bogs are part of their
glacial inheritance. The ice ground out basins atop the plateaus and
the meltwater flooded them. Since the basins had neither streams
nor springs to feed them, the water was poor in nutrients. Few
plants could grow. Sphagnum, better known as peat moss, could

store mineral nutrients by soaking up and holding some twenty times its weight in water. It floated out over the water in a spring-green mat of small, red-tipped leaves. Dead sphagnum growth, its cells still holding water, sank to the bottom and remained there, since the basins had no outlets. With sphagnum choking the surface, the waters became as poor in oxygen as they were in nutrients. Without oxygen, what fell to the bottom didn't rot, so the basins filled up with the waterlogged sphagnum which, thickened over time with insect skeletons, bits of plants and bones of animals, formed a soaking bed of peat upon which lay an illusory mossy meadow. For although a few spruces, tamaracks, or clumps of sedge may take root, this is not solid ground.

Stepping onto the quaking sphagnum mat of a Pocono bog, one can imagine oneself, though only at two thousand feet, on the appropriately quaverous summit of a shaky world: a place of hardy, often rootless species of sometimes delicate beauty, of sometimes carnivorous appetites; an unstable place, but so slow to change that after twelve thousand years a bog can be considered a still-maturing ecosystem.

What has slowed time in the bog is the lack of oxygen and nutrients. Sundews and pitcher plants thrive because they can capture and digest insects. Evergreens survive because they retain food in their needles. But they grow slowly: a hundred-year-old black spruce may be only a few inches thick. Decomposition is so slow that an inch of peat may take a hundred years to form. Time in a bog passes like time on that Einsteinian spaceship traveling near the speed of light—the aging process slows until time hardly seems to pass at all.

This was a relief after Todd, Roger Spotts, and I had spent an afternoon in the county's pickup truck, viewing the ruin that a bulldozer can wreak in a wetland in a matter of hours, and taking notes on the violations of developers for whom time is measured in interest payments. The investigative barnstorming has left us all pretty exhausted. Todd's tour up into the Pocono hills went like this:

"All wetland, used to all be wetland. All fill. You talk to old-timers who used to hunt bear and trap and hunt ducks in here. Now it's a shopping mall. Lake Valhalla, on the right, all constructed in a wetland. There's a heavy nutrient load into this lake from all the adjoining development. It's all on-lot septic. Now Valhalla is in a rather advanced stage of eutrophication. In the summertime you can almost walk across it. Was all wetland. Like most of our lakes in the Poconos. This was all wetland where there's now the Shaw-nee Racquetball Club. This was wetland in here where the Toyota dealership is. This was wetland here. This was all wetland. This is a town-house project going in. There's an illegal wetland fill on the left. An excavating company put a road right through the middle of the damn thing. These were bogs. Bogs on your right."

Common practice in the Poconos was to extract the peat, then sell the mined bed for lakefront development.

Todd stops and pulls a map out of the glove compartment. He takes another toothpick—he's trying to quit smoking, and the truck is littered with toothpicks.

"This is called the plateau. There's two systems here. There's the Long Pond system and the Lost Lake system. Here's scrub-shrub and forested wetlands, and here's mucky-peat wetlands. All glaci-ated stuff. Now here was a very controversial project called the Estates at Emerald Lakes. All in here. This was once wetland. Now it's a lake. This whole thing has been wiped out. We'll ride through there. Here you see Lake Naomi, which used to be wetlands. Still-water Lake used to be wetlands. Tamaqua Lake used to be wet-lands. One developer is proposing a big project in here. This whole shootin' match could be gone. This used to be a wetland. This used to be a wetland."

He shakes his head, raises his eyes, makes a mock appeal: "I don't know why I come out here to torture myself."

He looks out again. "All the lakes in here used to be wetlands. So this system, one of the most diverse and unique in North America, is really under a lot of pressure. The hydrology in here is something, I mean there are places in here where water runs uphill."

The map quickly folded, we continued along Route 611, passing stretches of commercial development as dense as those of any metropolitan suburb, the blocky shopping centers looking like desert barracks amid the low, sparse, gnarly scrub-oak scenery.

It is the same uncompelling barrens at Emerald Lakes—another looping maze of narrow hillside lanes.

"All right, where's the lake?" mutters a tight-lipped Todd. "We may never get out of here."

The lake is no lake. It's a dammed and drained wetland waiting to be flooded. Todd got involved because of the developer's permit problems. Instead of just damming and flooding the wetlands, the developer began dredging.

"He found sand."

"When the glacier came through here, it left sand," says Roger.

"Sand," says Todd, "is a hot commodity for septic systems. So they turned this wetland into a surface mine."

Homesites ring the "lake shores." But the only water is a trickling stream meandering through the middle of a low, broad, green plain that ends abruptly, leaving the stream to wind a muddy course through the mounds of sand and construction debris of the dredged lakebed.

Todd paces the silty stream remnant and finds it spills down a brambled slope of blueberry, and into another stream, itself now red and muddied. He digs a stick into the plume of silt. In some places it's more than a foot thick. He stalks back to the truck, climbs in, makes some notes, lights a cigarette, and slams the door.

"Just kind of embarrassing, don't you think? I mean, here are two dead wetlands. For second-home development to destroy something like this—is almost as stupid as smoking."

Higher yet, we drive along Sioux Court, Iroquois Trail, Minsi Trail, all remote cul-de-sacs amid the highbush blueberry. Water pools around the few scattered homes so that they seem to be afloat. Many people who bought lots here have been told they can't build on them. Their plaints always make the newspapers:

> *J—— R—— and his wife, L——, own a beautiful Pocono lot.*
> *And it's a good thing they enjoy the scenery because they*

can't build on it or sell it. Their third-acre lot contains a Pocono wetland.

The L——s spent $23,000 for two acres and dreamed of building a vacation house to escape their Paramus, N.J., home. But their land, like the majority of the five hundred acres that make up the Estates, has scattered areas of wetlands.

"You can't walk in there very far without mud and muck up to the knees," said Walter Burkhart. . . . "With the swamp, the mosquitoes and the bears," he said, "life in the Estates would be far from idyllic."

The development came to the DER's attention when Craig Todd, a resource conservationist with the County, went to the site and saw roads being constructed in wetlands.

"The biggest losers are the people in the community," B—— said. . . . "Craig Todd goes down the road and plays games."

We see bear tracks in one driveway. A turkey and half a dozen chicks pad off through the underbrush, feeding on grasshoppers.

"This place," says Roger, "is loaded with wildlife. With these uplands and wetlands interspersed, it's unparalleled wildlife habitat. See, this yellow bloom of bird's-foot trefoil feeds deer and rabbits."

"You name the critter," echoes Todd, "he's in here." He shakes his head as he drives through. "This is the high part of the project. There's a sand mound. There's wetland. You know, twenty years ago people wouldn't even have considered building up here because it's such a pain in the butt. But now that you're running out of easy places to develop, you get into sensitive areas, and the degradation increases at an exponential rate. Two hundred and seventy subdivision reviews so far this year. We can't keep up. We're just outgunned. I mean, this is a mess."

Roger continues, playing the analytical Watson to Todd's risible Holmes. "There's coyote, bear, deer, bobcat, wild turkey. I've seen goshawks, broad-winged hawks, red-tailed hawks, red-shouldered hawks, snowshoe hares. Loaded with them."

Todd sets his jaw, narrows his eyes. He lets off steam: "You're pissing me off, Roger. I'm getting stressed out." If he took it all so seriously, he reminds me, he'd never have lasted so long at the job. But I only half-believe him.

We drive along a dirt road between lots to come up to the quaking wetland. This was the road Todd spotted and had its construction stopped. We climb down from the truck and stare out at the floating tundra.

"Moose habitat," says Roger. "A lot of boreal species. Black spruce, red maple, blueberry. Marsh fern. Cinnamon fern. Cotton grass, cranberry, bog rosemary."

We squat close around a square foot of bog, like rug merchants examining an exotic weave.

"Here's sundew."

"Sundew."

"Look at it, son of a gun, here's hundreds of them."

"This is a leatherleaf here, with the leaves pointing up."

"Boy, there's a lot of sundew."

"Look at all the cranberry."

"You see," says Todd, smiling, "their argument was that these are little lakes in a raised upland, but I said, 'No, these are little islands in a giant lake. I mean, you're telling me these wetlands aren't connected hydrologically? You're telling me they're all standing on their own? And I'd walk them through here and I'd say, 'Listen.' And you could hear water running underneath your feet!"

Developers in the Poconos, says a New York *Daily News* real-estate report, "know how to ease you into a home filled with the rustic peace that nature allows in this area. . . .

"Quiet country living, a myriad of recreational activities and excellent school systems far from urban crime.

"But don't let that isolating quiet scare you. . . . The community is close to all the urban conveniences one could wish for."

Our development, boasts one builder, is "carved from one of Mother Nature's loveliest forests."

Prince Maximilian found the "Pokono" to be a "lonely, wild, and grand" wilderness, where the forest "rises in awful gloom," presenting a vista of "solemn and sublime grandeur."

From nearly that same rise, Roger, Todd, and I look out across the steep-sloped, wooded mesa lands of the Poconos. Far to the east, the Kittatinny runs its endless blue ridge. Between, every slope seems to have its little cluster of houses. Todd can name the developments.

"All the woodland is broken up. Look at the houses perched on the sides of the hills. I mean, the least you can do is give the illusion you're protecting it. Unbelievable."

THE RIVER MASTER

ALONG THE DELAWARE, A DROUGHT CAN BECOME THE FOCUS OF SOME predictable theatrics. First the portentous warnings. Then, at a public meeting in front of reporters and cameras, the dour-faced Commission gathers to declare a crisis. The chief hydrologist, under the glare of lights, sets out charts on easels to compare normal precipitation with what he calls "the present precipitation deficit." Then the official pronouncement that "Whereas . . . Whereas . . . So be it resolved by the Delaware River Basin Commission that, one, a state of emergency shall exist in the state of the water supplies of the Delaware River Basin . . . two, the Delaware River Master is requested to cooperate with the administration of this resolution and the conservation orders issued hereunder together with such parts of the Supreme Court decree of 1954 . . . three, any person, association, corporation, public or private entity violating or attempting or conspiring to violate any provision of this resolution or any conservation order or regulation shall be punishable . . ." Then the reading of the regulations. Things have got so bad that only greens and tees on golf courses may be watered, while fairways must go dry, public fountains must cease flowing, only commercial car washes can wash cars, and customers in restaurants must ask for water before having it served to them. The audience expresses concern. Politicians, in asides to reporters, exhort their constituents to try to go along with these measures, acknowledge that things might get worse, and threaten to find new sources of water—perhaps the Tocks Island Dam must be built after all, perhaps the $20-billion water tunnel from New York City to the Great Lakes will at last be undertaken, perhaps the Hudson ought to be tapped. The newspapers and nightly newscasts report on ways to save water: shower together, run dishwashers only when full. This past year the Commission passed a regulation that all new toilets in the Delaware River Basin must be designed to use half the water used by older toilets. They assert that if all four million toilets in New York City were converted, 200 million gallons of water a day would be saved. The problem is that the active life of a toilet is thirty years, which means the replacement rate will be a gradual one. So toilets, they admit, won't be the only answer.

This is what passes for a drought emergency along the Delaware. In any larger context—say, translated for the amusement of no-mads in the African Sahel or Ethiopia—it would make us all look gluttonous and hysterically self-absorbed, complaining how na-ture's shortchanged us when we each use, in one way or another, some two hundred gallons of water a day. When our emergency passes, the Commission is back to business as usual, granting allo-cations of water to every new request from industries or housing developers, looking for new places to build dams, and seeming gen-uinely amused when private citizens appear at their meetings to question the commissioners' inexplicable generosity in the light of their recently serious concerns. Not that these commissioners don't know that houses, roads, and parking lots increase runoff while they reduce the amount of water able to sink down to recharge the vaults of natural underground storage, an estimated 2,000 billion gallons in the Delaware basin, which dwarfs the 300 billion gallons stored in reservoirs. Not that they don't know the runoff from new development is silt-laden and then becomes contaminated with pesticides and fertilizer, septic waste, the wash of oil and rock salt from new roads, the leachate from new landfills, the leaks from gas stations and dry cleaners. And not that they haven't ever acted to benefit the river. But by their nature as appointees of the governors of the states they represent, they tend to drift with the prevailing political flow. When politicians call for dams, the Delaware River Basin Commission wants dams. When politicians call for clean waters, they vote for clean waters. When asked if they believe in development over clean waters, or waters over development, they will say they want both, and take as an accolade the fact that they are able to please no one at all.

The truth is that the commissioners only reflect the will, or lack thereof, of their constituents. The truth is that the Delaware has plenty of water. It supplies some ten percent of the population of the entire country with water from a watershed that takes up only one percent of the country's land. How much more can one ask of a river? The truth is that we have no stomach or imagination for finding a way to conserve when we can foresee no real prospect of ever having to do without. The separate states want, industry wants, electric companies want water to support new development. Homeowners don't want to give up pesticides and fertilizers—why should farmers? Trout fishermen want cold water released from the reservoirs. Shad fishermen fear the cold water will kill off the most productive shad spawning grounds. They want warmer upstream waters. Canoeists want more water of any temperature so their weekend relaxation won't be dampened in shallow, rocky rapids. Everyone is interested in everyone else conserving. And they all come banging on the River Master's pipes.

Who appointed the River Master? In 1931 the U.S. Supreme Court settled a brewing tempest among the Delaware River basin states and allowed that New York City, already bringing much of its water down from the eastern slopes of the Catskills, could tap into the western Catskills' upper Delaware watershed. ("A river is more than an amenity, it is a treasure," wrote Justice Oliver Wen-dell Holmes. "It offers a necessity of life that must be rationed among those who have power over it." And with that the court wrested control of the river out of nature's realm forever and laid it in the laps of politicians, lawyers, and engineers. For the next fifty years Holmes's dictum would be cited by every thirsting self-interest along the river. "No one less than Oliver Wendell Holmes . . ." they would begin.) The city could take 440 million gallons a day for its reservoir on the East Branch Delaware. But the Depres-sion and World War II delayed construction. By the time the city was ready to begin holding water behind its first Delaware dam, it realized it would need more water than it had been guaranteed, more than the East Branch could provide. In 1953, with a West Branch reservoir in mind, it went back to the Supreme Court.

The court doubled New York's allocation, but it also provided that the city must release enough water from its reservoirs to main-tain a flow of 1,750 cubic feet per second at the U.S. Geological Service's gaging station on the main branch of the river at Mon-tague, New Jersey. This, the court hoped, would provide enough water for the needs downstream. One particular concern was that the diminished flow of fresh water would allow the salt water of the bay to move farther upstream, perhaps further damage the seed-beds of Delaware Bay oysters, and even contaminate the drinking water supplies of Camden and Philadelphia. The salt line had al-ready been moving up due to the rise in sea level and the deep dredging of the shipping channel. To make certain New York City honored its responsibilities, the court mandated the office of the River Master.

But nature did not give up control so easily. Its own fluctuations in weather and rainfall, combined with New York City's demand-ing withdrawals, played havoc with attempts to control the flow. While the natural flows were always subject to natural fluctua-tions, the persistence of bass and shad in the upper river meant that enough water flowed to support a substantial fauna. Zane Grey, who, in his early writing years, lived on the upper Delaware at its confluence with the Lackawaxen, believed the Delaware provided the best bass fishing in the East. But the bass took a beating when the reservoirs came on line. According to a New York State Department of Environmental Conservation report, "minuscule conservation releases" left the upper river in "a perpetual drought." What water was released came from the bottom of the dam and was cold. The bass were killed. Trout began to thrive. (Before this time, trout, according to the 1935 New York State Biological survey, provided "indifferent fishing" in the main river. They might descend in the early spring to feed in fast riffles or in deep, cool, spring-fed pools, but they remained mostly in the upper tributaries.) Then, in the 1960s, as the city began to fill its new West Branch reservoir in the midst of an increasingly severe natural drought, the upper Delaware experienced "the worst aquatic habitat" in its history. With fewer releases, however, the waters warmed. The trout declined. The bass returned. The habitat of the river now hinged on the whims of the dam releases. When releases were called for, the temperature of the upper Delaware rarely went over fifty degrees. When held back, summer water temperatures could rise into the eighties. Since both reservoirs' waters came down into the main stem, as far as the Supreme Court ruling was concerned, one's waters was as good as the other's. But the land around the West Branch reservoir, acquired later, had been far more developed, and the water quality began to decline. Rather than risk sending it down to the city, it was more often used to fulfill the River Master's flow requirements.

The Delaware River Master I meet in his dimly lit, wood-furnished office in Milford, Pennsylvania, is William Harkness. He is stout and sturdy, formally casual in blue V-neck sweater, and seemingly as implacable as his gaze behind his silver-rimmed eyeglasses. He is a disciplined engineer who faces a daily hydrological puzzle: how to take all the water sources of the upper Delaware, natural and unnatural, and have them combine at Montague to make a flow of 1,750 cubic feet per second. This is not a matter of simple addition. The first problem is that, flow-wise, the New York City reservoirs are anywhere from thirty-three to sixty hours away from Montague. This means that Harkness has to calculate what the flow at Montague will be three days ahead, and then request his releases accordingly. A forecast of rain, of course, complicates matters. Further complicating the problem are releases from two tributary reservoirs used for power generation. Since both are designed to boost the general supply in times of high power demands, especially to cover the extra load from running air conditioners in hot weather, Harkness must take their releases, one eight hours from Montague and the other sixteen hours away, into account. The power companies send him two-day advance weather forecasts. Natural flows change with the seasons.

"A large oak tree may take up as much as fifty gallons of water a day in hot weather. In fall they lose their leaves and the runoff increases."

Seasonal differences alone can account for the disparity between the July flow of six hundred cubic feet per second and a cloudy November day's flow of two thousand, as it was on the day of my visit.

"People from the Colorado basin would wonder what our problems could be, with all of the rain we have, when they have twelve inches or less each year and all the irrigation demands. There are seven dams along the Missouri River, and one of them alone holds some seven billion gallons of water."

Why seventeen hundred and fifty cubic feet per second?

"Seventeen hundred and fifty cubic feet per second is one-half a cubic foot per second for every square mile of the nearly 3,500-square-mile upper basin watershed. It's a negotiated number that is hydrologically meaningless."

Especially since the original estimate of the daily flow the city's reservoirs could sustain was too high. With a more realistic look at the system, says Harkness, the flow at Montague might be only thirteen hundred and fifty cubic feet per second. During the drought years of the 1960s, the worst since the 1930s, perhaps the worst ever, the city couldn't give the River Master what he needed to meet his Montague flow.

"Fortunately," says Harkness, "it finally started to rain."

ONLY IN AMERICA

WERE HE HERE TODAY, BENJAMIN FRANKLIN MIGHT BE ONE PERSON less than enthusiastic over the return of the bald eagle to the Delaware River valley.

> *For my own part, I wish the Bald Eagle had not been chosen as the Representative of our Country; he is a Bird of bad moral Character; he does not get his living honestly; you may have seen him perch'd on some dead Tree, near the River where, too lazy to fish for himself, he watches the Labour of the Fishing-Hawk; and, when that diligent Bird has at length taken a Fish, and is bearing it to his Nest for the support of his Mate and young ones, the Bald Eagle pursues him, and takes it from him. With all this Injustice he is never in good Case; but, like those among Men who live by Sharping and Robbing, he is generally poor, and often very lousy. Besides, he is a rank Coward; the little King Bird, not bigger than a Sparrow, attacks him boldly and drives him out of the District. He is therefore by no means a proper emblem for the brave and honest Cincinnati of America. . . .*

Franklin suggested a native animal might make a better symbol: the turkey, for one.

> *The Turk'y is in comparison a much more respectable Bird, and withal a true original Native of America. Eagles have been found in all Countries, but the Turk'y was peculiar to ours; the first Species seen in Europe being brought to France by the Jesuits from Canada, and serv'd up at the Wedding Table of Charles the Ninth. He is, though a little vain and silly, it is true, but not the worse emblem for that, a Bird of Courage, and would not hesitate to attack a Grenadier of the*

*British Guards, who should presume to invade his Farm Yard
with a red Coat on.*

Franklin made his suggestion in 1784. (Although he was right
about the bird being a native of North America; the first turkeys
may have come to Europe when Cortez subjugated the Aztecs, who
had already domesticated the turkey in Mexico.) The American
woodlands may have supported some ten million of the birds when
the colonists arrived. But by the 1840s the wild turkey had all but
disappeared in the Northeast, a victim of hunting and the clear-
cutting of the forests.

Another of Franklin's nominations for national symbol was also
nearly wiped out. "I observed on one of the drums belonging to the
marines now raising," he wrote on the eve of the Revolution in
1775, "there was painted a Rattle-Snake, with this modest motto
under it, 'Don't tread on me.'

*It occurred to me that the Rattle-Snake is found in no other
quarter of the world besides America, and may therefore have
been chosen, on that account to represent her. . . . I recollected
that her eye excelled in brightness, that of any other animal, and
that she has no eye-lids—She may therefore be esteemed an
emblem of vigilance.—She never begins an attack, nor, when
once engaged, ever surrenders: She is therefore an emblem of
magnanimity and true courage . . . she never wounds till she
has generously given notice, even to her enemy, and cautioned
him against the danger of treading on her.—Was I wrong, Sir,
in thinking this a strong picture of the temper and conduct of
America? . . . The Rattle-Snake is solitary, and associates
with her kind only when it is necessary for their preservation—In winter, the warmth of a number together will preserve
their lives, while singly, they would probably perish—The
power of fascination attributed to her, by a generous construction, may be understood to mean, that those who consider the
liberty and blessing which America affords, and once come
over to her, never afterwards leave her, but spend their lives*

with her.—She strongly resembles America in this, that she is beautiful in youth and her beauty increaseth with her age, "her tongue also is blue and forked as the lightning, and her abode is among impenetrable rocks."

One would have thought the rock reaches in which they wintered the better part of several months, in dens called hibernacula, some fifteen to twenty feet back in the rock, below the frost line, would have kept them not only warm but safe. But when they emerged in May, posses of snake hunters would be waiting for them, and would slaughter them for their skins, their rattles, for money—most states had bounties on them—or simply for sport. Farmers killed them. Miners killed them. Timbermen killed them. Quarrymen killed them. This was no great challenge. The timber rattlesnakes emerged and lay coiled, basking, and were shot or beaten to death on the spot. The "hunting" would cease in the summer, when the snakes dispersed from their dens into the woods, traveling ranges of up to two to three miles to find food, always meat, and mostly mice. In the forest they coil up next to a log where tongue and heat-sensing pit between the eyes (for which they are known as pit vipers) can catch the tang of prey in the air, and wait. The paths themselves are well-worn ones, since the young seem to follow the scent trails of older snakes. With the coming of fall the snakes return to their natal dens, the females to bear their young. Then it was that the "roundups"—sometimes to support the local volunteer fire company or ambulance corps—and the killings began again.

Not that there were ever very many people getting bitten. Even today, when more people die of insect bites than of all snakebites, there is little sympathy for the timber rattler. And while the collecting craze has died down, along with the decline of roadside serpentariums (where people may have gotten the idea that pit vipers were snakes found in dirt pits), the new, and perhaps final threat to the timber rattler may be the development of new communities on the last wild and impenetrable rocks where the snakes den. The final demise of the snakes could come quickly. Like other long-lived

reptiles—the timber rattler may live twenty years in the wild—
they mature late. The female doesn't have her first litter until she
is at least five years old, and she can give birth only once every
three years. Development endangers the rattlers not only at their
dens but on their summer migrations, when they must cross the
new roads and backyards. They are left exposed, either basking on
open blacktop or coiling next to a suburban woodpile. Then the
snakes seem to bring out another aspect of the American temperament.

By canoe from Hancock, passing the points of origin of the spring
races of timber rafts, one weaves a winding way between steep,
wooded slopes. At their stony bases often lie a wrack of toppled
trees that took root in the thin soil but were unable to gain a secure
footing in the rock beneath. They make a shattered frame for the
picturesque little streams that cascade over the rubble of crumbled
shale eroded from the faces of these one-to-two-thousand-foot
ridges. Many of the ridges were disfigured a hundred years ago
when their hard blue stone was quarried to build the sidewalks of
eastern cities. Ospreys and bald eagles are these days more and
more common sights, soaring above. And the high, south-facing
ledges hold the last refuges of the Delaware River valley's timber
rattlesnakes.

New houses are being built on these ridges, with views overlooking the panorama of the Pocono plateau and ribboning river below.
Much to the chagrin of the developer, the protection of the rattlesnakes is being championed by a squarely built, bearish young man,
Randy Stechert, who roams over the stony upper Delaware ridges
finding the dens, marking and releasing the snakes, and then distributing handbills to the new homeowners telling them that rattlesnakes live nearby and that the snakes are a threatened species
protected by law.

"Unfortunately," he tells me, "people will look back at you
proudly and say, 'Let me tell you something, it sure as hell is endangered if it's on my property.' "

Besides, said one particularly scornful fellow we talked to, what do we need the rattlesnakes around for? The dinosaurs were here and now they're gone, too.

"There's development everywhere," he continued as we looked across the river at the mist rising from the hills. "I grew up around here, and now it's finally being developed. Now people somehow expect us to provide them with free scenery."

"But," Stechert argues, "they're coming up here and taking *your* scenery."

"Well, I know. But what the hell, they're all Americans. I mean, you got people comin' up here, they build a goddamn house, then they want to build a green wall around it to prevent everyone else from comin' in. I don't go along with that shit. We're all Americans!"

"But wouldn't you like to look out at those hills and see what's there now instead of roads and houses?"

"Sure. Sure, there's a lot of things I'd like to see, buddy. I tell you, if I had the chance I'd stop the world right now. But I don't want to happen here what happened in the Adirondacks, where they just control everybody's property. Like the National Park Service would like to do here. They make this a Wild and Scenic River and expect the people who live along it to provide the free scenery. What the hell—it's their goddamn land. It's the only thing they've got."

Along the road we have seen signs of the sort we might see while driving through an occupied military zone: "National Park Service, Get Out of Town," and "Beware, You Are Now 17 Miles Into the NPS Dictatorship."

"It's a fucking free country, but these environmental bastards come along and they expect everybody to keep everything the way it is. But they're makin' their livin'."

He turns, scuffles his feet in the gravel roadbed in which we stand, and squints up at us both.

"I been studyin' this shit for a long time. There are two sides to this shit. They try to make these developers and businessmen look like assholes. Well, if it wasn't for the free-enterprise system, most of the people in the world would be starvin', let alone just half of 'em. But then you get these goddamn bureaucrats runnin' around—like you—" He looks up at an open-faced Stechert, then to me. "Got to be some gainful employment for these people instead of meddlin' in everybody's goddamn backyards. I don't go for it. You wonder what you fight wars for. I don't like people goin' around tellin' other people how to live."

Stechert makes a stab at a defense.

"Too many people will bring all new problems, from waste to—"

"But they're Americans! They live in this country!"

"But what about the right to open space and clean air—"

"We're all entitled to everything! I'll tell you somethin'. Any of your friends—wherever they're from—bring 'em up. As many as you can. Because, goddamn it, if they're interested in freedom and liberty the way I am, hey, man, we're all here for that. Just don't send anybody up here tellin' me how to live. I been around too goddamn long for that."

Stechert just nods and bids good-bye. The fellow follows a little, wanting to know what Stechert will do with the snakes when he finds them.

"Well, I don't take them out. I mark them and release them and I hope I scare them enough that they stay away from people."

The man must feel that he's been a bit too hard on us. He relents.

"I can feel this warming trend, you know. We have too many people. We're burnin' up too much shit." He cackles. "But it's goin' to keep goin'! If Congress passed every bill that's supposed to protect the critical components of our environment, the air and water—it wouldn't make a five-degree difference in thirty years! Our system is not politically attuned to savin' the goddamn environment. 'Hey, you can't use your car. You can't do this.' 'Fuck you. I'm goin' to vote for somebody else.' You know what I'm sayin'? Jesus Christ, they need a crisis! Before they give up the airspace, two planes have got to collide, you know?"

As we wave good-bye he continues laughing, as if we have amused him a great deal.

"Apparently," says Stechert, "he had some steam he wanted to blow off."

Stechert himself is a kind of American original. He finished high school in Ridgewood, New Jersey, and decided he had no interest in college. So he took a job with the Ridgewood Cab Company and in his spare time began turning a longtime interest in snake collecting into a serious study of reptiles of the nearby Ramapo, Shawangunk, and Pocono mountains, populations that many more-worldly herpetologists had neglected. At the time the timber rattlesnakes were not protected, but Stechert knew firsthand just how threatened they were.

"It was a slightly shady beginning," he admits. "This guy, a snake hunter of the old school, took me out snake hunting when I was thirteen. He showed me some timber rattlesnakes, and I went hunting with him for the next four years. This guy was the scourge of the timber rattlesnake. He'd been collecting more than forty years, and I estimate that this man took maybe four thousand rattlesnakes from New York State alone. And knowing eighty percent of the dens in the state, I estimate there's now only some seven thousand snakes left altogether. By the time I was seventeen I was getting a little distressed, because he'd take me to some beautiful sites and we'd see three or four rattlesnakes and he'd say, 'Well, I used to come here and I used to see two dozen.' And I'd say, 'Isn't that a shame?' He'd nod, say 'Yeah.' And I'd say, 'Then why did you do it? Why didn't you lose some?' His stock answer was an asinine one, which was, 'Well, if I don't take them, somebody else will.' So it was the old story of the pupil turning on his mentor. He and I had a falling-out, and I started snake hunting on my own and marking them and leaving them there."

Even while working on snake surveys for the state of New York, and showing scientists more used to looking at snakes in books and laboratories how to find them in the wild, Stechert clung to the security of his cabdriving. "I don't think I have to tell you," he says, "the length, breadth, and depth of professional snobbism toward a basically untrained individual such as me is truly bottomless. But they can be as snobby as they want, when it comes to being out in the woods, they're lost. That's my forte.

"I have been told by some researchers in colleges or with the state that I'm lucky to be able to get out into the field when I want, which is what I love.

"The cab company has been good to me. Only once, when one dispatcher didn't like my taking time off, did I have any problem. Fortunately, I consider one of my claims to fame that I outlasted him. He had said to me, 'Randy, you take time off again and you ain't comin' back.' Well, the next time I came back he had a kind of smile on his face and said, 'Randy, why don't you go down to the garage, the owner wants to talk to you.' So I went down to the garage, and my friend Dave could hardly look me in the eye. He said, 'Randy, they gave your car to another driver and we don't have anything for you.' I said, 'What do you mean?' I even had gotten a driver to take my place when I was gone. He said, 'We don't have a place for you.'

"Now, I'm not normally a very volatile person, but"—he laughs as he recalls the moment—"I said, 'I'm not leaving. I'm not leaving.' I said, 'You come out in the yard and find a car for me right now.' And I embarrassed him. And he gave me the worst car we had. And I drove back to the office and I walked in and the dispatcher said, 'What are you doin' back here?' And I said, 'I work here, remember?' And I think I really ruined his day."

It had been a long, damp morning climbing and trying to keep up with the agile Stechert as we hunted for signs of rattlesnakes, traipsing through the waist-high undergrowth of an especially warm and verdant spring, until we were soaked to the skin. When the sun finally came out, one could see why the snakes chose to den on these rock ledges: they fairly glowed. Even with the light filtered through the trees (chestnut oak, and, as Stechert put it, "the handsome big-ass white pine"), the warmth suffused the entire slope. Even Stechert seemed to breathe a little easier as we worked our way across the jagged faces of the slate, sideslipping where the ledges were too narrow to gain a good footing, skidding often on the moss- or lichen-covered stone, formations stuck here and there with plumes of sweet fern—what Stechert said has been called rattlesnake fern. Stechert even took off his shirt and, crouching to get a glimpse over the edge of one high ledge, looked about as bearlike as a man could. Then, standing, sunlit, with snake stick in his hand, bare hairless chest glistening with perspiration, he struck an Indianlike pose as he paused and surveyed the scene with dark green, skeptical eyes.

"All they have to do, you know, is stick a coil out and it will heat them up with just that little exposed."

The mountains shade the river below us, and we can see canoes going by, red canoes in a gray-green vale with their paddlers still in yellow rain slickers. A thousand feet up we can hear their voices.

This seventy-five miles of Wild and Scenic River between Hancock and Port Jervis, New York, can be crowded with canoes and rafts. Many come downriver with music blaring from portable radios and drifting coolers full of beer. No one wants to call the people a nuisance, thus one official report stated that "crowding and overuse are not significant problems on the upper Delaware." The real problems, it said, are "litter, disposal of human waste, trespass on private lands, alcohol abuse, water pollution, lack of adequate utilities and conveniences for visitors, overfishing, inadequate trip planning, disturbance of wildlife, and impact on vegetation."

"I came up here one hot spring day," says Stechert, "and found a rattler and a copperhead coiled up right next to each other. They live in harmony. Another day I found five rattlesnakes coiled up here. It is a place that looks ready-made for rattlesnakes."

He came down from the ledge, moved on, stalking. He turned, looked, still crouched, pivoting from his hips, and pulled aside the low-growing vines with his stick. He stopped me with a hand and then pointed down into the brush. There lay coiled a dark timber rattler, its patchwork skin blending with the patchwork of light on the forest floor. The snake did not move.

"It will stay still," whispers Stechert. "If it thinks it can, it will try to inch off. If we make a grab for it, it will shoot away."

I was willing to stay and watch it. It was maybe two feet long and had, to me, the quiet, wary stillness of a cat resting with its head up and eyes narrowed.

Stechert took a short step closer, stick at ready. The snake seemed to stiffen.

"I want you to see," he said, "how much it takes to get a snake like this to actually strike."

He put the stick down near the snake's head. It seemed to focus on it. And then I became aware of the buzzing that was its tail rattling. But instead of raising up, the snake tucked its head into its body, away from the stick, like a dog wincing from a lifted rolled newspaper.

Then Stechert hits the stick down in front of the snake, and it strikes swiftly, with wide watery glistening jaws. Just as quickly, Stechert clamps it in the jaws of the stick and sweeps it up. The snake is hissing now as Stechert examines it. He declares it a healthy two-year-old male. With a marker he colors in the bottom of the rattles, a quick method he has found successful in marking the snakes. He puts the snake back down on the ground and releases it, but it doesn't move, even as Stechert makes out his field notes. My own thoughts are confused. I'm standing here, three feet away from a rattler, and I wonder if it's considering its own revenge.

"We're Paul Bunyon to this snake," says Stechert. "He doesn't want to mess around with us, because he knows he'll most likely come out the loser. He just wants to get away. The human attitude is astounding. A simple little animal causes so much consternation."

He makes his notes on the snake and the site: rock, fern, pitch pine, early afternoon after rain, warm haze, and on the rocks near the snake, Stechert points out a bright red mosslike formation of British Soldier lichen, a touch Ben Franklin himself would have appreciated. The snake lies patiently as Stechert photographs this threatened American scene.

THE PHILOSOPHY OF EEL WEIR HOLLOW

HANCOCK, EQUINUNK, LONG EDDY, CALLICOON WERE UPRIVER towns, timber towns, rafting towns, canal towns, railroad towns, tall-tale towns. As the large-eared, rheumy-eyed, mustachioed nineteenth-century Delaware River raconteur raftsman George "Boney" Quillen, the "Wit of the Delaware River," put it:

Here's to the grand old Delaware, with bumpers of old rye
whiskey and its jolly raftsmen so happy and strong:

How often portrayed by the hand of Nature we see
The lives of men there written on brooklet, river and tree.
So let us call Hancock "Manhood," where the branches join so fair,
They come from east and west to form the majestic Delaware.

Rafts come thus far single and each its mate does meet
And being joined together, they form a double fleet.
And now they're joined together by many an oaken tie,
They look like bride and groom together as thus side by side they lie.

But they know not of the crooked course and the rapids they
*   must run*
Ere they pass old Trenton bridge and the trip of life
*   is done.*

There was John Geer, the rattlesnake man, who once collected forty-five rattlers in two hours, and whose personal fail-proof cure for snakebite died with him. It may have been something akin to the following cure described in the nineteenth-century *History of Wayne County:*

Rye whiskey, applied externally and internally, is pronounced
to be a sure antidote for the bite of this snake. The philosophy of

the matter is, that the man must take more poison than the snake had in him. The dose for an adult is one quart of pure whiskey, but, as this can seldom be found, one pint of adulterated whiskey will do.

There was fiddler Charlie Freer, who called the Fireman's Dance, and Zebadee Asa Kelly and his son, bearded and unshorn as any Tennessee mountain men, who ran one of the more popular dance halls. Old man Kelly lived to be ninety-nine.

The last two days I have been holed up here on the East Branch in a place known as Eel Weir Hollow, just north of where the two branches meet to form the Delaware at Hancock. The weather's been autumnal: dark, damp, rainy, misty, the river beginning to rush more swiftly by the hour below the gray-green hemlock-wooded ridge. It's just what we've been waiting for. And if the night is moonless, all the better, for then the eels will be driven up from stream and creek bottoms to begin their fall run down the river and out to the sea. Then we will move out to stand on the stone-and-wood weir in the middle of the river rushing about us in the seamless darkness, to bring in what we hope will be a good night's catch.

In the meantime, we wait by the woodstove in Ray Turner, Jr.'s stone-and-wood cabin, speaking with Turner and his dad of what's here and what's gone in this last frontier; of the cool East Branch waters, the trout, and the mysterious passage of the eels themselves. Ray junior has a full, jutting, mountain man's beard bleached light red by the sun. He has a quixotic temperament, by turns surly, sentimental, impetuous, and philosophical. Nature and the river give him a good deal of pleasure. There has been eating and drinking and last-minute stonework on the weir, taking out the canoe to check and recheck for signs of the run. The elder Turner, long and lithe, has been recounting, in an upriver fashion, life along the river as he recalls it. For instance, in the telling of how bare the hills were when he was young:

"My brother was an undertaker embalmer and he got called out one time when some woodchoppers used a still from the acid factory and the still had enough wood alcohol left in it so that there was eighteen dead woodchoppers on the road. Everybody helped out, but there was one fella in a shack on a hill. We went up and found him sittin' froze to a chair. I was just a little guy, and when we started to carry him down the hill I slipped and lost him and, jeez, he broke free of the chair and went barrel-assin' down the hill with no trees to stop him. We picked him up—he still looked like he was sittin'—and sat him right up with us in the hearse and drove off."

Turner senior recalls fishing with Charlie Howard, an engineer who worked on the construction of the New York City subway, a man so thin "he made you think of an old blue heron.

"He chose to leave the city and become a river rat. His mother was affluent, so he could afford to play at it. He was an alcoholic—I guess that goes along with bein' a river rat—and he lived as a squatter in an old hovel on the East Branch, right by where Ray's eel rack is. I stayed up fishing with him in 1933 and got a dose of bedbugs that almost perty near killed me."

Nearby, he recalls, lived Ralph "Shep" Shepherd, who piloted rafts from the East Branch out into the main river but who drowned, and not, some thought, accidentally.

Rafting was a colorful but rough occupation. The captain of a raft, wrote folk historian Leslie C. Wood, had only four commands at his disposal: "Jersey!" "Pennsyvanya!" "Holt!" and "Holt, t'other way!"

"I shall never forget," goes one account, "the feeling that came over me as the big fleet of medium-sized logs swung out into the boiling muddy stream and started on what I anticipated would be an adventurous and fascinating journey." The traveler was sixteen at the time, which was 1888, and on his first trip on his father's raft.

All went well until we reached Foul Rift. The river had raised to considerable height by the fast melting snow and was running wild. As we entered the Rift a fleet was about a fourth of a mile ahead of us. When approximately two and a half miles down the rift we saw this raft catch on a rock which protruded above the water to such an extent that the whole raft climbed the jagged rocks, broke into pieces and was lost. As we swiftly passed, we could see the men struggling in the boiling water—it was a terrifying experience—but we were powerless to render them any assistence as we had to maneuver our fleet to keep from meeting the same fate as the current ran very strongly toward those jagged rocks when the river was high.

Eel Weir Hollow is some fifteen hundred miles from the Sargasso Sea, a deep, relatively still region of ocean that stretches from Bermuda halfway across the Atlantic. Ocean currents sweep around its edges and bring in the seaweed from which the Sargasso takes its name. The sea itself turns constantly in slow, sweeping cyclones called gyres, which keep the weed and collected wrack moving into its center and then out toward its edges. The wrack bears a great deal of sea life, from snails to fish larvae to young sea turtles. They are swept in from the ocean, drift with the great gyres, and then, having grown in the relative safety of the sargassum weed, move back out into the open ocean again. This is where the eels of Eel Weir Hollow were born. This is where the full-grown eels are heading in the floodwaters of the autumn new moon. Biologists believe the deep waters beneath the Sargasso are the spawning grounds for all the Atlantic's migrating eels, not only those that will find their way up every coastal river from Florida to Canada, but also those that will find their way the thousands of miles east to the rivers of Europe. This can't be said with finality, however, because no one has ever seen an adult eel anywhere in the Sargasso. Eels have been tracked downstream and off the coast, and then, somewhere off the continental shelf a few hundred miles offshore, they simply disappear. A few months later, in February and March, eel larvae, looking like tiny transparent flounder, surface in the Sargasso waters. The adults, it's assumed, have died after spawning. Although European and American eels may look alike, genetic studies have distinguished them as separate species, and they apparently spawn, or at least their larvae appear, in adjacent but distinct areas of the ocean.

For the next several months the American eel larvae drift off in the currents that eventually bring them out of the Sargasso and into the Gulf Stream. By fall, now some two and a half inches long, still transparent, but beginning to take on a more cylindrical shape, they begin to move toward the coast. What guides them? Experiments have shown that "glass eels," as the young are known as they enter the tidewater, can smell the difference between ebb and flood waters, and change their positions accordingly. Based on this and perhaps other stimuli, the young eels seem to set an internal clock that runs in rhythm with the tides. When the waters move upstream, the eels come up and move upstream along with them. Before the tide turns and runs back out, however, the eels have dropped to the bottom, where they'll wait until the flow moves upstream once again. In this way they make it up the Delaware beyond the falls at Trenton, beyond Hancock and Eel Weir Hollow. No one knows how the eels know their destinations. Some eels remain to grow in the bay while others go far upstream, even running through underground watercourses to lakes and beaver ponds. But with their long journeys ended, they begin their metamorphosis into hard-muscled, dusky yellow-green adults. In a few to a dozen years they will pick up with the fall flood waters to head back out to sea. Then they metamorphose once again, turning from green to black-backed and from yellow to silver-bellied. Their sexual organs mature, their digestive systems shrink. Their eyes enlarge the farther they come downstream, the better to navigate the dim deep waters, adding sight to an evidently extraordinary sense of smell that can follow to its source the distant odor of its birthplace.

The Delaware eel weir is usually two walls of rock that form a **V** with its point downstream. At the point is a wooden scaffold holding a ramp with a slatted floor. This is called the rack. As the eels come downstream, the walls funnel them toward the rack; the water pours out the end, the eels drop back onto the ramp, and then slide into a box beneath. The construction of the weir and rack reflect the ambitions of the builder and the conditions of the river. Some are shallow, with low walls and rack and box that sit right on the riverbottom; others, like Turner's, build up the level of the river within the weir, and lead to a large, sturdy wooden ramp on which the two of us could easily stand. Ray senior recalls a man who built a rack with a little shack on the back where he'd spend the nights during the eel run.

The younger Turner is of a philosophical turn of mind with regard to his stonework (he runs his own construction company), the nature of the river, the demands of a high-powered rifle (when things get boring, there is some shooting at treetops across the river, and the gunshots echo in the mist of the Hollow), and the art of the eel rack. He spends a long time with me out on the rack in the river, explaining in detail its construction. The ramp of the rack is slatted to allow small eels and fish to slip through. The ramp is set at about a thirty-degree angle and built in two stepped sections with a space of a foot or so between them. The water brings the eels up over the first section, and they land on the second and then slide back down the ramp and fall between the stairs, where the force of the water falling over the top ramp keeps them trapped.

One of the keys to a construction that will hold up through the high water is the stonework. It has to control the flow without bringing the whole river up through the rack.

"The first year I took two huge trees and angled them, and the force of the water was too great. The idea of the rock wall is that you have to give way. You have to give way to the river. You're not here to stop the river. You have to let it by. So the philosophy is to let the wall transmit the energy. Because when the water gets really serious here, it's cookin'. I mean, I've been out here when the water's been shootin' right out the back of the rack. That gets pretty hair-raisin'. And when the eels come . . ." He says he has taken as many as three thousand eels in a single night.

Turner will stand on the rack with a pair of old iron eel tongs given him by the daughter of "an exquisite old gentleman" who once worked a weir here in the Hollow. The heavy tongs, as long as bolt cutters, were hammered by a local blacksmith.

As we stand on the rack, the water running under us, he works hard to let me know his feeling for the dynamics of the flow.

"When we put in the trees, the water just pushed the whole thing out. Now you want it to go out in the winter. We'll catch eels up until the first freeze. Then you want the thing to go out. The philosophy behind that is that if they didn't get wasted every year, this whole area in front of the walls would get filled in with gravel. Like that big rock in the river over there. In front of it, it's three and a half feet deep, but behind it, it's six feet. So you want these rocks washed out."

In the house, with everyone anxious for the rain, Turner stokes the woodstove and opens a worn copy of Lao-Tsu to this verse:

> *Creating, yet not possessing*
> *Working, yet not taking credit.*
> *Work is done, then forgotten,*
> *Therefore, it lasts forever.*

This, Ray says somberly, is how he feels about the eel weir he and his crew have built of stone and wood. It is a wall that must give way, something that the winter ice will crush and the river will wash out.

> *That the yielding conquers*
> *the resistant*
> *and the soft conquers the hard*
> *is a fact known by all men,*
> *yet utilized by none.*

"How much remains depends upon the savageness of the ice when it goes out. It always seems to go out at night. Now, that's a charge. I don't know if you've ever heard or seen it. The ice just starts to move, and it sounds like someone's draggin' a giant-sized chain down the valley." The image calls for another beer all around.

"I like this river," Turner says with a flourish that comes out like a challenge. "I like to get down in it with a snorkel and mask so my belly's on the bottom. Being out in it brings me a lot of deep feelings, a lot of deep thoughts. This place brings me in touch with antiquity. I feel like the mentor of this generation. I carry the ball. No brag, just fact."

The metaphysics of the eel rack, the way it catches eels by allowing water to flow through it, has an elegance that I imagine John Roebling, whose suspension bridge supported itself as it crossed the river, would appreciate. Not far downstream from Hancock, at Minisink, just downstream from where the Lackawaxen enters the Delaware, is the oldest of Roebling's remaining bridges. Built in 1847, it still extends from its original stone anchorages and is suspended from its original cables. It seems that timber rafts often rammed the coal-filled canal boats crossing the Delaware. The solution was to bring the boats up to the level of the bridge-aqueduct by a system of locks, float the boats across the river, then bring them down on the other shore. The problem was that a bridge with stone columns would block the flow and threaten the rafts. Roebling's suspension bridge allowed the rafts and river to pass beneath, and the canal boats to cross above. Standing on this bridge today, its woodwork restored, one feels the same light sense of lift as when one stands on the Brooklyn Bridge, a lightness that comes as much from the airiness of the structure above as from the undisturbed river running below.

Just upstream of the Roebling bridge at Minisink is an eel weir built by Orson Davis, Jr., whose father was once maintenance mechanic on the Roebling bridge, and who still lives in the little house on the hill above the bridge. Davis senior tells me his son's eel rack is constructed so that when the eels drop onto the rack a piece of tubing leads them from the rack into a box by the shore. Then his son cleans them and hangs them in a makeshift smokehouse that looks like a sealed-up outhouse connected by stovepipe to a wood-burning stove. Davis senior, who married the daughter of the previous bridge caretaker, now stokes the fires for his son, who works away during the week. Roebling's Delaware Bridge, Davis tells me, has survived nearly a hundred and fifty years of winter ice and spring high waters. Even when the great hurricane and flood of 1955 took everything else out with it, the river came up to the bridge and flowed through. No brag, as Turner might say, just fact.

The rain has begun, and there is no moon. We paddle the canoe hard upstream to the rack and tie it there. We climb up onto the rack and try to see the river. We can feel it rising up on the rack. Turner shines a flashlight down to our feet, then off.

"I like to see brown water—just a little on the creamy side instead of real deluge, soil-brown." He shines the light down again, considers the color, and nods. He turns the light off.

"Sometimes, with high water, under the right moon, they'll all put their hats on in one night and that's it, they're gone."

With that image in mind and the two of us standing on the latticework of the rack and the river beginning to rise and race under our feet, I have the feeling of standing on a station platform, bidding the departing eels farewell.

And in my mind I see them traveling downstream below the rattlesnake ridges, along all the river bends I could recall, down through the ghostly Minisink woodlands and the Walpack farms, past Durham Furnace, Easton, Lambertville, below the Trenton bridge, down the rocky falls to tidewater, where, in a couple of weeks, we could stand on the piers at Philadelphia and tip our hats to them as they pass. A few days, a month, later, they'll head out of the Delaware Bay and be off on their long, unseen oceanic journey. The whole scheme "flashing to me such a hint of the whole spread of Nature with her eternal unsophisticated freshness, her never-visited recesses of sea, sky, shore—and then disappearing into the distance."

In the darkness Turner says to me what I'd heard everywhere on my Delaware journeys.

"Not many places like this. That's why I'm here."

NOTES

vii   Langston Hughes, "Old Walt," in *Selected Poems of Langston Hughes* (New York: Random House/Vintage, 1990).

vii   Walt Whitman, "A Hint of Wild Nature," in *Walt Whitman: Complete Poetry and Collected Prose* (New York: Literary Classics of the United States, Inc. 1982).

4—9   Horseshoe crab information from Koichi Sekiguchi (ed.), *Biology of Horseshoe Crabs* (Tokyo: Science House Co. Ltd., 1988); and from conversations with, and published work of, Mark Botton of Fordham University, Robert Loveland of Rutgers University, and Carl N. Shuster, Jr., of the Virginia Institute of Marine Sciences.

6—7   Bird migrations and population estimates from J. P. Myers, "Delaware Bay: A Spectacle of Spring Passage," *The Nature Conservancy Magazine*, March/April 1989; also from Larry Niles and Kathleen Clark at the New Jersey Department of Environmental Protection. The Western Hemisphere Shorebird Reserve Network has taken great interest in preserving the Delaware Bay shore.

7—8   "ON ABOUT HALF A MILE . . . "; "WE SAW SEVERAL . . . ." George H. Cook, "Geology of County of Cape May, State of New Jersey," part 2, *Economic Geology*, 1857, 105—112.

10   "EXPERIENCE HAS SHOWN . . ." Peter Kalm quotes here and throughout are from *Peter Kalm's Travels in North America, the English Version of 1770* (New York: Dover, 1987), "a republication in a single volume of the two-volume 1966 Dover edition, which was an unabridged republication of the work originally published by Wilson-Erikson, Inc., in 1937." This version, some seven hundred pages long, includes only those sections that take him through the United States and Canada. "Travels," however, is hardly sufficient to describe the kind of resource that Kalm's book is. The title page of the 1770 English translation tells it better: "Travels into North America; containing Its Natural History, and a circumstantial Account of its Plantations and Agriculture in general, with the Civil, Ecclesiastical and Commercial State of the Country, The Manners of the Inhabitants, and several curious and Important Remarks on various Subjects . . . Enriched with a Map, several Cuts for the Illustration of Natural History, and some addi-

tional Notes." Had it not already been used, this was, in fact, going to be the title of this, my own book of travels on the Delaware. In any case, Kalm's is as indispensable a study to the natural historian as Alexis de Tocqueville's *Democracy in America* is to the political scientist. Since different versions of Kalm's book may have different pagination, I will note the excerpt by the date of its entry. This first is from 2 May 1749.

10—11   BUT ACROSS THE RIVER . . . History of Port Penn from Port Penn Historic District National Register of Historic Places nomination form, published by the National Park Service of the United States Department of the Interior, and on microfilm at the Delaware State Bureau of Archaeology and Historic Preservation.

11   THE SIZE OF THEIR BANDS . . . This matter of the numbers of Native Americans at contact is still much argued. The consensus appears to be that along the Delaware the groups were relatively few and far between. I have referred to Marshall Joseph Becker, "Lenape Population at the Time of European Contact," *Proceedings of the American Philosophical Society* 133, no. 2, 1989.

11   AS ONE INCREDULOUS . . . The Delaware diarist is quoted in "Papers Relating to the Colonies on the Delaware," *Pennsylvania Archives* 5 (1877), 130—133.

11   "WHEN WE SPEAK TO THEM ABOUT GOD . . ." Campanius quoted in C. A. Weslager, *New Sweden on the Delaware 1638—1655* (Wilmington: Middle Atlantic Press, 1988), 104.

12   "THE OLD SWEDE . . ." Kalm, 27 March 1749.

14—16   AS LATE AS THE CIVIL WAR . . . 31 May 1749: "About noon I left Philadelphia and went on board a small yacht which sails continually up and down upon the river Delaware, between Trenton and Philadelphia. We sailed up the river with fair wind and weather. Sturgeons leaped often a fathom into the air. We saw them continuing this exercise all day, till we came to Trenton." The leaping sturgeon quote ("MANY YEARS AGO . . .") is from *Report of the Fish Commissioners, State of Pennsylvania*, for the years 1892—94, and published in 1895, page 284. Much of the report is devoted to the sturgeon fisheries, and much of it is taken from John A. Ryder's history of the sturgeon industry in *Bulletin of the U.S. Fish Commission* for 1888, 231—328. The history here comes from both of these sources, as well as from my interview with Beck.

17   John O'Herron took me out on the river along the sturgeon route. O'Herron, in studies of the river, tracked sturgeon tagged with radio transmitters even into the middle of winter, dodging ice floes in the falls at Trenton. Other recent sturgeon information came from *NOAA Technical Report NMFS 14, Synopsis of Biological Data on Shortnose Sturgeon*, Acipenser brevirostrum, *LeSeur 1818* (Washington, D.C.: U.S. Department of Commerce, 1984).

19 "MAN GETS ACCUSTOMED . . ." In some cases Tocqueville can also be of value to the natural historian. This quote comes from "A Fortnight in the Wilds," in *Journey to America*, quoted in Michael Williams, *Americans and Their Forests: A Historical Geography* (Cambridge, England: Cambridge University Press, 1988).

21—24 A TIDAL MARSH . . . This geological, botanical, zoological, and paleontological reconstruction was developed from a few sources. Modern archaeologists spend a great deal of time on such ecological reconstructions of their sites. One of the primary resources for such studies along the East Coast, cited repeatedly by Delaware Valley archaeologists, is Victor Carbone's "Environment and Prehistory in the Shenandoah Valley," which was his Catholic University doctoral dissertation published in 1976. Carbone died not long after. My other sources all make use of his work, and in private conversations all acknowledged his prescience in these kinds of studies. Carbone's work is available from University Microfilms of Ann Arbor, Michigan.

Other sources include Jay Custer, *Delaware Prehistoric Archaeology, An Ecological Approach* (Newark: University of Delaware Press, 1984); John C. Kraft and Frank Daiber in *The Delaware Estuary: Rediscovering a Forgotten Resource*, edited by Tracey L. Bryant and Jonathan R. Pennock for the University of Delaware Sea Grant College Program, Newark, Del., 1988; and an unpublished cultural/ecological chronology of the Middle Atlantic region by Michael Stewart, professor of archaeology at Temple University.

24 IN LENAPE MYTH . . . Creation legends from Paul A. W. Wallace, *Indians in Pennsylvania* (Harrisburg: Pennsylvania Historical and Museum Commission, 1989), 73—75.

26—27 DUSKY, SCABROUS, ALGAE-COVERED . . . Snapping turtle evolution and biting mechanism from paleontologist and turtle researcher Peter Meylan; also from David Alderton, *Turtles and Tortoises of the World* (New York: Facts on File, 1988), 110—113.

33—37 "THE RIVER WAS LOW . . ." Charles Conrad Abbott, *A Naturalist's Rambles About Home* (New York: D. Appleton and Co., 1890).

38—39 The recognized authority on muskrats is Paul Lester Errington, whose works include *Muskrats and Marsh Management* (Lincoln, Nebraska: University of Nebraska Press, 1961) and *Muskrat Populations* (Ames, Iowa: Iowa State University Press, 1963).

41 THE FIRST RECORDED FUR TRADE. . . . Information on Indians and trapping comes from Herbert C. Kraft, both from conversations and from his book *The Lenape* (Newark: New Jersey Historical Society, 1986), which combines his own lifetime of archaeological research along the Delaware with the work of others into a wonderfully respectful and readable history of the river natives.

41–42 ABLE TO LIVE UP TO THE EDGE . . . Robert J. Naiman et al. "Alteration of North American Streams by Beaver," *BioScience* 38, no.11 (December 1988).

42 BY THE TIME THE STEEL TRAP . . . Richard Gerstell's *The Steel Trap in America* (Harrisburg, Pa.: Stackpole Books, 1985) is a one-of-a-kind book and my major source for trap history. Gerstell, like Errington, takes a long perspective on trapping. They both respect the tradition but recognize some of the modern concerns.

42 "BEAVERS WERE FORMERLY . . ." Kalm, 8 February 1749.

44 "IF THE EUROPEANS . . ." Kalm, 22 September 1750.

45 "NO GOVERNOR OF DELAWARE . . ." Recited in an address by President Franklin D. Roosevelt at the dedication of a Printz memorial at Wilmington in 1938, and reported by Weslager in *New Sweden on the Delaware*, 79.

45 "THEY MAKE THEIR NESTS . . ." Kalm, 8 February 1749.

46–47 THE LARGEST DEALER . . . Oneida information from Gerstell, *The Steel Trap in America*.

49–50 THE EARLIEST SCIENTIFIC REPORT ON PHRAGMITES . . . Few studies on phragmites have been done in this country. My information here comes from Erik Kiviat, who has studied the Hudson River marshes. His paper, "Common Reed (*Phragmites australis*)," was part of a series (no. 29) developed by The Exotic Plant Committee of the New York chapter of The Wildlife Society and published by the Department of Natural Resources, Cornell University Agricultural Experiment Station, Ithaca, New York, 1980.

63–82 Although the material in this chapter comes from a few days' conversations with Bernie Herman, he has written a great deal on the subject. His book, *Architecture and Rural Life in Central Delaware* (Knoxville: University of Tennessee Press, 1987), combines his obsession with architectural detail with his insights into the culture that produced them. A collection of essays from the University of Delaware Museum Studies Program, titled *After Ratification: Material Life in Delaware, 1789–1820*, Herman et al., (Newark, Del.: University of Delaware, 1988) also looks at how the world that people build for themselves reflects their view of life. Herman served as an editor and has two essays in this book, but the book as a whole would serve as a good model for approaching the cultural history of nearly any area.

68 IN 1812 DELAWARE PASSED A LAW . . . Delaware law from Leipsic and Little Creek, Delaware Historic District National Register of Historic Places nomination form, published by the United States Department of the Interior, National Park Service, and on microfilm at the Delaware State Bureau of Archaeology and Historic Preservation. New York law from John M. Kochiss, *Oystering from New York to Boston* (Middletown, Conn.: Wesleyan University Press, 1974), 10.

69—70 THESE DIKES WERE MAINTAINED . . . David Grettler, "The Landscape of Reform: Society, Environment, and Agricultural Reform in Central Delaware, 1790—1840," an unpublished Ph.D. dissertation, Dept. of History, University of Delaware; also from conversations with the author.

70 "THE HAVOC WROUGHT . . ." Bernard L. Herman, "Fences," in *After Ratification*.

72—73 THE WAR OF 1812 . . . Henry Adams, *History of the United States of America During the Administration of James Madison* (New York: Library of America, Volume Three, 1986), 1287—88, 1294.

75 THE OYSTER INDUSTRY . . . "White Gold," from Bryant and Pennock, *The Delaware Estuary*, 82—83.

76 A SYSTEM OF ROTATING OYSTER BEDS . . . National Register nomination. Louise Heite and James E. Valle in Bryant and Pennock, *The Delaware Estuary*, 25—26. Oyster bed quote from Kochiss, *Oystering from New York to Boston*, 7.

77 DELAWARE FARMS WORTH $5,000 . . . Farm prices from conversation with Herman.

79 GOSPILL'S PHILADELPHIA BUSINESS DIRECTORY . . . Cited in National Register nomination.

79 THE HARVEST RANGED . . . Data from Stewart Tweed in Bryant and Pennock, *The Delaware Estuary*, 85—86.

79—80 FINALLY, IN 1958 . . . MSX biology from Susan Ford in Bryant and Pennock, *The Delaware Estuary*, 84—85.

80 AN AGGRESSIVE . . . PLAN . . . Jack Dukes participated in the farmers' resistance to the oil companies. Much of the Delaware River shore is now under the protection of Delaware Wildlands, a nonprofit organization that, under the stewardship of Rusty Harvey, a rough-and-ready conservationist, duck hunter, and decoy carver, buys, protects, and manages undeveloped lands.

82 THE LAST CONGREGANT . . . Alston information from "A Story of Odessa Quakers," a pamphlet written and privately published in 1967 by John S. Walker of Wilmington. Hicksite material from Robert W. Doherty, *Hicksites, Pennsylvania History* 33, no. 4 (October 1966).

83—85 For the theories regarding fish migration, I have made use of several papers presented at a 1986 international symposium on "Common Strategies of Anadromous and Catadromous Fishes." The papers were collected and published under that collective title by the American Fisheries Society, Bethesda, Maryland, in 1987. Four papers were especially helpful here: Robert M. McDowall, "The Occurrence and Distribution of Diadromy among Fishes," pp. 1—13; Mart R. Gross, "Evolution of Diadromy in Fishes," pp. 14—25; Keith R. Maurice et al., "Increased Spawning by American Shad Coincident with Improved Dissolved Oxygen in the Tidal Delaware River," pp. 79—88; and Michael J. Dadswell et al., "Influences of Origin, Life History, and Chance on the Atlantic Coast Migration of American Shad," pp. 313—330. These shad studies owe a great deal to work done in the late 1960s and early 1970s by Mark Chittendon, Jr., who, in a sense, rediscovered the Delaware River shad. His papers include "Trends in the Abundance of American Shad, *Alosa sapidissima*, in the Delaware River Basin," *Chesapeake Science* 15, no. 2 (June 1974), 96—103; and "Dynamics of American Shad, *Alosa sapidissima*, Runs in the Delaware River," *Fishery Bulletin* 73, no. 3 (1975).

85 "THE SHAD, WHICH WERE VERY NUMEROUS . . . *Judd's History of Hadley, Massachusetts*, cited in *Report of the Fish Commissioners, State of Pennsylvania, 1895*, 274. The Englishman's theory is from the same report, p. 282.

96—97 A REPORT, LONG WITHHELD . . . Environmental report titled *Technical Review and Evaluation of Thermal Effects Studies and Cooling Water Intake Structure Demonstration of Impact for the Salem Nuclear Generating Station*, by Martin Marietta Environmental Systems. Available from New Jersey Department of Environmental Protection, Trenton, N.J.

105 "THE LITTLE BOY . . ." From Joel Chandler Harris, *Told by Uncle Remus: New Stories of the Old Plantation* (New York: Grosset & Dunlap, 1905).

106—107 THE DELAWARE RIVER LED TWO LIVES . . . Slave trade information from Donald D. Wax, "Negro Imports into Pennsylvania," *Pennsylvania History* 32, no. 3 (July 1965), and "Africans on the Delaware: The Pennsylvania Slave Trade, 1759—1765," *Pennsylvania History* 50, no. 1 (January 1983).

106—107 "LIKELY NEW NEGROES . . . Newspaper ads from the *Pennsylvania Gazette*, 11 September 1760; nearly any date can be chosen to see similar notices.

107—111 ON MAY 6, 1762 . . . The material on the development of the black community in Wilmington comes from Wade Paul Catts, "Slaves, Free Blacks, and French Negroes: An Archaeological and Historical Perspective on Wilmington's Forgotten Folk," an unpublished master's thesis. The Willing, Morris and Company notice is from the *Pennsylvania Gazette*, 6 May 1762, and the subsequent quotation is from slave dealer Thomas Riche. Both are cited in Catts's study.

109 Henry Adams found L'Ouverture a fascinating character and devoted an entire chapter to this ex-slave's struggles against Napoleon in his *History of the*

United States of America During the Administration of Thomas Jefferson, vol. 1 (New York: Library of America, 1986), 258.

110 "EXCEPT FOR A FEW MEN . . ." Ibid., 267—68.

110 "FOR SOMETIMES VIGILANCE . . ." Ibid., 267—68.

111 IT WAS TWO . . . Du Bois cited in Charles L. Blockson, *Pennsylvania's Black History*, (Philadelphia: Portfolio Associates, Inc., 1975). Blockson also tells the histories of Allen and Jones.

111—120 IN 1813, PETER SPENCER . . . History of Spencer and the Wilmington Big Quarterly from Lewis V. Baldwin, "Festivity and Celebration: A Profile of Wilmington's Big Quarterly," *Delaware History* 19, no. 4 (Fall/Winter 1981).

113 "AN' YO' ENEMIES . . ." Paul Laurence Dunbar, "An Antebellum Sermon," 1895, in *Literature in America: A Century of Expansion* (New York: The Free Press/Macmillan, 1971).

114 SOMETIMES ALL IT TOOK . . . Springtown material from Maria Boynton, "Springtown, New Jersey: Explorations in the History and Culture of a Black Rural Community," unpublished Ph.D. dissertation, 1986.

120—121 "I BATHED IN THE EUPHRATES . . ." Langston Hughes, "The Negro Speaks of Rivers," in *Selected Poems of Langston Hughes* (New York: Random House/Vintage, 1990).

121—123 FOR SOME FIFTY MILES . . . A natural history drawn from several sources. Once again from Kraft and Daiber, *The Delaware Estuary*; from Michael Stewart's unpublished manuscript; and a great deal from work by Robert Simpson, Ralph Good, Mary Leck, and Dennis Whigham, researchers who spent a great deal of time on the freshwater marshes of the Delaware. Papers by the four include "The Ecology of Freshwater Tidal Wetlands," *BioScience* 33, no. 4 (April 1983), and "Plants of the Hamilton Marshes: A Delaware River Freshwater Tidal Wetland," *Bartonia* 54 (1988). Mary Leck's husband, Charles Leck, studied the birds of the same marshes. His "Breeding Bird Communities in a Tidal Freshwater Marsh" was published in *The Bulletin of the New Jersey Academy of Sciences* 22, no. 1 (Spring 1977). I also visited the marshes with both Mary Leck and Robert Simpson. Good, Whigham, and Simpson also edited *Freshwater Wetlands: Ecological Processes and Management Potential* (New York: Academic Press, 1978). From this collection I made particular use of the paper "Biomass and Primary Production in Freshwater Tidal Wetlands of the Middle Atlantic Coast." Information on plants also came from Alfred E. Schuyler of the Academy of Natural Sciences of Philadelphia.

123—125 RICHARD ORSON OF RUTGERS . . . Orson's dissertation on the Woodbury Creek and tidal marshes is in press.

127   It too often happens . . . Charles Conrad Abbott, *A Naturalist's Rambles* "Live six months on the Delaware . . ." from *Abbott's Recent Rambles* (Philadelphia: J. B. Lippincott, 1892) 305, cited in Lucy Aiello, "Charles Conrad Abbott, M.D., Pick and Shovel Scientist," *New Jersey History*, 1967, 208—16.

127—132   Abbott, Dr. Abbott . . . Information on Abbott from Aiello (see above) and Herbert Kraft. Kraft sent me a draft copy of his yet-unpublished archaeological conference presentation, "Charles Conrad Abbott, the Trenton Gravel Implements and the Early Man Controversy." Information on the history of the site also from Kraft, *The Lenape*, and from the lifetime of work done on the site by Dorothy Cross, published in *Archaeology of New Jersey*, vol. 2, *The Abbott Farm* (Trenton: The Archaeological Society of New Jersey and the New Jersey State Museum, 1956).

127—128   "If I have seen . . ." Charles Conrad Abbott, *Wasteland Wanderings* (New York: Harper & Brothers, 1887). Abbott, *A Naturalist's Rambles*, 6—7.

128   "Startling . . ." Abbott, *Wasteland Wanderings*, 77.

128—132   Many in the archaeological establishment . . . Controversy details from Kraft, "Dr. C. C. Abbott: Right for the Wrong Reasons," paper presented at the Fiftieth Anniversary meeting of the Archaeological Society of New Jersey, Trenton, New Jersey, 1981.

129   "many men of many minds . . ." Abbott, *Recent Archaeological Explorations in the Valley of the Delaware, 1892*. Cited in Cross, *The Abbott Farm*, 4.

130   "Penn's thrifty followers . . ." Derivation of names, from Abbott, *Wasteland Wanderings*, iv.

131   "These dusky-skinned natives . . ." Abbott, *A Naturalist's Rambles*, 8.

132—133   Even as the glaciers . . . details from Stewart, Custer, Carbone, Kraft, Cross.

133   And in 1914 . . . Fire details from Aiello, "Charles Conrad Abbott." Information on scavenging amateurs from conversation with Michael Stewart.

136—137   Here, in the spring . . . Stewart, et al. (see above).

138—141   "The bark growing . . ." Gladys Tantaquidgeon, *Folk Medicine of the Delaware and Related Algonkian Indians* (Harrisburg: Pennsylvania Historical and Museum Commission, 1972).

140   The Swedes poured . . . Information on Swedish *badstus* from C. A. Weslager, *New Sweden on the Delaware* (Wilmington: Middle Atlantic Press, 1988), 154.

148—149 GEOLOGY AND THE RIVER . . . Jessie Rose Turk, "History of Falls from Trenton, New Jersey, in the Nineteenth Century: The Significance of Location in the Historical Geography of a City," unpublished doctoral dissertation, 1964. Daenckaerts quotation, cited in this paper, is from his *Journal of a Voyage to New York in 1679—80*, first published in *Memoirs of the Long Island Historical Society* 1 (1867).

150—155 BUT THE QUAKERS . . . Most of the details in these pages come from a two-part journal article by the late Philadelphia historian Hannah Benner Roach, "The Planting of Philadelphia: A Seventeenth-Century Real Estate Development," *Pennsylvania Magazine of History and Biography* 62, nos. 1, 2 (January and April 1968). Also important in the development of this chapter were conversations—held, it seems, in every lively quarter of the city—with then city archaeologist Carmen Weber. Penn's remarks come from *Some Account of the Province of Pennsylvania*, published in Albert Cook Meyers, *Narratives of Early Pennsylvania, West New Jersey and Delaware, 1630—1707* (New York: 1912) 202—215.

154 IF GEOGRAPHY . . . Results of freezing river from Philip C. F. Smith, *Philadelphia on the River* (Philadelphia: University of Pennsylvania Press, 1986), a collection from the archives of the Philadelphia Maritime Museum.

155 PENN WAS FORCED . . . Penn and his family and financial problems are from John B. Trussell, Jr., *William Penn, Architect of a Nation* (Harrisburg: Pennsylvania Historical and Museum Commission, 1983).

157—158 BEFORE THOSE BAD TIMES . . . Information on Fishtown, especially industrial data, from *Workshop of the World: A Selective Guide to the Industrial Archaeology of Philadelphia* (Wallingford, Penn.: Oliver Evans Press, 1990). Here I made use of Philip Scranton's introduction and the chapter on Fishtown industries by Stuart Paul Dixon.

158 "ONE OF THE PLEASANTEST . . ." From a 1708 letter from Penn to James Logan, in "Penn Treaty Park," brochure published by Philadelphia Fairmount Park Commission, 1982.

158—159 "THE SUBJECTS OF RIDICULE . . ." In Francis Burke Brandt, *The Majestic Delaware* (Philadelphia: Brandt and Gummere, 1929) Henry Adams, *History of the United States of America During the Administration of Thomas Jefferson.* (New York: Literary Classics of the United States, 1986) Vol. 1, 48—53.

159—160 TAKE MARTIN LANDENBERGER . . . Factory outputs and industry counts from Dixon in *Workshop of the World* (see above).

160 "HOW DEAR TO MY HEART . . ." Verse from "Will Kensington Ever Come Back?" by Billy Brady. This poem was published in the Fishtown Civic Associ-

ation's collection of memoirs and miscellany published to celebrate Fishtown's three hundredth anniversary in 1982. The verse is "from an undated news clipping found in a drawer." Many of the items from the views of Fishtown in this section come from this same collection, along with those of Milton Ginn.

161 "QUITE AN EXCITEMENT . . ." Whitman, *Walt Whitman: Complete Poetry and Collected Prose*, "FOR TWO HOURS . . ." Ibid., 832—833.

162 ALFRED JAMES REACH . . . Dixon, in *Workshop of the World* (see above), and from interview with Bill Deane, archivist at the Baseball Hall of Fame in Cooperstown, New York.

165 TO A WRITER . . . During my visit, Ginn repeated (and embellished) this story, which he had told to columnist Kitty Caparella of the *Philadelphia Daily News*, and which appeared in that newspaper on 14 July 1981.

168—169 WROTE PENN . . . Penn, *Some Account of the Province of Pennsylvania* (see above).

169 AMERICANS . . . SEEMED . . . Quote regarding Americans' "aversion to trees" from Isaac Weld, *Travels Through the States of North Amaerica and Provinces of Upper and Lower Canada During the Years 1795, 1796, and 1797.* (London: John Stockdale, 1799). Cited in Michael Williams, *Americans and Their Forests* (Cambridge, England: Cambridge University Press, 1988).

171 "INTERFACES OF WELL-DRAINED SOILS . . ." John Milner Associates, Inc., *A Phase I Archaeological Survey of Proposed Industrial Development Parcels, Eastwick Urban Renewal Area, Philadelphia County, Pennsylvania* (West Chester, Pa.: John Milner Associates, Inc., 1984).

171—172 THE EFFORTS TO MAKE . . . Weber's research on the Hertz lot was conducted for the preparation of the designation form for the Philadelphia Register of Historic Places.

172—173 "SHIPWRIGHTS, CARPENTERS . . ." Penn, *Some Account of the Province of Pennsylvania* (see above).

173—174 BUT WHEN THE BRITISH . . . Information for these pages came from conversations with Weber and with Walter Licht, dean of the History Department, University of Pennsylvania.

174 "IN A VERY LITTLE SPACE . . ." Edward Johnson, *Johnson's Wonder-Working Providence* (1654), cited in Williams, *Americans and Their Forests*, 82.

174—175 DURHAM BOATS . . . Durham boat history from J. A. Anderson, "Navigation of the Upper Delaware," paper read before the Bucks County Historical Society at Doylestown, Pennsylvania, on 16 January 1912 and published in 1913 by MacCrellish & Quigley, Doylestown.

175 "SCORCH'D BEFORE . . ." From Benjamin Franklin's 1744 pamphlet, "Pennsylvanian Fireplace," cited in I. Bernard Cohen, *Benjamin Franklin's Science* (Cambridge: Harvard University Press, 1990). Data on charcoal production and forests from Williams, *Americans and Their Forests*, 342—43. "Insatiable maw," ibid., 108, a quote from Johann David Schoepf, *Travels in the Confederation (1783—1784)*.

175 "THROUGH THE THICK SULPHUROUS . . ." Description of ironmaster from Arthur C. Bining, *Pennsylvania Iron Manufacture in the Eighteenth Century* (New York: Augustus M. Kelley, 1970), 55.

175 "IRON IS ALWAYS SWEET . . ." Cohen, *Franklin's Science*, 203.

175—176 DANIEL SKINNER CLAIMED . . . Skinner story from Anderson, "Navigation of the Upper Delaware," but also, along with other rafting lore, in William Heidt, Jr., "History of Rafting on the Delaware," a paper read before the Minisink Valley Historical Society in 1922 (Port Jervis, N.Y.: New York Gazette Printers), and in Terry A. McNealy, "Rafting on the Delaware: New Light from Old Documents," *Bucks County Historical Journal*, 1977.

177 THE "ARK" APPEARED . . . Anderson, "Navigation of the Upper Delaware."

177—178 WITH THE SEAGOING TRADE . . . Railroad and canal conglomeration from Turk, *History of Falls from Trenton*.

178 COAL PRODUCTION . . . Figures and ownership details from Stephen R. Crouch, "The Coal and Iron Police in Anthracite Country," in *Hard Coal, Hard Times: Ethnicity and Labor in the Anthracite Region*, edited by David L. Salay (Scranton: The Anthracite Museum Press, 1984), 101. Waste of coal from Earl and Dorothy Selby, "Clean-up on the Delaware," *Colliers*, 5 January 1946.

179 "THE SIGNS OF ARTIFICIAL IMPROVEMENT . . ." George Perkins Marsh, "Address Delivered before the Agricultural Society of Rutland County," in Williams, *Americans and Their Forests*, 18. Floating Church pictured in Francis Burke Brandt, *The Majestic Delaware*.

180—187 ALONG THE DELAWARE . . . Disston biography from Harry Silcox, from both correspondence and conversations and from his essays on Tacony and Disston in *Workshop of the World*, 8-1—8-12; also from Silcox, "Henry Disston's Model Industrial Community: Nineteenth-Century Paternalism in Tacony, Philadelphia," *Pennsylvania Magazine of History & Biography* 114, no. 4 (October 1990), and *Henry Disston and Sons, 1840—1955: The Rise and Fall of America's Mightiest Saw Works*, an unpublished manuscript. Other information on Disston from Roy E. Goodman and David G. Orr in *Workshop of the World*, 9-3—9-7.

183—184 HIS SON, HAMILTON . . . The story of "Ham" Disston and the ecological ruin of Florida is told in great detail by Mark Derr in his *Some Kind of Paradise: A Chronicle of Man and the Land in Florida* (New York: William Morrow, 1989).

187—189   WHEN THOMAS MELLON EVANS . . . The Evans quotations are from his own speech to the Newcomen Society, a copy of which was on file at The New York Historical Society. Evans's business practices were chronicled in the business press over the years.

189—190   THE STORY GOES AROUND . . . The local press in Pittsburgh also chronicled Evans's personal life. The account of his second wife's suicide was developed from a couple of these, notably the *Pittsburgh Post-Gazette*, May 23, 1977.

190   AND THE ORIGINAL . . . Information on Shuman from Silcox and from "Tacony," a pamphlet of historical information compiled by Robert Van Dervort (Philadelphia: Free Library of Philadelphia, 1982).

191   DURING WORLD WAR I . . . Shipyard information and the "hoggie/hoagie" connection from Philip C. F. Smith, *Philadelphia on the River* (Philadelphia: Philadelphia Maritime Museum, 1986).

192   NO TRANSFER . . . Walter Licht's own book (with Philip Scranton) on Philadelphia industry is indispensable: *Work Sights: Industrial Philadelphia, 1890—1950* (Philadelphia, 1986).

199   "THERE HAVE BEEN GREAT CHANGES . . ." Thomas Sharf & Thompson Westcott, *History of Philadelphia*, 1609—1884 (Philadelphia, 1884).

200—201   THE REPORTER UNDERESTIMATED . . . The story of the river's decline has been written often. The most authoritative account is Richard C. Albert, "The Historical Context of Water Quality Management for the Delaware Estuary," *Estuaries* 11, no. 2 (June 1988) 99—107. "Clean-up on the Delaware," *Collier's*, 5 January 1946, gives details of the first efforts to slow the ruin; this also seems to be the first mention of the pilots joking about smelling the river. More-scientific writing on past and present water quality and concerns is in *Ecology and Restoration of the Delaware River Basin*, Shydmal K. Majumdar, Willard Miller, Louis E. Sage, et al., eds, (Easton, Pa.: Pennsylvania Academy of Science, 1988). Good general essays are in Bryant and Pennock, *The Delaware Estuary*.

205—206   "IT IS A COUNTRY . . ." Mahlon Stacy, quoted in the *Report of the Pennsylvania Fish Commissioners*, Harrisburg, Pa., 1895, 259—61.

206—207   THE FALLS OF THE DELAWARE . . . Geological assessment from Turk, "History of Falls."

207   "THE INHABITANTS . . ." Kalm, 28 October 1748.

207—209   TRENTON MERCHANTS . . . Trenton stores and industrial and canal history from Turk.

209—210   IN 1890 TRENTON . . . John Cumbler, *A Social History of Economic Decline: Business, Politics, and Work in Trenton* (New Brunswick, N.J.: Rutgers University Press, 1989).

209   FERDINAND ROEBLING . . . Roebling history from Hamilton Schuyler, *The Roeblings: A Century of Engineers, Bridge-builders and Industrialists* (New York: AMS Press, 1972), reprint of 1931 edition published by Princeton University Press. Also from U.S. Environmental Protection Agency report, *Record of Decision on Roebling Steel Superfund Site, on Roebling Steel Company, March 1990*. And from Clifford Zink, project proposal, *The Trenton Roebling Project, Redevelopment Plan for the John A. Roebling's Sons Company Historic Industrial Sites, August 1989*.

210   IT WAS . . . THE WIRE AGE . . . John Kimberly Mumford, *Outspinning the Spider: The Story of Wire and Wire Rope* (New York: Robert L. Stillson Co., 1921).

211—212   Roebling balance sheets from Schuyler, *The Roeblings*.

213   ALL THAT WAS NEEDED . . . Ibid., 367—73.

215   "THE WHOLE TRACT . . ." Ibid., 369.

216—217   NEW INVESTIGATIONS . . . Contamination of Roebling site from EPA Superfund Report (see above).

219—220   "NINE O'CLOCK . . ." Clifford Zink, "The Invention Factory: An Interactive Museum/Learning Center," pamphlet.

221—222   IN 1867 . . . Cuban Giants information and information on Trenton's black history from Jack Washington, *In Search of a Community's Past: The Black Community in Trenton, New Jersey, 1860—1900* (Trenton, N.J.: Africa World Press, 1990).

227   FERDINAND ROEBLING, JR. . . . Family history from Schuyler, *The Roeblings*.

230   BUT IT SOON BECAME EVIDENT . . . Upstream fish spawning hypothesized by Mark Chittendon in "Present and Historical Spawning Grounds and Nurseries of American Shad," *Fishery Bulletin* 74, no. 2 (1976), and reported by the Delaware Basin Fish and Wildlife Management Cooperative in a 1980 paper, "Strategic Management Plan for the American Shad in the Delaware River Basin."

233—242   Frank Carle's work on dragonflies appears in scientific journals. "Evolution of the Odonate Copulatory Process" was published in *Odonatologica* 11, no. 4 (1 December 1982), 271—86. "Thoughts on the Origin of Insect Flight" appeared in *Entomological News* 93, no. 5 (1982), 159—72. "Environmental Monitoring Potential of the Odonata" appeared in *Odonatologica* 8, no. 4 (1 December 1979), 319—23.

243—244 "WE HAD ONLY . . ." "NATURE PRESENTS HERSELF . . ." Both quotes are cited in Martin Willever Wilson, "A History of the Delaware Water Gap," a master's thesis published in part under the title "Delaware Water Gap: Birth and Death of a Resort Town," in *Pennsylvania Folklore* 35, no. 2: 80—92.

244—245 THE WATER GAP . . . Preston's history of the Gap appears repeatedly from its first publication in *Hazard's Register*. My information about Preston comes from F. J. Stephens, *The Preston Letters*, an essay privately published in 1976, copies of which are cataloged in the Sinclair Collection at Rutgers University. Luke Brodhead wrote his own brochure on the Water Gap, titled *The Delaware Water Gap: Its Scenery, Its Legends, and Its Early History* (Philadelphia: Sherman & Co., 1867).

247 "THE PRACTICE OF GARDENING . . ." Herbert Kraft, *The Lenape* (Newark: New Jersey Historical Society, 1986).

248—250 WHEN PENN DIED . . . Biographical details from Trussell, *William Penn*. The Walking Purchase story has been pieced together from several sources, but the suggestion that Indians who were never signatories to the original treaty, and whose ancestors had never lived in the lands in question, had tried to make their own gains by now claiming rights to that treaty's territories, comes from Marshall Becker. In his "The Moravian Mission in the Forks of Delaware: Reconstructing the Migration and Settlement Patterns of the Jersey Lenape During the Eighteenth Century Through Documents in the Moravian Archives," *Unitas Fratrum* 21, no. 22 (1987), 88—172, Becker presses his point that the so-called "river" Indians were of many different backgrounds. In the case of the Walking Purchase, the "self-appointed King of the Delawares," Teedyuscung, tried to take advantage of the whites' tendency not to differentiate between one native culture and another. Teedyuscung, writes Becker, claimed that "his 'land and inheritance' had been taken by fraud. These allegations appear to have become the basis for the myth that the 'Walking Purchase' was a land fraud perpetrated by the colonials, when the reverse is more nearly the case."

Becker's point is this: "Teedyuscung's land claims and his pretense to being the representative of many nations had no basis in reality and had no effect on the day-to-day cultural interactions of these native people. As these many groups withdrew from these conflicts and moved west or north, most managed to maintain their cultural integrity as well as their traditional rivalries. These difficulties emphasize the observation that cultural differences manage to persist through time." The Penns' own machinations are more evident.

250 BY 1846 . . . Francis Parkman, *The Oregon Trail* (New York: New American Library Signet Classics, New York, 1950), 26.

251—252 "WHEN IT WAS DAY . . ." David Pietersz de Vries, *Narratives of New*

Netherland, 1609—1664, edited by J. Franklin Jameson (New York: Charles Scribner's Sons, 1909), and cited in Kraft, *The Lenape*, 223—24, although Kraft notes that some doubts have been cast upon the accuracy of de Vries's reporting.

252—253   THE LENAPE PRINCESS . . . The version of the Winona legend I have used was written by Mrs. E. S. Swift and appeared in Brodhead, *The Delaware Water Gap*.

253   AT THIS POINT . . . Joel Cook, from his Delaware tour section of *Brief Summer Rambles Near Philadelphia* (Philadelphia: J. B. Lippincott, 1882).

254—255   "THERE ARE FIFTY . . ." Mark Twain, *Life on the Mississippi*, in *Mark Twain, Mississippi Writings* (New York: Library of America, 1982), 574.

254   "ANTIQUATED WAYSIDE INNS . . ." *The New York Times*, 12 May 1877, cited in Wilson, "History of the Delaware Water Gap."

254—255   "A POOR OLD MAN . . ." Maximilian, Prince of Wied, *Travels in the Interior of North America*, translated from the German by H. Evans Lloyd (London: Ackermann and Co., 1843), 34. Description of Dutot's court appearance from Robert Brown Keller, *History of Monroe County*, (Stroudsburg, Pa.: Monroe County Publishing Co., 1927).

255—256   THE RAILROAD . . . Rail information from Thomas Taber and Thomas Taber III, *The Delaware, Lackawanna & Western Railroad in the Twentieth Century, 1899 to 1960* (Muncie, Pa.: Thomas Taber III, 1980), and *Lehigh Valley Transit Company*, published by the Lehigh Valley chapter of the National Railway Historical Society.

256   "THE HEALTHFUL INFLUENCE . . ." Brodhead, *The Delaware Water Gap*.

257   DOCTOR F. WILSON HURD . . . Anecdotal material from Wilson, "History of the Delaware Water Gap," and from collections of the National Park Service archives at Delaware Water Gap National Recreation Area, Marshall's Creek, Pennsylvania.

259—260   "AN OLD MAN . . ." Archer Butler Hulbert and William Nathaniel Schwarze, eds., "David Zeisberger's History of the Northern Indians," *Ohio State Archaeological and Historical Quarterly* 19, nos. 1—2 (1910), and cited in Kraft, *The Lenape*, 177.

261   "WHEN A BOY . . ." Wi-tapanoxwe reminiscence from Gladys Tantaquidgeon, *Folk Medicine of the Delaware and Related Algonkian Indians* (Harrisburg: Pennsylvania Historical and Museum Commission, 1972), 19.

278—279   SOME OF THE NUMBERS . . . These figures came from the first announcements of the Tocks Island plan as reported in *The New York Times*, 1 May 1961.

In subsequent years the specifications of the project would change often. The best account of the Tocks Island project is in Richard Albert, *Damming the Delaware: The Rise and Fall of Tocks Island Dam* (University Park, Pa.: Pennsylvania State University Press, 1987). Albert is head of Water Quality Planning and Analysis for the Delaware River Basin Commission, and I thank him for his comments to me in conversation with regard to Tocks, access to his news clipping files, and his permission to quote from his book in this chapter.

281   THE MAJOR RESERVOIRS . . . *New Jersey v. New York*, 283 U.S. 336 (Opinion) and 283 U.S. 805 (Decree), 25 May 1931, cited in Albert, *Damming the Delaware*, 23. The court record takes up sixty volumes.

294–295   "AS MORE AND MORE LAND . . ." Quote and accounts from Albert, ibid., 134–42.

306   "ALL THE STREAMS . . ." Brodhead, *The Delaware Water Gap*.

310–312   "THEY FLEW OVER . . ." Stevenson Whitcomb Fletcher, *Pennsylvania Agriculture and Country Life 1640–1840* (Harrisburg: Pennsylvania Historical and Museum Commission, 1971).

316   "THE SURROUNDINGS . . ." Brodhead, *The Delaware Water Gap*.

316–317   THE SOURCE OF THE DELAWARE . . . Statistics on watershed area from Majumdar et al., *Ecology and Restoration*.

319   IN 1889 . . . Good reading on the Pocono flyfishing community can be found in Ernest Schweibert, *Remembrances of Rivers Past* (New York: Macmillan 1972).

322–323   TWO POCONO RESORTS . . . Information on Rand and Tamiment from the Tamiment Collection, New York University.

324   IN 1945 . . . Information from the Pocono Mountains Vacation Bureau, Stroudsburg, Pa.

326   WHEN BIG-TIME REAL-ESTATE . . . Rise, decline, and rise of the resort and development industry from conversations with Pocono developers.

327   SOON THE VACATION HOMES . . . Estimates by the county planning offices. Monroe County figures from *Monroe 2030: The Monroe County Comprehensive Master Plan and Policy Recommendations*, June 1989, Monroe County, Pennsylvania.

327   THE OWNERS OF BUSHKILL FALLS . . . Concerns of Bushkill Falls from conversations with Charles Eyer, a Peters descendant, and Bushkill owner and attorney Charles Bensinger.

343–345   "FOR MY OWN PART . . ." Benjamin Franklin, in a letter to Sarah Bache, 26 January 1784, and (page 498) in a letter to *The Pennsylvania Journal*, 27 December 1775, both from *Writings of Benjamin Franklin* (New York: Library of America, 1987), 1088, 744.

353—354 HANCOCK, EQUINUNK ... Song and characters from Leslie C. Wood, *Holt! T'other Way!* an upriver folk history published by the author in Middletown, N.Y., 1950.

356—357 EEL WEIR HOLLOW ... Eel life history remains a mystery. For this account I depended on work by Robert C. Kleckner and James McCleave of the University of Maine, and the U.S. Fish and Wildlife Service life history of the American eel in *Life Histories and Environmental Requirements of Coastal Fishes and Invertebrates* Biological Report 82 (Washington, D.C.: 1987).

Index